C000180329

# CIVIL REMEDIES

# Civil Remedies

BENJAMIN ANDOH, BA, LLM, PhD, PGCTLHE, Barrister
*Senior Lecturer in Law, Southampton Institute*

and

STEPHEN MARSH, BA, LLB, LLM, PGCE
*Senior Lecturer in Law, Southampton Institute*

Dartmouth
Aldershot • Brookfield USA • Singapore • Sydney

© Benjamin Andoh and Stephen Marsh 1997

All rights reserved. No part of this publication may be reproduced, stored in a retrieval system, or transmitted in any form or by any means, electronic, mechanical, photocopying, recording, or otherwise without the prior permission of Dartmouth Publishing Company Limited.

Published by
Dartmouth Publishing Company Limited
Gower House
Croft Road
Aldershot
Hants GU11 3HR
England

Dartmouth Publishing Company
Old Post Road
Brookfield
Vermont 05036
USA

**British Library Cataloguing in Publication Data**
Andoh, Benjamin
Civil Remedies
1.Remedies (Law) - England
I.Title II.Marsh, Stephen
344.2'07

**Library of Congress Cataloging-in-Publication Data**
Andoh, Benjamin, barrister, 1951-
Civil remedies / Benjamin Andoh, and Stephen Marsh.
p. cm.
Includes bibliographical references and index.
ISBN 1-85521-788-0 (hb). -- ISBN 1-85521-792-9 (pb)
1. Remedies (Law)--Great Britain. I. Marsh, Stephen, 1949- .
II. Title.
KD7576.A96 1996
347.41'077-dc20
[344.10777] 98-41977
CIP

ISBN 1 85521 788 0 (Hbk)
ISBN 1 85521 792 9 (Pbk)

Printed and bound in Great Britain by
Biddles Limited, Guildford and King's Lynn

# Contents

## PART II: NON-COMPENSATORY DAMAGES



## PART III: COMPENSATORY DAMAGES

## PART IV: EQUITABLE REMEDIES

# Table of Cases

Landom Trust Ltd. v Hurrell [1995] 1 All E.R. 839. 38
Lane v Capsey [1891] 3 Ch. 411. 19
Lane v Holloway [1968] 1 Q.B. 379. 62
Langen & Wind Ltd. v Bell [1972] Ch. 685, [1972] 1 All E.R. 296, [1972] 2 W.L.R. 170. 215
Lavery v Pursell (1888) 39 Ch. D. 508. 231
Law v Redditch Board (1892) 1 Q.B. 127. 38
Lazard Bros. & Co. Ltd. v Fairfield Properties Co. (Mayfair) Ltd. (1977) 121 Sol. J. 793. 234
Lazenby Garages Ltd. v Wright [1976] 2 All E.R. 770, [1976] 1 W.L.R. 459. 129
Leaf v International Galleries [1953] 1 Q.B. 646, 1 All E.R. 693. 291, 296
Lee v York Coach and Marine [1977] R.T.R. 35. 25
Leeds Industrial Co-operative Society Ltd. v Slack [1924] A.C. 851, [1924] All E.R. 259. 284, 288
Lemmon v Webb [1895] A.C. 1. 16, 17
Lewin v Guest (1826) 1 Russ. 325. 230
Lewis v Avery [1972] 1 Q.B. 198. 297
Lexmead (Basingstoke) Ltd. v Lewis [1982] A.C. 225, [1981] 2 W.L.R. 713, [1981] 2 Lloyd's Rep.17, *sub nom.* Lambert v Lewis [1981] 1 All E.R. 1185. 94, 112
Liesbosch Dredger v Edison S.S. [1933] A.C. 449. 96, 99, 115, 116, 117, 118, 198
Lim Poh Choo v Camden Health Authority [1980] A.C. 174. 146, 154
Lindenau v Desborough (1828) 8 B.& C. 586. 294
Lipkin Gorman v Karpnale [1991] A.C. 548. 306
Lister v Stubbs [1890] 45 Ch. D. 1. 254, 255
Litchfield-Speer v Queen Anne's Gate Syndicate (No. 2) Ltd. [1919] 1 Ch. 407. 278
Livingstone v Minister of Defence [1984] N.I. 356. 6
Llanover, The (1947) P. 80. 198
Lloyd v Director of Public Prosecutions [1992] 1 All E.R. 982. 4, 15
Lloyd v Stanbury [1971] 1 W.L.R. 535, [1971] 2 All E.R. 267. 125
Lloyds and Scottish Finance Ltd. v Modern Cars and Caravans (Kingston) Ltd. [1966] 1 Q.B. 764. 100
Lock International v Beswick [1989] 3 All E.R. 373. 276
Lombard North Central plc v Butterworth [1987] 1 All E.R. 267, [1987] Q.B. 527. 41

# Table of Statutes

**Table of statutory rules, orders and statutory instruments**

**European legislation**

# Preface and Introduction

The original stimulus for the writing of this book was the creation of a civil remedies unit on the undergraduate law programmes at Southampton Institute. It is, therefore, hoped that the text will provide a comprehensive yet concise guide to students who study the subject as a discrete unit both at first-degree and postgraduate levels. Additionally, the writers intend the book to be a useful extension to the the more general texts on contract and tort whilst also providing readily accessible information to students at the professional stage where, of course, the subject of remedies is a central issue.

Civil remedies may be classified into two broad categories: judicial and non-judicial remedies. The latter are obtained by a court action, the former are pursued outside the courts e.g., self-help and out-of-court settlements. The subject area may be further classified into: (a) "legal" remedies, e.g., damages at common law or under statute, and equitable remedies, e.g., specific performance, (b) private law remedies, e.g., damages for personal injuries, and public law remedies, e.g., those granted by judicial review of administrative action and (c) provisional remedies, e.g., interlocutory injunctions and provisional damages, and permanent remedies, e.g., final injunctions.

The book examines the whole area of remedies available in a civil action. There is detailed coverage of the non-judicial remedy of self-help, the consensual remedies, the judicial remedies of compensatory and non-compensatory damages for breach of contract and tort, the factors limiting an award of damages and the equitable remedies of specific performance and injunction. However, the following topics have been treated in outline only: rescission and rectification of a contract, restitutionary remedies, tracing subrogation and judicial remedies against administrative bodies. This is because first, they have all been comprehensively treated by textbooks on contract, restitution and administrative law respectively, and secondly, they were deemed to belong conventionally to those three subject areas.

Enforcement of judgements is not considered because the methods of enforcement, which include execution against goods, garnishee orders, attachment of earnings, administration orders, charging orders, etc., are not remedies, *strictu sensu*.

The book has a total of six parts, comprising twelve chapters. Part one deals with self-help (chapter 1) and the non-consensual remedies of liquidated damages and penalties, etc. (chapter 2). Part two concentrates on the non-compensatory damages, namely nominal, contemptuous and exemplary damages; mention is made of aggravated damages because, although they are compensatory in intent, they appear to be non-compensatory. Part three focuses on compensatory damages. This is a large topic and, to ease assimilation, has been broken down into several sections: factors limiting an award of damages (chapter 4), compensatory damages for breach of contract (chapter 5), compensatory damages for tort - personal injuries and death (chapter 6) and other aspects of compensatory damages - for mental distress, inconvenience and loss of reputation, and other losses in tort (chapter 7). Part four is concerned with the main equitable remedies: specific performance (chapter 8), injunctions (chapter 9), other equitable remedies - equitable damages, rescission and rectification (chapter 10). The remaining parts are very short dealing in outline only with the subject-matter. Part five considers a number of miscellaneous remedies not already addressed in the text - restitutionary remedies, tracing and subrogation (chapter 11). Lastly, part six looks at judicial review (chapter 12).

At the end of the chapters on the topics treated in detail are exercises to give students and other readers extra stimulation. Further tasks relating to damages, the Mareva injunction and the Anton Piller order can be found in the appendices section which, for the purposes of illustration, also contains a number of draft pleadings.

As the saying goes, "life is what happens to you when you are busy making other plans". After we had submitted the camera-ready copy of the book to the publishers, the Damages Act 1996 was passed. It came into force on 24th September 1996 and gives effect to the Law Commission's recommendations in its *Report on Structured Settlements and Interim and Provisional Damages* (Law Commission No. 224, September 1994). Since the Act concerns damages for personal injuries, it was thought necessary, under the present circumstances, to give a brief account of it here as an annex.

Benjamin Andoh
Stephen Marsh

September 1996

*ANNEX*

*The Damages Act 1996*

Under section 1 of the Act the court, when determining the return to be expected from the investment of damages awarded for future pecuniary loss, is to take account of any rate of return prescribed by the Lord Chancellor. However, it can take account of a different rate of return if that is more appropriate in a particular case. Section 2 empowers the court to make orders by which damages may be paid periodically. According to section 3, if provisional damages are awarded to a person and he then dies of his injuries, his dependant/s can still make a claim in respect of the death under the Fatal Accidents Act 1976. But, when assessing the loss suffered by the dependant/s, the court will take into account that part of the total damages awarded to the injured person (the deceased) which related to future pecuniary loss in respect of any period after the date of his death. Under section 4, where, following a structured settlement, an annuity has been purchased for a person, that person is given full protection under the Policyholders Protection Act 1975 if the insurer goes into liquidation. Section 5 then sets out the meaning of structured settlements. Under section 6 a Minister has power to guarantee a structured settlement entered into by a public body. Lastly, section 7 concerns interpretation and section 8 the short title, extent and commencement of the Act.

# Acknowledgements

Help, encouragement and advice have been given by many people in the course of producing this book and we are grateful to all those concerned. In particular, we would like to thank a number of colleagues in the law faculty at Southampton Institute: the Dean, Professor Jeremy Cooper for his support and interest, Irene Clark for her assistance in formatting some of the text, Dawn Black and Mark Wing. Thanks also to Edwin Gogo and Eunice Mensah; and to His Honour Judge Geoffrey Jones for his valuable comments on the draft pleadings contained in the appendices. Any errors in the text are the responsibility of the authors.

# PART I
# SELF-HELP AND THE CONSENSUAL REMEDIES

# 1 Self-help

## Introduction

Self-help is the oldest kind of remedy. Loosely speaking, it is do-it-yourself justice without recourse to the courts (e.g., an aggrieved person taking the law into his own hands).[1] As such, it is essentially a non-judicial remedy.[2] It may be said to belong to the class of rights or remedies by operation of law, e.g., tortious remedies like the right to retake goods, the right to eject a trespasser, the right to abate a nuisance, etc. In this chapter various aspects of self-help will be looked at, namely: its advantages and disadvantages, self-defence, ejection of a trespasser, abatement of a nuisance, the recapture of goods, necessity as self-help, the set-off, right of retainer of debt due to an estate, and self-help in contract. Under self-help in contract the following selected topics will be covered: avoidance of a voidable contract, termination of a contract after breach of a condition, the lien, self-help under the Sale of Goods Act 1979 and under the Consumer Credit Act 1974, and a mortgagee's right to sell mortgaged property.

## Advantages and disadvantages

There is no doubt that self-help is advantageous because of its very nature. When compared with litigation:

(i) it is *cheaper*; it avoids payment of court fees and other legal expenses;

(ii) it is *summary* (*speedier*); it avoids delay and complications; and

---

1. It could also be instantaneous.
2. In early law, because of its nature and advantages, self-help could not fully be restrained. See W.S. Holdsworth, *A History of English Law*, 3rd ed. (Methuen: London, 1923), vol. II, p. 100.

(iii) it also *saves effort* because it makes unnecessary the duty to mitigate one's loss, a topic discussed later in the text.

These are very desirable attributes indeed.

However, it is a risky remedy as the person exercising it may, in the course of doing so, exceed his rights. In *R. v Chief Constable of Devon and Cornwall, ex. p. C.E.G.B.*,[3] where protestors unlawfully obstructed or interfered with a survey of private land by a statutory board, the Central Electricity Generating Board, the Court of Appeal reviewed the powers and duties of the police where a landowner or person with rights over land exercises the right of self-help. It held, *inter alia,* that the objectors deliberately broke the law by their wilful obstruction of the operations of the "Electricity Board", which breach entitled the Board to use reasonable force in order to remove the protestors and that using self-help in those circumstances was likely to cause a breach of the peace. So, the police had a right to be there to intervene, if necessary. Lawton L.J. issued this warning about self-help: "... the most important reason for not using self-help, if any other remedy can be used effectively, is that as soon as one person starts to, or makes to, lay hands on another, there is likely to be a breach of the peace." Other cases illustrating how risky self-help can be include *Burton v Winters and Another*[4] and *Lagan Navigation Company v Lambeg Bleaching, Dyeing and Finishing Co. Ltd.*,[5] discussed below.

Where, in the course of exercising self-help, a person violates the rights of another person, he may be liable in conversion if he appropriates the other's property, as in *Mills v Brooker*.[6] Where he commits contempt of court, he may be fined or imprisoned (*Burton v Winters*), where he violates the criminal law in another way (e.g., acting in breach of s.6, Criminal Law Act 1977 (looked at later in this chapter) or causing criminal damage by way of breaking a wheelclamp in order to retrieve his car, as in *Lloyd v D.P.P.*[7]), he may be imprisoned, etc., and, where he uses excessive force in self-defence, he may be liable for trespass to the person. Therefore, persons who exercise self-help without caution (i.e., where there is no emergency or in a way that unjustifiably affects the rights of other people) are likely in the

3. [1982] Q.B. 458, 473.
4. [1993] 1 W.L.R. 1077.
5. [1927] A.C. 226.
6. [1919] 1 K.B. 555.
7. [1992] 1 All E.R. 982.

long run to face a financial penalty or disadvantage (*via* damages or payment of a fine) or the label of "person convicted of an offence".

Another case which illustrates how risky self-help can be is *Revill v Newbery*.[8] There the defendant, aged 76, was sleeping in a shed in his garden. He heard the plaintiff and another man trying to break in at 2.00 a.m.. He loaded his shotgun and poked the barrel through a small hole in the door. He then fired the shotgun at a range of about five feet and hit the plaintiff on the upper arm, through the armpit and into the chest. The defendant was held liable in negligence and for breach of the occupier's duty to trespassers under the Occupiers' Liability Act 1984: the force he used was excessive and unreasonable. Also, he could not rely on the defence of *ex turpi causa non oritur actio* (i.e., illegality)[9] or accident although the plaintiff was found to have been contributorily negligent (he was two-thirds to blame).

## Examples of self-help

### 1. Self-defence

Self-defence here means (i) defence of one's person and (ii) defence of the person of another. Defence of one's property is dealt with below under ejection of trespassers and retaking of goods.

### (i) Defence of one's person

At common law a person can use reasonable force to defend himself. If he uses force that is unreasonable, then he may be in breach of the law; under the civil law he may be liable for trepass to the person (battery and/or assault): *Anderson v Marshall*.[10] If he is provoked and uses unreasonable force, he cannot plead provocation as a defence but only as a mitigating

---

8. (1995) *The Independent*, Nov. 10; [1996] 1 All E.R. 291.
9. Illegality is not a defence under the Occupiers' Liability Act 1984. As Millett, L.J. said in his concurring judgement, if the defence was available, no trespasser could claim under the Act even if the force used against him was excessive or unreasonable.
10. [1835] 13 S. 1130.

factor to reduce his damages.[11]

It cannot be over-emphasised that the force used must be reasonable or commensurate with the force used by the one against whom a person acts in self-defence. The reasonableness of the force used is a question of fact. Thus, every case may be different. For example, in *R. v Jones*[12] a lady driver, after causing damage to another person's car, was arrested but was later remanded on bail. After she had refused to have her fingerprints taken, the police obtained a magistrates' court order authorising them to take her prints. The police then took her to the police station. There she resisted attempts by the police officers to take her fingerprints forcibly; in her struggle with them she bit two of them. However, the Court of Appeal quashed, *inter alia,* her conviction for assaulting those police officers because, apart from the finding that the officers acted unlawfully in attempting to take her fingerprints at the station (and not at the court building where the prints could only have been legally taken following the magistrates' court order), there was no evidence that the force she (the appellant) used to resist the officers was unreasonable.

On the other hand, in *Revill v Newbery* the defendant, by shooting the plaintiff, a burglar who was trespassing on his land, used unreasonable force. He did not, therefore, act in self-defence. Evans L.J., in his concurring judgement in the Court of Appeal, stated that the defendant's negligence, as found by the court, implied that the violence he used against the plaintiff exceeded the reasonable limits which self-defence allowed.

One interesting question is whether a person can claim self-defence against an innocent bystander, a non-attacker. In other words, if D attacks P and P throws a punch back at D but D quickly moves out of the way and E, a bystander, is hit instead, can P claim self-defence even though he was not defending himself against E? The answer seems "no". On that view P will be liable for battery because what is required is not the intention to injure someone. Rather, what is required is intention to hit or touch someone plus the actual touching.[13] He may be liable in negligence as well if E can establish the three elements of duty, breach and damage. After all, self-defence is not a (recognised) defence to negligence.

---

11. *Anderson v Marshall; Murphy v Culhane* [1977] Q.B. 94; *Barnes v Nayer* (1986), *The Times*, Dec. 19.
12. [1978] R.T.R. 137, C.A..
13. See *Livingstone v Minister of Defence* [1984] N.I. 356.

### (ii) Defence of the person of another

At common law reasonable force may be used by a person to defend another person. Thus, in *R. v Duffy*[14] the appellant's defence was that what she did was to assist (defend) her twin sister. The judge directed the jury that self-defence was not open to her and she was convicted of unlawful wounding. But the Court of Criminal Appeal disagreed and, quashing her conviction, held that there was a general right, even as between strangers, to prevent a crime and that whether her claim of defence was true should have been left to the jury.

In addition, there is a statutory "right" (i.e., power, not duty) to defend another person. That is contained in s.3(1), Criminal Law Act 1967 which provides that "a person may use such force as is reasonable in the circumstances to prevent the commission of a crime, or to effect or assist in lawfully arresting offenders, suspected offenders or persons at large unlawfully".[15]

A case which illustrates the requirement of reasonableness of the force used in arresting an offender, etc., is *Allen v Metropolitan Police Commissioner*.[16] There two police officers, who were much taller and younger than the middle-aged appellant and had put armlocks on him, etc., were held to have used, together with their colleagues, more force than was reasonable in the circumstances for the purpose of arresting him and taking him to the police station.

## 2. The ejection of trespassers/intruders (defence of property)

The right of self-help may also be exercised to eject from property human and animal trespassers and to prevent encroachment.

*Human trespassers and trespass by encroachment*

A person may use reasonable force to defend any property (realty or personalty) from being trespassed against. But, that person must actually be

---

14. [1967] 1 Q.B. 63. This criminal case is only an illustration.
15. Such as escaped prisoners.
16. (1980) Crim. L.R. 441.

in possession of that property or have the right of possession of it before he can lawfully defend it himself. Put simply, the person who can sue for trespass to the property in question is the person who can rightfully exercise self-help to defend that property.

Again, the force used must be reasonable (*Revill v Newbery*). The defender of property can only use force if the trespasser did the same.[17] Conversely, where trespass to land is made without any violence, the trespasser must first be asked to leave and, if he does not leave, then, reasonable force can be used to eject him.[18]

An interesting question which may be posed here is: Can a person shoot another person who is burgling his home/ property? The answer seems to be "yes" and "no". *Dicta* in *Murphy v Culhane*[19] suggest the answer is "yes". There Lord Denning said:

> "... suppose that a burglar breaks into a house and the householder, finding him there, picks up a gun and shoots him - using more force, maybe, than is reasonably necessary. The householder may be guilty of manslaughter ... But I doubt very much whether the burglar's widow could have an action for damages. The householder might well have a defence either on the ground of *ex turpi causa non oritur actio* or *volenti non fit injuria.*"

However, *Revill v Newbery*, as can be seen above, suggests the answer is "no" unless the burglar himself had a gun and was about to use it. In any case, *Murphy v Culhane* was decided before the Occupiers' Liability Act 1984 was passed. Therefore, today, in the light of that Act and of *Revill v Newbery*, Lord Denning's view might be differently expressed.

Where there is trespass by encroachment, e.g., building a wall, shed or other structure on one's land in such a way that it protrudes on neighbouring property, the affected party may be entitled to use a form of "self-help" by abatement (similar to abatement of a nuisance). But, this is only justifiable in emergency situations or in cases which are clear and simple, and do not really require or justify litigation, as illustrated by

---

17. Or had already violently attacked the property and was likely or about to attack it again. See *Attorney-General's Reference No. 2 of 1983* [1984] Q.B. 456.
18. *Collins v Renison* (1754) 1 Say. 138; *Polkinhorn v Wright* [1845] 8 Q.B. 197; *Webster v Watts* [1847] 11 Q.B. 311.
19. [1977] Q.B. 94, at 98.

*Burton v Winters.*[20] That case is a classic example of the stubbornness and contumacious behaviour of a plaintiff in defiance of a judicial order. In other words, it shows how risky self-help can be. There the defendants built a garage (on their property) but the garage encroached upon the land of their neighbour, the plaintiff, by about 4.5 inches. The plaintiff sued her neighbours for trespass and nuisance and sought a mandatory injunction to compel them to remove the encroachment. The claim for an injunction was refused by the court which instead granted a declaratory judgement and adjourned the claim for damages to enable a valuation to be made regarding how much the plaintiff's property had fallen in value as a result of the encroachment. But the plaintiff was very impatient and disobedient to the court: she decided to exercise self-help and, so, trespassed on the defendants' land and built a brick wall in front of their garage. An injunction was issued against her but she ignored it; she also ignored subsequent injunctions to the extent that eventually a two-year suspended sentence of imprisonment was activated against her. Her appeal against that was dismissed with costs by the Court of Appeal. The case is so graphic an illustration of the riskiness of self-help that it is worth giving a chronological account of the events that happened there:

12-12-90: Plaintiff (B)'s claim for a mandatory injunction (to compel the defendants to remove a 4.5-inch encroachment) was dismissed.

18-2-91: B failed in appeal against dismissal of claim for injunction.

18-12-91: B was denied leave to appeal to the House of Lords.

14-3-92: B started to build a brick wall in front of the defendants' garage on the defendants' side of the boundary. She was therefore trespassing, etc.

21-4-92: An injunction was issued against B not to trepass, etc.; but, she continued to trespass.

14-5-92: B was committed to prison for 14 days by the judge (of the County Court). The sentence was suspended on condition

20. [1993] 1 W.L.R. 1077.

that she removed the wall.

| | |
|---|---|
| 15-5-92: | B removed her wall from the defendants' land. |
| 16-5-92: | B rebuilt her wall on the defendants' land. Therefore, the court activated the 14-day prison sentence against her and committed her to prison for 12 months. |
| 17-7-92: | The Court of Appeal allowed B's appeal against the committal order, but issued an injunction to restrain her from trespassing or interfering with the defendants' property. |
| 25-7-92: | B, in breach of the injunction, put bricks in the defendants' garden and made a hole in the roof of the defendants' garage. |
| 14-8-92: | The Judge sentenced B to two years' imprisonment but suspended it on condition that she did not breach the injunction anymore. Just before then, on 11-8-92, B and her friend had used a sledge hammer to make a hole in the defendants' garage and had been arrested by the police for criminal damage. |
| 21-8-92: | B removed the repairs the defendants had made to the roof of their garage. |
| 31-8-92: | B tried to rebuild the wall in front of the defendants' garage: a clear trespass. |
| 2-10-92: | The two years' suspended prison sentence was activated against B. She was committed to prison for two years. |
| Dec. 1992: | Her appeal against the two-year sentence, imposed on 14-8-92, was dismissed. |

According to the Court of Appeal, she retained her right to claim damages for the reduction in the value of her property. The dismissal of her appeal was on two grounds:

(i) First, her right of self-redress lapsed when the judge refused her claim for a mandatory injunction; she should, therefore, not have taken the law into her own hands. Lloyd L.J. said, at p. 1082:

> "Self-redress is a summary remedy, which is justified only in clear and simple cases, or in an emergency. Where a plaintiff has applied for a mandatory injunction and failed, the sole justification for a summary remedy has gone. The court has decided the very point in issue. This is so whether the complaint lies in trespass or nuisance. In the present case, the court has decided that the plaintiff is not entitled to have the wall on her side of the boundary removed. It follows that she has no right to remove it herself."

(ii) Secondly, according to the House of Lords in *Lagan Navigation Co. v Lambeg Bleaching, Dyeing and Finishing Co. Ltd.*,[21] the law does not favour the remedy of abatement. In the course of his judgement, to show that the remedy of self-help, where warranted, must be exercised without delay, Lloyd L.J., at p. 1081, quoted from Blackstone's *Commentaries on the Laws of England*, Book III, ch. 1, as follows:

> "And the reason why the law allows this private and summary method of doing one's self justice, is because injuries of this kind, which obstruct or annoy such things as are of daily convenience and use, require an immediate remedy; and cannot wait for the slow progress of the ordinary forms of justice."

His Lordship also referred to the statement of Greene J. in *Moffet v Brewer*,[22] which was as follows:

> "This summary method of redressing a grievance, by the act of an injured party, should be regarded with great jealousy, and authorised only in cases of particular emergency, requiring a more speedy remedy than can be had by the ordinary proceedings at law."

---

21. [1927] A.C. 226, at p. 244.
22. (1848) Iowa 1 Greene 348, 350.

*Entry on land by owner, etc., to eject an intruder*

Again at common law a person in immediate possession of land which has been intruded upon by another person can use reasonable force to enable him to gain entry into the premises in question so as to eject the intruder. Note that reasonable force must be used in the ejection, as happened in *Hemmings v Stoke Poges Golf Club*.[23]

However, two statutory provisions do affect the common law, even if to a limited extent:

(a) first, ss.2 and 3, Protection from Eviction Act 1977 forbid landlords from evicting tenants without a court order, and also from harassing tenants in order to make them quit (moreover, s.27, Housing Act 1988 provides for damages to be awarded against a landlord for wrongfully evicting a tenant, a residential occupier); and

(b) according to s.6, Criminal Law Act 1977, it is an offence (punishable by imprisonment and/or fine) for anyone (except a displaced residential occupier), without lawful authority,[24] to use or threaten violence to secure entry to any premises occupied by another person. "Displaced residential occupier" is defined by s.12(3), Criminal Law Act 1977 as "any person who was occupying any premises as a residence immediately before being excluded from occupation by anyone who entered those premises, or any access to those premises, as a trespasser ... so long as he continues to be excluded from occupation of the premises by the original trespasser or by any subsequent trespasser". However, according to s.12(4), "a person who was himself occupying the premises in question as a trespasser immediately before being excluded from occupation shall not ... be a displaced residential occupier of the premises" for the purposes of that part of the Act.

---

23. [1920] K.B. 720.

24. Thus, there is protection for court officers who are executing court orders and also police officers using lawful violence or threat of violence in exercising their power of arrest or search.

*Landlord's peaceable re-entry to terminate a lease*

In *Re A Debtor (No. 13A-10-1995)*[25] there was a twenty-five-year lease of premises, the rent for which was payable in advance quarterly on certain dates. The lease provided, *inter alia*, for the landlords' re-entry and determination of it if the tenants defaulted in paying the rent or any part of it for 14 days beyond the date it was due, whether the landlords formally asked for that payment or not. The tenants failed to pay the rent within the specified time. After a warning letter to the tenants the landlords issued a writ claiming payment of the arrears of rent. The tenants responded by obtaining an interim order from the county court under section 252 of the Insolvency Act 1986, which barred the commencement of legal proceedings without the leave of the court. The landlords later re-entered the premises peaceably after entering judgement (in their action) in default of defence, which entitled them to such entry; they also obtained a county court declaration that their re-entry did not require the court's leave and also that the re-entry forfeited the lease because the tenants had failed to pay the rent in question within the period specified in the lease. When the tenants appealed, it was held, *inter alia*, that the landlords' subsequent peaceable re-entry on to the premises in order to terminate the lease was a self-help. Since self-help was a non-judicial remedy not requiring assistance by the courts, it did not come under "other proceedings" or "other legal process" under section 252(2)(b) of the Insolvency Act 1986. Therefore, the landlords could rightly re-enter the premises without leave of the court.

*The setting of traps, etc., against trespassers*

According to s.31, Offences Against the Person Act 1861, it is unlawful to set man-traps, spring-guns, etc., likely to cause death or physical injury. But, such weapons or traps may be set at night for the purpose of protecting residential property. The duty owed to trespassers under s.1(4) of the Occupiers' Liability Act 1984 must, however be discharged. That duty is to take reasonable care to see that a trespasser does not suffer injury on the premises as a result of any danger there. An example of such reasonable care is a clear warning of the danger in question. Breach of the duty in the absence of any applicable defence like *volenti non fit injuria* (provided for by

25. [1995] 1 W.L.R. 1127.

s.1(6)) will make an occupier liable under the Act.

Also, it may be reasonable under the Animals Act 1971, s.5(3), to leave a fierce watch dog loose as a deterrence to trespassers or to protect one's property if there is proper warning of the dog's presence, as happened in *Cummings v Grainger*.[26]

*Non-human trespassers (right of distress damage feasant)*

In the case of non-human trespassers there is what is known as the right of "distress damage feasant". That is the right of a person in occupation of land:

(a) to seize any chattels (e.g., goods, cattle, etc.) which are on his land unlawfully and doing damage there, and

(b) to detain them until he has been compensated by their owner for the damage so caused.

Today the right of distress over trespassing animals (specifically livestock) may be said to be governed by the Animals Act 1971. This is because the right at common law to seize and detain animals has been abolished by section 7 of that Act, which has put a statutory procedure in its place as follows:

- The occupier may detain any livestock (which term, according to section 11, covers cattle, horses, asses, mules, hinnies, sheep, pigs, goats, poultry, etc.) that has strayed onto his land and which is then not under any person's control (s.7(2)). However, that detention must end:

  (a) after 48 hours unless the occupier has given notice to a police station and to the animal's owner, if known (s.7(3)), or

---

26. [1977] Q.B. 397; [1976] 3 W.L.R. 842, C.A.. But, it is unlawful to use unchained guard dogs to protect property other than a dwelling house and farms: *Hobson v Gledhill* [1978] 1 W.L.R. 215. The Guard Dogs Act 1975 governs the keeping of guard dogs.

(b) if sufficient compensation is paid to the occupier (s.7(3)(b)), or

(c) if, where compensation is not required or due under s.4 of the Act,[27] a person entitled to possession of the animal claims it.[28]

- After 14 days have passed the occupier has the right to sell the livestock in a market or by public auction (s.7(4)). However, if proceedings have already started for the return of the livestock or for a claim for damage caused by it, or for the expense of keeping it, there can be no sale.[29] After the sale the occupier must, after deducting his expenses and satisfying his claim, pay the balance to the owner.

In *Arthur and Another v Anker,*[30] the facts of which were similar to those in *Lloyd v D.P.P.*, Sir Thomas Bingham, Master of the Rolls, doubted whether the self-help remedy of distress damage feasant applied to afford a defence to a "landowner" who clamped a car parked on his land without his permission, the car-owner having seen a warning notice that cars parked there without appropriate authority would be clamped. The reasons of the Master of the Rolls for his doubt included the following:

---

27. Which provides:
"(1) Where livestock belonging to any person strays on to land in the ownership or occupation of another and -
(a) damage is done by the livestock to the land or to any property on it which is in the ownership or possession of the other person; or
(b) any expenses are reasonably incurred by that other person in keeping the livestock while it cannot be restored to the person to whom it belongs or while it is detained in pursuance of section 7 of this Act, or in ascertaining to whom it belongs;
the person to whom the livestock belongs is liable for the damage or expenses, except as otherwise provided by this Act.
(2) For the purposes of this section any livestock belongs to the person in whose possession it is."

28. Section 7(3)(b) and (c).

29. Impliedly, therefore, if the damage caused is more than the proceeds of the sale, the occupier of the land can sue the animal's owner for the balance.

30. (1995) *The Times*, December 1.

(i) the remedy was aimed at stopping or preventing damage to one's land or anything on it (which the clamping of a parked car did not achieve); and

(ii) unlawful parking alone was not enough (something more, such as actual damage of or on the land, was required).

In addition, s.9, Animals Act 1971 authorises the putting down of a dog if it is worrying or about to worry livestock, and if there is no other way of ending or preventing the injury or there is no ascertainable owner in control of that dog.

## 3. Abatement of a nuisance

Any victim of a private nuisance has the right to abate that nuisance by doing something on his own property; e.g., he may cut the branches of his neighbour's tree which project over or into his land.[31] However, he must not appropriate what he severs, otherwise he will be liable for conversion. Thus, in *Mills v Brooker*,[32] where the plaintiff's Bramley's Seedling apple trees had branches overhanging the defendant's land and the defendant picked apples off those branches and sold them, the defendant was held liable for conversion. Lord Lush's judgement, agreeing with that of Avery J., is quite instructive. He said (at pages 558-9):

> "The owner of a fruit tree, the branches of which grow over the boundary of his land, is the owner of the fruit of the overhanging branches while it is still growing on the tree. It is equally his property after it has been detached from the tree, whether it has fallen from being ripe, or been blown off by the wind, or been severed by the act of man. The adjoining owner is entitled to sever the overhanging fruit in the exercise of a right of abatement of the nuisance, but the exercise of that right cannot divest the owner's right of property in the fruit so severed. It may be that the owner could not justify entering upon the adjoining land for the purpose of recovering the fruit, but as soon as the adjoining owner carries off the fruit and sells it he is guilty of a conversion and liable for the full value."

---

31. *Lemmon v Webb* [1895] A.C. 1; see also *Pickering v Rudd*, 1 Stark. 56; 4 Camp. 219.
32. [1919] 1 K.B. 555.

The right to abate a nuisance, however, is subject to the following conditions:

(i) It must be exercised in a peaceful way. If the abator is entering adjoining land to exercise the right and his entry is refused, he can only use force to enter if the circumstances are most exceptional (e.g., in a fire or other life-threatening emergency).[33] As Best J. said in *Earl of Lonsdale v Nelson*:[34]

> "The security of lives and property may sometimes require so speedy a remedy as not to allow time to call on the person on whose property the mischief has arisen, to remedy it. In such cases an individual would be justified in abating a nuisance from omission without notice. In all other cases of such nuisances, persons should not take the law into their own hands, but follow the advice of Lord Hale and appeal to a court of justice."

(ii) Notice must be given to the creator of the nuisance to remedy it, otherwise the abator may be technically a trespasser. But, no notice is required (a) where the nuisance is one of omission and it is very urgent (i.e., the security of lives and property does not allow time for notice to be given), or (b) if the nuisance can be abated without entry on to the land of the offender, as in *Lemmon v Webb* (a case which is authority for the proposition that, where a person's land is overhung by trees growing on the land of his neighbour, he can, without giving notice and providing he does not trepass on that neighbour's land, cut those overhanging branches).

(iii) Unnecessary damage should not be done by the abator. This is illustrated by the *Lagan Navigation case*. There the appellants were, under a local Act of 1843, required to keep the navigation and locks, etc., of a canal in an efficient state. They raised their embankments to protect their lock from damage and keep it in an efficient state for navigation purposes. The respondents, who owned the adjacent land, considered the raised embankments were causing the canal to flood on to their land. They, therefore, during a heavy flood, entered the appellants' land without giving them notice, and removed a portion of the embankments in order to allow

33. Use of force in the absence of any emergency is a breach of the criminal law (though probably not the civil law because the court may not allow his neighbour to sue successfully and thus take advantage of his unreasonable wrongdoing).

34. (1823) 2 B. & C. 302, 311 (quoted in the *Lagan Navigation case* [1927] A.C. 226, at 245).

escape of the flood water. The appellants commenced proceedings against them and sought damages and an injunction restraining them from interfering with those embankments. The respondents claimed their action was justified because it was to abate a nuisance and they also sought damages and a mandatory injunction to force the appellants to remove those banks. The House of Lords held (endorsing the decision of the judge at first instance, which the Court of Appeal had reversed) that, since there was no evidence of the appellants negligently exercising their statutory power, they were not liable for the flooding of the respondents' lands. So, the appellants were granted the injunctive relief they sought and the respondents' counterclaim was dismissed with costs. The respondents' taking the law into their own hands was, accordingly, inadvisable, thereby illustrating how risky self-help can be. Lord Atkinson described their behaviour (at page 246) as "high-handed and violent". His Lordship pointed out that they failed to prove that they did no unnecessary damage and also that they had no choice but to cut those banks.

The abator must also cause as little damage as possible to the wrong-doer, to any innocent party or to the public. Therefore, where there are two ways of abatement, the less mischievous one should be followed. Also, in order to abate, if the abator has a choice of interfering with the property of the wrong-doer or with that of an innocent third party, he must choose to interfere with the wrong-doer's property: *Roberts v Rose*.[35]

(iv) If an occupier has already been to court and his application for a mandatory injunction has been refused, he cannot thereafter take the law into his own hands by exercising self-help to achieve the same end. This is clearly shown by *Burton v Winters*.

*Abatement by persons with a right of common*

Persons with a right of common (i.e., the right to take some part of the natural products of the land/water which belongs to another person, which right can be exercised together with him or others) may abate a nuisance on

---

35. (1865) L.R. 1 Ex. 82, 89; see also *Lagan Navigation Company v Lambeg*.

the common if a *prima facie* unlawful act is the nuisance. An illustration of this is *R v Dyer*.[36] There Dyer and others were convicted of malicious damage to a notice board and the scaffolding supporting it on Felton Common in the parish of Winford, Somerset. They submitted that they, as commoners, had the right to remove the notice board because it had not been proved to be lawfully on the common. But that submission of theirs was overruled by the court. They, therefore, appealed to the Court of Criminal Appeal, which quashed their conviction because their submission should not have been overruled but, rather, should have succeeded. Goddard L.C.J., in his judgement pointed out that the district council concerned (Long Ashton R.D.C.) had power under s.1(1) of the Commons Act 1899 to make bye-laws and regulations for preventing nuisances and preserving order on the common, but not for permitting nuisances or boards to be placed there. The notice board in question had nothing to do with the common: it was partly an advertisement for contractors working nearby and partly a sign directing people to the site where those contractors were working. Therefore, according to The Lord Chief Justice (at p. 160):

> "ARLETT V ELLIS (1827) 7 B. & C. 346 and DAVIES V WILLIAMS (1851) 16 QB 546, are ample authority for the saying that 'if an erection is placed on a common without lawful authority, the commoners are entitled to remove it'."

This abatement by commoners may extend to the demolition of a building erected on the common by a trespasser. Even if the trespasser is living in the building, that right may still be exercised as long as he has previously been given reasonable notice to remove the building: *Davies v Williams*.[37]

## 4. The retaking/recapture of goods

Put simply, if someone trespasses on another person's land, wrongfully takes that person's property away and puts it on his land (i.e., is detaining another person's property on his land without lawful justification), the owner has the right to use reasonable force to enter the other person's land and retake his

---

36. [1952] 36 Cr. App. R. 155.
37. [1885] 116 Q.B. 546; see also *Lane v Capsey* [1891] 3 Ch. 411.

property.[38]

However, if someone borrows another person's property (e.g., typewriter) and he refuses to return it after the owner has expressly requested its return to him, the owner cannot enter the other person's property without his permission or forcibly[39] and retake the typewriter. This is because the typewriter did not get on to the non-owner's property by his own wrongful act initially and, therefore, if the owner does so, he will be trespassing and/ or may be liable in conversion[40] or possibly break the criminal law, especially if he does not have proof of ownership of that typewriter. Here it is worth noting that, according to the New Brunswick Supreme Court in *Devoe v Long*, a person has no right to retake property by force from another person who originally obtained it lawfully.

Unfortunately, the law is not clear about the position of a person on whose land the goods happen to be but who is not responsible for their being there and had not committed any tortious act in relation to them. However, in *Anthony v Haney*[41] Tindall C.J. said, *obiter,* that under certain circumstances the owner of the goods could recover them from the innocent person's land, for example:

(i) if the goods accidentally happen to be on that innocent person's land,

(ii) where a person takes the goods feloniously and their owner follows them to the land of the innocent party, or

(iii) where the innocent party refuses to hand the goods back to their owner or to answer the owner's demand for them.[42]

The right to retake property is also limited by the Consumer Credit Act 1974 as regards "protected goods". That will be looked at later in this

---

38. *R v Milton* (1827) 1 M. & M. 107; *Devoe v Long* (1951) 1 D.L.R. 203.

39. According to the Law Commission's Working Paper 54: "a forcible entry to recover a chattel, which involved an application, display or immediate threat of force likely to dissuade a person from fear of violence to his person from offering lawful resistance to the entry, should never be regarded as reasonable."

40. *Mills v Brooker*; see now Torts (Interference with Goods) Act 1977, s.1.

41. (1832) 8 Bing. 186, at 192-3.

42. Tindall C.J., at pp. 191-2, went on to stress the important requirement that the owner must first not only allege or show ownership of the goods but also must explain how they happened to be on the innocent person's land.

chapter.

## 5. Necessity as self-help

Sometimes a person may act to preserve life and/or property against a natural force (a non-human assailant), e.g., a flood. Thus, it may be lawful for a landowner to build a barrier to prevent flood water entering his land, even though the barriers will have the effect of causing water to enter his neighbour's property.[43]

What he cannot do lawfully, however, is:

(a) to assist actively the discharge of flood waters from his land on to his neighbour's land (i.e., he must beware of nuisance or liability under the rule in *Rylands v Fletcher*, the rule that anyone who brings on to his land something which is not there ordinarily but that is likely to do mischief if it escapes, and it escapes and causes mischief, he will be liable therefor even though he is not at fault,[44] or

(b) to obstruct a regular stream or the course of ordinary flood water.[45]

An interesting, debatable issue is the entering of another's property for the purpose of making repairs so as to avoid damage to one's own adjoining property. According to cases like *John Trenberth v National Westminster Bank*,[46] an occupier of property damaged by natural or other causes must have a licence or easement (e.g., a right of way) before he can lawfully enter the property of his neighbour for the purpose of making repairs. Also, on the authority of *Bradburn v Lindsay*,[47] a defendant cannot claim that a plaintiff ought to mitigate his loss by entering his (the defendant's) land and abating the nuisance, etc.

---

43. *Gerrard v Crowe* [1921] 1 A.C. 395; *Lagan Navigation Co. v Lambeg*.
44. See *Rylands v Fletcher* (1868) L.R. 3 H.L. 330. According to the *Cambridge Water Co. v Eastern Counties Leather* [1994] 1 All E.R. 53, the damage caused must be reasonably foreseeable.
45. Therefore, if flood water on A's land draws away naturally and does damage to B's land, A will not be liable. For example, strict liability under the rule in *Rylands v Fletcher* will not lie because A did not bring the water on to his land.
46. (1979) 123 *S.J.* 388.
47. [1983] 2 All E.R. 408.

Logical though it may be, this aspect of the law, it is submitted, is highly unsatisfactory because it does not consider necessity, e.g., the preservation of property. It should be possible for such an occupier to make those repairs on his neighbour's land providing he does no damage or gives an undertaking to compensate his neighbour for any damage. It is, therefore, not surprising that the Law Commission has recommended that such an occupier should be able to apply to the court for a right of access to his neighbour's land in order to do preservation work to his own property.[48] It is also submitted that in an emergency, in order to save life or limb in circumstances where going to obtain a right of access from the court will waste time, the occupier of land should be able to enter his neighbour's property to do any repairs necessary (providing he causes no damage there).

## 6. The set-off

The set-off is another important kind of self help. It is a cross-claim by a person against another who has a claim against him. For example, if D owes P money but has some claim against P, D can in general "set off" his claim against the debt; this may cancel or reduce the sum of money he, D, owes P. Therefore, if D owes P £4,000 and P owes D £3,000, then if P asks D for his £4,000, D can "set off" the £3,000 owed to him by P and pay P only the balance of £1,000. If he can do this without going to court, the advantages of self-help can be clearly seen - it is speedier and saves costs, etc.

According to R.S.C. (Rules of the Supreme Court), Ord. 18, r.17, the set-off is a defendant's claim to a sum of money, ascertained or not, which he relies on as a defence to the whole of the plaintiff's claim or part of it. Therefore, in civil litigation the set-off is specifically pleaded by way of a defence (as a shield rather than a sword). It is a cross-claim, as shown by *Eller v Grovecrest Investments Ltd.*,[49] where it was held that a tenant's cross-claim for damages could be used by way of set-off as a defence against a landlord's claim to distraint on the tenant's chattels for rent due.

The counterclaim, too, is a cross-claim just like the set-off. But the counterclaim is in substance also a cross-action. It does operate "not merely

---

48. See para. 3.42 of *Law Commission No. 151, "Rights of Access to Neighbouring Land"*, 1985.
49. [1995] 2 W.L.R. 278.

as a defence, as does the set-off, but in all respects as an independent action by the defendant against the plaintiff".[50]

## 7. The right of retainer of debt due to an estate

A personal representative can retain out of a pecuniary legacy (i.e., money left by will) or share of residue a debt which the beneficiary under the will in question solely owes to the estate. However, a partnership debt cannot be retained out of a legacy given to one of two or more partners because that partnership debt is not owed solely by the particular partner-legatee. *Turner v Turner*[51] is authority for this. In that case A and B were partners. The partnership owed money to the estate of their deceased aunt. B was a legatee under the will of the deceased aunt. (There were other legatees but their legacies were not in question.) The question was whether the partnership debt owed to the estate of the deceased aunt of the partners should be paid out of B's legacy. It was held that, although a legatee who owed money to the estate of the testator must first pay that debt to the estate before he could receive anything from that estate (as his legacy), that rule did not apply if the debt was owed to the testator's estate by a partnership and the legatee was only one of the partners.

This right of the personal representative is different from the right of set-off in an action because, unlike the set-off in an action, it exists:

(a) even if the debt in question is statute-barred,[52] and

(b) on the principle that the beneficiary is regarded as having in his hands the estate's assets for which he has to account, and that the beneficiary cannot claim any part of the estate's assets until he has returned to the estate the portion of the assets he holds.[53]

---

50. *Per* Cockburn, C.J., in *Stooke v Taylor* [1880] 5 Q.B.D. 569, at p. 576.
51. [1911] 1 Ch. 716.
52. *Re Akerman* [1891] 3 Ch. 212.
53. Also, the right differs from the personal representative's "right of retainer", i.e., the right to repay a debt to himself in preference to other creditors of the same degree. That "right of retainer" was abolished by s.10, Administration of Estates Act 1971.

## 8. Self-help in contract

Self-help in the law of contract may seem slightly less problematic and not as highly risky as that in tort. However, that view is wrong because in fact self-help in contract is equally fraught with danger in that, if the party exercising the right is not careful enough to ensure he is doing the right thing, he himself will be a wrong-doer or a party in breach of contract or a statutory provision, e.g., the creditor under a hire purchase agreement who retakes protected goods without a court order.

The following are all examples of self-help in contract:

(a) the right of the innocent party to avoid a voidable contract,

(b) the innocent party's right to terminate (or treat as at an end) a contract if the other party has breached a condition of it,

(c) the lien,

(d) rights of the parties under a contract for the sale of goods (governed by the Sale of Goods Act 1979) and under hire purchase agreements (governed by the Consumer Credit Act 1974), and

(e) a mortgagee's right of resale.

### (a) Avoidance of a voidable contract

Misrepresentation has the effect of making a contract voidable. Therefore, avoidance of a voidable contract may be illustrated by the case of a person who, having been induced by a misrepresentation by another person to enter into a contract with him, has discovered the misrepresentation and wants to avoid the contract.[54]

---

54. If the representee's argument that misrepresentation justifies avoiding the contract is accepted by the representor, self-help has triumphed.

## (b) Termination of contract after breach of condition

A non-breaching party may wish to terminate a contract because of the other party's breach of it, e.g., where there is a seven-day late delivery of perishable goods by the seller and the buyer wishes to treat the contract as at an end by refusing to accept (and pay for) the goods. Support for this can be found in, for example, s.36, Sale of Goods Act 1979, which provides that "unless otherwise agreed, where goods are delivered to the buyer, and he refuses to accept them, having the right to do so, he is not bound to return them to the seller, but it is sufficient if he intimates to the seller that he refuses to accept them".[55]

A party may also choose to withhold performance until the other party has performed his part of the bargain either fully or partly. For example, P can refuse to pay D, who is obliged to him by contract to do some work for him, until D has done all or part of that work.[56]

The point, therefore, is that, if the non-breaching party or party exercising self-help is happy just to avoid the bargain and is not challenged (i.e., if the other party does not go to court), then self-help will have been successful and both time and expense will have been saved by both parties. But, where the matter does go to court, self-help fails and judicial remedies, with consequent involvement of time, expense and effort, take over.

## (c) The lien

The lien is a right to retain property in one's possession until something is done by the owner of that property, e.g., until a debt is paid by him. There are three types of lien: common-law lien, equitable lien and statutory lien.

*Common-law lien*

The common-law lien is a person's right to retain another person's property

---

55. However, in *Lee v York Coach and Marine* [1977] R.T.R. 35 the buyer of a second-hand vehicle, which was not of merchantable quality, could not reject it because it was too late to do so after she had used it. Therefore, her remedies did lie in damages.

56. *Miles v Wakefield Metropolitan District Council* [1987] 1 All E.R. 1089.

until a debt owed to him has been paid or his claims are satisfied. It gives no right to sell or alienate the property and is, therefore, only a mechanism for forcing a debtor to pay. There are two types of common-law lien: general and particular.

A general common-law lien enables retention of goods until their owner has paid all claims the possessor of the goods has against him. Those claims do not have to relate to those goods only. For example, a solicitor in possession of title deeds, which belong to his client, can retain them until he has been paid all his fees by that client (or by someone else on his behalf) for all professional services up to that point in time. Accountants also have the same general lien.[57] A banker, too, has by mercantile custom a general lien over any commercial paper deposited by a customer (or someone else on his behalf) in the ordinary course of banking business.[58]

In the case of a particular common-law lien the claim/s must relate to the particular goods retained. For example, a watch repairer has a lien on the watch a person takes to him to repair. It is a particular lien because it is a security only for the particular debt in respect of that particular watch.

However, whereas the particular lien is favoured by the law, the general lien is not. This is probably because of the potential problems the exercise of a general lien can give rise to. The general lien could be risky if improperly exercised, e.g., where an inn-keeper (unlawfully) retains the car of a guest for failure to pay his bill at the inn.

*Equitable lien*

The equitable lien, on the other hand, does not depend on possession; it gives a charge upon property until any claims in question have been satisfied. An example of it is a vendor of land's lien on it until payment of the full purchase price.[59]

---

57. *Woodworth v Conroy* [1976] 2 W.L.R. 388.
58. Thus, valuables deposited for safe-keeping are not included.
59. For various other equitable liens see, for example, P.V. Baker (ed.), *Snell's Equity*, 29th ed. (London: Sweet and Maxwell, 1990), pp. 457-467. They include the solicitor's lien on property recovered, the lien of a purchaser for his purchase money, and the lien of trustees and of personal representatives on the trust property for their expenses.

*Statutory lien*

Such a lien is created by a statute. For example, under s.41, Sale of Goods Act 1979, the unpaid seller has a lien over goods until payment therefor has been made by the buyer. The right arises if the agreement does not provide for any credit term, if any credit term provided for has expired, or if the buyer has become insolvent.

Moreover, according to the Consumer Credit Act 1974, (i) if a hire purchase agreement[60] is cancelled, the debtor/hirer has a lien over any goods in his possession until payment of any sum repayable to him has been made (s.72), and (ii) if a "part-exchange agreement" (i.e., an agreement whereby a consumer gives up goods belonging to him in part exchange for other goods) is cancelled, the consumer is entitled to have returned to him by the negotiator (credit-broker or supplier) the goods he gave up initially. Those goods must be in substantially as good a condition as they were in when the negotiator received them and they must be returned to the consumer within ten days. Otherwise, a part-exchange allowance must be paid to the consumer. Until performance of that obligation the consumer has a lien on the ("negotiator's") goods in his possession (s.73).

*A further example of the lien: the innkeeper's lien*

At common law an innkeeper has a lien (for the unpaid bill of a guest) on any personal property or chattels which the guest brings into the inn as part of his luggage in his capacity as a guest. That lien is in respect of the guest's boarding and lodging during the time of his stay.[61] The lien also covers stolen and wrongfully obtained goods unless the innkeeper knows of the facts. Thus,

---

60. Defined by section 189(1), Consumer Credit Act 1974 as "an agreement other than a conditional sale agreement, under which:
    (a) goods are bailed or (in Scotland) hired in return for periodical payments by the person to whom they are bailed or hired, and
    (b) the property in the goods will pass to that person if the terms of the agreement are complied with and one or more of the following occurs:
        (i) the exercise of an option to purchase by that person,
        (ii) the doing of any other specified act by any party to the agreement,
        (iii) the happening of any other specified event".

61. *Mulliner v Florence* [1878] 3 Q.B.D. 484.

in *Marsh v Police Commissioner,*[62] where a guest at an inn was unable to pay his bill but gave a stolen ring to the innkeeper as security for the payment of that bill, it was held that the lien of the innkeeper attached to the ring. Referring to *Gordon v Silber,*[63] Lord Goddard stated in his leading judgement: "the authorities seem to be perfectly clear and uniform on the point - that an innkeeper's lien will attach to property brought by a guest to the hotel although the property has been stolen." In *Gordon v Silber* the defendants were a married couple (Mr. Martin Silber and his wife, Lady Lucy) who stayed at the plaintiffs' hotel, the Hotel Metropole. Lady Lucy brought into the hotel a large quantity of luggage, her own (i.e., separate) property. Her husband was given credit by the hotel's proprietors and so he made payments on account. There was unpaid balance of the hotel bill and the plaintiffs detained the luggage (the separate property) of Lady Lucy in exercise of their lien in respect of that unpaid balance. The court held that they could rightly exercise that lien even though the goods in question were the separate property of the wife. According to Lopes L.J. (at p. 492):

> "The plaintiffs as innkeepers were bound to receive the defendants and their goods, and were bound, so long as the defendants remained guests at the hotel, to keep safely and securely their goods; and the plaintiffs would have been liable in damages if these goods had been lost. How did the plaintiffs receive them? They knew of no distinction between the goods of the husband and wife, and could not inquire into their respective titles to the goods. They received them as the goods of Mr. Martin Silber and his wife, who became their guests. Suppose Mr. Martin Silber had stolen the goods, still if the plaintiffs received them with their guests the lien would have attached."

However, now according to the Hotel Proprietors' Act 1956, s. 2(2), a hotel proprietor (just like an innkeeper) has no lien on (i) any guest's vehicle, (ii) any property left in that vehicle, or (iii) any horse or live animal or its equipment, e.g., harness. He also "shall not as an innkeeper be liable to make good to any guest of his any loss of or damage" to such property.[64]

---

62. [1945] K.B. 43.
63. [1890] 25 Q.B.D. 491.
64. Section 1(1) provides: "An hotel within the meaning of this Act shall, and any other establishment shall not, be deemed to be an inn; and the duties, liabilities and rights which immediately before the commencement of this Act by law attached to an innkeeper as such shall, subject to provisions of this Act, attach to the proprietor of such an hotel and shall not attach to any other person."

## (d) Sale of Goods Act 1979

This statute gives to the unpaid seller of goods (in addition to the lien) the right of stoppage *in transitu* whereby, if he has knowledge that his buyer has become insolvent, he can stop the goods in transit, i.e., assume control over them again and retain them until he has been paid. The seller must, however, do so before the goods have been delivered by the carrier, etc., to the buyer or his agent.[65]

The Act also gave the unpaid seller the right to resell the goods if they are perishable.[66]

Furthermore, where the seller has reserved title to the goods until payment of the contract price or of any debt owed him, he can repossess the goods if the buyer is a company which goes into liquidation or receivership.[67]

## (e) The Consumer Credit Act 1974

Generally, if a person (B) wrongfully possesses or controls another person (A)'s goods, A has a right to retake them using reasonable force, if necessary. However, under the Consumer Credit Act 1974, there are certain limitations on the right of a creditor to retake/repossess goods. These limitations constitute the "debtor's protection against snatch back". The protection of the debtor is three-fold:

(i) *Notice is required.* Notice before termination is required in both default and non-default cases. In a default case (i.e., where the debtor fails to make payment/s to the creditor), notice gives the debtor a chance to remedy the default and, therefore, stop the threatened cancellation. A non-default case is where one or more of certain specified events occurs, e.g., the debtor's alienation of the goods before property in them has passed to him.

(ii) *Entry on premises.* The creditor/owner cannot enter any premises to take possession of goods subject to a regulated hire purchase, conditional sale or consumer hire agreement without a court order.

---

65. S.44, Sale of Goods Act 1979.
66. *Ibid.*, s.48.
67. *Aluminium Industrie Vassen B.V. v Romalpa Aluminium Ltd.* [1976] 2 All E.R. 552.

Such entry without a court order is actionable as a breach of statutory duty (section 92 (3)).

(iii) *Protected goods*. The creditor is not entitled to repossess protected goods without a court order. Goods are protected when:

(a) the debtor is in breach of a regulated hire purchase or conditional sale agreement relating to goods; and

(b) the debtor has paid to the creditor one-third or more of the total price and

(c) the property in the goods remains in the creditor (s.90 (1)).

If the creditor breaches s.90, the consequences are as follows: the agreement is terminated, the debtor is released from all liability, and the debtor is entitled to recover from the creditor all the money he has paid under the agreement (section 91).

### (f) The mortgagee's right to sell property mortgaged

A mortgage, according to Lindley M.R. in *Santley v Wilde*,[68] is "a conveyance of land or an assignment of chattels as a security for the payment of a debt or the discharge of some other obligation for which it is given". It is different from a charge which is not a conveyance of property but only gives a person (the chargee) certain rights over the property in question as security for the loan. The person who mortgages the property (asks for the loan, i.e., the borrower) is the mortgagor and the "person" to whom the property is mortgaged (the lender) is the mortgagee.

According to the Law of Property Act 1925, ss.101-107, a mortgagee of property has the right to sell the property out of court (i.e., without any judicial order - a kind of self-help) and free from the equity of redemption.[69]

---

68. [1899] Ch. 474.

69. The equity of redemption is an equitable interest in the land/property and is made up of the total of the rights of the mortgagor in the property, including the right to redeem the land. That equitable interest can be alienated or conveyed, etc., like any other interest in land. It arises as soon as the mortgage in question is made.

This statutory power of sale arises if: (a) the mortgage was made by deed (s.101(4)), (b) the money payable under it is due (either because the date fixed for redemption (the legal date) has passed or, in the case of payments by instalments, because of non-payment of instalments,[70] and (c) one of the following conditions has been satisfied:

(i) the mortgagor has been served with notice requiring payment by him of the mortgage money, and he has thereafter failed to pay part or all of it for three consecutive months (Law of Property Act 1925, s.103(i)), or

(ii) some (e.g., monthly) interest under the mortgage has not been paid for two or more months (s.103(ii), Law of Property Act 1925), or

(iii) the mortgagor has breached some provisions of the Law of Property Act 1925 or of the mortgage deed (e.g., to insure or repair the property), apart from the covenant to pay the mortgage money or interest.

**Conclusion**

From the foregoing the remedy of self-help (whereby an aggrieved party can give justice to himself without going to court) can be seen to be a right which ordinary people exercise almost daily. It is interesting to note that this "D.I.Y." justice is the oldest kind of remedy. It is evident in the Mosaic Law and in other laws. It covers not only the defence of one's self and property, the ejection of a trespasser, the abatement of a nuisance, the recapture of goods, necessity, the set-off, and the right of retainer of debt/s due to an estate, but also the right to do one's self justice in the law of contract (examples of which include the avoidance of a voidable contract, termination of a contract upon the other party's breach of a condition, the lien, a mortgagee's right to sell property mortgaged, an unpaid seller's right under the Sale of Goods Act 1979 and parties' rights under the Consumer Credit Act 1974, etc.). Because self-help avoids appearance in court, it is less

70. Where only payment of the interest is in arrears but the principal is not yet due, as in the case of an endowment mortgage, there is no power of sale without a court order: *Wilkinson's case* [1977] Ch. 99.

costly than judicial proceedings - in fact it is cheap. It is also speedy indeed. Moreover, it saves effort in that the person exercising it is does not have any duty to mitigate his loss because he is not going to court. However, as shown by cases such as *Burton v Winters* and *Mills v Brooker*, etc., it can be a very risky remedy indeed because its careless or unreasonable exercise can lead to violation of the law and/or the rights of another person, for which action may be taken against the wrong-doer.

The consensual remedies may arguably be classified under self-help. According to Blackstone, self-help, the "redress of private injuries which is obtained by the mere act of the parties", is of two types: (i) that arising from the act of only the injured party, and (ii) that arising from the joint act of all the parties together.[71] Therefore, the justification for treating separately the consensual remedies is that they do arise, not from the act of only the aggrieved or injured party but rather, from the joint act of all the parties concerned. They are looked at in the next chapter.

---

71. Blackstone, *Commentaries on the Laws of England*, vol. III, 2, 15.

**Exercises**

1. "Self-help is cheap and risky." Discuss this statement with particular reference to the abatement of nuisance and trespass to land.

2. Collier has returned from holiday to discover that his neighbour, Summer has planted a tree, some branches of which overhang into Collier's garden. When windy the branches brush against Collier's greenhouse and he is fearful that damage may be caused. Additionally, Summer has built a wall on the boundary line at the front of the two houses which encroaches by three inches upon Collier's drive. Collier has approached Summer about both of these matters and has been told by his neighbour that the tree and the wall cost him a lot of money and he was not prepared to listen to any complaints.

   Advise Collier of any remedies available to him, giving reasons for your advice.

# 2 The consensual remedies

## Introduction

The development of a general theory of contract in the nineteenth century reflected a *laissez faire* approach in which binding agreements took the form of bargains, the content of which was essentially a matter for the parties, the courts having no role to play unless the agreement had been broken. This philosophy of freedom of contract, based on individualism, provides that the parties to a contract not only have the right to rely on their own skill and judgement to agree the terms of the contract but also have the opportunity to determine the levels of compensation payable in the event of a breach. Such an award of an agreed sum payable on breach, or liquidated damages, needs to be distinguished from an action for an agreed sum.

## Action for an agreed sum

A contract may specifically provide that an agreed sum is payable in return for some performance under the contract by the other party, e.g., goods are sold for an agreed price or work is done for an agreed remuneration. An action may arise where such payment is not forthcoming. Such an action is a claim for specific relief for it is a claim for the specific enforcement of the defendant's positive contractual obligation to provide a specified sum of money. By comparison, in an award of damages the court estimates compensation in money for damage or injury sustained by the plaintiff. Note that, since the plaintiff, in an action for an agreed sum, recovers precisely and only that sum, there is no reference to questions of mitigation of loss or the inability to claim for loss which is considered too remote.[1]

If the plaintiff chooses to terminate the contract, he will not be able to claim for any sum which was due to be paid after the date of such termination. Instead such sums will be considered as part of any assessment of damages to be awarded for wrongful repudiation. If the plaintiff chooses

1. Although see Treitel, *The Law of Contract*, 9th ed. (1995), pp. 916-918.

to treat the contract as still in existence, he may claim the agreed sum, as long as he has completed those obligations which give rise to the claim. If the plaintiff has not done all that is required of him, then he is unable to claim for the agreed sum and may only claim damages.[2] Where the plaintiff chooses to disregard the defendant's repudiation and continue the contract, he may claim for an agreed sum under the contract rather than sue for damages. In *White & Carter (Councils) Ltd. v McGregor*,[3] the plaintiff advertising agents agreed with the defendants to display advertising plates on letter bins for a period of three years at a price per litter bin per week. On the same day the defendants repudiated the agreement but this was not accepted by the plaintiffs who then carried out their obligations for the full three years. The House of Lords held that the plaintiffs were entitled to disregard the defendant's repudiation and treat the contract as remaining in full effect and so claim for the contract price.

In a contract for the sale of goods the seller has a statutory right to an action against the buyer for the price of the goods.[4] Such a right is a personal one against the buyer only rather than against the goods so that, if the property in the goods has passed to the buyer, the seller can exercise no control over them. To circumvent this limitation sellers frequently insert a "Romalpa" clause which provides that the title to the goods remains the seller's until the goods have been paid for.[5]

## Liquidated damages

The parties to a contract may make a genuine assessment of the losses which are likely to result from an anticipated breach of contract, and stipulate that such a sum shall be payable in that event. Such a provision for liquidated damages enables a party to know in advance exactly what his liability will be. By convention a provision for liquidated damages is treated as an aspect of contractual damages, yet the remedy is similar to an action for an agreed

---

2. *Denmark Productions v Boscobel Productions* [1969] 1 Q.B. 699.
3. [1962] A.C. 413. Since this was a claim for an agreed sum, the the rule regarding mitigation which is applicable to damages was not relevant. The distinction, in these circumstances, is difficult to justify.
4. S.49 (1) Sale of Goods Act 1979.
5. For "reservation of title" clauses see *Aluminium Industrie Vaassen B.V. v Romalpa Aluminium Ltd.* Also, *Clough Mill Ltd. v Martin* [1984] 3 All E.R. 982.

sum as both constitute the enforcement of the defendant's promise to pay a sum of money. However, there is an important distinction to be drawn between the two. A liquidated damages clause represents the estimated loss incurred and the consequent agreed sum payable in the event of a breach of contract whereas, an action for an agreed sum is not reliant on any attempt at estimating loss and payment will be enforced even it exceeds the loss actually suffered.

Liquidated damages are an estimate of the loss that will be caused to one party if the other breaches the contract. Conscious of the distinction that has to be drawn between freedom of contract and inequality of bargaining power, there is a fundamental question of whether the court should enforce what the parties have agreed. If the court considers that the sums payable are a genuine pre-estimate of the actual loss suffered, then the court will sustain such a claim. That is, it is not guided by the usual principles used in the assessment of unliquidated damages despite the fact that the sums agreed may be more or less than the actual loss caused by the breach.

A liquidated damages clause takes effect in the event of a breach. The plaintiff is prevented from claiming more by way of an action for unliquidated damages.

**Penalty or liquidated damages?**

If the sums stipulated are a genuine pre-estimate of loss, then, in an action for breach of contract, the court will enforce claims for such sums. As stated above, this will be so even where the loss suffered is more or less than the sums stipulated. However, where the clause is a penalty clause, it is disregarded. A penalty clause contains an agreed sum which is usually out of proportion to the damage inflicted on the innocent party. Here, the sum stipulated represents a threat to one party with the intention of ensuring performance of the contract by him. Such penalties are said to hold a party *in terrorem* (as a warning against breaking the contract). In these circumstances the court will ignore the sum which constitutes the penalty and award a sum which represents the actual loss suffered by a party as a result of the breach.

The parties' choice of the words "penalty" or "liquidated damages" is not, of itself, conclusive. In *Cellulose Acetate Silk Co. Ltd. v Widnes*

*Foundry (1924) Ltd.*[6] a pre-estimated sum of £20 per week, payable on late performance, was described in the contract as a penalty. As a result of a 30-week delay the plaintiff lost £5,850, yet the agreed amount was awarded since its object was not to act *in terrorem*. The parties must have known that the actual loss would be more than £20 per week. Thus, it is interesting to note that an agreed damages clause may be valid even though it was deliberately set at less than the estimated loss, for a party may properly limit his liability.[7] It is the construction of the clause itself and the surrounding circumstances which are of importance. With these in mind the court may decide that a clause described as a penalty is, in fact, a liquidated damages clause and vice versa.[8]

The onus of proving that a sum is a penalty lies on the party who is sued for it, and that of showing it is liquidated damages on the party who is suing.[9]

Lord Dunedin laid down the basis on which the courts decide whether a pre-estimated sum is a penalty or liquidated damages in *Dunlop Pneumatic Tyre Co. v New Garage & Motor Co. Ltd.*[10] as follows:

1. A sum will be a penalty if it is "extravagant and unconscionable in amount in comparison with the greatest loss that could possibly follow from the breach". For example, a clause in a building contract valued at £50 which provides that the builder should pay £1 million in the event of failing to do the work.[11]

2. It will be held to be a penalty if the breach consists only of a party not paying a sum of money and failure to do so results in that party incurring liability to pay a larger sum. Thus, liability to pay £500 for failure to pay £10 on the due day would be considered a penalty.[12]

---

6. [1933] A.C.20.
7. Note that this would not amount to a pure limitation clause for, although it fixes the maximum payment possible in the event of a breach, it also sets a minimum amount payable. Thus, the defendant would still have to pay the stipulated amount even if the plaintiff had lost less.
8. See *Kemble v Farren* (1829), *Wall v Rederiaktiebolaget Luggude* [1915] 3 K.B. 66.
9. *Robophone Facilities v Blank* [1966] 1 W.L.R. 1428.
10. [1915] A.C. 79, at pp. 87-8.
11. See *Clydebank Engineering Co. v Don Jose Ramos* [1905] A.C. 6.
12. See *Betts v Burch* (1859) 4 H. & N. 506.

3. There is a presumption that it is a penalty when a single lump sum is made payable by way of compensation on the occurrence of one or more or all of several events, some of which may be serious, some minor.[13] Thus, in *Wilson v Love*[14] a clause in a lease which stipulated that a tenant should pay £3 "for every ton of hay or straw which shall be sold off the premises during the last twelve months of the tenancy" was held to be a penalty since the value of hay was greater than straw. It seems that this presumption applies even where the actual breach gives rise to a loss which makes the sum stipulated appear to be a reasonable pre-estimate.[15]

4. "It is no obstacle to the sum stipulated being a genuine pre-estimate of damage that the consequences of breach are such as to make precise pre-estimation an impossibility." In *Dunlop*, the plaintiffs supplied tyres to the defendants who agreed that, *inter alia*, they would not re-sell the tyres below list price, £5 liquidated damages being payable for each tyre sold in breach of the agreement. It was held that the sum amounted to liquidated damages for, although it might have been disproportionate to the harm caused, that is a price war damaging Dunlop's selling organisation, the harm to Dunlop was impossible to estimate and the sum stipulated was not extravagant. Similar circumstances prevailed in *Ford Motor Company v Armstrong*,[16] in which an agreed sum, payable in the event of breaching a number of obligations including not to sell any car below the listed price, was held to be a penalty partly because of the fact that it was made payable for a number of different breaches and also because its size precluded it from being a genuine pre-estimate of the possible damage suffered as a result of a breach.

5. Subject to 1 and 2 above, if there is only one event upon which the agreed sum is to be paid, the sum is liquidated damages. An illustration of this is *Law v Redditch Local Board*,[17] where a contract for a sewage works construction provided that, if the work

---

13. See *Ford Motor Co. v Armstrong* (1915) 31 T.L.R. 267; and *Landom Trust v Hurrell* [1955] 1 All E.R. 839.
14. [1896] 1 Q.B. 626.
15. *Ariston S.R.L. v Charly Records*, *Financial Times*, March 21, 1990.
16. (1915) T.L.R. 267.
17. [1892] 1 Q.B. 127.

was not completed by a stated date, the contractor should pay £100 and £5 for every seven days thereafter on which the work was uncompleted.

The issue of whether a clause amounts to liquidated damages or a penalty should be judged at the time the contract was made and not at the time of the breach.[18] However, in *Philips Hong Kong v A.-G. of Hong Kong*,[19] a case concerning a road construction contract, the Privy Council, whilst accepting this view, considered that reference to what had actually happened might provide valuable evidence of what could reasonably have been expected. Indeed, it might provide a better guide than hypothetical examples of when the plaintiff's actual loss would be substantially lower than that suffered.

Hence, as Lord Woolf stated, the courts should normally uphold what the parties have agreed. This observation was based on the need for certainty, particularly in commercial contracts, and, it seems, the general approach in this context should be biased towards categorising such clauses as liquidated and enforceable. This is justified in a commercial context where the parties enjoy equality of bargaining power and need to know that what they have agreed is binding. Lord Woolf stated that:

> "...the fact that two parties who should well be capable of protecting their respective commercial interests agreed the allegedly penal provision suggests that the formula for calculating liquidated damages is unlikely to be oppressive...".[20]

**Where the sum stipulated is greater than the actual loss**

A liquidated damages clause is effective in the event of a breach, the plaintiff not recovering more than the sum stipulated. The plaintiff can recover the stipulated sum even though the actual loss is less or even nil. In *Clydebank Engineering and Shipbuilding Co. Ltd. v Castaneda*,[21] the House of Lords rejected the argument of the sellers of four torpedo boats to the Spanish navy that their late delivery saved them the destruction of the

18. *Dunlop Motor Co. v New Garage & Motor Co.* [1915] A.C. 79.
19. (1993) 61 B.L.R. 41.
20. *Ibid.*, at p. 59. This echoes Lord Roskill in *Export Credits Guarantee Department v Universal Oil Products Co.* [1983] 2 All E.R. 205.
21. [1905] A.C. 6.

fleet by the Americans and precluded them from having to pay liquidated damages.

If the sum stipulated is a penalty, then, although it remains a term of the contract, the plaintiff can only recover the amount to which he would have been entitled if the contract had not contained the penalty clause. This was the decision of the Court of Appeal in *Jobson v Johnson*[22] in which the defendant purchased shares in a football club for an intial payment of £351,688 to be followed by six monthly instalments of £40,000. It was agreed that non-payment of the second or later instalments would result in the purchaser returning the shares to the vendors for only £40,000. After paying £140,000, the defendant defaulted. It was held that the clause amounted to a penalty since it was not a genuine pre-estimate of the loss and the vendors should not be compensated beyond their actual loss.

**Where the sum stipulated is less than the actual loss**

Where the liquidated damages clause has underestimated the actual loss suffered by the innocent party, then only the stipulated sum is recoverable. As stated above, this will be so even where the amount stipulated is deliberately set at a sum less than the estimated loss.

It is possible for a stipulated sum to be deemed a penalty even though the plaintiff's loss is greater than the amount set by the clause, for example, where a single lump sum is made payable on the occurrence of one or more, or all, of several events some of which may cause serious loss, some minor. To follow the usual rule and disregard the penalty would clearly benefit the plaintiff. In *Wall v Rederiaktiebolaget*,[23] it was decided that shipowners could ignore a penalty clause and sue for their actual loss which was greater than the penalty. In *Cellulose Acetate*,[24] a case in which the clause under scrutiny could have been considered as either a penalty or as liquidated damages, the issue was left open whilst in *Robophone Facilities*[25] Diplock J. considered the question to be unclear and unresolved. Treitel[26] concludes that generally such a clause would be disregarded under

---

22. [1989] 1 W.L.R. 1026.
23. [1915] 1 W.L.R. 1428.
24. [1933] A.C. 20.
25. [1966] 3 All E.R. 128.
26. Treitel, *The Law of Contract*, 9th ed. (Sweet and Maxwell, 1995), p. 902.

the rule in *Wall's* case. However, although this view may be explained by the need to judge the clause in question by reference to the time at which the contract was made, it would seem wrong to invalidate the penalty clause and allow the party who imposed it to retrieve his actual loss when, in the same circumstances, the party who underestimated by way of a liquidated damages clause would receive no more than that which had been agreed. Such an approach would allow the plaintiff who had not genuinely attempted to estimate the loss to take the benefit of a penalty clause and to ignore it when it would be to his detriment.

**Actual loss recoverable?**

It follows that, as long as the clause in question is a genuine pre-estimate of the loss, then the sum stipulated is recoverable. According to Diplock L.J. in *Robophone Facilities v Blank*,[27] this seems to be the case even where part of the loss was beyond the defendant's reasonable contemplation and consequently too remote. This was because the clause would put the other on notice of special loss. However, it should be noted that the Law Commission[28] provisionally thought that the reference point for determining whether or not a stipulated sum is a genuine pre-estmate would be the damages which a court would award in the absence of such a clause, that is, those damages which are legally recoverable. The Court of Appeal also took a restrictive attitude towards losses not legally recoverable in *Lombard North Central plc v Butterworth.*[29]

Diplock L.J. and the Law Commission again took opposing views regarding the impact on a liquidated damages clause of the rule concerning mitigation of damage. It may be arguable that, where a genuine pre-estimate of loss has been attempted, then the actual sum agreed, rather than the legally recoverable loss, should be awarded. That is, no reference need be made to whether the plaintiff mitigated his loss. Yet this approach is open to criticism for it may well over-compensate his loss. Alternatively, it would encourage waste arising out of the failure to mitigate. In a Canadian case the plaintiff was found to be under a duty to mitigate and was only able to

---

27. [1966] 1 W.L.R. 1428, *per* Diplock L.J., at 1448.
28. Law Commission Working Paper No. 61.
29. [1987] 1 All E.R. 267.

claim legally recoverable damages.[30]

As far as liability in contract is concerned, the Unfair Contract Terms Act 1977 limits the ability of a party to "exclude or restrict" liability.[31] Although a liquidated damages clause must be a genuine pre-estimate of loss it may, in the event, increase liability as well as restrict liability. Nor, as the *Widnes Foundry*[32] case shows, can a liquidated damages clause be regarded as a limitation clause because the defendant does not have to pay any more than the sum agreed where the actual loss is higher, but he pays the stipulated sum even where the loss is less. It follows that such clauses are probably not subject to the Act.

From 1 January 1995 the E.C. Directive on Unfair Terms in Consumer Contracts[33] has applied in the U.K. under the Unfair Terms in Consumer Contracts Regulations 1994. The scope of the Regulations is limited to contracts between a seller or supplier of goods and services on the one hand and a consumer on the other. Further, the Regulations are limited to clauses in contracts which have not been individually negotiated, that is, standard form contracts.[34] Any term which is considered unfair is not binding on the consumer. Regulation 4 deems "unfair" any contractual term which causes a "significant imbalance" in the rights and obligations arising under the contract to the detriment of the consumer. This has to be "contrary to the requirement of good faith" and includes a term which requires "any consumer who fails to fulfill his obligation to pay a disproportionately high sum in compensation".[35]

It should follow that, if an "agreed damages" clause is considered to be "unfair" under the Directive, it will also be regarded as a penalty and, therefore, invalid at common law. Note that the common law is not restricted to standard form contracts for the sale of goods and services. However, as Treitel observes, the Directive appears to be wider in scope than the common law in that it may apply to sums payable otherwise than on breach. Failing to "fulfill his obligations" may cover a situation where the consumer is not necessarily in breach.[36] In such a circumstance the term may be regarded as "unfair" under the Directive.

---

30. *Elsey v J.G. Collins Insurance Agencies Ltd.* [1978] 83 D.L.R. (3d) 1.
31. S.13(2)(a).
32. *Cellulose Acetate Silk Co. Ltd. v Widnes Foundry (1924) Ltd.* [1933] A.C. 20.
33. 93/13/EEC.
34. Regulation 3 (1).
35. Schedule 3 para. 1(e).
36. Treitel, *The Law of Contract*, 9th ed. (Sweet and Maxwell, 1994), pp. 905-6.

**Rules regarding liquidated damages and penalties are applicable only to breaches of contract**

Liquidated damages and penalties are payable in the event of a breach of contract. However, as observed in the previous section, a contract may provide for the payment of money on an event which is not a breach. In such a situation the rules regarding liquidated damages and penalties do not apply.

Thus, in *Alder v Moore*,[37] an injured footballer received £500 from the Association Football insurance scheme. He agreed "to take no part as a playing member in any form of professional football in the future and that in the event of an infringement of this condition I will be subject to a penalty of the amount stated above (i.e., the amount paid)". Subsequently, he started playing professional football again and the plaintiff insurers sought the return of the £500. The Court of Appeal held that "the sum did not represent a penalty because the defendant had not broken the contract since he had made no promise not to play again".[38] The rules regarding penalties were not applicable and the plaintiff could claim the amount in question.

Again, *in Export Credits Guarantee Department v Universal Oil Products Co.,*[39] the House of Lords held that the main reason for not enforcing a penalty clause is to prevent a plaintiff recovering a sum that bears little or no relationship to the loss which he incurred as a result of the breach. It is not the function of the court to interfere with a contractual clause which merely causes a bargain to be burdensome to one party.

In that case, a construction project was financed by a banking consortium. The finance was provided in return for promissory notes issued by the companies ordering the construction. The plaintiffs, E.C.G.D., guaranteed payment of the promissory notes to the banking consortium in return for a promise by the defendants, who were builders involved in the construction, that they would reimburse E.C.G.D. any sums paid under this guarantee if the defendants defaulted in the performance of their obligations under the construction contracts. The promissory notes were dishonoured and the defendants refused to reimburse the plaintiffs, even though they had been in breach of their construction contract at the time the promissory notes

---

37. [1961] 2 Q.B. 57.
38. Devlin J. (dissenting) considered that the defendant had, in fact, made a promise not to play again. The distinction drawn between the two positions is a fine one.
39. [1983] 2 All E.R. 205.

were dishonoured. The defendants argued that the reimbursement clause was a penalty clause since the obligation to pay arose regardless of the scale of the loss caused by the breach. This was rejected by the House of Lords who held that, since the sum was payable on the breach of another contract with a third party and not payable on a breach of contract between the parties, it could not amount to a penalty.

## Deposits and part payments

### *Deposits*

A deposit is a payment made in advance of the contract being performed. It is payable before a breach occurs rather than after, as in the case of a penalty. If the contract is performed, then the amount of the deposit is set-off as part payment against the price. If the contract is not performed and the payee is at fault then the payee must return the deposit without prejudice to his liability under the contract. Conversely, the general rule is that the payee can keep the sum paid if the payor defaults. This is the case even if the amount is greater than the loss he suffers as a result of the breach.[40]

Where the deposit has not been paid, although due, the payee may recover it. In *Damon Cie Naviera S.A. v Hapag-Lloyd International S.A., The Blankenstein,*[41] an unpaid deposit of $236,500 was enforced even though the payee's overall loss amounted to only $60,000.

Thus, at common law, unless the contract provides otherwise, a deposit is generally not recoverable. However, note that it has been suggested[42] that, if the deposit exceeds in amount any conceivable damage that its holder can have suffered, a court may order part of it to be returned on the ground that retention of the full payment would be unconscionable. Also, according to s.49(2) of the Law of Property Act 1925, "where it thinks fit", the court has a wide discretion to order the return of the deposit paid under a contract for the sale of land.

---

40. *Howe v Smith* (1884) 27 Ch. D. 89.
41. [1985] 1 All E.R. 475.
42. Cheshire, Fifoot and Furmston, *The Law of Contract*, 12th ed. (Butterworths, 1991), p. 627; Treitel, *The Law of Contract*, 9th. ed., (Sweet and Maxwell, 1995), p. 906; *Stockloser v Johnson* [1954] 1 All E.R. 630.

Recently, *in Workers Trust and Merchant Bank Ltd. v Dojap Investments Ltd.*,[43] the Privy Council considered that:

> "It is not possible for the parties to attach the incidents of a deposit to the payment of a sum of money unless such sum is reasonable as earnest money.[44] The question, therefore, is whether or not the deposit ... in this case was reasonable as being in line with the traditional concept of earnest money or was in truth a penalty intended to act in terrorem."[45]

Note that the test for such a limitation on the general principle that a deposit is not recoverable differs from that applicable to penalties. In the former case the test is based on the reasonableness of the sum in question but in the latter on whether or not it is a genuine pre-estimate of the loss.

*Part payments*

A part payment is a payment of part of the contract price and as such is generally recoverable upon termination of the contract. This would be subject to any set-off there may be for performance done before the contract was terminated.[46]

It is usual that, in a contract of sale, the seller's right to part payment is conditional upon delivery of the subject-matter. The House of Lords took a contrary view in *Hyundai Heavy Industries Co. Ltd. v Papadopous,*[47] and held that an advance payment could not be recovered. The decision has been explained by the fact that the money was viewed as unconditional payment for the work that was already in progress.[48] In *Rover International Ltd. v Cannon Film Sales Ltd.* (No. 3)[49] Kerr L.J. made the distinction on the basis of whether there was any consideration in the nature of part performance for which the part payment was payable or whether the part payment was payable in advance of any performance which was

---

43. [1993] All E.R. 370.
44. That is, money given in token of a bargain made.
45. *Ibid.*, *per* Lord Browne-Wilkinson, at p. 374.
46. *Dies v British and International Mining and Finance Corporation* [1939] 1 K.B. 724.
47. [1980] 2 All E.R. 29.
48. Beatson, "Discharge for Breach: The Position of Instalments, Deposits and Other Payments Due Before Completion," (1981) 97 *L.Q.R.* 29.
49. [1989] 3 All E.R. 423.

required from the defaulting party. Using this argument, in *Dies* there was a total failure of consideration (i.e., performance), whereas in the *Hyundai* case the defendants had had the benefit of the work completed before the contract was terminated.

## Forfeiture and relief from forfeiture

Typically, a forfeiture clause is to be found in a contract for the sale of goods where the purchase price is payable in instalments and it is agreed that, in the event of non payment by the purchaser of an instalment, he must return the goods and forfeit any instalments already paid.

The court does have an equitable power to grant relief from forfeiture.[50] Thus, if the forfeiture clause is considered punitive, oppressive or unconscionable, relief should be granted. Where the purchaser is in a position to pay the sums due, equitable relief may be granted extending the time for payment.[51] In a case where the equitable remedy of specific performance would not be ordered because damages would be an adequate remedy, then equitable relief against forfeiture would also not be granted. In *Scandinavian Trading Co. v Flota Petrolera Ecuatoriana, The Scaptrade*,[52] the House of Lords would not grant relief against forfeiture in favour of a charterer of a ship for an order of specific performance is not normally given in time charter contracts, damages being an adequate remedy in the case of breach. A time charter is a contract for services and, therefore, does not concern the forfeiture of proprietary or possessory rights in land. In *Sport International Bussum B.V. v Inter-Footwear Ltd.*[53] this restricted view, that relief from forfeiture could only be granted where proprietary or possessory rights were being forfeited, was followed. However, in *B.I.C.C. plc v Bundy Corporation*,[54] the Court of Appeal took the view that such relief should not be confined to contracts for the sale of land and could be granted where the proprietary or possessory interest is in

---

50. See *Stockloser v Johnson* [1954] 1 Q.B. 476.
51. *Starside Properties Ltd. v Mustapha* [1974] 2 All E.R. 567. Note that the Law Commission (Working Paper No. 161, "*Penalty Clauses and Forfeiture of Monies Paid*"), recommended that rules relating to penalty clauses should apply also to forfeiture clauses.
52. [1983] 2 A.C. 694.
53. [1984] 2 All E.R. 321.
54. [1985] 1 All E.R. 417.

goods.

Note that relief is also available on a statutory basis. The Consumer Credit Act 1974, s.100(1) and (2), gives protection to the consumer similar to relief from forfeiture where the agreement in question is a regulated agreement. Also, the Law of Property Act 1925, s.49(2) provides that, in a contract for the sale of land, the court has a wide discretion to order the return of the deposit paid under a contract for the sale of land where specific performance is not granted or where the purchaser claims the return of his deposit.

**Exercises**

1. "Where parties to a contract have agreed that, in the event of a breach of contract thereof, the party in breach shall pay a certain amount of money, it is only desirable that the parties be held to their agreement, irrespective of whether that contractually agreed amount is a penalty."

   (a) Why do the courts intervene in such matters?
   (b) What guidelines do they follow?
   (c) What is the effect of a clause being held a penalty?

2. Rex agreed to purchase shares in Regina plc, a manufacturing company, for £500,000 and to make an initial payment of £140,000 followed by six instalments of £60,000. If Rex defaulted on any of the payments, he had to transfer the shares back to the vendor for £100,000 in accordance with clause 13 of the agreement. After paying £260,000, Rex defaulted.

   Advise Rex.

3. Warmup Ltd. contracted with the multinational company, A.B.C. plc, to design, supply, install and commission a computerised central heating system in A.B.C. plc's four regional headquarters in the U.K. The work to be done in each of the four buildings had a specific date for completion. Warmup Ltd. was to be paid a total of £2 million on completion of all the work. A clause in the contract provided that failure by Warmup Ltd to complete the work on any one building on time would result in their being paid £750,000 for the entire contract because time was of the essence. Warmup Ltd. have just failed by 5 days to complete the work on the fourth building and are worried about financial ruin. They have already satisfactorily completed work on the other three buildings.

   Advise Warmup Ltd.

4. Explain why the courts enforce liquidated damages clauses. Given the concept of "freedom of contract" should penalty clauses also be enforceable?

# PART II
# NON-COMPENSATORY DAMAGES

# 3 Non-compensatory damages

## Introduction

The usual objective of damages for tort and breach of contract is to compensate the plaintiff for the loss he has suffered. In tort it is to put the plaintiff in the position he would have been in if no tort had been committed; but, in contract it is to put the non-breaching party in the same position he would have been in if the contract had been performed.

However, in certain circumstances the court may award damages that do not aim to compensate the plaintiff. These are called non-compensatory damages and are of three types: nominal, contemptuous and exemplary.

Aggravated damages may also be awarded, but those damages are compensatory in intent, even if they appear non-compensatory. They are awarded where the Court feels the plaintiff has, as a result of the defendant's conduct, suffered more anguish and loss of dignity than the victim of a tort usually suffers. That is why the compensation ordered therefor is fairly high (for example, £500 for deceit in *Archer v Brown*,[1] and £7500 for trespass to the person in *Treadaway v Chief Constable of West Midlands*).[2]

## 1. Nominal damages

Nominal damages are awarded where a person's legal rights have been violated but no actual loss has been suffered by him. They may be awarded for a breach of contract (as in *Kenny v Preen*,[3] where 40 shillings were awarded, and *C. & P. Haulage v Middleton*,[4] where the award was only £10) or for a tort, even if actionable *per se*, i.e., without proof of damage (*Constantine v Imperial Hotels Ltd.*,[5] where only five guineas were awarded).

---

1. [1985] 1 Q.B. 401.
2. *The Independent*, September 9, 1994; *The Times*, October 25, 1994.
3. [1963] 1 Q.B. 499.
4. [1983] 3 All E.R. 94.
5. [1944] 1 K.B. 693.

They are described as non-compensatory because their award is for the wrong itself, but not as compensation to the plaintiff for his loss. They are small: usually £2, as in *The Kismet*[6] although lower or higher amounts (as in *C. and P. Haulage v Middleton*) may be awarded.

Nominal damages only declare that the plaintiff has been wronged by the defendant. Today that purpose is already being served by the remedy of declaration.[7] Therefore, nominal damages are no longer needed and can safely be abolished. Besides, the fact that a plaintiff has been awarded nominal damages does not necessarily mean he is a successful plaintiff so far as costs are concerned (as shown by *Anglo-Cyprian Trade Agencies v Paphos Wine Industries Ltd.*,[8] where costs of the action were awarded to the defendants). Thus, the plaintiff may still pay costs at the discretion of the court.[9]

## 2. Contemptuous damages

Contemptuous damages are awarded where the court feels that, although the defendant has committed the wrong complained of, the plaintiff's case has no merit and should not have been brought before it. Often called derisory damages, they are usually awarded by a jury in defamation cases, and the amount awarded is very small - usually the smallest coin "in the realm". Thus, in both *Dering v Uris*[10] and *Pamplin v Express Newspapers Ltd. (No. 2),*[11] which are cases on defamation, contemptuous damages of one half penny were awarded. That amount virtually constitutes a declaration of the plaintiff's rights; it is also a reprimand of him.

Since a declaratory judgement only states the plaintiff's rights but does not rebuke him, it cannot be a suitable alternative to contemptuous damages. Therefore, one can say that contemptuous damages, by virtue of their admonition of the plaintiff, still have a place in English law.

---

6. [1976] 2 Lloyd's Rep. 585.
7. See Rules of the Supreme Court, Order 25, r.5. A declaratory judgement conclusively declares the rights of the parties but does not attach any coercive order.
8. [1951] 1 All E.R. 873.
9. S.51(1), Supreme Court Act 1981. See also *Texaco Ltd. v Arco Technology Inc.* (1989) *The Times*, October 13, 1989.
10. [1964] 2 Q.B. 669.
11. [1988] 1 All E.R. 282.

## 3. Exemplary damages

Exemplary damages are also known as punitive damages because their purpose is to punish the defendant for his wrong-doing. The cases in which they are awarded are limited. In addition, their purpose, among other things, has led to much controversy, raising important questions concerning the role of the civil law, etc. This section will look at when they may be awarded, the further restrictions on their award and the case for and against them.

*When exemplary damages may be awarded*

### a. Breach of contract

Exemplary damages are not awarded for breach of contract on its own. *Addis v Gramophone*,[12] and *Kenny v Preen*[13] (where a landlord breached his covenant of quiet possession) are cases in point. Nevertheless, if the breach of contract is also a tort, exemplary damages may be awarded: *McMillan v Singh*,[14] where there was a breach of covenant of quiet possession as well as a tort (nuisance).

In *Addis v Gramophone* the defendants employed the plaintiff as their manager in Calcutta, paying him 15*l* a week plus commission. Under the contract they could dismiss him after giving him six months' notice. They gave him such notice in October 1905. They then at that time appointed another person to act as his successor; they also started taking steps to hinder the plaintiff's acting as manager. All that constituted a breach of contract (wrongful dismissal). The House of Lords held that damages awarded could not include compensation for (a) the way in which the plaintiff was dismissed, (b) the plaintiff's injured feelings or (c) the loss he might suffer because the dismissal would make it more difficult for him to get another job. Lord Loreburn L.C. said (at p. 491):

---

12. [1909] A.C. 488.
13. [1963] 1 Q.B. 499. See also *Perera v Vandiyar* [1953] 1 W.L.R. 672.
14. (1984) 134 *New Law Journal*, 1087. See also *Warner v Clark* (1984) 134 New Law Journal 763 and *Millington v Duffy* (1985) 135 *New Law Journal*, 708, where the plaintiff withdrew his claim for exemplary damages and the Judge said that, had that claim not been withdrawn, it would have succeeded.

"... the rule as to damages in wrongful dismissal, or in breach of contract to allow a man to continue in a stipulated service, has always been ... too inveterate to be now altered, even if it were desirable to alter it."

It is submitted, respectfully, that this aspect of the law is or should not be too inveterate or firmly established to be altered because the law changes in response to changing socio-economic conditions. There is, therefore, no reason for not amending the rule in *Addis v Gramophone*, especially today when, owing to advances in technology in relation to record-keeping, etc., a dismissed employee can be "blacklisted" for a long time and, as a result, face much difficulty in finding another job, with possibly grave financial consequences. This view is supported by *Maw v Jones*.[15] There the employer of an apprentice, engaged at weekly wages, summarily dismissed him. The plaintiff's damages were not limited to one week's wages. According to Lord Coleridge C.J.: "The plaintiff by reason of his being dismissed during his apprenticeship with a slur on his character naturally would experience a greater difficulty in getting employment elsewhere."[16] Unfortunately, the majority of the House of Lords in *Addis v Gramophone* disagreed with this.

It has been argued, however, that exemplary damages should be awarded for deliberate breaches of contract where the criminal law cannot punish the defendant. This is because a breach of contract, just like a tort, is a breach of a civil obligation; so, if it is proper to penalise by exemplary damages a person who calculatedly commits a tort to make a profit which may exceed any damages that may be awarded against him (as in *Broome v Cassell*[17]), then such damages should be awarded against a person who deliberately breaches his contract where the criminal law does not apply.[18]

## b. Tort

The law on exemplary damages in tort was restated in *Rookes v Barnard*[19] by the House of Lords. That was a case which concerned the economic tort of

---

15. [1890] 25 Q.B.D. 107.
16. *Ibid.*, at p. 198.
17. [1972] A.C. 1027.
18. N.J. McBride, "A Case for Awarding Punitive Damages in Response to Deliberate Breaches of Contract", *Anglo-American Law Review*, vol. 24, no. 3, 1995, 369-90.
19. [1964] A.C. 1129.

intimidation. There the plaintiff was a skilled draughtsman. He resigned his membership of his trade union, the Association of Engineering and Shipbuilding Draughtsmen, and refused to rejoin it even though there was a closed-shop agreement in operation at his particular office. His co-workers threatened, through their union, to withdraw their labour unless he was dismissed. His employers, British Overseas Airways Corporation ("the Corporation"), fearing other employees in other trade unions would, in sympathy with the first union, also withdraw their labour, suspended and later dismissed him. He sued the defendants for damages for using unlawful means to induce the Corporation to dismiss him and/or conspiracy (by threatening strike action) to have the Corporation dismiss him. The House of Lords held, *inter alia,* that, as happened, the defendants were liable for the tort of intimidation because it covered threatening a breach of contract as well as threatening to do a criminal or tortious act. Lord Devlin, in his leading judgement, laid down that in only three categories could exemplary damages be awarded, namely:

(i) where there is "oppressive or unconstitutional action by the servants of the government",

(ii) where "the defendant's conduct has been calculated by him to make a profit for himself which may exceed the compensation payable to the plaintiff", and

(iii) where they are expressly allowed by statute.

No exemplary damages were awarded in that case because the facts did not fall within any of the three categories (a new trial on the question of damages was ordered). The decision was confirmed by the House of Lords later in *Broome v Cassell.*

The three categories will now be looked at in some detail.

### (i) "Oppressive, arbitrary or unconstitutional action by government servants"

"Servants of the government", according to Lord Diplock in *Broome v Cassell* (at p. 1130), covers "all persons purporting to exercise powers of government, central or local, conferred upon them by statute or at common law by virtue of the official status or employment" which they hold. Earlier cases within this category are eighteenth century cases (concerning civil liberties).[20]

These days actions against the police for trespass to the person and malicious prosecution provide ample illustration of this first category. For example, in *Marks v Chief Constable of Greater Manchester*,[21] at the time of a demonstration during the visit of Sir Leon Brittan to Manchester, the police arrested and maliciously prosecuted the plaintiff for obstructing a police officer in the execution of his duty. The plaintiff was awarded exemplary damages of £50,000 as well as compensatory damages. Again, in *Hajivassiliou v Commissioner of Police*[22] the plaintiff, a Ph.D. student who was a Cypriot, after being stopped by the police for speeding, was arrested, assaulted (hit twice and knocked down by a police officer) and detained at the police station for two hours. The injuries he sustained included a swollen left forehead and scratches to his neck. He was awarded, on top of compensatory damages, exemplary damages of £4,000. Furthermore, in *Treadaway v Chief Constable of West Midlands*, where the police assaulted and "tortured" the plaintiff, exemplary damages of £40,000 were awarded.[23]

This first category, however, according to *A.B. v South West Water Services Ltd.*,[24] does not include nationalised bodies set up under a statute for a commercial purpose like the supply of water. In that case the defendants accidentally contaminated with chemicals a drinking water system. The plaintiffs who, as a result of drinking the contaminated water, suffered various ailments, sued the defendants for damages for public nuisance,

---

20. Like *Wilkes v Wood* (1763) Lofft. 1 (a case on trespass: a search of the plaintiff's premises under a general warrant issued by the Secretary of State, which was illegal) and *Huckle v Money* (1763) 2 Wils. K.B. 205; 95 E.R. 768, a case on false imprisonment by a messenger of the King.
21. *The Guardian*, December 6, 1991.
22. (1991), *Legal Action*, 17.
23. Some other cases where exemplary damages were awarded against the police are *Cusworth v Chief Constable of South Yorkshire Police*, *The Guardian News Report*, July 10, 1991; *Reynolds v Chief Constable of Wiltshire*, *The Guardian News Report*, February 14 and 15, 1991; and *Cumber v Chief Constable of Hampshire Constabulary*, *The Times*, January 28, 1995; and *Makanjuola v Metropolitan Police Commissioner and McCarthy*, *The Times*, August 8, 1989. See also Clayton and Tomlinson, "Civil Actions against the Police: recent developments in the law", *Legal Action*, Oct. 1993, 15-18, and Ghandhi, "Punitive Damages against the Police", *Solicitors' Journal*, vol. 134, no. 13, March 30, 1990, pp. 357-8.
24. [1993] Q.B. 507; [1993] 1 All E.R. 609.

negligence and breach of statutory duty under the Water Act 1945 and the Consumer Protection Act 1987. Although the plaintiffs were entitled to recover compensatory damages for what they had suffered, their claim for exemplary damages failed because:

(a) according to *Broome v Cassell*, no exemplary damages were available for torts for which such damages had not been awarded before 1964 and, so, negligence, public nuisance and the two statutory duties did not qualify for the award of that type of damages;

(b) the South West Water Authority, which was succeeded by the defendants, was performing functions, not of an executive or governmental nature but rather, of a nationalised body supplying water commercially; therefore, the defendants did not come within the first category set out by Lord Devlin in *Rookes v Barnard*; and

(c) the plaintiffs had not shown the defendants' conduct was cynically calculated to make a profit exceeding any damages that might be awarded against them.

**(ii) Where the defendant's conduct is calculated to make a profit**

The second category covers cases where the defendant has calculated his conduct in order to make a profit for himself which may be more than any compensation payable to the plaintiff. Thus, exemplary damages have been awarded for libel, trespass or nuisance relating to landlords' harassment or wrongful eviction of tenants and tortious interference with the plaintiff's business.

**(a) Libel**

In *Broome v Cassell* the defendants published defamatory material against the plaintiff (a distinguished retired naval officer), who sued them for libel. Shortly before the trial the plaintiff gave notice of his intention to claim exemplary damages, too. Although the defendants did not give evidence, they knew, according to the documents disclosed by them, that the plaintiff had objected to certain passages relating to his conduct and had threatened to sue for defamation, and also that the material in question had been considered by some high-ranking naval experts as defamatory. Nevertheless, the defendants went ahead and published the book with only minor changes of the passages the plaintiff had complained of. The court at first instance, finding that the defendants' conduct had been calculated to make a profit which might well exceed any compensatory damages that might be awarded to the plaintiff, awarded the plaintiff compensatory damages of £15,000 and exemplary damages of £25,000. Although the Court of Appeal agreed with the award and the reasons therefor, it also held that, because *Rookes v Barnard* was inconsistent with previous decisions of the House of Lords and was decided *per incuriam*, it was not binding. When the defendants appealed against the exemplary damages awarded, the House of Lords held, *inter alia,* that *Rookes v Barnard* was not decided *per incuriam* and was not inconsistent with any previous decision/s of the House. To their Lordships the award of exemplary damages in the case fell within Lord Devlin's second category. In Lord Hailsham's view, the requirement is that the defendant must know the act to be done is illegal or must have reckless disregard for whether it is illegal or not, and he must have decided to go ahead with it because he considered the prospects of material advantage would exceed those of material loss. Lord Diplock, at p. 1130, stated the two-fold purpose of exemplary damages, as regards that second category of Lord Devlin in *Rookes v Barnard*, namely, reversing the defendant's unjust enrichment and teaching him, the tortfeasor, that tort does not pay. In his words:

> "... to restrict the damages recoverable to the actual gain made by the defendant if it exceeded the loss caused to the plaintiff, would leave a defendant contemplating an unlawful act with the certainty that he had nothing to lose to balance against the chance that the plaintiff might never sue him or, if he did, might fail in the hazards of litigation. It is only if there is a prospect that the damages may exceed the defendant's gain that the social purpose of this category is achieved - to teach a wrong-doer that tort does not pay."

### (b) Trespass/nuisance re wrongful harassment or eviction of tenants

*Drane v Evangelou*[25] provides a good illustration of this. There the defendant rented a flat to the plaintiff for £25 a week. The plaintiff applied to a Rent

25. [1978] 2 All E.R. 437.

Officer for the rent to be fixed. Before the Rent Officer fixed the rent, the defendant gave the plaintiff notice to quit. That notice was of no effect, however, because the plaintiff had statutory protection from eviction at that time. The Rent Officer reduced the rent to £16 a week. Six days later the defendant took matters into his own hands: he and his colleagues entered the flat in the plaintiff's absence, put the plaintiff's things out in the back yard and prevented his return to the flat. The plaintiff had to stay with friends and store his things in a garage because the defendant moved his parents-in-law into the flat. The defendant was held liable for trespass and exemplary damages were awarded against him for acting cynically in disregard of the plaintiff's rights in order to secure the property he coveted and had to be shown that tort did not pay.

Another illustration is *Guppy's (Bridport) Ltd. v Brookling and James*,[26] which concerned landlords who were converting a building into self-contained flats. To achieve their aim, they sought to get their tenants out of the building quickly without offering them alternative accommodation; so, they attempted to evict them indirectly ("constructively"): during the conversion works they removed all the toilet and washing facilities from the building and disconnected the water supply to the outside toilet as well as cut off the building's supply of electricity. Those two tenants (aged mid-60's and 80, respectively) were awarded, *inter alia,* exemplary damages of £1,000 each for unlawful eviction (nuisance).

Similarly, in *Ramdath v Daley*,[27] where the plaintiff was evicted unlawfully (in an "extremely bad" and "brutal" manner by his landlord and his landlord's son who acted as his agent), was threatened with violence and also had the locks of his accommodation changed, exemplary damages were awarded against the landlord because he had been warned about the legal position before the tenant was evicted. Exemplary damages were, however, not awarded against the agent, son of the landlord, because there was no evidence that he, the agent, had made a profit for himself from the eviction.

### (c) Tortious interference with the plaintiff's trade

This may be illustrated by *Bell v Midland Railway*.[28] In that case the

---

26. (1983) 269 *Estates Gazette*, 846.
27. (1993) 20 *Estates Gazette*, 123
28. (1861) 10 C.B.N.S. 287.

defendants, who wanted to increase their trade, interfered with the plaintiff's business by wrongfully preventing trains from running to or serving the plaintiff's wharf. Exemplary damages of £1,000 were awarded against them.

### (iii) Where expressly authorised by an Act of Parliament

An example of such a statute is the Reserve and Auxiliary Forces (Protection of Civil Interests) Act 1951.[29] Section 13(2) of that Act provides:

> "In any action for damages for conversion or other proceedings which lie by virtue of any such omission, failure or contravention, the court may take account of the conduct of the defendant with a view, if the court thinks fit, to awarding exemplary damages in respect of the wrong sustained by the plaintiff."

*Further restrictions on exemplary damages*

No exemplary damages will be awarded:

(i) *if the tort is not one for which exemplary damages could be awarded before Rookes v Barnard in 1964.* According to Lord Hailsham and Lord Diplock in *Broome v Cassell,*[30] this was a restriction on exemplary damages because Lord Devlin, in *Rookes v Barnard*, intended, not to extend their availability but rather, to limit it. There are, however, some contradictory judicial views on this point; for example, as regards infringement of patent (a tort for which exemplary damages were not awarded before 1964): whereas in *Morton-Norwich Products v Intercen*[31] Graham J. thought that exemplary damages could be awarded if the circumstances were exceptional, they were held irrecoverable in *Catnic Components v Hill and Smith Ltd.*[32]

This restriction was stated by Lord Stuart-Smith in *A.B. v South West Water*[33] to be what, *inter alia*, *Rookes v Barnard* and *Broome v Cassell* had

---

29. 14 & 15 Geo. 6, ch. 65. Another (debatable) example is s.17(3), Copyright Act 1956 (now s.97(2), Copyright, Designs and Patents Act 1988).
30. [1972] A.C. 1027, at 1130-1.
31. [1981] F.S.R. 337.
32. [1983] F.S.R. 512.
33. [1993] 1 All. E.R. 609; [1993] Q.B. 507.

decided. However, as Howarth has observed (rightly, in the present authors' view), that was not precisely what Lord Devlin said in *Rookes v Barnard*; rather, Lord Devlin said that exemplary damages were awardable where there was "oppressive, arbitrary or unconstitutional action" by government servants, where the tort was done calculatedly by the defendant in order to make a profit perhaps in excess of any compensatory damages payable to the plaintiff, and where a statute had expressly authorised them.[34] Therefore, a more acceptable reason for denying the award of exemplary damages in *A.B. v South West Water* would have been the failure of that case to fall within any of the three categories specified in *Rookes v Barnard*.

Unfortunately, *A.B. v South West Water* was applied in *Deane v Ealing London Borough Council*[35] by the Employment Appeal Tribunal to the effect that no exemplary damages can be awarded for race discrimination. There the appellant, a white employee of the Ealing London Borough Council, was appointed a Principal Housing Officer in the absence of the Director of Housing. The Director of Housing refused to confirm the appointment because only an Asian with Asian language skills, not a white officer, could meet the special needs of the Asian people in that area. The appellant made a complaint against the Council and the Director of Housing personally for unlawful discrimination on the ground of race, contrary to s.1(1)(a) of the Race Relations Act 1976. It was held (by the Employment Appeal Tribunal, to whom the appellant appealed against the first ruling), *inter alia,* that exemplary damages could only be awarded in respect of torts in existence before 1964 but not for the statutory tort of race discrimination, which came into existence in 1976.

(ii) *If doing so will result in double punishment because a defendant has already been punished under the criminal law in respect of facts on which the plaintiff is basing his tortious action.* Examples of this are *Devonshire and Smith v Jenkins*[36] (where the defendant had already been penalised by a fine) and *Archer v Brown*[37] (where the defendant had already been imprisoned for the act complained of).

---

34. D. Howarth, *A Textbook on Tort* (Butterworths, 1995), pp. 598-601.
35. [1993] I.C.R. 329.
36. (1979) *LAG Bull.* 114, C.A.
37. [1984] 2 All E.R. 267.

(iii) *Where the plaintiff's own conduct has led to the tort*, as in *O'Connor v Hewitson.*[38] There the plaintiff and two brothers, after drunken behaviour, were arrested and put in police cells. There they behaved in an aggressive manner, shouted abuse at the police, banged and kicked at the cell doors virtually without stopping between 2.30 a.m. and 6.00 a.m. The plaintiff was assaulted (struck) by a police sergeant in an attempt to restrain him and remove his shoes and jacket to prevent him from injuring himself. The plaintiff's claim for, *inter alia,* exemplary damages for assault failed because of his own conduct (provoking the police) which resulted in the assault.

(iv) *If the court thinks compensatory damages are sufficient to punish the defendant. Dicta* in *Rookes v Barnard*[39] *and Broome v Cassell*[40] support this.

(v) *If they are not pleaded specifically.* This is because exemplary damages should be specifically pleaded if they are sought; otherwise, they will not be awarded: Rules of the Supreme Court,[41] Order 18, r.8(3) (as regards High Court proceedings) and County Court Rules, Order. 6, r.1B and *Ogunlolu v Bird*[42] (as regards County Court proceedings).

It should finally be noted that provocation is a factor that could reduce an award of exemplary damages.[43]

## 4. The case for and against exemplary damages

Some of the arguments against, and for, exemplary damages will now be looked at. After each argument a brief comment will be made.

### The case against

(a) *Exemplary damages confuse the function of the civil law with that of the*

38. (1979) *Crim. L.R.*, 46.
39. [1964] A.C. 1129, at 1228 (by Lord Devlin).
40. [1972] A.C. 1027, at 1089 (by Lord Reid).
41. Hereafter referred to as "R.S.C.".
42. (1993), unreported, *New Law Journal*, July 14, 1995, pp. 160-1.
43. *Lane v Holloway* [1968] 1 Q.B. 379; *Fontin v Katapodis* [1962] 108 C.L.R. 177.

*criminal law.*

However, that is not really true because the aim of the criminal law includes not only punishment but also deterrence, protection of the public, rehabilitation, etc. Exemplary damages do not go that far; they only punish and deter.

Moreover, it is not always desirable to say that punishment is best left to the criminal law because not all criminal activities are pursued by the criminal law. In other words, a satisfactory system is not always provided by the criminal law.

(b) *They entail punishment without the protections (evidential and procedural safeguards such as the presumption of innocence and the higher standard of proof) available to an accused person in a criminal case. It might be argued that similar protections should be given to defendants in civil actions, who are likely to pay exemplary damages. Indeed, in Broome v Cassell Lord Reid had this to say (at page 1087):*

> *"It is no excuse to say that we need not waste sympathy on people who behave outrageously. Are we wasting sympathy on vicious criminals when we insist on proper legal safeguards for them?"*

But again that is not a strong point because in a criminal case the liberty of the accused is often at stake. Moreover, a criminal prosecution may lead to a serious stigma for the accused, not to mention the grave negative effect a criminal conviction can have on a person's prospects of employment. That is very rarely the position in a civil case. A defendant in a civil case, therefore, does not need the same protection/s as the accused in a criminal trial.[44]

(c) *Some defendants (especially, those in business) do not really feel punished because they pay the damages from their insurance.*[45]

This is, however, hardly the fault of exemplary damages.

(d) *They result in the plaintiff receiving an undeserved windfall (as pointed*

---

44. G.S. Pipe, "Exemplary Damages after Camelford", *The Modern Law Review*, vol. 57, 1st Jan. 1994, pp. 97-8.

45. According to Anderson, "the ability to insure frustrates the punitive goal". See Anderson, "An Exemplary Case for Reform, *Civil Justice Quarterly*, vol. 11, July 1992, p. 254.

*out in Broome v Cassell by Lord Reid*[46] *and Lord Diplock*[47]).

But, the question to answer in response to this is whether the plaintiff does not deserve the money since, e.g., as in *Broome v Cassell*, he is the victim of the defendant's tort and has put his own resources at risk in taking legal action.[48]

(e) *They are no longer necessary because non-pecuniary harm (i.e., injury to feelings, mental suffering, etc.) is now compensated for more freely.*

Nevertheless, they are still needed since in certain cases (false imprisonment, defamation, etc.) the compensatory principle is inadequate and artificial because of the difficulty in identifying and quantifying the compensation.

(f) *They are so uncertain that they are immeasurable. In defamation cases, for example, assessment of damages is often by a jury. The outcome of such cases is, therefore, difficult to predict. Also, some exemplary damages awarded in defamation cases are excessive when compared with damages for personal injuries.*

However, the award of damages varies with the circumstances of each case and, so, measurement, even if possible, will not necessarily lead to uniformity. Besides, under section 8 of the Courts and Legal Services Act 1990, the Court of Appeal can now substitute an award of its own in jury cases without the parties' agreement, if it thinks the award is excessive.[49]

(g) *Where there are multiple plaintiffs claiming, there can be problems.*[50] *Must the defendant be ultra-penalised in order to satisfy every plaintiff?*

This is, however, not a very sound criticism because the aim is to punish the defendant once for what he has done to all those plaintiffs ("as plaintiffs, a group" (not in respect of each plaintiff) - after all, each plaintiff may be awarded compensatory damages). Thus, exemplary damages here will

---

46. [1972] A.C. 1027, at 1086.
47. *Ibid.*, page 1126.
48. Pipe, *op. cit.*, pp. 98-9.
49. *Rantzen v Mirror Group Newspapers* [1993] 4 All E.R. 925; *John v MGN Ltd. The Times*, December 14, 1995; (1996) 2 All E.R. 35; see also R.S.C., Order 59, rule 11(4).
50. Anderson, *op. cit.*, p. 256.

be the icing on the cake, a bonus (not compensation), to each plaintiff.[51]

(h) *Regarding vicarious liability, it is contrary to penal philosophy to penalise an employer who did not sanction the wrongful act of his servant and did not do the act himself.*

But, part of the answer to this criticism lies in the rationale behind, or justification for, vicarious liability.[52] In addition, the application of vicarious liability to exemplary damages is advantageous to plaintiffs. This is because they may not have to state the identity of the particular servant (of an employer) whose act or omission is the basis of the claim. Thus, in *Racz v Home Office*,[53] although the plaintiff could not identify the prison officers who had assaulted him, he was able to sue their employer, the Home Office.

(i) *It is questionable that exemplary damages are not awarded for breach of contract on its own unless the breach also constitutes a tort. As already mentioned, it has been argued that there should be exemplary damages for deliberate breaches of contract which the criminal law will not punish because, just like tort, a breach of contract is also a breach of a civil obligation.*[54] *Jurists (e.g., Oliver Wendell Holmes) who think a breach of contract is not a breach of a civil obligation*[55] *are yet to answer satisfactorily why specific performance is ever ordered (by the court of equity which upholds good conscience).*[56]

In *Broome v Cassell* Lord Reid (at page 1088) expressed the view that the civil wrongs for which exemplary damages are awardable should not be

---

51. Nevertheless, where all the claims cannot be dealt with at the same time, there could be a problem since the amount awarded to punish the defendant will be determined by reference to the overall sum with which the defendant will compensate the plaintiffs.
52. Such as employers, being more able to pay damages, recouping their losses by claiming insurance or by price increases, having a reason to encourage their employees to take care and gaining financially from their employees' work. See Anderson, *op. cit.*, pp. 254-5.
53. [1992] T.L.R. 624.
54. McBride, *op. cit.*, pp. 388-90.
55. With respect, that viewpoint is not tenable because Tort and Contract belong to the civil (not the criminal) law. Indeed, as Burrows says, "Tortious and contractual obligations are the two main types of obligations recognised in English law". See A. Burrows, *Remedies for Tort and Breach of Contract*, 2nd. ed. (Butterworths, 1994), p.3.
56. McBride, *op. cit.*, pp. 389-390.

expanded because firmly established authority did not require that.

(j) *The three categories stated in Rookes v Barnard are equally questionable*:

(i) *According to A.B. v South West Water, nationalised establishments created by statute for commercial activities like supply of water are not within category one.*

However, because of the monopolistic position such utilities enjoy, perhaps they should be subjected to exemplary damages if they break the law.

(ii) *Limiting the second category to torts where the defendant calculatedly acts to make a profit he reckons will exceed any damages he may pay is illogical because, as Lord Salmon said in Broome v Cassell:*[57]

> *"Why should the man who commits a tort calculating that he will make more money out of it than damages or costs which he will have to pay be less favourably regarded by the law than the man who, out of venomous malice, commits a tort in order to break an innocent neighbour regardless of the cost?"*

If so, perhaps the ambit of exemplary damages should be widened to include such deliberate tortfeasors.

(iii) *Disparity exists in the amounts awarded, especially, against the police. Some critics would like to see consistency of awards.*

But, the problem here is that this will be very difficult, if not impossible, because every case is not the same. Also, the same argument can be made against compensatory damages but, obviously, that does not prevent their award.

(k) *The other restrictions on exemplary damages make them "unprincipled".*[58]

---

57. [1971] 2 Q.B. 354 (C.A.), at p. 387.
58. Law Commission Paper No. 132 (1993), para. 6.5.

*Thus they offer a type of "palm-tree justice".*[59] *The temporal delineation (or discrimination) against some torts (those which did not attract exemplary damages before 1964) is not justified*[60] *- it is artificial. Is it not anomalous that the law should punish a man who wrongs his fellow in order to make a profit or better himself but not the man who wrongs his neighbour in order to make that neighbour's position worse?*[61]

If so, then the scope of exemplary damages can be extended to remove these illogical, arbitrary restrictions.

**The case for**

(i) *There is no line dividing the functions of the criminal law and those of the civil law. Punishment, deterrence and condemnation (all aims of the criminal law) are also quite legitimate aims of the civil law. Exemplary damages confirm that tort has a very important role to play in deterring acts like trespass to the person, defamation, etc..*

However, not all tortfeasors will be deterred. As already noted, employers who are insured do not really feel the sting of exemplary damages.

(ii) *There is the need for exemplary damages to punish certain types of conduct, which the criminal law either does not punish or does punish inadequately. For example, it has been argued that the police rarely initiate proceedings against police officers and that the Police Complaints system is less effective than civil proceedings.*[62] *There is also the argument that fines which the criminal courts impose when health and safety regulations are not complied with are inadequate, especially, where the breach causes death or*

---

59. A term used by Lord Reid in *Broome v Cassell* [1972] A.C. 1027, at p. 1087. According to Lord Buckley in *Newgrosh v Newgrosh*, 100 L.J. 525, it is "justice which makes orders which appear to be fair and just in the special circumstances of the case". It is also "an expression used to describe a form of justice dispensed by a cadi sitting under a palm-tree without the advantage of books or precedents": *Jowitt's Dictionary of English Law*, 2nd. ed. (Sweet and Maxwell, 1977).
60. For this and other reasons one can say that all is not well with exemplary damages.
61. See *Uren v John Fairfax and Sons Pty.* (1966) 40 A.L.J.R. 124. See also *Broome v Cassell* [1971] 2 Q.B. 354, 387.
62. See R. Clayton and H. Tomlinson, *Civil Actions Against the Police* (2nd. ed., 1992), pp. 11 ff..

*serious injury.*[63]

The Law Commission, however, recognises that: "If the penalty exacted by the criminal law is thought to be an inadequate response to particular conduct it is arguable that the attention of law reformers should be directed to improving the criminal law and that individuals should not be free to sidestep it by use of civil proceedings."[64]

(iii) *They prevent the defendant from unjustly enriching himself.*[65]

But, this is not so in every case. It is limited to only the second of the three categories specified in *Rookes v Barnard.*

(iv) *They pacify plaintiffs and, so, discourage them from being vengeful.*[66]

This pacification, however, comes late because it takes quite some time before a case is tried. A vengeful and impatient plaintiff, therefore, is likely not to be discouraged from vengeance. The pacification argument, thus, is only applicable *after* award of the exemplary damages (not before).

(v) *They are needed where compensation is inadequate, ineffective or artificial. Compensation may be artificial (in torts like false imprisonment nuisance, trespass to land via harassment, discrimination, defamation, etc.) because of the difficulty in identifying or describing the "loss" and, therefore, in measuring it.*[67] *Therefore, the provisional view of the Law Commission was "that the argument that exemplary damages have a useful role to play is persuasive".*[68]

In this respect exemplary damages complement compensatory damages.

---

63. See, for example, M. Whitfield, "Cost pressures keep safety on the sidelines", *The Independent*, 9 December 1992.

64. Law Commission, *Aggravated, Exemplary and Restitutionary Damages*, Consultation Paper no. 132 (H.M.S.O., 1993), para. 5.33.

65. *Broome v Cassell.*

66. This is one of the functions of exemplary damages identified by Anderson, *op. cit.*, p. 235 (the others are punishment, deterrence and counteracting any shortfall in the system of compensation). Vengeance, however, is risky because it may lead to the avenger himself breaking the law.

67. Law Commission Consultation Paper 132 (1993), para. 5.19.

68. *Ibid.*, para. 5.38.

**Reform measures**

Some of the suggestions for reform of the present law include the following:

(a) that exemplary damages should be abolished totally;

(b) that they could be partially abolished by removing their availability from problem areas like defamation;[69]

(c) that they be retained but extended to cases of general flagrant disregard of the plaintiff's rights or cases where there was, at the time of the tort, a relationship of inequality between the parties, as in employer-employee, citizen-state official, citizen-newspaper situations, etc.;[70]

(d) that they be extended to other torts, e.g., negligence (as in America);

(e) that they should also be extended to contract;[71]

(f) that there should be statutory detailing of instances where wrongful conduct will lead to an award of exemplary damages, e.g., deliberate designing of unsafe products, and breaches of health and safety regulations causing personal injuries;[72] and

(g) that exemplary damages be replaced with the restitutionary remedy of claim for money had and received (whereby the plaintiff will

---

69. Their abolition in defamation cases has been called for years ago by (i) the Faulks Committee in 1975 (*Report of the Committee on Defamation*, Cmnd. 5909 (1975), and (ii) a Working Group of the Supreme Court Procedure Committee in 1991 (*Supreme Court Procedure Committee Report on the Practice and Procedure in Defamation* (1991)).

70. J. Beatson, "More Proposals on Damages Law Reform from the Law Commission: Punitive and Other Non-Compensatory Damages", *Quantum*, Issue 6/93, Nov. 11, 1993, pp. 1-2. See also Alan Reed, "Exemplary Damages: A Persuasive Argument for their Retention as a Mechanism for Retributive Justice", *C.J.Q.*, vol. 15, April 1996, 130-140.

71. McBride, *op. cit.*

72. Law Commission Paper No. 132 (1993), para. 6.15. See also paras. 6.8-6.35 regarding the suggestion that exemplary damages could be put on a more principled basis by a legislative scheme and by the taking of other measures.

waive the tort and instead seek the defendant's surrender of the money with which he has enriched himself by his tort).[73]

**Exercises**

1. Should nominal damages and derisory or contemptuous damages be abolished?

2. "The law relating to exemplary remedies is far from satisfactory."

   Discuss critically with reference to decided cases.

3. "Exemplary damages confuse the role of the civil law with that of the criminal law."

   Discuss.

4. Do you think exemplary damages are anomalous and should be made available both in all tortious actions and in claims for breach of contract?

5. Eastcountry Water Services plc, a privatised water company, is the statutory body authorised to supply water to an area of the east of England. Six months ago, the company carelessly released two dozen tons of aluminium sulphate into the water supplied to the town of Eastwich. If ingested, aluminium sulphate can cause bodily harm and 200 inhabitants of Eastwich did indeed suffer illness as a consequence of drinking the tainted water. As a result, they wish to sue Eastcountry Water Services plc for negligence, nuisance and breach of statutory duty under the Consumer Protection Act 1987 and the Water Act 1993.

   Advise the inhabitants of their chances of receiving non-compensatory damages if they are successful in their action.

---

73. Anderson, *op. cit.*, p. 259. But, the problem here is that the defendant must have enriched himself with the property of the plaintiff or proceeds thereof (see *Phillips v Humfray* (1883) Ch.D. 429).

# PART III
# COMPENSATORY DAMAGES

# 4 Factors limiting awards of damages

## Introduction

The following factors may be said to limit a plaintiff's entitlement to damages: remoteness of damage, causation (intervening causes), duty to mitigate, contributory negligence and impecuniosity. It must be noted that the first two and the last of these factors can actually exclude entitlement to an award. There are also other factors (e.g., *volenti non fit injuria* and illegality) which seriously affect a plaintiff's entitlement to damages in that their presence acts as a defence and results in the failure of the plaintiff's case. Since those factors are, therefore, related primarily to the liability of the defendant, they are omitted in this chapter. The limitation of actions is, however, included at the end of the chapter for one very important reason: a plaintiff must commence his action within the period specified by the Limitation Act 1980, otherwise, subject to exceptions, the action will not proceed and the issue of damages will not arise in the first place.

## 1. Remoteness of damage

It is, of course, perfectly reasonable to make the contract-breaker or the tortfeasor responsible for the damage he has caused. However, not every type of damage caused to the plaintiff will be recoverable for, if the loss is too remote from the breach of duty, then an award of damages will not be forthcoming. In contract loss will be too remote if it was not in the defendant's reasonable contemplation whilst in tort damages will not be awarded for loss which was not reasonably foreseeable by the defendant.

### *Remoteness of damage in contract*

Loss, to be recoverable, must have been in the reasonable contemplation of the defendant. The test for remoteness in contract was originally laid down by Alderson B. in *Hadley v Baxendale*.[1] The plaintiff, a mill owner at Gloucester, agreed with the defendant carriers that the latter would transport a broken crankshaft to the manufacturers at Greenwich. The crankshaft was delayed in transit due to the negligence of the defendants and, as a result, the mill was closed for longer than would have been the case if the contract had been performed as agreed. The mill owner claimed for the profits lost as a result of the delay. It was held by the Court of Exchequer that such loss was not recoverable for the defendants could not reasonably have been expected to know that the mill was out of action and, therefore, that delay in delivering the crankshaft would cause lost profits. Alderson B. held that:

> "Where two parties have made a contract which one of them has broken, the damages which the other party ought to receive in respect of such breach of contract should be such as may fairly and reasonably be considered arising naturally, that is according to the usual course of things from such breach of contract itself, or as may reasonably be supposed to have been in the contemplation of both parties, at the time they made the contract, as the probable result of the breach of it."[2]

Thus, under *Hadley v Baxendale*, damages are recoverable for two categories of loss:

a) normal loss which is an inevitable result of the breach, and

b) special loss recoverable only if, at the time of the contract, the defendant had knowledge of the special circumstances giving rise to the loss.

In the case the loss suffered was not a natural consequence of the breach for the millers could well have had a spare crankshaft, and so have prevented any stoppage of production. That is, the defendant could not reasonably have foreseen the loss. The only circumstances here communicated by the plaintiffs to the defendants at the time the contract was made were that the article to be carried was the broken shaft of a mill and that the plaintiffs were the millers of the mill. The special circumstances, that is, the fact that the mill was idle and delay would lead to further loss,

---

1. (1854) 9 Exch. 341.
2. *Ibid.*, at 354.

were not known to the defendant. Therefore, such loss could not have been in the defendant's reasonable contemplation and was not compensatable.

The two "limbs" of the ruling in *Hadley v Baxendale*, which concerned normal and special losses, were subsumed into one in *Victoria Laundry (Windsor) Ltd. v Newman Industries Ltd.*[3] Here, the plaintiffs, launderers and dyers, wishing to expand their business, ordered a boiler from the defendants telling them that they intended "to put it into use in the shortest possible space of time". The boiler was delivered five months after the agreed date and the plaintiffs claimed for profits lost as a result of their inability to expand the business, including those they had expected to make from especially lucrative dyeing contracts entered into with the Ministry of Supply. The Court of Appeal held that the defendants knew that the boiler was required for immediate use and were, therefore, liable for lost profits ordinarily resulting from such use. However, this did not include the loss resulting from the lucrative dyeing contracts since the defendants did not know of such contracts and could not reasonably have foreseen the particular loss. Asquith L.J. set out the general principles applicable in assessing damages for breach of contract. In so doing, he suggested that liability for losses depended on a reasonable foreseeability test:

> "In cases of breach of contract the aggrieved party is only entitled to recover such part of the loss actually resulting as was, at the time of the contract, reasonably foreseeable as liable to result from the breach. What was at the time reasonably foreseeable depends on the knowledge then possessed by the parties or, at all events, by the party who later commits the breach ... In order to make the contract-breaker liable under either rule [in *Hadley v Baxendale*], it is not necessary that he should actually have asked himself "what loss is liable to result from a breach". Parties at the time of contracting contemplate, not the breach of the contract, but its performance and it suffices that, if he had considered the question, he would, as a reasonable man, have concluded that the loss in question was liable to result. ... Nor, finally, to make a particular loss recoverable, need it be proved that on a given state of knowledge the defendant could, as a reasonable man, foresee that a breach must necessarily result in that loss. It is enough if he could foresee it was likely to so result."[4]

The phrase, "reasonably foresee as liable to result", impliedly suggested that the appropriate test for remoteness was the same as the test

---

3. [1949] 2 K.B. 528.
4. *Ibid.*, at 539-40.

of foreseeability in tort.[5] However, whether the low degree of probability required in a tort action was applicable to the test of remoteness in contract was considered and rejected by the House of Lords in *The Heron II*.[6] The defendant owner of the Heron II agreed to carry a cargo of sugar from Constanza to Basrah. The plaintiffs, sugar merchants, intended to sell the cargo immediately on its arrival. Instead of taking the normal 20 days, the defendants, in breach, took nine days longer. During those nine days, the sugar market fell and the plaintiffs suffered loss of profit.

It was held that the plaintiffs were entitled to damages for loss of profit. However, the House of Lords considered it inappropriate that the loss was merely reasonably foreseeable. A higher degree of probability was required than in a tort action but the Law Lords used various formulations to express its measurement. They each used different phrases to describe the requisite degree of probability. Lords Pearce and Upjohn considered that there must be a "serious possibility" or a "real danger" or a "very substantial" probability of loss. Lord Morris regarded loss which was not too remote as that which is "not unlikely to occur" or "liable to result". Lord Hodson also used the expression, "liable to result" whilst, for Lord Reid, the plaintiff may not recover loss which, although a real possibility, was only likely to occur "in a small minority of cases".

Although it is diffcult to draw clear distinctions between the various approaches, the Law Lords were adamant that for a loss to be recoverable, the degree of probability of such loss must be higher in contract than in tort.

The matter was further considered by the Court of Appeal in *H. Parsons (Livestock) Ltd. v Ingham & Co. Ltd.*,[7] in which a bulk-storage hopper "fitted with ventilated top" was supplied and erected by the defendants for the plaintiffs, pig farmers. The hopper was to be used for the storage of pig-nuts. In breach, the ventilator sealed during transit, was left closed. As a consequence, some of the pig-nuts stored therein went mouldy and many pigs fed with the nuts died. The plaintiffs sued for the loss of the pigs and lost sales.

The Court of Appeal upheld the first instance decision finding the defendants liable for all the losses directly caused. However, Lord Denning M.R. said that the higher degree of probability laid down in the *Heron II* applied where the plaintiff's claim was for mere loss of profit. His approach

---

5. See the section on remoteness of damage in tort below.
6. *Sub nom. Koufos v Czarnikow* [1969] 1 A.C. 350.
7. [1978] Q.B. 791.

was to distinguish between claims for economic loss as opposed to those for physical harm rather than distinguish between claims in contract and tort. If the claim was for physical damage caused by the breach then a lower degree of probability, that is, the same test as in tort, would suffice. This denotes a stricter test on claims which are inherently speculative, for instance lost profits, and a more lenient test for claims which lend themselves more readily to accurate measurement, as in physical damage. Thus, in the case, the fact that the physical harm to the pigs could be foreseen as a "slight possibility" was sufficient to make the defendants liable to compensate.

Lord Scarman (Orr L.J. concurring) also found for the plaintiff but rejected Lord Denning's distinction between physical damage and financial loss. Liability in the case rested on the fact that, using the test in the *Heron II*, the chance that the pigs might become ill as a result of the breach was a "serious possibility".

In addition, Lord Scarman considered it absurd that the test of remoteness should differ according to whether the action was in tort or contract. Yet, he also took the view that the formulations for each are different since the relationship between the parties in a contract situation differ from that in tort. This is because a contracting party may protect himself against unusual risks by pointing them out to the other party before the contract is made. Treitel[8] tentatively reconciles these opposing positions by suggesting that, where the same facts give rise to liability in both contract and tort, the plaintiff may rely on the more favourable tort test whereas, if the cause of action is confined to contractual liability, then the stricter test applies.

The law on remoteness of damage in contract is, therefore, unclear although, until the House of Lords decides differently, the stricter rule as expressed in *Heron II* would seem to prevail. In *Balfour Beatty Construction (Scotland) Ltd. v Scottish Power plc*[9] the House of Lords considered the state of knowledge which could be imputed to the defendants, given the capacity in which they were contracting. It was held that an electricity company could not be presumed to have known that, if their power supply to the plaintiff construction company failed, the consequent interruption of a continuous pour of concrete would lead to the construction of an aqueduct being halted and the work in hand being demolished. The House held that,

8. *Law of Contract*, 9th ed. (Sweet and Maxwell, 1995), p. 873.
9. [1994] S.L.T. 807.

although parties as businessmen could be assumed to have all reasonable acquaintance with the ordinary course of business,[10] businesses could not, as a general rule, be presumed to know about the other's business affairs, particularly where the activity was a complicated one.

However, the nature of the trading relationship between the contracting parties is clearly of importance when the court is deciding who should bear responsibility for loss arising out of a breach. This can explain the different decisions in *Hadley v Baxendale* and *The Heron II*. In the latter case, the carrier regularly transported the plaintiff's goods, whereas in the former, he had little knowledge of the plaintiff's business. This approach encourages parties to make available to each other information concerning the risks associated with the agreement so that they may be more likely to recover in the event of a breach.

Note, however, that the extent of loss does not have to be in the defendant's contemplation.[11] It is the *kind* of loss which must be foreseen and in *Brown v K.M.R. Services Ltd.*[12] a Lloyd's name succesfully sued his agent for breach of contract when, in advance of the Lloyd's crash, the latter made him a member of a high-risk syndicate. Gatehouse J. stated (at pages 398-99):

> "It is most unlikely that any professional member of Lloyd's foresaw the magnitude of the financial disasters that struck in the middle to late 1980's ... But losses of the type that occurred were undoubtedly foreseeable and in fact foreseen even though their scale was not. That is enough for the plaintiff ... The plaintiff's losses were the natural and obvious result of his being a member of the 'disaster' syndicates."

Note also, that the defendant is liable for special losses only if made aware or warned of the special circumstances which would give rise to them. It has been asserted that the special circumstances "must have been brought home ... in such circumstances that the defendant impliedly undertook to bear any loss referable to the breach".[13]

In *Horne v Midland Railway*[14] the defendant railway company contracted to deliver a consignment of boots to London. The delivery was

---

10. This is a reference to the *dictum* of Alderson B. in *Hadley v Baxendale*.
11. *Parsons v Uttley Ingham* [1978] Q.B. 791 and *Wroth v Tyler* [1974] Ch. 30.
12. [1994] 4 All E.R. 385.
13. *British Columbia and Vancouver Island Spar, Lumber and Sawmill Co. Ltd. v Nettleship* (1868) L.R. 3 C.P. 499, at 509.
14. (1873) L.R. 8 C.P. 131.

delayed by a day and as a result the plaintiffs lost the opportunity of selling the boots at a price higher than the usual market price. The defendants were not liable to reimburse this exceptional loss. Blackburn J. said that, in order that notice of special circumstances may have any effect, it must be given in such a way that an actual contractual obligation arises on the part of the defendant to bear the unusual loss.[15] However, later cases make it clear that there need be no express agreement to accept responsibility to compensate for the special loss.[16] The defendant is liable for the loss irrespective of any actual agreement to bear it.[17]

This suggests that mere notice of special circumstances can lead to liability and the fairness of this position may be questioned. The vulnerability of the defendant to a literal application of this approach was recognised in *Kemp v Intasun Holidays Ltd.*[18] Here, a casual remark to a travel agent by a customer about his wife's medical condition was not sufficient to make her subsequent illness, whilst on holiday, reasonably contemplatable. However, compare this case with *Jackson v Chrysler Acceptances Ltd.*,[19] where the purchaser of a new and defective car was able to claim, not only for those defects but also, for a holiday abroad interrupted by the car's breakdown. The latter claim was justified by the fact that the purchaser had told the car dealer, at the time of contracting, of his intention to use the car for such a holiday soon after taking delivery.

### *Remoteness of damage in tort*

As with contract, where breach of a tortious duty causes damage to the plaintiff, the plaintiff may recover damages as long as the damage was not too remote a consequence of that breach. The legal position in relation to remoteness of damage has been dominated by two different approaches to the concept. Two leading cases provide the opposing principles in question.

---

15. *Ibid.*, at 141. The decision may be explained on the basis that the defendants had no knowledge of the special price which the plaintiffs would have been able to charge had the delivery been on time.
16. E.g., *Robophone Facilities v Blank* [1966] 1 W.L.R. 1428.
17. *G.K.N. Centrax Gears Ltd. v Matbro Ltd.* [1976] 2 Lloyd's Rep. 555.
18. [1987] F.T.L.R. 234
19. [1978] R.T.R. (C.A.).

*The direct consequence test*

In *Re Polemis*[20] the servants of the defendant charterers dropped a plank into the hold of a ship while unloading cargo. The cargo included petrol and the falling plank caused a spark which ignited petrol vapour resulting in an explosion which completely destroyed the ship. The defendants argued that the damage was too remote on the ground that it was unforeseeable that a falling plank would result in an explosion. The Court of Appeal rejected the argument that liability for damage is limited to the foreseeable consequence of an act. Some damage to the plaintiff was foreseeable and although the kind of damage, that is damage by explosion and fire, was not foreseeable, it was a direct consequence of the breach of duty.

*The foresight test*

The direct cause test was attacked because it furnished no guidelines for monitoring liability. It is irrelevant, according to the direct cause test, that the loss is totally outside of a class of possible damage which might be seen as a risk of harm created by the defendant. Thus, without a clear criterion of directness, the limits to be placed on liability are purely arbitrary.[21]

In *The Wagon Mound*[22] fuel oil, carelessly spilled into the harbour by the defendants, floated around the plaintiff's wharf. This was ignited by drops of molten metal from welding operations carried out by the plaintiffs on the dock above, which had landed on cotton waste in the water. Both the wharf and the two ships docked there were badly damaged in the fire which resulted. The Privy Council considered the direct cause test of *Polemis* to be unjust and the test of foreseeability was substituted.

---

20. *Re Polemis and Furness Withy & Co. Ltd.* [1921] A.C. 388.
21. However, Fleming, (*The Law of Torts*, 1992, Law Book Co., pp. 207-8), observes: "ominous as the Polemis formula ... might at first sound, it was rarely taken to extravagant lengths ... . In practice, save in a few isolated instances, the Polemis formula was reserved for cases where the harm fell broadly within the hazard that made the defendant's conduct negligent but where, because the stage was set for it, its *extent*, exceeded the bounds of reasonable foresight. Even then, it was subject to the overiding requirement, evolved largely as a counterweight, that only a 'foreseeable plaintiff' was entitled to redress because only to him ... would a 'duty' of care be owed. Thus unless *some* injury to *him* was foreseeable, he would not be entitled to claim for any injury, still less for all direct injury."
22. *Overseas Tankship (U.K.) Ltd. v Morts Dock and Eng. Co. Ltd.* [1961] A.C. 388.

This limited the liability of the defendant to those consequences which are reasonably foreseeable at the time of the breach of duty. Viscount Simonds stated:

> "It is a principle of civil liability, subject only to qualifications which have no present relevance, that a man must be considered to be responsible for the probable consequences of his act. To demand more of him is too harsh a rule, to demand less is to ignore that civilised order requires the observance of a minimum standard of behaviour. The depth of foresight required ... is the foresight of the reasonable man which alone can determine responsibility."[23]

The Judicial Committee held that there was no liability in negligence since damage by fire to the plaintiff's wharf could not reasonably have been foreseen by the defendants when they carelessly discharged oil into the harbour.

The modern test then is based on reasonable foreseeability. However, when are remote consequences foreseeable to the reasonable man? According to Lord Denning M.R.:

> "It is not necessary that the precise concatenation of circumstances should be envisaged. If the consequence was one which any reasonable person might foresee (and was not of an entirely different kind which no one would anticipate) then it is within the rule that a person who has been guilty of negligence is liable for the consequences."[24]

The Wagon Mound criterion is somewhat vague and the effect of dealing with this shortcoming has been to considerably weaken the impact of the test. The courts have in fact waivered between strictly adhering to the foreseeability limitation, with the risk of depriving an innocent victim of recovering, and recognising that abandoning the test could lead to liability which is entirely disproportionate to the breach in question. With this loose application of the doctrine, it is hardly surprising that Salmond commented: "This doctrine of remoteness of damage is one of very considerable obscurity and difficulty."[25]

What is clear is that the introduction of the foreseeability test has had a less than radical impact. This can be illustrated by reference to the

---

23. *Ibid.*, at 422-3.
24. *Stewart v West African Terminals* [1964] 2 Lloyd's Rep. 371, at 375.
25. Salmond, *Law of Torts*, 20th ed. (Sweet & Maxwell, 1992), p. 522.

following limiting characteristics:

a) the kind of damage suffered and the manner in which it was inflicted, and

b) the extent of the damage suffered.

*The kind of harm suffered and the manner in which it was inflicted*

The case of *Hughes v Lord Advocate*[26] provides a major modification to the *Wagon Mound* test for here the House of Lords held that neither the precise way in which the injury occurs nor the exact nature of the damage suffered need be foreseeable. All that is necessary is that the accident or damage is of a similar kind to that which could be anticipated as likely to happen.

In *Hughes* two young boys, aged eight and ten, entered a tent which had been erected over a manhole by the defendant's employees. The tent was surrounded by paraffin lamps, one of which was taken by the eight year old, who tripped and fell into the hole igniting the paraffin vapour. Quite unpredictably, a violent explosion followed, and the boy suffered terrible burns. But, the defendants argued that the way in which the damage was inflicted was not foreseeable. The House of Lords held the defendants liable because damage by burns, albeit caused by explosion rather than fire, was foreseeable. It was within the risk created by the negligence.

A rational application of the requirement that only the kind of damage in question need be foreseeable to establish liablity is dependent upon a recognition of the different kinds of damage which exist. This is not apparent and, as such, can lead to difficulties. In *Doughty v Turner Manufacturing Co. Ltd.*[27] the Court of Appeal held that the plaintiff's burns, suffered as a result of the defendant's employee dropping an asbestos cover into a vat of molten liquid causing it to erupt, amounted to damage which was too remote. The damage, that is a burn resulting from an unexpected and violent chemical reaction, was of an entirely different kind from that caused by the foreseeable risk of splashing.

In *Tremain v Pike*[28] the rat population on the defendant's farm had grown unduly large. The plaintiff, a herdsman, contracted Weil's disease

---

26. [1963] 1 All E.R. 705.
27. [1964] 1 Q.B. 518.
28. [1969] 1 W.L.R. 1556.

after contact with rats' urine. This was held to be too remote since it was different in kind from foreseeable consequences such as rat bites or food poisoning. Such a decision suggests that the classification of kinds of damage will need to be precise. Yet, it is interesting to contrast this approach with the decision in *Bradford v Robinson Rentals*.[29] There, the plaintiff driver recovered for frostbite sustained as a result of driving the defendant employer's unheated vehicle in extreme winter conditions. The foreseeable kind of damage was injury from the cold, for example, cold and chillblains, and frostbite, though in itself unforeseeable, fell within that category.

*The extent of the damage suffered*

In *Bradford v Robinson Rentals* the chances of the driver sustaining frostbite in the south west of England were very low, even in very cold winter conditions, yet the court considered it foreseeable enough to satisfy the *Wagon Mound* test. This decision is illustrative of the principle, already referred to in the case of contractual claims, that, provided the *kind* of damage is foreseeable, the plaintiff may claim for loss which is more extensive than could have been foreseen. Another example may be found in *Vacwell Engineering v B.D.H. Chemicals*[30] in which the defendants supplied a chemical and carelessly failed to give warning that it was liable to explode in water. Extensive damage was caused when the plaintiff's scientist placed the chemical in water and a violent explosion ensued. The defendants were held liable since a minor explosion and, therefore, some property damage was foreseeable.

*The "egg shell skull" principle*

A further application of the principle that remoteness is restricted to the kind, rather than the extent, of damage caused is the rule that the defendant must take his victim as he finds him. This rule is often referred to as the "egg shell skull" rule and requires the defendant to compensate his victim

---

29. [1967] 1 W.L.R. 337.
30. [1971] 1 Q.B. 88.

even though the latter suffers from a particular weakness[31] which exacerbates his injuries making them worse than could have been foreseen.

In *Smith v Leech Brain & Co. Ltd.*[32] the defendant's negligence caused the plaintiff to suffer a burn on the lip. The plaintiff had a predisposition to cancer and the burn made the cancer develop resulting in his death. In an action under the Fatal Accidents Act 1976 the widow established that the employers were liable.[33]

It is arguable whether the "egg shell skull" rule is an independent doctrine or just an application of the distinction drawn above between kind and extent of damage. Lord Parker's judgement in *Smith v Leech Brain* suggests the latter. He said (at page 415):

> "The test is not whether these employers could reasonably have foreseen that a burn would cause cancer and that he would die. The question is whether these employers could reasonably foresee the type of injury he suffered, namely the burn. What in the particular case is the amount of the damage which he suffers as a result of that burn depends on the characteristics of the victim."

*Degree of foreseeability*

In *Wagon Mound (No. 2)*[34] the owners of the two ships that were being repaired at the wharf of the plaintiffs in the first *Wagon Mound* case sued the owners of the Wagon Mound, the ship from which fuel oil was spilled. The action was in nuisance and negligence and the court found liability on the ground that, although the reasonable man would find the risk of fire highly improbable, the possibility of it was foreseeable. Compared with *Wagon Mound (No. 1)*, it seems that a lower likelihood of damage is

---

31. The rule also applies, but with a qualification, in nervous shock cases. See *Brice v Brown* [1984] 1 All E.R. 997, where it was held that as long as the victim was a person of "normal disposition and phlegm" the fact that he might become more seriously ill than would normally be expected would not prevent a successful claim for the full extent of the injury. See also *Page v Smith* [1995] 2 All E.R. 736.
32. [1962] 2 Q.B. 405.
33. For an interesting application of the rule, see *Meah v McCreamer* [1985] 1 All E.R. 367.
34. *Overseas Tankship (U.K.) Ltd. v The Miller Steamship Pty. Ltd., (The Wagon Mound No. 2)* [1967] 1 A.C. 617.

required.[35] According to the Privy Council, it is sufficient that it is a:

> "real risk, one which would occur to the mind of a reasonable man in the defendant's position and which he would not brush aside as far fetched."[36]

The effect of this judgement is that, while the actual damage may not be reasonably foreseeable, a defendant may still be liable if there is a mere possibility of that damage, and the defendant was negligent in doing the act which caused it. This makes a substantial change to the *Wagon Mound (No. 1)* rule in that it extends the application of the test of foreseeability of damage to possibility rather than probability. It is not necessary that the chances of damage resulting should be greater than the chances that no damage will occur. Indeed, even if the risk is small, it would be unreasonable not to act in response to it, unless there was some valid reason.

*Applicability of the Wagon Mound test*

It is well established that the *Wagon Mound* test applies to the torts of negligence and nuisance. However, what of other torts?

*Torts based on intentional conduct*

It seems that the appropriate approach to remoteness for those torts in which the defendant intends to do harm is that, once causation has been established, the defendant is liable for the natural and direct consequences of the tort i.e., all the damage flowing from the tort. This is because the deliberate wrongdoer should be made answerable for his actions and not be able to avoid such responsibility merely because the consequences were unforeseeable. Thus, in *Doyle v Olby (Ironmongers) Ltd.*,[37] the Court of Appeal held that, in the tort of deceit, the defendant is liable for all the actual losses directly flowing from the fraudulent statement.

---

35. In the *Wagon Mound (No. 1)*, the plaintiffs did not argue that it was foreseeable that the oil would ignite, lest they be held contributorily negligent, a complete defence in N.S.W. at the time.
36. *Wagon Mound (No. 2), per* Lord Reid, at 643.
37. [1969] 2 Q.B. 158. "It does not lie in the mouth of the fraudulent person to say that they could not have been foreseeable" (*per* Lord Denning, at p. 167).

Stanton observes that a similar test for remoteness may well apply to the tort of battery.[38] He supports this contention by reference to the Canadian case, *Allen v Mount Sinai Hospital*,[39] in which Linden J. said: "In battery, however, any and all damage is recoverable, if it results from the wrongful act, whether it is foreseeable or not." This view was echoed, *obiter dictum*, by Bristow J. in *Chatterton v Gerson*.[40] However, in the later New Zealand case, *Mayfair v Pears*,[41] the court was unwilling to lay down a clear rule regarding remoteness and trespass, and considered that the intention behind the concept of remoteness was to "limit the amounts recoverable by the plaintiff to those that are not only connected to the act but which are reasonable having regard to its nature and the interests of the parties and society". In the case the defendant, who had trespassed by parking his car in the plaintiff's garage, was found not liable for damage caused when the car unforeseeably caught on fire.

Strict liability torts present further problems, since the appropriate test for remoteness is not clear. The Privy Council stated that its decision in the *Wagon Mound (No. 1)*, did not embrace the rule in *Rylands v Fletcher*.[42] However, in the recent case of *Cambridge Water Co. v Eastern Counties Leather*,[43] the House of Lords decided that the rule was essentially an extension of the law of nuisance to cases of isolated escape and so it would be logical to extend the same requirement as to liability. Thus, the defendant must have reasonably foreseen the consequences of the escape in question.

In cases of breach of statutory duty, the harm suffered must be within the scope of the class of risks at which the statute is directed.[44] If the damage is so within, it does not matter that the damage did not occur in exactly the same way as that contemplated by the statute. Thus, in *Donaghey v Boulton and Paul Ltd.*,[45] the fact that the plantiff fell through a *hole* in a roof, as opposed to through *fragile* roofing, did not make the damage suffered too remote since the object of the statutory duty was to

---

38. K.M. Stanton, *The Modern Law of Tort*, (Sweet & Maxwell, 1994) p. 101.
39. (1980) 109 D.L.R. (3d) 634.
40. [1981] Q.B. 432.
41. [1987] N.Z.L.R. 459.
42. (1868) L.R. 3. H.L.330.
43. [1994] 1 All E.R. 53; [1994] 2 W.L.R. 53.
44. See *Gorris v Scott* (1874). L.R. 9 Exch. 125.
45. [1968] A.C. 1.

prevent workmen falling to the ground from unsafe roofing and, therefore, the damage suffered was within the ambit of the statute.

Lastly, with regard to the tort of defamation, the decision of the Court of Appeal in *Slipper v BBC*[46] has clarified the position in respect of damage caused by the wrongful act of a third party. In the past such loss was considered too remote[47] but now, if the damage suffered by the plaintiff was a reasonably foreseeable consequence of the defendant's act, then the defendant will be liable. The case itself was concerned with liability for the foreseeable repetition of a defamatory statement.

**Distinction between actions in contract and tort**

In *Parsons v Uttley Ingham*,[48] Lord Denning discussed the issue of remoteness, not in terms of whether the claim was pursued in contract or tort but whether the damage caused was physical or non-physical; the former giving rise to the application of the *Wagon Mound* test and the latter the application of *The Heron II*. The reader should refer back to the earlier discussion of this point.

## 2. Intervening causes

It may be established that the defendant was in breach of his duty and this was followed by loss to the plaintiff. However, the defendant may escape liability altogether or incur partial liability if he can show that some other factual cause, intervening after the breach, was the sole or part cause of the plaintiff's damage. Such a *novus actus interveniens* would be considered too remote and breaks the chain of causation between the defendant and the plaintiff.

Although intervening causes may be classified as below, there are no clear principles to guide the judiciary. Where the *novus actus* is the intervening wrongful conduct of a third party who is found to be more responsible for the loss to the plaintiff than is the defendant's breach, then fairness dictates that the defendant be relieved of liability. It is not always so straightforward, for example, when the intervening act is a natural event

46. [1991] 1 Q.B. 432.
47. *Vicars v Wilcocks* (1806) 8 East 1.
48. [1978] Q.B. 791.

or attributable to a non-culpable third party. Here, the court will not be so willing to conclude that the chain of causation has been severed.

*Intervening natural events*

For reasons of policy the courts have been resistant to allowing a natural and intervening event to break the chain of causation for to do so would mean that the plaintiff would have no-one to sue.

However, an intervening and unforeseeable natural event may make the damage too remote and exonerate the defendant. The chain of causation will be broken where the natural event causes the damage simply because the defendant's breach of duty has placed the plaintiff or his property in a position where the damage can be caused. Conversely, the chain of causation will not be broken if the intervening natural event merely increased the posibility of further damage being incurred or made the plaintiff more prone to damage.

In *Carslogie Steamship Co. v Royal Norwegian Government*[49] the defendant's ship was responsible for colliding with and causing damage to the plaintiff's ship. Temporary repairs were made and then the plaintiff's ship set sail for the United States, a voyage which would not have been made but for the collision. Storm conditions were encountered on the journey and the ship suffered further damage. The House of Lords considered that the storm damage "was not in any sense a consequence of the collision, and must be treated as a supervening event occurring in the course of a normal voyage". The only contribution made by the defendant's breach of duty to the storm damage was that the plaintiff ship owners had voluntarily put to sea at a time when, subsequently, the ship found itself in the Atlantic during the storm. In the circumstances the damage suffered was not within the foreseeable risk created by the defendant's negligence but was a consequence of one of the ordinary natural hazards of shipping.

Thus, where the negligence of the defendant combines with a natural event and together this causes injury to the plaintiff, liability will not arise if, firstly, the defendant's negligence alone would have failed to produce the injury and, secondly, the natural event is an extraordinary occurrence which

---

49. [1952] A.C. 292. See also *Monarch S.S. Co. Ltd. v A./B. Karlshamms Oljefabriker* [1949] A.C. 196; *Smith v London and South Western Rly. Co.* (1870) L.R. 6 C.P. 14; *Toledo & Ohio Central v Kibler* 119 N.E. 733 (1918).

could not be reasonably anticipated or reasonably guarded against. That is: "the negligence is not followed by the injurious results in natural and probable sequence, but only by the occurrence of something abnormal and not to be anticipated."[50]

*Intervening act of a third party*

A defendant may escape liability if, subsequent to his breach of duty, an entirely independent act by a third party causes damage to the plaintiff. A negligent intervention by a third party may be something which is not reasonably foreseeably and may break the chain of causation but it is not clear whether something less than negligence will have the same effect. In *Knightly v Johns,*[51] Stephenson L.J. stated that: "negligent conduct is more likely to break the chain of causation than conduct which is not", so suggesting that it could. However, in *Robinson v Post Office,*[52] Orr L.J. indicated that any conduct which fell short of negligence could not amount to a *novus actus interveniens*. The decision as to whether the damage sustained should be attributed to one or other or to regard each as joint causes of the damage will depend on the facts for firm rules on this issue are not evident.

In *The Oropesa*,[53] after a collision between two ships, for which both captains were partly responsible, the captain of one sent a boat to the other to discuss how his vessel could be saved. The boat overturned in the high seas and a crew member drowned. The Court of Appeal did not consider this subsequent action a *novus actus*, Lord Wright taking the view that:

> "To break the chain of causation it must be shown that there is something which I will call ultroneous, something unwarrantable, a new cause which disturbs the sequence of events, something which can be described as either unreasonable or extraneous or extrinsic."[54]

In *Rouse v Squires*[55] a driver, A, negligently "jack-knifed" his lorry blocking

---

50. *Bevan On Negligence* (4th ed.) p. 80.
51. [1982] 1 W.L.R. 349.
52. [1974] 2 All E.R. 737.
53. [1943] P. 32.
54. *Ibid.,* at 59.
55. [1973] Q.B. 889; [1973] 2 All E.R. 903.

the road. A car ran into the obstruction and the plaintiff stopped to help. Subsequently another lorry, driven negligently by B, collided with the crashed vehicles killing the plaintiff. The Court of Appeal held that lorry driver A was responsible for the death since, although B's negligence was the main cause of the plaintiff's death, A had created a continuing hazard which was to be considered a contributory cause. Indeed A's contribution was measured as 25%.

It is instructive to contrast the above case with *Knightley v Johns*.[56] Here, the defendant negligently overturned his car in a one way road tunnel. The police inspector in charge at the scene of the accident, realising that he had omitted to follow standing orders and close the entrance to the tunnel, instructed the plaintiff constable to ride his motor cycle back against the traffic and prevent more entering. In the process the plaintiff was hit by a car. The Court of Appeal held the defendant not liable, Lord Stephenson taking the view that the reasonable hypothetical observer would anticipate some human errors on the part of the police operation but the ordinary course of things had taken an extraordinary course when the inspector had made such a departure from common sense procedure in not closing the tunnel immediately.

According to Hart and Honore,[57] for the intervening act to break the chain of causation it must be free, deliberate and informed, otherwise it should be treated as a natural and probable consequence of the defendant's breach of duty and his responsibility should not be displaced. It follows that, if the intervenor was not fully responsible for the act in question, for example, where he is a child or mentally disabled, it is not likely to be considered a *novus actus*.

Thus, in *Kirkham v Chief Constable of the Greater Manchester Police*,[58] an action was brought under the Fatal Accidents Act 1976 against the police by the widow of a man who committed suicide whilst on remand. She established that the police had failed to inform the prison authorities of his clinical depression. The Court of Appeal held that the suicide, though a voluntary act, was a foreseeable consequence of the breach of duty and did not amount to a *novus actus interveniens*.

Similarly, an action may not amount to a *novus actus* where the intervenor had a choice of action but the choice was not a fair one to make.

---

56. [1982] 1 W.L.R. 349; see also *Wright v Lodge* [1993] 4 All E.R. 299.
57. *Causation in the Law*, 2nd ed., (Oxford; Clarendon, 1985), p.136.
58. [1990] Q.B. 283.

An illustrative case can be considered. In *Scott v Shepherd*[59] the defendant threw a lighted squib into a busy market house which landed on a stall. In self protection, the stallholder tossed the squib onto the adjacent stall and this pattern was repeated until the squib which was thrown in the direction of the plaintiff, exploded in his face, consequently blinding him. The defendant was held liable for trespass, the intervenors acting in the agony of the moment in order to safeguard themselves from injury.[60]

What of situations where the intervening conduct consists of a deliberate and wrongful act of a third party? It seems that such wilful misconduct is much more likely to constitute a *novus actus*. In *Lamb v Camden Borough Council*[61] the defendant's negligence caused a water main to burst which lead to the plaintiff having to vacate her house. Subsequently squatters moved into the house which they damaged. It was held that the defendants were not liable for the actions of the squatters because, even though what happened was foreseeable, it was not likely.[62]

Note that Lord Denning held that it was a question of policy whether the damage was too remote given the availability of insurance to the plaintiff and the fact that he could have taken greater precautions to prevent the entry of squatters.[63]

This requirement for a higher degree of likelihood than mere foreseeability is based on a recognition that it would be unfair to make a careless wrongdoer too easily responsible for the wilful misconduct of others. However, the law is prepared to make responsible those who negligently provide an opportunity for others to cause deliberate harm. In *Home Office v Dorset Yachts Ltd.*,[64] due to the negligence of the prison authorities, a number of Borstal boys escaped and, in the process, caused damage to nearby property. The boys' actions did not amount to a *novus actus*. Lord Reid observed that, for such behaviour to break the chain of

---

59. (1773) 2 Wm. Bl. 892.
60. This "doctrine of alternative danger" has been held to apply to danger to property - *Sutherland v Glasgow Corporation* (1951) S.C. 1.
61. [1981] Q.B. 625.
62. *Ibid.*, *per* Lord Oliver at 642. See also *Ward v Cannock Chase District Council* [1986] Ch. 546, where similar facts produced a different decision, and note, *Smith v Littlewoods Organisation* [1987] 1 All E.R. 710. Note that in *Perl v Camden B.C.* [1983] 3 All E.R. 161 the Court of Appeal held that there was no general duty owed to protect one's neighbours against, for example, the possibility of burglars gaining access via one's premises.
63. *Ibid.*, at 637.
64. [1970] A.C. 1004.

causation, it would have to be very unlikely. In the circumstances it was very likely that yachts would be damaged by such boys attempting to make good their escape from an island.

Liability may be imposed for the intentional wrongdoing of a third party where the defendant is duty-bound to ensure that the action which constitutes the wrongdoing does not occur. Thus, in *Stansbie v Troman*[65] a painter employed to decorate the plaintiff's house left the house unattended and unlocked against instructions. During his absence, jewellery belonging to the plaintiff was stolen and the Court of Appeal held that the decorator was liable for the loss since the negligent act in question was the failure to ensure that the very thing that did happen should not happen. There was a direct connection between the duty to leave the house locked and the damage suffered which outweighed the fact that the theft was not very likely.

In *Smith v Littlewoods*[66] Lord Goff summed up (at page 279) the situation illustrated by *Stansbie v Troman:*

> "When a duty is cast upon a person to take precautions against the wrongdoing of third parties, the ordinary standard of foreseeability applies and so the possibility of such wrongdoing does not have to be very great before liability is imposed. I do not myself subscribe to the opinion that liability for the wrongdoing of others is limited because of the unpredictability of human conduct."

*Intervening act of the plaintiff*

Usually a plaintiff's act which, in conjunction with the defendant's breach of duty, causes the plaintiff to incur injury will constitute contributory negligence, for which see below. However, the defendant may bear full or part responsibility for the plaintiff's damage where the latter's subsequent acts follow naturally from the breach. In order for the plaintiff to break the chain of causation his actions must be unreasonable.

In *McKew v Holland and Hannen and Cubitts (Scotland) Ltd.*[67] the defendant had negligently injured the plaintiff's leg which, as a result, occasionally gave way under him. Subsequent to the accident, and accompanied by his daughter whose hand he was holding, the plaintiff was

---

65. [1948] 2 K.B. 48.
66. [1987] A.C. 241.
67. [1969] 3 All E.R. 1621.

descending a steep stairway which had no handrail. His leg gave way and, pushing his daughter to safety, he jumped to avoid falling. As a result he broke his ankle. The House of Lords held that the plaintiffs were not liable for the broken ankle, the defendant's unreasonable behaviour in taking such a risk amounting to an intervening act which broke the chain of causation. Lord Reid said:

> "In my view the law is clear ... if the injured man acts unreasonably he cannot hold the defender liable for injury caused by his own unreasonable conduct. His unreasonable conduct is novus actus interveniens. The chain of causation has been broken and ... one may say that unreasonable conduct of the pursuer and what follows from it is not the natural and probable result of the original fault of the defender or of the ensuing disability."[68]

Contrast the above with *Wieland v Cyril Lord Carpets Ltd.*,[69] where the plaintiff's neck was injured through the defendant's negligence and, because of her surgical collar, she was unable to adjust her bi-focal spectacles. As a result she tripped whilst descending a staircase. It was held that, in the circumstances, her behaviour was entirely reasonable. The plaintiff's second accident occurred soon after the collar was fitted and, so, she had not fully appreciated the difficulties associated with wearing bi-focals with such restricted movement, and the court considered climbing the stairs reasonable in the circumstances. Therefore, responsibility for her injuries caused by the fall rested on the defendant.

In *Emeh v Kensington and Chelsea and Westminster Area Health Authority*[70] Waller L.J. considered that the degree of unreasonable conduct required, before the plaintiff's act eclipsed the defendant's wrongdoing and broke the chain of causation, must be "very high". The defendant negligently performed a sterilisation operation on the plaintiff who subsequently became pregnant. In a claim for the upkeep of the child the Court of Appeal held that it was not unreasonable conduct for the plaintiff not to have sought an abortion, particularly as by the time she discovered her condition, she was 20 weeks pregnant and any operation would have been both traumatic and risky.[71]

---

68. *Ibid.*, at 1623.
69. [1969] 3 All E.R. 1006. See also *Quinn v Burch (Builders) Ltd.* [1966] 2 Q.B. 370.
70. [1985] Q.B. 1012, [1984] 3 All E.R. 1044.
71. Slade L.J. said that, generally, to refuse an abortion, even where the pregnancy is in early term, would not be unreasonable. See page 95 below.

The concept of *novus actus* can arise in contract and so a plaintiff is unable to claim damages for damage loss arising out of a breach which has been exacerbated by a supervening event unattributable to the defendant contract-breaker. In *Beoco Ltd. v Alfa Laval Co. Ltd.*[72] the intervening event was that of the plaintiffs themselves. The first defendant installed a heat exchanger for the plaintiffs. The latter, on discovering that the heat exchanger leaked, contracted the second defendant to repair the fault. The plaintiffs then used the equipment without checking whether it could function safely. Had they done so, it would have been clear that the heat exchanger was still defective. Shortly afterwards an explosion occurred. In a claim against the first defendant for breach of contract the Court of Appeal held that the plaintiffs' unreasonable conduct was the cause of the subsequent explosion, and so broke the chain of causation.

It follows that in "rescue cases", as in *Haynes v Harwood*,[73] where a policeman was injured in attempting to stop a runaway horse which had been negligently left unattended, the courts are reluctant to conclude that the act of the rescuer amounts to a *novus actus* for danger invites rescue.[74] Of course, a rescuer who behaves with careless disregard for his own safety may break the chain of causation but the courts are aware of the pressure on the rescuer to take swift action in the agony of the moment. Action which, in retrospect, might seem unwise is nevertheless something which the defendant could reasonably anticipate. Lord Denning, in *Videan v British Transport Commission*,[75] summarised the position (at page 868) that: if the rescuer's act is not wanton interference and he is killed or injured, he can recover damages.[76]

---

72. [1994] 4 All E.R. 464. See two other contract cases; *Compania Naviera Maropan v Bowaters* [1955] 2 All E.R. 241 and *Lexmead (B.) Ltd. v Lewis* [1982] A.C. 225.
73. [1935] 1 K.B. 147.
74. "The cry of distress is the summons to relief. The law does not ignore these reactions of the mind in tracing conduct to its consequences ... The risk of rescue, if only it be not wanton, is born of the occasion. The emergency begets the man. The wrongdoer may not have foreseen the coming of a deliverer. He is accountable as if he had." *Per* Cardozo J. in *Wagner v Int. R..R..* (1921) 133 N.E. 437.
75. [1963] 2 All E.R. 860.
76. See, however, *Cutler v United Dairies Ltd.* [1933] 2 K.B. 297, where the "rescue" was not reasonably necessary and did break the chain of causation. But, in *Jones v Boyce* (1816) 1 Stark 493, where the plaintiff broke his legs by jumping from a coach which due to the defendant's negligence seemed about to overturn but, in the event, did not, the chain of causation was not broken as the plaintiff's action was reasonable.

A duty is thus owed to the rescuer, independent of any duty to the rescued. In *Videan* it was held that a stationmaster who rescued his son, who had been trespassing on the railway line, was owed a duty of care, even though the boy himself was not.

## 3. Duty to mitigate

The defendant's breach of duty allows the plaintiff to sue for compensation. However, subsequent to such breach, the plaintiff is obliged to to take reasonable steps to minimise his loss. Much of the case law on this topic is concerned with breach of contract, of which more below, but the general principles also embrace actions in tort.

*Unreasonable inaction*

To describe the responsibility to mitigate as a "duty" is misleading for, in this respect, the plaintiff owes no duty to another. More accurately, the plaintiff may choose to incur losses which were avoidable by taking positive steps, but he will be prevented from passing the cost of such unreasonable inaction onto the defendant.[77] Note that the effect of the "duty" can be to limit the liability of the defendant to compensate for damage which in fact is foreseeable and as such it is more far reaching than the doctrine of causation. It is for the defendant to prove that the plaintiff has acted unreasonably in this regard.

What should reasonably be expected of the plaintiff is a question of fact in each case but the standard of reasonableness is not a high one. This is because it is the defendant who has committed the wrong and consequently placed the plaintiff in difficulty. The burden of proof is upon the defendant to prove that in all the circumstances the plaintiff has responded unreasonably. The case of *Emeh v Kensington and Chelsea and Westminster A.H.A.*,[78] referred to earlier in the context of *novus actus*, serves equally well as an illustration of the doctrine of mitigation. The plaintiff's refusal to have an abortion following an unsatisfactory sterilisation operation was not considered unreasonable in the circumstances.

---

77. Reference to mitigation also covers unreasonable action. See p. 99 below.
78. [1985] Q.B. 1012.

By contrast, in *The Flying Fish*[79] the plaintiffs' ship was damaged when it collided with that of the defendant's negligently operated vessel. The plaintiffs' ship's captain unreasonably refused help and as a result the ship was destroyed. In an action for the loss of the ship the plaintiffs were able only to claim for the original damage suffered in the collision. The claim for the additional loss was not sustained on the grounds that the plaintiffs should have mitigated such loss.

Unreasonable refusal of medical treatment for injuries, incurred as a result of the breach of duty and which leads to an increase in their severity, will limit the plaintiff's claim to compensation for losses arising from the original extent of the injury.[80] However, in *Selvanayagam v University of West Indies*[81] the risk involved in having the recommended treatment made the plaintiff's refusal of it reasonable.

It may be that the plaintiff has to spend money or incur expense in order to mitigate damage. If reasonable means have been chosen so to do the plaintiff may seek reimbursement. This would be the case even if the ultimate cost were greater than if the plaintiff had remained passive and taken no steps to minimise the loss.[82] Mitigation in this respect is concerned with the *actions*, reasonable or otherwise, of the plaintiff. This will be considered later. However, there is no requirement for the plaintiff to spend money, risk capital or pay for something which is beyond his means.

In *Dodd Properties Ltd. v Canterbury City Council*[83] the plaintiffs' property was damaged by the defendant's negligent pile driving in 1970. At issue was whether the plaintiffs could claim for the necessary repairs at trebled 1978 prices or at pre-inflation 1970 prices. The Court of Appeal held that the higher cost was claimable since it was reasonable for the plaintiffs to wait and see whether their action was successful for, without the award of damages, they could not afford to pay for the remedial work.

Most illustrations of the duty to mitigate are to be found in contract. Lord Haldane L.C., in *British Westinghouse Electric and Manufacturing Co. v Underground Electric Railways Co. of London*,[84] laid down that a duty is imposed on the plaintiff to take all reasonable steps to mitigate loss which

---

79. *Anderson v Hoen, The Flying Fish* (1865) 3 Moo PCCNS 77.
80. *McAuley v London Transport Executive* [1957] 2 Lloyd's Rep. 500 (P.C.).
81. [1983] 1 W.L.R. 585.
82. *The Oropesa* [1943] P. 32; *Kirkham v Boughey* [1958] 2 Q.B. 338.
83. [1980] 1 All E.R. 928. See also *Robbins of Putney Ltd.* [1971] R.T.R. and distinguish *Liesbosch Dredger v Edison S.S.* [1933] A.C. 448.
84. [1912] A.C. 673.

is a consequence of the breach and neglecting to take such steps will bar a claim for that loss which results from such neglect. In *Dunkirk Colliery v Lever* James L.J. stated:

> "The person who has broken the contract is not to be exposed to additional cost by reason of the plaintiffs not doing what they ought to have done as reasonable men, and the plaintiffs not being under any obligation to do anything otherwise than in the ordinary course of business."[85]

The following cases provide examples of the court's interpretation of the meaning of unreasonable inaction in a contractual context. In *Payzu Ltd. v Saunders*[86] the plaintiffs failed to pay on time for the first consignment of goods ordered and the defendants, in breach of contract, refused to deliver any more under the contract unless the plaintiffs agreed to pay cash when ordering subsequent instalments. The plaintiffs refused this offer buying goods elsewhere but at a higher price. The Court of Appeal held that whether a loss is avoidable by reasonable action is a question of fact not law and, in the circumstances, the plaintiffs should have accepted the defendant's offer, which represented the best alternative available, and so mitigated their loss. Damages were awarded, but only to represent the loss the plaintiffs would have suffered if they had paid cash, that is, the cost of the period of credit they would have lost if they had paid cash.[87]

There is no duty to pursue a complicated and difficult piece of litigation against a third party in order to minimise loss resulting from a breach of contract. In *Pilkington v Wood*[88] the defendant solicitor, who had negligently transferred property with a defective title to the plaintiff buyer, argued that the latter should take legal action against the vendor for having conveyed a defective title. This was rejected by the court. Harman J., applying *Payzu v Saunders,* held that the defendant should not be allowed to protect himself from the consequences of his own carelessness by placing such an unreasonable burden on the plaintiff.

In *Brace v Calder*[89] the plaintiff was a manager employed on a two

---

85 (1907) 9 Ch. D. 20, 25.

86. [1919] 2 K.B. 581.

87. See also *The Solholt* [1983]1 Lloyd's Rep. 605 (buyer having to mitigate by accepting late delivery with some alteration in the price to reflect the costs of delay).

88. [1953] Ch. 770.

89. [1895] 2 Q.B. 253.

year contract by a partnership which, upon dissolution, wrongfully dismissed him. The business was immediately transferred to two of the original partners who offered to re-employ the plaintiff on the same terms as before. This offer was refused and the plaintiff sought damages to reimburse him for the salary which he would have received if the contract had gone its full term. The Court of Appeal was unanimous in holding that only nominal damages were payable for the plaintiff had acted unreasonably and imprudently by allowing his pride to cause him to reject the offer of continued employment. Clearly if the offer of re-employment involves less advantageous conditions of work, for example, reduced status or the plaintiff has lost confidence in his employers, its refusal would be understandable and reasonable.[90]

In cases of unfair dismissal before an industrial tribunal it is not appropriate for the employer to argue that, where it is alleged that the employee has failed to mitigate his loss since being dismissed, it is for the tribunal, sitting as an industrial jury, to fill any evidential vacuum in this regard. Where the tribunal is asked to consider this issue, the burden of proving failure to mitigate is on the person who asserts it and, therefore, the employer must provide the necessary evidence, either from cross-examination or from evidence called.[91]

The reputation of a business is paramount and, not surprisingly, in commercial contracts the innocent party is under no obligation to act in such a way that would place his reputation or public relations at risk. In *London and South of England Building Society v Stone*[92] the plaintiffs had loaned money to the purchasers of a house. The house was subsiding but this fact was not discovered by the negligent defendants when they surveyed the property. The borrowers had agreed to keep the house in good repair but the plaintiff building society refused to mitigate by enforcing this covenant against the borrower. The Court of Appeal, in an action in both contract and tort, accepted the argument that to pursue such a claim would have damaged the reputation of the plaintiffs.[93]

Lack of funds may prevent the plaintiff from being fully able to mitigate his loss in the event of a breach. For example, a seller of goods may not have sufficient finance to hold on in an attempt to secure the same

---

90. See *Yetton v Eastwoods Froy Ltd.* [1967] 1 W.L.R. 104.
91. *Ministry of Defence v Hunt and others* [1996] I.R.L.R. 139.
92. [1983] 3 All E.R. 105.
93. See also *James Finlay & Co. Ltd. v Kwik Hoo Tong* [1929] 1 K.B. 400.

price for the goods as a defaulting purchaser had promised to pay. Selling at a price lower than the original contract price would not be seen as a failure to mitigate[94] but rather reasonable conduct in the circumstances.

*Unreasonable action*

Discussion of the principle so far has been confined to situations where the focus has been on the inaction of the plaintiff, reasonable or otherwise, in response to the defendant's breach of duty. Generally, the plaintiff's unreasonable action will be considered in the context of an intervening cause breaking the chain of causation but, where the unreasonable conduct in question is an incurring of expense after the breach, it will be treated as an aspect of the duty to mitigate.

As with cases of inaction, the courts will be conscious of the fact that it is the defendant's breach of duty which has placed the plaintiff in the position which has caused him to act. Thus, the fundamental question is, with this in mind, whether the plaintiff has acted reasonably in all the circumstances. In *Banco de Portugal v Waterlow & Sons Ltd.*[95] Lord Macmillan observed:

> "where the sufferer from a breach of contract finds himself in consequence of that breach placed in a position of embarrassment the measures which he may be driven to adopt in order to extricate himself ought not to be weighed in scales at the instance of the party whose breach of contract has occasioned the difficulty. It is often easy after an emergency has passed to criticize the steps which have been taken to meet it, but such criticism does not come well from those who have themselves created the emergency."[96]

In the case the defendants agreed to print bank notes for the plaintiff bank. In breach the defendants delivered the notes to a criminal who put them into circulation in Portugal. In consequence the bank undertook to exchange all notes in circulation and, in so doing, increased the loss resulting from the breach. When sued for the costs involved, the defendants argued that they

94. *Robbins of Putney Ltd. v Meek* [1971] R.T.R. 345, distinguished from *The Liesbosch* [1933] A.C. 449 in which impecuniosity was deemed a factor limiting the award of damages. See the section on this below, at p. 115.

95. [1932] A.C. 452.

96. *Ibid.*, at 506.

were responsible only for the cost of printing new notes. However, the House of Lords held that, because of the bank's commercial obligations, its actions had been quite reasonable and deserving of compensation.

It follows that, if the plaintiff's actions, although reasonable, were not in fact the most cost-effective way of responding to the problem, the court will discount any argument in this vein put forward by the defendant. In *Gebruder Metelmann GmbH & Co. v N.B.R. (London) Ltd.*, Browne Wilkinson L.J. echoing Lord Macmillan in the *Banco de Portugal* case, stated:

> "If there are two methods of mitigating damage, both of which are practicable and reasonable in the circumstances known to the innocent party at the time the mitigating action is required, it is not possible to say that the innocent party acted unreasonably in selecting one of these methods just because, in the light of later events, it turns out that the loss would have been less had the other method been adopted."[97]

Further, even if the action taken by the plaintiff to mitigate actually results in increased damage, then as long as the conduct in question is deemed reasonable at the time action was taken, the extra loss will be recoverable.[98]

Compare the above with the case of *Compania Financiera Soleada SA v Harmoor Tanker Corpn. Inc., The Borag*,[99] in which the Court of Appeal held that the plaintiffs had incurred unreasonably high interest charges when taking out a loan in order to seek the release of a ship held by the defendants in breach of contract.

## Anticipatory breach of contract and mitigation of loss

In cases of anticipatory breach the plaintiff has a choice of accepting the defendant's repudiation and suing immediately or awaiting the date of performance before action is taken. If he anticipates the breach, then he will be under the usual duty to mitigate.[100] If he does not wish to accept the repudiation, he is under no duty to mitigate.[101]

---

97. [1984] 1 Lloyd's Rep. 614, at p. 634.
98. *Lloyds and Scottish Finance Ltd. v Modern Cars and Caravans (Kingston) Ltd.* [1966] 1 Q.B. 764.
99. [1981] 1 All E.R. 856.
100. *Melachrino v Nickoll and Knight* [1920] 1 K.B. 693.
101. [1960] 2 All E.R. 239.

However the latter rule should be read in the light of the decision in *White & Carter (Councils) Ltd. v McGregor*.[102] The plaintiff advertising contractors agreed with the defendants that for a period of three years they would make litter bins, place notices on the bins advertising the defendant's business and supply them to local councils. Although the defendants cancelled the contract as soon as it was agreed, the plaintiffs, refusing to accept this breach, carried out their obligations for the full three years. They then claimed the full contract price. The majority of the House of Lords held that, where the plaintiff opts to await the date for performance, as on the facts, the duty to mitigate arises only when that date for performance has arrived. If it were otherwise, the choice of the plaintiff to accept or ignore the repudiation would be unduly restricted. Nevertheless, in the case, Lord Reid placed two apparent limitations on this principle. Firstly, the plaintiffs could perform the contract without the co-operation of the defendant and, secondly, that the choice to affirm the contract was available only to the plaintiff who had a legitimate interest, financial or otherwise, in the contract being performed, as opposed to claiming damages.[103] The meaning of "legitimate interest" was not fully explained except that reference was made to the application of the *de minimis* principle.

In *Clea Shipping Corpn. v Bulk Oil International Ltd., The Alaskan Trader,*[104] a case concerned with a contract for the charter of a ship, Lloyd J. held that the plaintiff owner's refusal to accept the defendant charterer's repudiation by maintaining the ship at anchor with a full crew ready to sail for a period of eight months was wholly unreasonable. Although conscious of the importance of certainty in commercial contracts, Lloyd J. took the view that there comes a point at which the court will cease, on general equitable principles, to allow an innocent party to enforce his contract to its strict legal terms. On the facts he found that the plaintiffs had no legitimate interest in pursuing their claim for hire rather than a claim for damages.

In view of his decision on the matter of legitimate interest, Lloyd J. found it unnecessary to consider the plaintiff's need to show that he could continue to perform without the co-operation of the defendants. However,

---

102. *White and Carter (Councils) Ltd. v McGregor* [1962] A.C. 413.

103. The legitimate interest approach appears to have been accepted in *Attica Sea Carriers Corpn. v Ferrostaal Poseidon Reederei GmbH, The Puerto Buitrago* [1976] 1 Lloyd's Rep. 250, Court of Appeal, and *The Odenfeld* [1978] 2 Lloyd's Rep. 357.

104. [1984] 1 All E.R. 129.

this issue had been considered further in *Hounslow London Borough Council v Twickenham Garden Developments Ltd.*[105] Contractors working for a local authority refused to accept the latter's repudiation of the contract and continued with the work on the site. In considering the right of the contractors to insist on doing this, Megarry J. regarded the concept of "co-operation" as including *passive* as well as *active* co-operation. The contractors had *de facto* possession of the land on which the work was carried out and, in that respect, the contractors could perform the contract without any "co-operation" by the local authority. But, completion of the contract required the passive co-operation of the local authority in that its execution would require them to "stand impotently aside" whilst a perhaps ill-advised contract was executed on their property which they had delivered into the possession of the other party.

In *White and Carter* neither active nor passive co-operation was required of the defendants for the plaintiffs to complete their side of the bargain. However, this interpretation of the concept of co-operation restricts the impact of the decision in *White and Carter* for, in most contracts, some form of passive co-operation will be needed from the repudiating party if the innocent party is to be able to perform all his contractual obligations. Therefore, in most cases, by refusing co-operation, the party in breach can compel the innocent party to restrict his claim to damages.

In a case of anticipatory breach, where the plaintiff accepts the defendant's repudiation, the date at which damages are to be assessed will be at the date when the plaintiff missed the opportunity to mitigate rather than at the date of performance. In *Kaines (U.K.) Ltd. v Osterreichische Warenhandelsgesellschaft Austrowaren Gesellsschaft gmbH*[106] a contract to supply oil in September was repudiated and accepted by the buyers in June. The market price which rose and fell between the two dates was higher in September, when the buyers purchased a replacement supply, than it had been in June. The Court of Appeal confirmed Steyn J.'s decision that, given the volatility of the market, the plaintiffs should have bought in June and the damages were fixed at the price being charged at that time.

---

105. [1970] 3 All E.R. 326, [1971] Ch. 233.
106. [1993] 2 Lloyd's Rep. 1.

## 4. Contributory negligence

Where the plaintiff is partly responsible for the loss or event which causes his loss he is said to be contributorily negligent. As a consequence, the defendant has a partial defence and any damages recoverable from him will be limited. Contributory negligence differs from the duty to mitigate in that the former is usually concerned with the conduct of the plaintiff before or at the time of the breach of duty,[107] whereas the latter obligation arises after the breach.

*Contributory negligence and tort*

The original common law rule provided a complete defence to tortious liability,[108] although its application to breach of contract was unclear. However, the Law Reform (Contributory Negligence) Act 1945 provides that contributory negligence constitutes a partial defence, and in so doing, reduces the amount of damages payable by the defendant in proportion to the extent of the plaintiff's contributory negligence. Whether the statute applies to breach of contract will be dealt with later in this section. For the moment its impact on tortious liability will be considered.

*Fault*

Section 1(1) provides:

> "Where any person suffers damage as a result partly of his own fault and partly of the fault of any other person or persons, a claim in respect of that damage shall not be defeated by reason of the fault of the person suffering the damage, but the damages recoverable in respect thereof shall be reduced to such extent as the court thinks just and equitable having regard to the claimaint's share in the responsibility for the damage."

With regard to the defendant, section 4 provides that "fault means

---

107. Although see *The Calliope* [1970] 1 All E.R. 624, in which the doctrine of contributory negligence was applied to conduct subsequent to the tort.
108. However, the plaintiff could recover by way of the rule of "last opportunity". See *Davies v Mann* (1842) 10 M. & W. 546.

negligence, breach of statutory duty or other act or omission which gives rise to liability in tort". It follows that fault attaches to the defendant whenever he commits a tort. Section 4 also refers to the plaintiff's fault as any act or omission which would, apart from the Act, give rise to the defence of contributory negligence. This is less clear for two views of its meaning are possible. The first is that it is applicable only to those torts for which, prior to the Act, contributory negligence was a defence at common law. Such an approach would exclude intentional torts, for example deceit and intentional trespass to the person.[109] The second, and more expansive, view is that the section can be interpreted in such a way that the partial defence embraces all torts. That is, the defence is applicable where the plaintiff's conduct would have given rise to the total defence of contributory negligence at common law if he was suing for a tort to which the defence clearly applied.

Note that the Tort (Interference With Goods) Act 1977 s.11, provides that contributory negligence is not available as a partial defence to an action in conversion or intentional trespass to goods.

*Standard of care*

It is unnecessary for the defendant to establish that the plaintiff owed him a duty of care. However, what is required is proof that, on the balance of probabilities, the plaintiff did not, in his own interest, take reasonable care of himself and thereby contributed to his own injury.[110] This employs the same objective test and reference to similar factors as those used to assess breach of duty in negligence claims. Thus, according to Lord Denning in *Jones v Livox Quarries Ltd.*:[111]

> "A person is guilty of contributory negligence if he ought reasonably to have foreseen that if he did not act as a reasonable, prudent man, he might be hurt himself; and in his reckonings he must take into account the possibility of others being careless."[112]

---

109. As in *Alliance & Leicester Building Society v Edgestop Ltd.* [1993] 1 W.L.R. 1462, a case of deceit.
110. Mummery J. in *Nance v British Columbia Electric Railway Co. Ltd.* [1951] A.C. 601, at 616.
111. [1952] 2 Q.B. 608.
112. *Ibid.*, at 615.

The real question is whether he was acting as a responsible person with reasonable care.

The following cases provide illustrations of a number of different situations in which the plaintiff did not take reasonable care with regard to his own safety. In *Owens v Brimmell*[113] the plaintiff was found 20% contributorily negligent having accepted a lift in a friend's car after sharing a night of heavy drinking with him. The act of plying his friend with drink was a contributory cause of the accident which occurred on their return home. The plaintiff must have appreciated at some part of the evening that to continue drinking would be to expose him to the risk of being driven by someone so much under the influence of drink as to be incapable of driving safely, or he gave little, if any, thought to the consequences or was recklessly indifferent to them.

Rather than be a cause of the accident, the plaintiff's conduct may place him in a situation which is inherently dangerous and where risk of injury is foreseeable. This may be the case, for example, where a pedestrian carelessly steps into the road and is knocked over by a car being driven without due care.[114] In *Jones v Livox Quarries Ltd.*[115] the plaintiff, a quarry worker, rode on the towbar at the back of a "traxcavator" which was hit from behind by a dumper truck. He was seriously injured and judged 20% to blame. Similarly, in *Davies v Swan Motor Co. (Swansea) Ltd.*[116] the plaintiff's husband, who was killed, was found to be contributorily negligent in riding on the back of a dustcart which collided with a bus, the accident being caused by the negligence of both drivers.

In *Froom v Butcher*[117] the plaintiff car driver failed to wear his seat belt and was injured in a collision caused by the negligence of the defendant driver. The Court of Appeal found that the plaintiff was partly responsible for the damage which he sustained. By failing to take reasonable precautions, the plaintiff had placed himself in a position which, though not dangerous in itself, had increased the risk of injury. Similarly, riding a motor cycle with one's helmet unfastened[118] or, for that matter, without a helmet[119] amounts to contributory negligence.

---

113. [1976] 3 All E.R. 765.
114. *Fitzgerald v Lane* [1989] A.C. 328 - 50% reduction in plaintiff's damages.
115. [1952] 2 Q.B. 608.
116. [1949] 2 K.B. 291.
117. [1976] Q.B. 286.
118. *Capps v Miller* [1989] 2 All E.R. 333.
119. *O'Connell v Jackson* [1972] 1 Q.B. 270.

As already noted, it is an objective standard of care which the plaintiff is expected to reach. However, a less rigorous approach is employed in a number of situations. First, in *Gough v Thorne*[120] Lord Denning considered that a very young child cannot be guilty of contributory negligence. In that case a thirteen year old girl was waiting to cross the road when she was waved across by a lorry driver who had stopped for her. She was then knocked over by a car negligently driven by the defendant. Lord Denning said:

> "A judge should only find a child guilty of contributory negligence if he or she is of such an age as reasonably to be expected to take precautions for his or her own safety; and then he or she is only to be found guilty if blame should be attached to him or her."[121]

Thus, children are to be judged according to the standards of ordinary children of their age although it is not resolved whether the test is entirely objective or whether the court should take into account the child's actual maturity, experience and mental ability.

Again, in *Yachuk v Oliver Blais Co. Ltd.*[122] a boy of nine was not found contributorily negligent when he set fire to, and was injured by gasolene, negligently supplied to him by the defendant. He did not know, nor could a child of his age be expected to know the dangerous properties of gasolene. Nevertheless, in *Morales v Eccleston*[123] an eleven year old boy, who was kicking a ball in the middle of a street with traffic in both directions, was found 75% responsible when knocked over by the defendant's car.[124]

A second situation requiring special treatment is that where the negligence of the defendant places the plaintiff in danger causing the latter to make an immediate decision regarding his personal safety. In hindsight it may be argued that his reaction was ill advised yet, in the agony of the moment, reasonable. In *Jones v Boyce*[125] the plaintiff coach passenger,

---

120. [1966] 1 W.L.R. 1387.
121. *Ibid.*, at 1390.
122. [1949] A.C. 386.
123. [1991] R.T.R. 151.
124. The Pearson Report (*Report of the Royal Commission on Civil Liability and Compensation for Personal Injury*, Cmnd. 7054, 1978) recommended that the defence of contributory negligence should not be available against children under the age of 12 injured in motor vehicle accidents.
125. (1816) 1 Stark 493.

reasonably, but mistakenly, fearing that the coach was about to overturn due to the negligence of the driver, jumped from the moving vehicle and broke his leg. The court held that the plaintiff was not contributorily negligent for, in the circumstances, he had acted reasonably and not rashly. Lord Ellenborough said:

> "The question is whether he was placed in such a situation as to render what he did a prudent precaution, for the purpose of self preservation ... it must appear that there existed a reasonable cause for alarm."[126]

Note that, as Salmond[127] suggests, the courts do not demand that the plaintiff displays the care of a superman but only that of ordinary nerve and presence of mind.

However, Lord Ellenborough considered in *Jones* that, even when the plaintiff is faced with a dilemma, he should not act in a rash and imprudent manner. A dramatic illustration is to be found in the Canadian case of *Holmis v Dubuc.*[128] A seaplane, having hit an object on the surface of a lake, began to fill with water. The pilot, fearing that the plane would sink, jumped into the lake without a life jacket and was drowned. In fact, had the pilot remained on board he would have survived for the plane did not sink. It was held that the pilot was 50% to blame for his own death. Surprisingly, the pilot's reaction was considered unreasonable.

As noted above, with regard to intervening causes, in rescue cases due consideration is given to the sense of moral obligation imposed on the plaintiff rescuer who is injured in the process. For danger invites rescue and the defendant who created the danger should not be too ready to criticise the plaintiff's response to the situation. In *Brandon v Osborne, Garrett & Co. Ltd.*[129] the defendants who were repairing a shop roof, negligently caused glass to fall onto the plaintiff's husband. Instinctively, the plaintiff grasped her husband's arm to pull him to safety and, in the process, was herself injured by falling glass. Had she remained in her original position she would have been unharmed but, not unreasonably, the court held that she had not been contributorily negligent.

Note that the circumstances may dictate a particular degree of skill is required of the injured plaintiff "rescuer"and failure to reach it can lead

---

126. *Ibid.*
127. Salmond, *Law of Torts*, 12th ed. (Sweet & Maxwell, 1992), p. 510.
128. (1975) 56 D.L.R. 3d 351.
129. [1924] 1 K.B. 548.

to a reduction in damages awarded. Thus, in one case, a guard was injured trying to help a passenger attempting to board a moving train. It was established that the guard was expected in such circumstances to apply the emergency brake, which he had failed to do. On reducing the damages awarded by 20%, Boreham J. expressed distaste at having to do so but recognised that there had been a failure by the man in authority to reduce the danger by doing what he was duty bound to do.[130]

*Causation*

Having established fault, as discussed above, it is then necessary for the defendant to prove a causal connection between such fault and the damage suffered.[131] The usual rules of causation apply. The "but for" test is very important. That is, would the harm have occurred but for the plaintiff's failure to take reasonable care? It is not necessary for the plaintiff's negligence to have been a cause of the accident itself, although often this will be the case. Rather, it is incumbent on the defendant to show that the plaintiff's conduct has been a legal and factual cause of the damage suffered.

The injury suffered must be within the sphere of risk created by the plaintiff's failure to take care and it seems the courts will not easily permit the defence to be rebutted by fine distinctions as to the foreseeable type of damage. In *Jones v Livox Quarries Ltd.*[132] Denning L.J. said:

> "Once negligence is proved, then no matter whether it is actionable negligence or contributory negligence, the person who is guilty of it must bear his proper share of responsibility for the consequences. The consequences do not depend on foreseeability, but on causation. The question in every case is: what faults were there which caused the damage? Was his fault one of them?"[133]

In *Jones* although the plaintiff did not foresee the possibility of being crushed, indeed the principal risk to which he exposed himself was falling off the traxcavator, the injury which he suffered was due in part to the fact that he chose to ride on the towbar of the traxcavator. Denning L.J.

---

130. *Harrison v British Railways Board and others* [1981] 3 All E.R. 679.
131. Lord Atkin, *Caswell v Powell Duffryn Associated Collieries Ltd.* [1940] AC. 152 at 165.
132. [1952] 2 Q.B. 608. See also *Stapley v Gypsum Mines Ltd.* [1953] A.C. 663.
133. [1952] 2 Q.B. 608, at 615.

compared these facts with the hypothetical case of the plaintiff being hit in the eye by a shot from a negligent sportsman. As regards the latter case he said:

> "I should have thought that the plaintiff's negligence would in no way be a cause of his injury. It would only be the circumstance in which the cause operated. But I cannot say that in the present case. The man's negligence was so mixed up with his injury that it cannot be dismissed as mere history."[134]

Thus, the plaintiff's lack of care was a factual cause of the loss which, in turn, was a type of damage within the sphere of foreseeable risk. That is, it was not too remote.

*Apportioning the loss*

Section 1(1) of the Law Reform (Contributory Negligence) Act 1945 provides that damages recoverable shall be reduced as the court thinks fit having regard to the plaintiff's share in the responsibility for the damage. Thus, if in a case of two cars colliding, the plaintiff is 25% responsible and the defendant 75% to blame, the plaintiff's damages will be reduced by 25%. The practical effect of this is that, in order to allocate proportionate blame to the parties, the courts consider both the respective blameworthiness of their conduct and the extent to which the plaintiff's conduct caused or increased his injuries (i.e., its causative potency).[135]

Blameworthiness is measured by reference to the objective rather than the moral standard. That is, the degree to which the plaintiff has departed from the standard of behaviour set by the reasonable man. Causative potency has an important role, for if it were not given consideration and reference was made to comparative blameworthiness only, in cases of strict liability a careless plaintiff would receive no damages from a defendant who, though liable, was without fault. Even so as discussed above, causation is a prerequisite under the Act but it is not susceptible to rational assessment.[136] Fleming[137] suggests that weight should be given to the comparative gravity of the risk each party took. Thus, what appears to be

---

134. *Ibid.*, at 616.
135. *Davies v Swan Motor Co.* [1949] 2 K.B. 291 *per* Denning L.J..
136. Treitel, *The Law of Contract*, 14th ed. (Sweet and Maxwell 1994), p. 185.
137. J. Fleming, *The Law of Torts*, 8th ed. (The Law Book Co., 1992), p. 274.

a trivial act of negligence can actually be fraught with danger and, in such circumstances, the larger share of blame should attach to the party who created the danger.

Note that, although apportionment of damages is an exercise in judicial discretion, room for manoeuvre is not unlimited. In *Pitts v Hunt*[138] Beldam J. considered *obiter* that a 100% reduction in damages was not possible under the Act, which presupposes fault on the part of both the defendant and the plaintiff and recovery of some damages by the plaintiff. To hold the plaintiff 100% responsible is not to hold that he shared in the responsibility for the damage.

*Multiple defendants*

Apportioning the loss is less straightforward where, rather than two, there are three or more parties involved. In *Fitzgerald v Lane*[139] the plaintiff pedestrian carelessly stepped into the road and was struck by a car being driven by the first defendant. The impact caused the plaintiff to fall into the path of a second car driven by the second defendant. Holding the three parties equally to blame, the Court of Appeal awarded the plaintiff two thirds of his damages. The House of Lords, whilst upholding the decision regarding relative responsibility for the plaintiff's injuries, considered the apportionment of contribution wrong.

Lord Ackner made clear that the proper approach should be in two stages. The first is whether the plaintiff was guilty of contributory negligence and, if so, the extent to which the recoverable damages should be reduced. Thus, as the plaintiff was held equally to blame with the defendants for his injuries, his damages should be reduced by fifty per cent. The second, is the amount of contribution recoverable between the two defendants having regard to the extent of their responsibility for the damage suffered by the plaintiff. This is an issue only affecting the defendants as between themselves and does not involve the plaintiff. Therefore, the defendants were liable each to pay half of the damages which had been reduced by fifty per cent. That is, each should contribute twenty five per cent of the total loss.

---

138. [1990] 3 All E.R. 344.
139. [1989] A.C. 328.

## Contributory negligence and breach of contract

The question of whether the Law Reform (Contributory Negligence) Act 1945 is applicable to the law of contract so as to reduce the plaintiff's damages or is confined to tortious matters was addressed by Hobhouse J. in *Forsikringsaktieselskapet Vesta v Butcher*.[140] He considered the matter by referring to three different ways in which the defendant may breach the contract:

### a. Breach of strict contractual duty

Here the Act has no application. Section 4 of the Act refers to "negligence, breach of statutory duty or other act or omission giving rise to liability in tort" which would not embrace the defendant's conduct. For example, if B Co. sells a defective electric drill to C, who is injured partly because of the defect and partly because of using it negligently, the Act would not apply as the defendant's behaviour cannot be described as negligent or as an act or omission giving rise to liability in tort.

The Law Commission Working Paper No. 114 proposed that the partial defence should apply to cases of strict liability but its report, *Contributory Negligence as a Defence in Contract* (No. 219, 1993), recommended the opposite view.

> "We have rejected the possibility of apportionment where there is liability for breach of strict contractual obligation for reasons both of principle and pragmatism. The reason of principle relates to a consideration of the position before the plaintiff is aware, or must be taken to be aware, of the defendant's breach of contract. If the defendant commits himself to a strict obligation regardless of fault, the plaintiff should be able to rely on him fulfilling his obligation and should not have to take precautions against the possibility that a breach might occur. ... The rules on mitigation, although not a perfect substitute for apportionment, mean that the plaintiff is not entitled to act unreasonably once he is aware of his loss or of the defendant's breach."

This recommendation has recently been affirmed by the Court of Appeal in *Barclays Bank plc v Fairclough Building Ltd.*,[141] in which the defendants

140. Affirmed by Court of Appeal, [1989] A.C. 852.
141. [1995] 1 All E.R. 289.

contracted to clean the plaintiffs' asbestos roofs. The work was conducted without appropriate precautions and high pressure hoses caused asbestos dust to contaminate the plaintiffs' property, the removal of which cost the plaintiffs £4 million. In an action against them for breach of contract, the defendants claimed that the plaintiffs had been contributorily negligent by not complying with a duty to ensure that adequate safety precautions were taken.

Beldam L.J. dismissed the existence of such a duty but made it clear that, even if such a duty were apparent, no reduction in damages would have been granted. He stated:

> "In my judgement ... in the present state of the law contributory negligence is not a defence to a claim for damages founded on breach of a strict contractual obligation. I do not believe the wording of the 1945 Act can reasonably sustain an argument to the contrary."[142]

Indeed, Simon Brown L.J. considered that the very imposition of a strict liability upon a defendant is inconsistent with an apportionment of loss that the Act would provide.

Note that contributory negligence will be a complete defence to an action for breach of a strict contractual term where the plaintiff's negligent conduct amounts to a *novus actus interveniens*. Thus, in *Lexmead (Basingtoke) Ltd. v Lewis*[143] the plaintiff farmer bought from the defendant seller a trailer with a faulty coupling which he continued to use even though he had knowledge of the defect. In time the coupling gave way and there was an accident. The House of Lords held that the defendant was not liable because the plaintiff's conduct amounted to an intervening cause.[144]

### b. Breach of duty of care imposed by the contract where there is no corresponding duty in tort

The view of the Court of Appeal in the *Vesta* case was that the Act does not apply where the defendant, although in breach of a contractual duty of care, does not breach any corresponding duty in tort. In a previous New Zealand case, *Rowe v Turner Hopkins and Partners*,[145] Pritchard J. considered that,

---

142. *Ibid.*, at 303.
143. [1982] A.C. 225.
144. See also *Beoco Ltd. v Alfa Laval Co. Ltd.* [1994] 4 All E.R. 464.
145. [1980] 2 N.Z.L.R. 550, at p. 556.

under the Act, "fault ... which gives rise to liability in tort" is required of the defendant and it follows that liability confined to contractual obligations does not come within the scope of the Act.

However, Brabin J. in *De Meza v Apple*,[146] a case of a careless auditor who failed to complete certificates for a client who, in turn was careless, took the view that the Act was available as a defence in cases of breach of a contractual duty of care only. However, although the case has been regarded as fitting within this category, it may be argued that the auditor's liability was both contractual and tortious.[147]

The Law Commission Report No. 219 (1993) recommended that damages should be apportioned in cases where the breach is restricted to a contractual duty to take care. Its reasoning was that there is a clear similarity between an action for breach of a contractual duty of care and an action for a breach of a tortious duty of reasonable care. It would seem undesirable that the availability should be dependent upon how the duty in question is classified. Here the plaintiff's damages should be reduced unless the contract expressly or by implication excludes this defence.[148]

### c. Breach of a contractual duty to take care and a duty of care in tort

In *Sayers v Harlow U.D.C.*[149] the plaintiff trapped in a lavatory because of a faulty lock "embarked on an exceedingly perilous manoeuvre"[150] in trying to climb over the cubicle wall to escape. The Court of Appeal applied the Act and the plaintiff's damages were reduced. Arguably, the case is authority for the view that the Act will operate where the defendant's conduct amounts to both a breach of contractual duty to take care and negligence. However, the reasoning is not clear enough to support the contention. Nevertheless, the Court of Appeal in both the *Vesta* case and *Barclays Bank v Fairclough* has confirmed that the Act does indeed apply to such circumstances.

The requirement for concurrent liability in negligence was evident

146. [1974] 1 Lloyd's Rep. 508.
147. Treitel, *Law of Contract*, 9th ed. (Sweet and Maxwell, 1994), p. 889.
148. Law Comm. No. 219 (1993), 7-15, 23-25.
149. [1958] 1 All E.R. 342.
150. *Per* Scrutton L.J.

in the recent case of *Gran Gelato Ltd. v Richcliff (Group) Ltd.*[151] Here, Sir Donald Nicholls V.-C. was concerned with whether s.1(1) of the Law Reform (Contributory Negligence) Act 1945 was applicable to the award of damages in an action under s.2(1) of the Misrepresentation Act 1967. It was held that contributory negligence applied to a claim in negligent misrepresentation under the statute and to negligent statement at common law under the principle in *Hedley Byrne*[152] for, as Nicholls V.C. stated:

> "Liability under the 1967 Act is essentially founded on negligence, in the sense that the defendant, the representor, did not have reasonable grounds to believe that the facts represented were true. ... This being so, it would be very odd if the defence of contributory negligence were not available to a claim under the Act. It would be very odd if contributory negligence were not available as a defence to a claim for damages based on a breach of a duty to take care in and about the making of a particular representation, but not available to a claim for damages under the 1967 Act in respect of the same representation."[153]

It seems that contributory negligence would not operate to reduce damages in a case where liability arises only under s.2(1) of Misrepresentation Act 1967 for, under this section, the defendant's liability is not equated with negligence but with fraud and the latter does not admit contributory negligence as a partial defence.

It has already been noted that the Law Commission has recommended that the partial defence of contributory negligence should be made available to cases within the second category, that is where the defendant is in breach of a duty of care imposed on him by the contract alone. Adoption of this suggestion would allow the courts to ignore the somewhat false distinction at present being drawn between unreasonable conduct in contract and tort. Such a view would be supported by the fact that, in contract, reference can be made to the plaintiff's unreasonable conduct when considering the limiting factors of *novus actus* and mitigation.

---

151. [1992] 1 All E.R. 865. Further support for this view is to be found in *AB Maritrans v Comet Shipping Co. Ltd.* [1985] 3 All E.R. 442 and *Basildon District Council v J.E. Lesser (Properties) Ltd.* [1985] 1 All E.R. 20. However, note *Alliance & Leicester Building Society v Edgestop* [1994] 2 All E.R. 865, in which the court distinguished *Gran Gelato* and held that apportionment is not available in an action for the tort of deceit.

152. *Hedley Byrne & Co. Ltd. v Heller & Partners Ltd.* [1964] A.C. 94.

153. [1992] 1 All E.R. 865, at 875.

## 5. Impecuniosity

In *Owners of Dredger Liesbosch v Owners of Steamship Edison*[154] the defendant's negligence caused the sinking of the plaintiffs' dredger which was required to complete a construction project. The plaintiffs' contractual obligations meant that a replacement dredger was necessary but a shortage of funds prevented the purchase of a substitute. Instead, a dredger was hired, but at greater cost in the long run due to the expensive financial arrangements involved. The House of Lords allowed the recovery of all losses incurred by the plaintiffs except those which arose from their weak financial position.

Lord Wright stated:

> "The respondents' tortious act involved the physical loss of the dredger; that loss must somehow be reduced to terms of money. But the appellants' actual loss in so far as it was due to their impecuniosity arose from that impecuniosity as a separate and concurrent cause, extraneous to and distinct in character from the tort; the impecuniosity was not traceable to the respondents' acts and in my opinion was outside the legal purview of the consequences of these acts ... In the present case if the appellants' financial embarrassment is to be regarded as a consequence of the respondents' tort, I think it is too remote, but I prefer to regard it as an independent cause, though its operative effect was conditioned by the loss of the dredger."[155]

The decision has not met with universal acceptance although it has never been overruled. Lord Wright's assertion that the decision is based on principles of causation and, for that matter, remoteness is, with respect, questionable.[156] Additionally, it is difficult to reconcile the case with a number of well accepted principles. First, the "thin skull" rule states that, if the plaintiff is particularly susceptible to injury, the defendant must nevertheless "take his victim as he finds him" and recompense him for the

---

154. [1933] A.C. 449.

155. *Ibid.*, at 460.

156. Indeed Lord Wright recognised this in the same case: "The law cannot take account of everything that follows a wrongful act; it regards some subsequent matters as outside the scope of its selection. ... In the varied web of affairs, the law must abstract some consquences as relevant, not perhaps on grounds of pure logic but simply for practical reasons." It is also arguable that the decision is logical in that, (a) the plaintiff did take an unreasonable action by hiring a bigger dredger which necessitated hiring further equipment and paying a higher fee and, (b) it did not lead to over-compensation of the plaintiff.

full loss sustained. Secondly, it is clear that negligently injuring a person may lead to loss of income and such damage is not too remote. However, the fact that the victim is a succesful executive and the resulting loss of income is very high does not negate or reduce liability for here the court is concerned only with placing a value on consequences which are not remote. It seems unfair that the plaintiff whose loss is exacerbated by his reduced, as opposed to privileged, circumstances should be treated less favourably.

Further difficulties flow from the decision, for impecuniosity will excuse a failure to mitigate loss. Indeed Lord Wright made specific reference to the speech of Lord Collins in *Clippens Oil Co. v Edinburgh and District Water Trustees,*[157] where the latter said:

> "It was contended that this implied that the defenders were entitled to measure the damages on the footing that it was the duty of the company to do all that was reasonably possible to mitigate the loss, and that if, through lack of funds, they were unable to incur the necessary expense of such remedial measures the defenders ought not to suffer for it. ... I think there would be force in the observation for in my opinion the wrongdoer must take his victim *talem qualem*, and if the position of the latter is aggravated because he is without the means ofmitigating it, so much the worse for the wrongdoer, who has got to be answerable for the consequences flowing from his tortious act."[158]

Lord Wright considered that Lord Collins was dealing here, not with the measure of damage, but with the victim's duty to minimise damage. However, the reasoning on this point is not clear and merely adds to the confusion. The case of *Robbins of Putney Ltd. v Meek*[159] is another example of a case where impecuniosity was considered an acceptable reason for not mitigating loss and has been referred to earlier in the section on mitigation.

The response of the judiciary over the years has, in the main, been to distinguish or even ignore the decision.[160] Nevertheless, the Court of Appeal, in *Dodd Properties (Kent) Ltd. v Canterbury City Council*, has made it clear that is bound by the decision until it is reviewed by the House

---

157. [1907] A.C. 291.
158. *Ibid.*, at 303.
159. [1971] R.T.R. 345.
160. As Kerr L.J. said in *Perry v Sidney Phillips & Sons* [1982] 3 All E.R. 705, "... the authority of what Lord Wright said in *The Liesbosch* is consistently being attenuated in more recent decisions of this court."

of Lords.[161] In that case the plaintiffs delayed repairing their business premises which had been damaged by the defendant's negligence. The period between the time when the cause of action arose and the time of the hearing was ten years during which the cost of repairs trebled. The Court of Appeal, allowed the claim, distinguishing the facts from those of *The Liesbosch*. The plaintiffs had opted to delay repairs on the basis of a reasoned commercial decision for they had considered it not worthwhile to incur expenditure, which they could ill afford, until they were sure that the defendants had been judged legally liable to compensate for the loss incurred. Financial stringency was not a cause of the decision to delay repairs but merely one factor which made it sensible to do so.

Subsequently there have been a number of cases in which *The Liesbosch* has been distinguished. A similar approach to that in *Dodd Properties* was followed with success in *Perry v Sidney Phillips*[162] whilst in *Jarvis v T. Richards*[163] and *Archer v Brown*,[164] the plaintiffs' impecuniosity was considered a foreseeable consequence of the defendant's actions.

The *Liesbosch* rule on impecuniosity may, therefore, be under severe pressure but one should not conclude that it is now of no consequence. Indeed, though the cases above illustrate the recent tendency of the judiciary to distinguish the rule, the Court of Appeal, without hesistation, and without reference to those cases, followed *The Liesbosch* in *Ramwade Ltd. v W.J. Emson*,[165] in which the plaintiff, whose lorry was damaged, hired rather than purchased a replacement. The defendant insurance brokers, who had been negligent and in breach of contract regarding the plaintiff's insurance policy, successfully contested the claim for reimbursement of hiring charges arguing that such loss flowed from the latter's impecuniosity.

Even so, the same Court, though differently constituted,

---

161. [1980] 1 W.L.R. 433. See also *Martindale v Duncan [1973]* 2 All E.R. 355, in which the plaintiff delayed having his car repaired until he was sure that the defendant would pay the cost. He recovered the cost of hiring a substitute vehicle during that period, the court accepting that his impecuniosity was not the sole reason for his delay.
162. [1982] 3 All E.R. 705. Indeed, Lord Denning M.R. considered that *The Liesbosch* should be restricted to its own facts.
163. (1980) 124 *Sol. Jo.* 793.
164. [1985] Q.B. 401.
165. [1987] R.T.R. 72; *The Times*, July 11, 1986.

distinguished the *Ramwade* case[166] in *Mattocks v Mann.*[167] This was another case concerned with the hiring of a vehicle by the plaintiff whose own car had been damaged by the defendant. It was held that in such an event the plaintiff should be able to claim for loss of use even where it arises from the plaintiff's impecuniosity. The Court recognised that the law had not stood still since the *Liesbosch* and a principle of law should not be applied regardless of the circumstances of the case in hand. Indeed, only in "exceptional circumstances was it possible to isolate impecuniosity of a plaintiff as a separate cause and as terminating the consequences of a defendant's wrong".[168] Nowadays it is accepted practice and, therefore, reasonably contemplated that, amongst other things, substantial repair costs would be the responsibility of the insurers.

The *Liesbosch* principle is clearly in need of review and clarification by the House of Lords is long overdue. It seems doubtful that it would actually survive such consideration.

## 6. Limitation of actions

As already stated, it is worth noting that the Limitation Act 1980 provides limitation periods within which a plaintiff must commence proceedings, i.e., serve a writ, if his action is not to be statute-barred and his right to a remedy extinguished. In outline, the provisions are as follows:

*Breach of Contract*

(a) An action for a breach of a simple contract must be brought within six years from the time the cause of action accrued.[169]

(b) An action on a "specialty" (a contract in the form of a deed) must be brought within twelve years from the time the cause of action accrued.[170]

---

166. On the basis that, in that case, the court felt able to isolate the plaintiff's lack of resources as the real cause of the claim for damages for the cost of hiring the vehicle.
167. [1993] R.T.R. 13.
168. *Ibid.*, *per* Beldam L.J., at p.19.
169. Limitation Act 1980, s.5.
170. *Ibid.*, s.8(1).

(c) In the event of fraud or mistake, the limitation period does not begin to run until the fraud or mistake has been discovered by the plaintiff or, with reasonable care, could have been discovered.[171]

(d) Written acknowledgement of the debt, or part payment of it, causes the time period to commence running again.[172]

*Tort*

(a) In contrast to contractual claims, where the time begins to run from the time of the breach, in tort the period of limitation does not commence until some damage has been incurred by the plaintiff.[173]

(b) An action in tort must be brought within six years of the cause of action.[174]

(c) In cases where the plaintiff has suffered personal injury or death, the limitation period is three years. The period runs from the time when injury or death occurred or, in the case of injury, from the date when the plaintiff had knowledge of such injury.[175]

(d) As with contract, where the defendant's fraudulent behaviour is the cause of action or conceals facts relevant to the action, the time period runs only from the time when the plaintiff has or ought to have discovered the fraud in question.[176]

(e) Where the action is brought under the Law Reform (Miscellaneous Provisions) Act 1934 the limitation period is three years from the date of

---

171. *Ibid.*, s.32(1).
172. *Ibid.*, s.29(5).
173. Where the tort is actionable *per se*, the time period runs from the date of the defendant's tortious act: *Duke of Brunswick and Luneburg v Harmer* (1849) 112 E.R. 75.
174. Limitation Act 1980 s.2.
175. *Ibid.*, s.11(1). Note that this section does not apply to intentional torts such as trespass to the person; *Stubbings v Webb* [1993] 1 All E.R. 322.
176. *Ibid.*, s.32(1).

death or, if longer, from the personal representative's knowledge of the death.

(f) Where the action is brought under the Fatal Accidents Act 1976, the period of limitation is three years from the date of death, or knowledge of the death of the person on whose behalf the action is brought, whichever is the longer.

(g) The Latent Damage Act 1976 inserted two new sections into the Limitation Act 1980 in regard to latent damage to negligently constructed buildings. S.14A of the Limitation Act 1980 provides a period of six years from the date on which the cause of action accrued or three years from the date on which the plaintiff knew or ought to have known facts about the damage whichever is the later. With respect to the latter, s.14B provides a "long-stop" of fifteen years from the date of the defendant's breach of duty, unless the defendant has been fraudulent or wilfully concealed the defect.

*Equitable remedies*

Equitable remedies are unaffected by the Limitation Act but the doctrine of laches applies. That is, "delay defeats equity" and, although no fixed time limit has been laid down, the plaintiff will be denied equitable relief if the court in the exercise of its discretion, considers that he did not, in the circumstances, act quickly enough in seeking the equitable remedy. With this in mind, the court will make reference to any hardship caused to the defendant by the delay and/or where the defendant has been encouraged by the plaintiff's delay to change his position. Additionally, consideration will be given to the impact upon third parties and generally the balance of justice between the parties in granting or not granting relief.

**Exercises**

1. Is the law on remoteness of damage clear? Does it need to be reviewed?

2. At Evelyn's engagement party her twin sister, Bridget, a third year law student, is talking to her boyfriend, Larry, a research economist. Teller, a professional stockbroker in the City of London, joins in the conversation. Bridget then asks Teller about the performance of the shares of Buy-me PLC and Teller said: "My advice to you, Bridget, is you can bet on it, but do not go beyond 5,000 shares." Bridget later buys 15,000 shares with her life's savings but loses heavily when the company goes into liquidation shortly afterwards.

   Advise Bridget. Would your advice be different if, ten days before the liquidation of the company, Bridget gets a message from Teller's secretary that Teller is sorry to say that Buy-me PLC may be going into liquidation within one month, but Bridget takes no notice of this information?

3. Max was injured in a road accident caused by Maureen. Max, on religious grounds, refused to have a blood transfusion which the doctor strongly advised. If successful, the treatment would have restored Max to his former earning capacity. Max sued Maureen. Maureen pleaded that Max's refusal to have a transfusion amounted to a break in the chain of causation.

   Advise Max.

4. Should loss resulting from a plaintiff's weak financial position be recoverable?

5. The Law Commission (Law Comm. No. 219, 1993) recommended that contributory negligence should be available as a defence in all actions for breach of contract.

   What is the present state of the law and do you agree that the partial defence should be made generally available in contractual actions?

# 5 Compensatory damages for breach of contract

## Introduction

Damages are awarded to the injured party to compensate him for the loss suffered as a result of the breach of contract. The remedy is available at common law as of right to the victim, unlike equitable remedies which are discretionary. Indeed, even where the innocent party has suffered no loss as a result of the breach, he will, nevertheless, receive an award, albeit of nominal damages.

Note that, although nominal damages are available, a victim of a breach who has suffered no loss may not recover damages which serve to transfer profits made from the breach by the contract breaker. This is so even where the profit has been made deliberately. In *Surrey County Council v Bredero Homes Ltd.*,[1] a Court of Appeal case, the defendant had been granted permission by the council to build 72 homes. Instead, five additional houses were built, the defendants gaining consequent extra profit. However, the plaintiff council suffered no loss as a result of the breach and received only nominal damages. Steyn L.J. stated (at page 715):

> "The introduction of restitutionary remedies to deprive cynical contract breakers of the fruits of their breaches of contract will lead to greater uncertainty in the assessment of damages in commercial and consumer disputes."

He added that such an extension of restitutionary remedies was against the public interest in that it would have a tendency to discourage economic activity and, because the burden would fall on insurance companies, it would, in turn, raise insurance premiums. Thus, the calculating contract-breaker has the opportunity to make significant profits which he would be able to retain. The fairness of this position is questionable but, even the

---

1. [1993] 3 All E.R. 705.

alternative, an award of damages, would, in such circumstances, "compensate" the plaintiff where no loss has been sustained.[2] However, this case is difficult to reconcile with *Wrotham Park Estate Co. Ltd. v Parkside Homes Ltd.*,[3] in which the plaintiffs sought an injunction against the defendant builders who had erected houses in breach of covenant. The application for an injunction was rejected and the plaintiffs, the value of whose land was not reduced by the breach, instead, received damages. In assessing the sum to be paid, the court considered the profit made by the defendant as a result of his breach and the amount which might reasonably have been demanded by the plaintiffs as a *quid pro quo* for relaxing the covenant. Treitel[4] observes that an explanation for the two decisions is that in *Bredero* all the houses in question had been sold and so the breach could no longer be restrained. Thus compensatory damages were not available in substitution for an injunction whereas in *Wrotham Park* they were.

Note that this explanation echoes the recommendation of the Law Commission Consultation Paper No. 132, "Aggravated, Exemplary and Restitutionary Damages", 1993, that exemplary damages should be awardable where the defendant had made a gain from his breach of contract and such gain was attributable to an interference with a proprietary or analogous right, or to deliberate wrongdoing which could have been restrained by injunction.

### Expectation loss

The basic measure of damages endeavours to compensate the plaintiff for the loss of his expectations which were created by the contract itself. That is, to place the plaintiff in the same situation, so far as money can, as if the contract had been performed.[5] Two points are worth noting. First, loss to the plaintiff includes harm to his person or property and economic loss

---

2. Note that there are a number of exceptions to the principle, e.g., wrongful use of confidential information or trade secrets and breach of a contractual and fiduciary obligation. See, in this regard, *Peter Pan Manufacturing Corp. v Corsets Silhouette* [1964] 1 W.L.R. 1073 and *Att. Gen. of Hong Kong v Reid* [1994] A.C. 324, *Mathew v T.M. Sutton Ltd.* [1994] 4 All E.R. 793.
3. [1974] 2 All E.R. 321.
4. Treitel, *An Outline of the Law of Contract*, 5th ed. (Butterworths, 1995), p. 355. See also *Jaggard v Sawyer* [1995] 2 All E.R. 189.
5. *Robinson v Harman* (1848) 1 Ex. 850. Note that the aim to compensate expectation losses is subject to the mitigation and the remoteness rules.

sustained. Secondly, the approach to expectation loss in contract, that is, placing the plaintiff in the position he expected to enjoy after the contract had been completed, differs from the award of damages in tort where the aim is to place the plaintiff in the position he would have been if the tort had not been committed.

The fact that measurement of expectation loss may prove very difficult and imprecise is not in itself a bar to recovery of damages.[6] Indeed, even where the loss claimed is of a speculative nature, the courts are willing to award compensation. In *Simpson v London and North Western Ry. Co.*[7] the defendants, in breach of contract, failed to deliver samples to a trade exhibition. The plaintiff exhibitor was awarded damages, despite the clear difficulty of accurately assessing the profits lost. A further illustration of the court's willingness to overcome the difficulties caused by such speculative claims is *Chaplin v Hicks*,[8] in which, due to the defendant's breach, the plaintiff was denied the opportunity to win a prize offered in a beauty contest. The plaintiff was awarded a sum which, though less than the prize money, reflected the lost chance of winning the money, a chance worth something. Fletcher-Moulton L.J. said (at page 229):

> "It is clear that, where in the minds of reasonable men, there has been a *de facto* loss, the jury have to do their best to estimate it."

However, there will be occasions when the expectation loss in question is so speculative that the court is unable to identify an assessable loss. In *McRae v Commonwealth Disposals Commission*[9] the plaintiff's tender for the purchase of an oil tanker of unspecified size lying on a named reef was accepted. After much expense incurred by the plaintiff, it transpired that the ship was not at the stated location. In addition to the purchase price, the plaintiff recovered only £3,000, this being the wasted cost of the salvage expedition. Since there was no more than a promise by the defendant to deliver a stranded tanker as opposed to any partcular ship in any particular

---

6. As in tort where, for example, loss caused by defamation and physical injury are difficult to assess.
7. (1876) 1 Q.B.D. 274.
8. [1911] All E.R. 224. Also, *Scally v Southern Health and Social Services Board* [1992] 1 A.C.294 - loss of chance of obtaining pension benefits dependent on the exercise of discretion by government department.
9. (1951) 84 C.L.R. 377 (Aus.).

condition, only nominal damages were payable in addition to recovery of the purchase price and the cost of the expedition.

## Reliance loss

It is possible for the plaintiff to claim damages, not for his loss of expectations as above, but instead for his expenditure which has been wasted as a result of the defendant's breach of contract. That is, the expenditure incurred by the plaintiff in reliance on the defendant's undertaking to carry out his contractual obligations.

If the plaintiff claims wasted expenditure, he is not limited to the expenditure incurred after the contract was concluded. He can also claim the expenditure incurred before the contract was agreed, provided that it was such as would reasonably be in the contemplation of the parties as likely to be wasted if the contract was broken. Such was the judgement of Lord Denning M.R. in *Anglia Television Ltd. v Reed.*[10] There, the plaintiff TV company successfully claimed for pre-contract expenditure on items such as director's fees, designer's fees and stage manager's fees incurred before abandoning a film production, in which the defendant actor contracted to appear. He repudiated and was found liable for the reliance loss incurred by the plaintiffs. Note that Anglia did not claim expenditure loss for it was not possible to forecast what their profit would have been if the actor had completed his contractual obligations.

It is not the function of the court to put the plaintiff in a better financial position than if the contract had been properly performed. The Court of Appeal has confirmed that, where the plaintiff is claiming reliance loss to avoid the consequences of a bad bargain, nominal damages only will be awarded. In *C. & P. Haulage v Middleton,*[11] as a consequence of a six-month leasehold agreement, the appellants made improvements to the premises for the purposes of their business. Wrongfully ejected ten weeks before the lease expired, the appellants were allowed by the planning authorities to use their own premises instead. On claiming for the expenditure on the improvements made, it was held that the appellants would have been unable, even if the contract had not been broken, to make sufficient profit to cover the outlay. Thus, to award reliance loss would be to place the appellant in a better position than if the contract had been

---

10. [1972] 1 Q.B. 60. See also *Lloyd v Stanbury* [1971] 1 W.L.R. 535.
11. [1983] 3 All E.R. 94.

honoured. Additionally, the fact that ten weeks rent was saved meant that the appellant had been able to mitigate his loss of profits. The onus is on the defendant to prove that the plaintiff has made a bad bargain and, therefore, the expenditure incurred by him is irrecoverable.[12] Generally, this would be a difficult task for the defendant who would have limited access to important information in this regard. However, this modification to the general rule as to the onus of proof is fair since it is the defendant who has prevented the plaintiff exploiting the right contracted for.

*Expectation or reliance loss?*

In *Anglia Television v Reed* Lord Denning M.R. considered that the plaintiff has a choice between claiming for loss of profits or for his wasted expenditure, but he must elect between them and not claim both.[13] This would follow where the profit in question is gross profit because the plaintiff would be required to pay for expenditure out of gross profits. Thus, to pursue both claims would lead to double recovery, that is, recovering twice for the same loss. However, if the combined claim refers to the recovery of net profits and wasted expenditure, then damages for both are recoverable.[14]

## Measure of damages

Measurement of the expectation loss requires an assessment of the damage caused to the plaintiff and an award of money which endeavours to place him in the position he would have enjoyed had the contract been performed as agreed. The approach is best illustrated by reference to contracts for the sale of goods.

---

12. *C.C.C. Films (London) Ltd. v Impact Quadrant Films Ltd.* [1984] 3 All E.R. 298.
13. Lord Denning cited *Cullinane v British "Reema" Manufacturing Co. Ltd.* [1954] 1 Q.B. 292 as authority for this proposition.
14. *C.C.C. Films (London) Ltd. v Impact Quadrant Films Ltd.* [1984] 3 All E.R. 298. See also *Hydraulic Engineering Co. Ltd. v McHaffie, Goslett & Co.* (1878) 4 Q.B. 670, where the plaintiff was permitted to claim for both reliance and expectation (net profits) losses.

**Non-delivery by the seller**

Section 51(3) of the Sale of Goods Act 1979 is concerned with damages for non-delivery of the goods by the seller and states that, where there is an available market for the goods in question, the measure of damges is, *prima facie*, to be ascertained by the difference between the contract price and the market or current price of the goods at the time or times when they ought to have been delivered or, if no time was fixed, at the time of the refusal to deliver.[15] Thus, what is awarded is compensation sufficient to enable the plaintiff to buy substitute goods in the open market. If the price of goods is greater than the contract price, then the damages awarded will reflect that difference. If the market price is less, then no loss has been sustained and only nominal damages are warranted.[16] Note that even where the buyer planned to re-sell the goods at a higher price than that prevailing in the market, his claim would be restricted by the above measurement on the grounds that he could obtain substitute goods at the market price which could then be re-sold at the same profit as originally expected. Indeed, even if the resale price was less than the market price, the value of the goods in the market independent of any circumstances peculiar to the plaintiff is taken.

If there is no available market, then alternative methods of quantifying the loss must be used. Inevitably, with no market price to act as a guide, any other approach will be speculative. Thus, where the buyer has agreed a re-sale, then the difference between the contract price and the re-sale price can represent the loss even where the seller was not aware of the sub-contract.[17]

Where late delivery of goods is rejected by the buyer, damages are assessed in the same way as for non-delivery.[18] However, a different

---

15. See *Shearson Lehman Hutton Inc. v Maclaine Watson & Co. Ltd. (No. 2)* [1990] 3 All E.R. 723, at p. 730, where Webster J.defined an "available market" as where "the seller actually offers the goods for sale... and there is one actual buyer on that day at a fair price ... Where there is no actual offer for sale but only a notional or hypothetical sale, there is no available market unless on that day there are in the market sufficient traders potentially in touch with each other to evidence a market in which the actual or notional seller could, if he wished, sell the goods".
16. L.J. Scrutton, in *Slater v Hoyle & Smith Ltd.* [1920] 2 K.B. 11.
17. *Stroud v Austin & Co.* (1883) Cab. & El. 119, *France v Gaudet* (1871) L.R. 6 Q.B. 199. However, see *The Arpad* [1934] P. 189, where reference was made to the market price of similar rather than the same goods (which were not available).
18. *The Almare Seconda* [1981] 2 Lloyd's Rep. 433.

approach was employed in the Privy Council case of *Wertheim v Chicoutimi Pulp Co.*,[19] where the late delivery was accepted by the buyer. The contract was to deliver wood pulp in November when the market price was 70s a ton. The pulp was delivered in the following July when the market price was 42s 6d a ton. The buyer had made a sub-contract at 65s a ton. The Privy Council allowed the sellers to take advantage of the sub-sale and awarded damages at only 5s a ton, ignoring the market price prevailing at the time. The decision is difficult to justify for, had the buyers bought substitute goods in the market, the court could have awarded 27s 6d by applying the usual rule and ignoring the existence of the sub-sale.[20]

In the case of defective goods delivered to and accepted by the buyer the usual principle applies, that is, damages are assessed by measuring the difference between the market value of the goods and their actual value which has been reduced by virtue of the defect.[21] If the market value of the defective goods has fallen by the date of delivery and the buyer is unable to reject them, which if he could he presumably would, only nominal damages in this regard would be awarded although, of course, he would recover compensation for the defect.[22]

## Non-acceptance of goods by buyer

The relevant section of the Sale of Goods Act 1979, s.50(3), is very similar in its construction to s.51(3), discussed above. It states that, where there is an available market for the goods in question, the measure of damages is *prima facie* to be ascertained by the difference between the contract price and the market or current price of the goods at the time or times when they ought to have been accepted or (if no time was fixed for acceptance) at the time of the refusal to accept.

In this respect, it is necessary to distinguish between a private seller and a dealer. A private seller may sell the goods in question to another buyer and recover the difference, if any, by which the actual market value obtained for the goods in question falls below the contract price agreed with the buyer who is in default. A dealer, on the other hand, may argue that,

---

19. [1911] A.C. 301.
20. See Treitel, *The Law of Contract*, 9th ed. (Sweet and Maxwell 1995), pp. 856-857 for a discussion of this point.
21. L.J. Scrutton, in *Slater v Hoyle & Smith Ltd.* [1920] 2 K.B. 11.
22. See *Taylor v Bank of Athens* (1922) 27 Com. Cas. 142.

although compensation assessed in this way will allow him to recover loss of profit arising from the original contract, he has nevertheless secured two sales yet received profit from only one.

The payment of compensation for "lost volume" was considered in *W.L. Thompson v R. Robinson (Gunmakers) Ltd.*,[23] Upjohn J. taking the view that the deciding factor was the existence or otherwise of an "available market". The defendant buyer refused to take delivery of a Vanguard car, a model for which supply exceeded demand and for which the price was fixed by the manufacturers. The manufacturers agreed to take the car back but the plaintiff sellers sought recovery of the lost profit on the sale. The defendants argued that nominal damages only should be payable. An available market for the car was a market or fair in the limited technical sense, within which market the price had been fixed by the manufacturers. However, it was held that there was no available market, the sale had been lost and the lost profit could be recovered. The sellers had sold one fewer car than they otherwise would. Upjohn J. defined available market as where:

> "the situation in the particular trade in the particular area was such that there was a demand sufficient to absorb readily all the goods that were thrust on it, so that if a purchaser defaulted the goods in question could readily be disposed of."[24]

In *Charter v Sullivan*[25] a contract to purchase a Hillman Minx was repudiated by the buyer. Demand for the car exceeded supply and, consequently, the plaintiff dealer was able to sell the car to another customer. It was held that nominal damages should be awarded since the dealer, being able to sell all the cars he could take delivery of, had suffered no loss directly and naturally resulting from the defendant's breach of contract. Today's highly competitive market should make such circumstances a rare occurrence.

The above two cases concern the sale of new cars. But, with secondhand models each one is different from the next even though they may be of the same make and year. There is no "available market" for a secondhand car rejected by the buyer and, therefore, according to Lord Denning M.R.,[26] the measure of damages is the estimated loss directly and

---

23. [1955] 1 All E.R. 154.
24. *Ibid.*, at 159.
25. [1957] 2 Q.B. 117.
26. *Lazenby Garages Ltd. v Wright* [1976] 2 All E.R. 770.

naturally resulting in the ordinary course of events from the buyer's breach of contract.[27] As such the buyer could contemplate, not that the seller would sell one car fewer, but at most, that the seller might have to sell to another purchaser at a price lower than that which he was originally offered by the buyer who is in breach. The possibility of the dealer selling a different car to the subsequent buyer was considered too remote. It follows that if, in fact, the seller manages to obtain a higher price than the original contract price, then no loss has been suffered and nominal damages only would be available.

**Cost of cure**

An alternative to the difference in value approach to the assessment of expectation loss is to consider the cost incurred by the innocent party in curing the breach. In contracts for the sale of goods the failure of the seller to deliver the goods, or to deliver goods of the appropriate quality, can be cured by the buyer buying substitute goods in the market. Here the difference in value (measured by the market price) and the cost of cure are the same. With regard to defective goods, the buyer may claim the cost of repairing the defect where the cost involved is reasonable.[28]

In building contracts the measure of the cost of cure, that is, the cost of engaging someone to complete the work, may differ from (that is, exceed) the measure of the difference in value. Wherever it is reasonable for the employer to insist upon re-instatement, the courts will treat the cost of re-instatement as the measure of damage.[29] The question of reasonableness has been considered in a number of recent cases.

In *C.R. Taylor (Wholesale) Ltd. v Hepworths Ltd.*[30] May J. referred with approval to McGregor on Damages[31] which states that the appropriate test in deciding between diminution in value and cost of re-instatement is the

---

27. That is, an application of s.50(2) of the Sale of Goods Act 1979, which states that, *prima facie* the measure of damages for non-acceptance is "the estimated loss, directly and naturally resulting, in the ordinary course of events, from the buyer's breach".
28. *Charterhouse Credit Co. Ltd. v Tolly* [1963] 2 Q.B. 683 (hire-purchase case).
29. Lord Cohen, *East Ham B.C. v Bernard Sunley & Sons Ltd.* [1965] 3 All E.R. 619.
30. [1977] 2 All E.R. 784.
31. 13th ed. (1972).

reasonableness of the plaintiff's desire to re-instate the property. In particular, where the cost of remedying the defect is out of proportion to the end to be attained, the damages should be measured by the value of the building had it been built according to the contractual specification less the value as it stands.

Most recently, the House of Lords has considered the issue in *Ruxley Electronics & Construction Ltd. v Forsyth.*[32] The defendant contracted with the plaintiff company for the construction of a swimming pool in his garden. The contract expressly specified that the maximum depth should be 7ft. 6in., but on completion the maximum depth was only 6ft. 9in. and the point where people would dive in was only 6ft. deep. The builders claimed the balance of the contract price and the defendant counterclaimed for breach. The diminution in value caused by the breach was nil, the depth of the pool being perfectly adequate for diving.

Lord Lloyd considered that it is first necessary to ascertain the loss the plaintiff has suffered by reason of the breach. If he has suffered no loss, he can recover no more than nominal damages, for the object of damages is always to compensate the plaintiff, not punish the defendant. If loss has been suffered, then the cost of re-instatement is not the appropriate measure of damages if the expenditure would be out of all proportion to the good to be obtained.[33]

Where the contract breaker has entirely failed to achieve the contractual objective it may well be reasonable to conclude that the loss is the necessary cost of achieving that objective. Lord Lloyd gave as an example a house whose construction is so defective that it is of no use for its designed purpose and must therefore be reconstructed. Furthermore it is the loss in relation to the particular contract which must be taken into account. Hence, if a party contracts for a folly to be built in his garden and it collapses shortly after completion, it would be irrelevant to argue that the erection of a folly, which contributed nothing to the value of the house, was a foolish thing to do. Lord Jauncey made reference to *Radford v De Froberville*,[34] in which Oliver J. said:

---

32. [1995] 3 W.L.R. 118.
33. Such principle expressed by Cardozo J. in *Jacob & Youngs Inc. v Kent* (1921) 230 N.Y. 239.
34. [1978] 1 All E.R. 33 at 42.

> "If he contracts for the supply of that which he thinks serves his interests, be they commercial, aesthetic or merely eccentric, then if that which is contracted for is not supplied by the other contracting party I do not see why, in principle, he should not be compensated by being provided with the cost of supplying it through someone else or in a different way ... ."[35]

However, as Beale[36] observes, the requirement to compensate so as to satisfy the plaintiff's interest will be less readily enforced where the plaintiff is a non-consumer. In *Channel Island Ferries Ltd. v Cenargo Navigation Ltd. (The Rozel)*[37] the plaintiff's ship was repaired but the defendant repairers were in breach because the vessel failed to qualify for a Class certificate. Nevertheless, the classification society did not insist on any remedial action and Phillips J. held that in the circumstances it was not reasonable to have the repairs done again and award damages on this basis. Rather, compensation should be given to reflect any diminution in the value of the ship. The employer's personal interest and preference in regard to the contract should be considered but:

> "where the contractual requirement is not an end in itself but is inserted into a commercial contract because it has financial implications ... the costs of remedial measures will not normally be recoverable as damages if they are disproportionate to the financial consequences of the breach."[38]

Normally, the courts are not concerned with what a plaintiff does with his damages. However, in the circumstances, intention is relevant to reasonableness, at least in those cases where the plaintiff does not intend to reinstate. In *Ruxley* Lord Jauncey and Lord Lloyd both recognised this, the latter stating, that if the owner of the swimming pool were to receive the cost of building a new one and retain the exisiting one, he would have recovered, not compensation for loss but, a very substantial gratuitous benefit, something which damages were not intended to provide. It was found as a fact that the owner did not intend to reinstate and an award based on cost of cure would, therefore, be unreasonable. Indeed, in such circumstances, even an undertaking by the owner to spend any damages which he may receive on rebuilding the pool made no difference for such

---

35. *Ibid.*, at p. 42.
36. Beale, *Damages for Rebuilding,* 95 *L.Q.R.* 111.
37. [1994] 2 Lloyd's Rep. 161.
38. *Ibid.*, at p. 166.

an undertaking would create a loss which does not exist so that the defendants would effectively be punished for their breach of contract and this is something which should not be allowed.[39]

It was held that, since there was no diminution in value of the pool, only nominal damages should be awarded in addition to the sum of £2,500 for loss of amenity.

The principle that a plaintiff cannot always insist on re-instatement where to do so would be unreasonable is not confined to building cases. In *Sealace Shipping Co. Ltd. v Oceanvoice Ltd., The Alecos M*[40] a ship was sold but delivered without the specified spare propeller. No market for secondhand propellers existed and the only way of obtaining a spare was to order the manufacture of a new one, albeit at great expense. The Court of Appeal upheld the Arbitrator's decision to award only the scrap value of the propeller as this was all the buyer had lost by reason of the seller's breach. Neill L.J. said that the award answered the question of what the buyers lost as a result of the non-delivery of the spare propeller to the vessel, and that loss was its value.[41] It was incumbent on him to make a substitute contract as soon as his cause of action had arisen.

Note that the cost of cure will be awarded only where it is appropriate to the liability which the defendant has assumed under his contractual obligations. In *Watts v Morrow*,[42] if the plaintiffs, who purchased a defective house, had recovered the cost of repairs from the defendant surveyors, they would have recovered damages for a breach of warranty as to the condition of the house when no such warranty that repairs would not be needed had been given.

## The date at which damages should be assessed

Prices do not remain constant and, because of the possibility of fluctuating values, there is a need to consider the point of time at which the plaintiff's costs or losses should be assessed. The principle usually applied is to assess damages as at the date of the breach. Indeed, in cases of contracts for

39. *Per* Lord Lloyd at p. 288.
40. [1991] 1 Lloyd's Rep. 120.
41. *Ibid.*, at p. 125.
42. [1991] 4 All E.R. 937.

the sale of goods this is the statutory requirement for, with respect to the non-acceptance of goods by the buyer, reference is to be made to the market price prevailing at the time when they ought to have been accepted. But, where the seller fails to deliver, reference is to be made to the market price prevailing at the time when the goods ought to have been delivered.[43] The principle is based on the duty of the plaintiff to mitigate his losses and therefore it is incumbent on him to make a substitute contract as soon as his cause of action arises.

There will be times when such an an approach is inappropriate and some later date should be referred to for the purposes of assessment. In *Johnson v Agnew*[44] Lord Wilberforce stated that the rule was not an absolute one, and where it would give rise to injustice, then the court had the power to fix another date appropriate to the situation. In his words:

> "In cases where a breach of a contract for sale has occurred, and the innocent party reasonably continues to try to have the contract completed, it would to me appear more logical and just, rather than tie him to the date of the original breach, to assess damages as at the date when (otherwise than by his default) the contract is lost."[45]

The case concerned a contract for the sale of land which the purchaser failed to complete on the agreed date. The vendors sought specific performance which, owing to a five month delay in drawing up the order, became impossible. The vendors were successful in their claim to treat the contract as repudiated and recover damages to be assessed at the date on which the equitable remedy became aborted and the contract was lost.[46]

On the facts, reference to a date other than that of the breach was appropriate and fair. It follows that there will be other situations where the court may depart from the general rule. Thus, for example, it may be unreasonable to expect the plaintiff to realise that a breach has occurred and, therefore, respond immediately, at the time of performance, as when defective goods are supplied in sealed packages or when the defect is hidden from the reasonable buyer, not manifesting itself until some time after

---

43. Sale of Goods Act 1979 ss. 50(3) and 51(3).
44. [1979] 1 All E.R. 883.
45. *Ibid.*, at 896.
46. Support for this approach was found in *Ogle v Earl Vane* (1867) L.R. 2 Q.B. 275, *Hickman v Haynes* (1875) L.R. 10 C.P. 598 and *Radford v de Froberville* [1977] 1 W.L.R. 1262.

purchase.[47] Additionally, the plaintiff, though aware of the breach, may be unable to take action until a later date by which time the market value of the goods in question may be higher than at the date of the breach. Also, in a time of high inflation, rapidly rising prices may make it unreasonable and perhaps impossible for a buyer to go into the market and purchase substitute goods with damages assessed at the time of breach. In *Wroth v Tyler*[48] the defendant reneged on a contract to sell a house worth £7,500 for £6,050. Specific performance was refused the plaintiff but damages were granted "in substitution for specific performance". The value of the house at the date of judgement was £11,500 and £5,500 damages were awarded to the plaintiff whose resources were limited to the original purchasing power of £6,000, a fact known to the seller. Thus, even though the buyer was aware of the rising market and consequent increase in damage, he was unable to enter the market and buy a substitute house and, in so doing, mitigate the loss. The Court of Appeal, confirming Megarry J.'s decision, held that the date on which the damages should be assessed was not the date of breach but the date of judgement.

**Anticipatory breach - assessment of damages**

As discussed above, where the victim of an anticipatory breach of contract is unwilling to accept the breach, he is under no duty to mitigate and the time at which damages are assessed is determined according to the principles so far described. That is, reference is made to the time at which the contract should have been performed.

Where the victim accepts the repudiation, he is under a duty to mitigate and the time for assessment then becomes the time at which substitute performance could reasonably have been arranged. The point was considered recently in *Kaines (U.K.) Ltd. v Osterreichische Warenhandelsgesellschaft Austrowaren Gesellschaft mbH.*[49] Here, a contract to supply oil was repudiated by the seller in advance of the delivery date. The purchaser accepted the breach but delayed buying a substitute supply by which time the price had risen substantially above the contract price.

---

47. Similarly, where defects in a building do not manifest themselves until after the work has been completed: *East Ham Borough Council v Bernard Sunley Ltd.* [1966] A.C. 406.
48. [1974] 1 Ch. 30.
49. [1993] 2 Lloyd's Rep. 1.

During the intervening period the market price had first risen and then actually fallen below that originally agreed. The Court of Appeal, confirming Steyn J.'s judgement, held that the buyer should have bought at the time of breach (June 18-19). Accordingly, the date on which the alternative contract should have been made was the time fixed for the assessment of loss. Bingham L.J. stated:

> "The Judge's conclusion that a reasonably prudent oil trader would have bought in a substitute cargo on June 19 in my opinion fixes the level of the plaintiff's damages on the facts of the case irrespective of what the plaintiffs did or failed to do at the time. Had the market price risen steadily after June 19, their failure to buy could not have increased the damages payable by the defendants. Had the price fallen steadily after June 19, their failure to buy would not have reduced the damages."[50]

## Tax and savings made

In *British Transport Commission v Gourley*,[51] a tortious action for personal injuries, the plaintiff, a successful engineer seriously injured in a railway accident, claimed £37,720 lost income. This sum, after tax would have been reduced to under £7,000. The House of Lords awarded the lower figure since, as damages for lost earnings are not taxable, the sum awarded should only be the net loss of income, that is, the plaintiff's actual loss. The prime concern was to avoid over-compensating the plaintiff. This was an action in tort but the same principles apply to contractual liability so that, for example, in an award for wrongful dismissal, savings in tax should be accounted for.[52]

The assessment of such a deduction can pose serious difficulties for the courts. The reader is referred to two employment cases, *Beach v Reed Corrugated Cases Ltd.*[53] and *Re Houghton Main Colliery Co.*,[54] which provide illustrations of the problems of accurately quantifying the deduction to be made. Cheshire, Fifoot and Furmston recognise the speculative nature of the principle: "The truth is that in such cases the assessment of the

---

50. *Ibid.*, at pp. 10-11.
51. [1956) A.C. 185.
52. *Beach v Reed Corrugated Cases Ltd.* [1956] 2 All E.R. 652.
53. *Ibid.*
54. [1956] 3 All E.R. 300.

amount to be deducted is a matter of guesswork rather than of calculation."[55]

Two conditions are attached to the operation of the principle in *Gourley*:

1. The damages which are awarded to the plaintiff must not themselves be subject to tax otherwise the injured party would pay double the amount due in tax and so be under compensated. Awards of damages for wrongful dismissal are not taxable below a certain limit (currently £30,000).[56] In *Parsons v B.N.M. Laboratories Ltd.*[57] the Court of Appeal decided that *Gourley* is applicable to awards below £30,000 and the damages should be reduced accordingly and, where the award exceeds £30,000, then the court should make a deduction from the first £30,000 of the award but not from the amount of the award which exceeds £30,000. However, note that in *Shove v Downs Surgical plc*[58] Sheen J. employed a different approach, first estimating the injured party's loss net of tax and then awarding a sum which included an amount equivalent to the estimated tax.

2. The loss for which the damages are awarded must represent a taxable income. Thus, the rule is applicable to loss of income but inapplicable to the loss of a capital asset which is not subject to a general liability for tax.

The decision has been criticised on a number of grounds. For example, it may actually be cheaper for the defendant to break the contract and pay compensation from which tax has been deducted than to perform his obligations. Again, the rule can have the effect of making the assessment of damages very speculative.[59] However, despite these and other criticisms, the Law Reform Committee[60] made no recommendations for change and the rule in *Gourley* remains intact.

---

55. *Cheshire, Fifoot and Furmston, Law of Contract*, 12th ed., (Butterworths, 1991) p. 611.
56. Income and Corporation Taxes Act 1988 ss. 148 and 188(4), as amended by Finance Act 1988, s.74.
57. [1964] 1 Q..B. 95.
58. [1984] 1 All E.R. 7.
59. For futher criticisms see Treitel, *Law of Contract,* 9th ed. (Sweet and Maxwell, 1995), p 862-3.
60. Law Reform Committee, 7th Report (1958) Cmnd. 501.

The decision was based on the principle that the plaintiff should receive no more damages than required to compensate him for the loss sustained. It follows that, if he has been able to make savings, then these should be considered by the court when making the award.

In *British Westinghouse Electric and Manufacturing Co. Ltd. v Underground Electric Railways Co. of London Ltd.*,[61] a House of Lords case, the appellants supplied turbines which did not meet the agreed specification. The plaintiffs replaced them with turbines which were more efficient and cheaper to run than those originally purchased even if the latter had met their specification. In an action by the appellants for the unpaid part of the purchase price, the respondents claimed for the cost of purchasing replacement turbines and the extra running costs incurred when using the inefficient turbines. The court acepted the first counter claim but regarded the second as being subject to a deduction reflecting the savings made by the respondents when using the more powerful replacement machines. Viscount Haldane stated:

> "... But when, in the course of business, [the plaintiff] has taken action arising out of the transaction, which has diminished his loss, the effect of the loss which he has suffered may be taken into account, even though there was no duty to act."[62]

Thus, it is appropriate for the court to consider what actually happened in the circumstances of the case and balance gain and loss. Viscount Haldane made reference in his judgement to *Staniforth v Lyall*,[63] in which a ship was chartered and abandoned by the defendants. It transpired that the captain of the ship was able to make a voyage home, which was more profitable than the original venture would have been. The Court of Common Pleas held that, in quantifying the damages, it was bound to bring into account the advantages from which the plaintiffs had benefitted because of the savings made after the breach.

---

61. [1912] A.C. 673.
62. *Ibid.*, at 689.
63. (1830) 7 Bing 169.

## Exercises

1. Distinguish between expectation loss and reliance loss with reference to decided cases.

2. Smart agreed to purchase a BMW car from Go-Ahead Motors. Later, when informed that the car was ready for collection, Smart told the garage that he had changed his mind and was not willing to accept or pay for the vehicle.

   Advise Go-Ahead Motors as to any damages they may claim from Smart.

# 6 Compensatory damages for tort - personal injuries and death

## Introduction

Unlike the position in contract where the purpose of an award of damages is to put the plaintiff in the position he would have been in if the contract had been performed, in tort the general position is that damages are awarded in order to put the plaintiff in the position he would have been in if the tort had not occurred (in other words, to compensate the plaintiff). This chapter deals with damages for personal injuries and awards for death. The award of damages for other losses in tort will be looked at in the next chapter.

## 1. Damages for personal injuries

Personal injury includes both mental injury, e.g., nervous shock, and physical injury. Physical injury covers disease or illness or other physical effects of a tort, e.g., head injury. Thus, in *Griffiths v Williams*,[1] a case of trespass to the person, damages of £50,000 were awarded for rape.

### *Classification of damages*

When a person suffers personal injuries as the result of another's negligence, for example, he can recover damages for his pecuniary loss (e.g., loss of earnings, medical expenses, etc.) as well as his non-pecuniary loss, e.g., pain and suffering (including mental distress), loss of amenity and the injury itself. Losses in respect of the pre-trial period and the post-trial period may be

---

1. *The Times*, November 24, 1995. See also *W. v Meah* (1986) C.L.Y. 1071.

claimed. Pre-trial loss of earnings and other losses during that period which are quantifiable (e.g., medical bills, fares to and from hospital, etc.) are claimable as *special damages* and should be pleaded as such in the statement of claim. Post-trial loss of earnings, damages for non-pecuniary loss, etc., are categorised as *general damages*.

Therefore, conventionally, damages for personal injuries are classified as:

(a) damages for *pecuniary loss* and *non-pecuniary loss*,

(b) *special* damages and *general* damages, and

(c) *pre-trial* damages and *post-trial* damages.

*Form and basis of the award of damages*

Since there is no jury in a personal injury hearing, it is the judge who states how much damages has been awarded and for which items of injury or loss.

The basis of awarding damages is compensation of the plaintiff for the pecuniary and non-pecuniary losses suffered by him as a result of the tort.

**(a) The lump sum**

Damages are paid once in a lump sum, except that:

(i) where there is a serious and substantial chance that the injured person's physical or mental state may, at some time in the future, deteriorate or he may suffer from some disease, the court can award *provisional damages* with a *proviso* that, if the deterioration, etc., occurs, further damages will be awarded at a later date: section 32A, Supreme Court Act 1981;

(ii) where the defendant has admitted liability but only challenges the amount of damages, and the defendant is a public authority or insured or has substantial resources, an award of *interim damages* may be made at the interlocutory stage of the court proceedings; and

(iii) where the defendant has liability insurance, it is possible for the parties to agree to a *structured settlement*.

**(b) Structured settlements**

*Structured settlements* consist of a lump sum to cover the past financial losses and existing needs of the plaintiff up to the time of the settlement, and a pension payable annually for the rest of his life. They have the following advantages:

(a) From the plaintiff's point of view, they provide certainty: the plaintiff does not have to manage a big sum of money and is not given the opportunity to waste it in one go; in other words, he is assured of regular payments for life.[2]

(b) Both the plaintiff and the defendant benefit because structured settlements save time and money.

(c) They are flexible: each structured settlement is designed to suit the needs of the individual plaintiff.

(d) They have tax advantages.

However, they also have some disadvantages.

(a) Forecasting still needs to be done (under a structured settlement experts and advisers are needed to plan a complicated budget for life).

(b) They do not provide 100% certainty because, e.g., if a plaintiff is not subject to the supervision of the Court of Protection, he can still dissipate the funds.

(c) The individual plaintiff may not in the first place want a structured

---

2. Law Comm. No. 224, para. 3.17.

settlement.[3]

*Pecuniary loss*

*Pre-trial and post-trial:*

### (a) Loss of earnings

The plaintiff may first wish to claim for loss of earnings where, as the result of the accident/negligence, he could not go to work and, therefore, suffers loss of earnings. Here tax[4] and his National Insurance contributions[5] would have to be deducted because damages should be compensatory but not punitive, and should represent the plaintiff's take-home pay (net earnings, i.e., after those deductions have been made).[6]

Assessment of the *pre-trial* loss of earnings is quite a straightforward process because that loss is precisely the plaintiff's take-home pay if he had not been injured.

When calculating the *post-trial* or future loss of earnings, however, the courts use the "multiplier system" - they first assess the "multiplicand"

---

3. See paras. 3.10 - 3.22, *Report on Structured Settlements and Interim and Provisional Damages* (Law Commission No. 224, Cm. 2646, H.M.S.O., 1994). See also Richard Lewis, "The Merits of a Structured Settlement: The Plaintiff's Perspective", *Oxford Journal of Legal Studies*, vol. 13, no. 4, 1993, 530-547; "Structured Settlements in Practice", *Civil Justice Quarterly*, vol. 10, July 1991, 212-219; "Structured Settlements: An Emergent Study", *Civil Justice Quarterly*, vol. 13, Jan. 1994, 18-28; *Structured Settlements: the Law and Practice* (Sweet and Maxwell, 1994). The Law Commission in 1994 (Law Comm. No. 224, Cm. 2646) proposed, *inter alia*, a new statutory scheme of structured settlements with features such as direct tax-free payments to the plaintiff as an annuitant (where the insurance company from which the annuities were bought for the plaintiff by the defendant or his insurer, carried on business in the United Kingdom as authorised), etc. Those proposals are reflected in the Damages Act 1996.
4. *British Transport Commission v Gourley* [1956] A.C. 185.
5. *Cooper v Firth Brown Ltd.* [1963] 2 W.L.R. 418.
6. Critics of this say that the state loses because the defendant does not pay the taxman the amount that the plaintiff would have paid in tax. See, e.g., Bishop and Kay, "Taxman and Damages: The Rule in Gourley's Case", *L.Q.R.*, vol. 105, 1987, 366). According to Howarth, however, that loss by the Inland Revenue "is plainly relational economic loss, and there is no one better placed to spread the loss than themselves". See D. Howarth, *A Textbook on Tort* (Butterworths, 1995), pp. 605-6.

(the plaintiff's net loss of income *per annum*) and multiply it by the "multiplier" (a figure which reflects the fact that the plaintiff would suffer the annual loss for a number of years). When working out what is the appropriate multiplier to use, the courts consider the various vicissitudes or uncertainties of life, how long he would have lived if he had not been injured, whether he would stay in the same job, his promotion prospects, loss of pension, lost earning capacity, etc. As may be deduced from the cases, the appropriate multiplier for a plaintiff aged about 35 is likely to be around 16 and the 18-20 range may be said to be the maximum.[7]

*The case of children*

Although it would seem that the younger plaintiff would have a higher multiplier, the position is different in the case of young children. When compared to adults, children's multipliers have been low because in their case there are far more uncertainties: they may not live long enough to be able to earn, etc. An example is *Croke v Wiseman*.[8] There, owing to medical negligence, the plaintiff, aged seven and a half at the date of trial, suffered brain damage and severe spastic quadriplegia when he was 21 months old. The judge took, for the plaintiff's loss of future earnings, an average wage of £5,000 per annum and applied a multiplier of 9, making a total of £45,000. The Court of Appeal held, *inter alia,* that the multiplier in respect of his loss of future earnings (post-trial loss of earnings) should be 5 instead because he might not, for example, become a wage-earner. Lord Denning, disagreeing with the award of the trial judge, said:

---

7. This judicial estimation of the multiplier, in the present authors' view, may be described as "judicial roulette" simply because it is not precise enough and the courts do not always use actuarial tables. The "Ogden Tables", *Actuarial Tables with Explanatory Notes for Use in Personal Injury and Fatal Accident Cases*, are standard tables of multipliers to assist the court and have been published by the Government (H.M.S.O.) since 1984. In response to the Law Commission's recommendation for legislative encouragement of judges to make more use of those tables in the future (Law Com. No. 224, para. 2.15), s.10, Civil Evidence Act 1995 has given them (the Ogden Tables) authority as evidence.
8. [1982)] 1 W.L.R. 71.

> "The judge awarded £45,000 to this baby for loss of future earnings. To my mind there is something odd about giving this tiny baby two separate items of damages: One for cost of "future care"; the other for loss of "future earnings." "Future care" is awarded on the footing that he is completely incapacitated and has to be kept at great expense all his future life. "Future earnings" are awarded on the footing that he was not incapacitated at all, and would be earning all his future life. I cannot think it right in principle that he should have both."[9]

For children who have never worked the multiplicand cannot be worked out as is done in the case of adults. Thus, the tendency of the courts is to take as the multiplicand of infants the national average earnings (*Croke v Wiseman*). Where the child has worked before, such as where he is a child actor or singer, the calculation of his lost earnings will be based on the actual earnings which he has lost and his likely future earnings

### (b) Expenses

*Medical and related expenses*

The plaintiff can recover his medical, hospital and nursing care costs as well as his travel costs to and from hospital, etc. If he receives or plans to receive private treatment, his claim for medical expenses will not be jeopardised or affected if he does not choose National Health Service treatment which is available. This is because of s.2(4), Law Reform (Personal Injuries) Act 1948, which provides:

> "In an action for damages for personal injuries (including such action arising out of a contract), there shall be disregarded, in determining the reasonableness of any expenses, the possibility of avoiding those expenses or part of them by taking advantage of facilities available under the National Health Service Act 1946 or the National Health Service (Scotland) Act 1947, or of any corresponding facilities in Northern Ireland."

The expenses for private treatment must, however, be reasonable. For example, if the plaintiff lives in Surrey and chooses private treatment in

---

9. *Ibid.*, p. 76.

Surrey, that may be said to be reasonable. But, it would be unreasonable of him to choose more expensive private treatment in Scotland or Switzerland without very special medical justification. That will constitute failure to mitigate his loss *via* unreasonable action.[10]

The plaintiff who is disabled can also claim for altering or converting his house to suit his disability.[11] However, if the capital value of the house is enhanced thereby, that increase will be set off against the cost of alteration.

Where he is disabled enough to need 24-hour care in hospital and he receives that care in a National Health Service hospital or some other hospital[12] but at public expense, any living expenses he saves as the result of staying in hospital will be set off against his damages (i.e., they will be deducted from his loss of earnings): s.5, Administration of Justice Act 1982.[13] Damages are also awardable for nursing care at home.

*Care provided by relatives, etc.*

Where the care of the plaintiff is provided by a relative who, e.g., has given up his job in order to do so, an amount to reflect reasonably that relative's loss can be claimed by the plaintiff, as happened in *Cunningham v Harrison*[14] (where a wife gave up her job to care for her husband).

Thus, the fact that the one providing the care has left his paid job in order to do so is considered although the total cost of care is taken to be not more than the going (commercial) rate.[15] It would really be unreasonable and unfair to the defendant if the cost of care is taken as, for example, the wages of the carer before he gave up his job, where that is in excess of the going (commercial) rate of care.

---

10. *Selvanayagam v University of West Indies* [1983] 1 W.L.R. 585, P.C..
11. *Roberts v Johnstone* [1989] Q.B. 878; [1988] 3 W.L.R. 1247.
12. *Lim Poh Choo v Camden Health Authority* [1980] A.C. 174.
13. If, as we shall see later, by virtue of the Social Security Administration Act 1992, the Secretary of State for Social Security can recoup social security benefits a plaintiff receives as a result of his disability or injury in the first five years thereafter, then there is a strong case for recouping from a defendant the cost of NHS treatment a plaintiff receives (freely, at state expense) through legislation, e.g., a Law Reform (Recoupment of Cost of National Health Service Treatment) Act.
14. [1973] Q.B. 942. See also *Donnelly v Joyce* [1974] Q.B. 454; [1973] 3 All E.R. 475 (where a mother gave up her job in order to care for the child-plaintiff, aged 6); and *Roberts v Johnstone* [1989] Q.B. 878 (where the adoptive mother was the carer).
15. *Housecroft v Burnett* [1986] 1 All E.R. 332.

Where, however, the carer who has given up his job is the tortfeasor himself, according to the House of Lords in *Hunt v Severs*,[16] it does not make sense for the defendant to pay to the plaintiff a sum which the plaintiff would then pay back to him. In that case the plaintiff was a passenger in the pillion of a motorcycle negligently driven by the defendant. As a result of an accident, she was seriously injured and became a paraplegic. The defendant later married her (but before the trial) and was caring for her. She sued the defendant and, liability having been admitted, the only dispute was about damages, especially, the travelling expenses of the husband-defendant to visit her in hospital and the value of the services provided to her by the defendant; those items were objected to by the defendant's insurers. The judge awarded the plaintiff the damages she sought because a tortfeasor's volunteering to care for the plaintiff does not mean the plaintiff could not recover the value of the defendant's services (in other words, on the basis of *Donnelly v Joyce*, recovery of the cost of the plaintiff's care should not be denied). The judge, when assessing the cost of the plaintiff's care and her future earnings, used a multiplier of 14 based on a life expectancy of 25 years. The defendant's appeal to the Court of Appeal failed for the same reason. There the plaintiff's multiplier was in fact increased to 15. However, the House of Lords overturned the decision of the Court of Appeal and allowed the defendant's appeal because: the plaintiff must recover the value of care (services) rendered him voluntarily by a family member so as to compensate the carer and, therefore, the plaintiff held the damages awarded on trust for the carer; however, where that carer was the defendant tortfeasor, he should not be required to pay to the plaintiff a sum of money only for the plaintiff to pay that same sum to him; therefore, the defendant's travelling expenses to visit the plaintiff in hospital and the value of the defendant's services were excluded from the plaintiff's award of damages. The House also reduced the multiplier used by the Court of Appeal from 15 to 14 because the earlier one (15) was based, not on a severely injured woman's expectation of survival, but on that of an average woman.

This decision has attracted critical comments from various quarters. It is an unsatisfactory decision. In effect it will encourage tortfeasors to enter into enforceable contracts for care to the plaintiffs (which has been thought by the Court of Appeal in *Cunningham v Harrison* as undesirable) or to provide no care to the plaintiffs in order not to reduce the total award of

---

16. [1994] 2 W.L.R. 602.

damages.[17] It also leaves possible problems unsolved, such as (a) where the carer-husband (relative) deserts the plaintiff or the plaintiff wishes another carer to care for her because she has, for example, divorced the original carer and does not wish to have intimate care from him anymore,[18] (b) the case of joint tortfeasors,[19] and (c) the possibility or rather indirect encouragement of plaintiffs to choose professional carers to care for them (since that care could be claimed for).[20] As Doggett puts it, "insurers may come to regret the ruling where the victim (aided and abetted by tortfeasor parent or spouse) pays for a £20,000 p.a. carer in preference to her parent or husband/wife for only £5,000 p.a.".[21] According to counsel for the plaintiff (at p. 354):

> "The result of a decision in favour of the defendant would reintroduce the need for a contract which *Donnelly v Joyce* [1974] Q.B. 454, 463-464 had been at pains to remove from the scene where the plaintiff was cared for by a member of his or her family. ... A decision for the defendant will, in effect, curtail the ordinary willingness of one human being to care for another and dam the springs of human kindness. It is important that the law should encourage family care for the injured. The courts should not fashion the law so as to discourage the giving of such care."

Unfortunately, those points were not accepted by the House of Lords.

It is suggested that the House of Lords could have been fairer to the plaintiff by awarding her damages for her care but ordering that the money should be held on trust for her while that care is being provided by the defendant-tortfeasor. Thus, if for whatever reason the defendant cannot or does not provide that care anymore, the plaintiff will have the means to afford hired help. If she dies "prematurely", the money will then revert to the "defendant" or his insurers, as the case may be.

---

17. See P. Matthews and M. Lunney, "A Tortfeasor's Lot is not a Happy One?", *Modern Law Review*, vol. 58: 3, 1995, p. 399.
18. Matthews and Luney, p. 403.
19. *Ibid.*, pp. 395-404; see also David Kemp, "Voluntary Services Provided by Tortfeasor to His Victim", *The Law Quarterly Review*, vol. 110, 1995, 524-6; and Roderick Doggett, "Hunt v Severs - A Pyrrhic Victory for Insurers?", *Quantum*, issue 3, May 6, 1994, 6-7.
20. Kemp, *op. cit.*, pp. 524-6; see also Doggett, *op. cit.*, 6-7.
21. Doggett, *op. cit.*, p. 6.

### (c) Other pecuniary losses

*The "lost years"*

This refers to the years the plaintiff would have been expected to be alive and earning money through work if he had not been injured. In other words, it is the number of working years the plaintiff may not live because, as a result of the accident, he may die sooner than was normally thought - "the years of which he has been deprived".[22]

Before 1980 damages for the lost years were not recoverable, as a result of the decision in *Oliver v Ashman.*[23] However, that is not now the position because of the House of Lords' decision in *Pickett v British Rail Engineering Ltd.*[24] The ruling in *Oliver v Ashman* was too harsh because it did not consider the plaintiff's lost opportunity to earn money and take care of his family. The better way, the House of Lords thought, was to award damages for loss of earnings during the lost years but deduct therefrom a sum which represents the plaintiff's personal living expenses, including what he spends *pro rata* on his dependants, etc. (*Harris v Empress Motors*). Therefore, damages for the lost years are now claimable. But, they can only be claimed by living plaintiffs.

In the case of children the courts have not been willing to make an award for the lost years simply because of the many uncertainties in their case, e.g., their future earning capacity is not certain. No wonder in *Croke v Wiseman,*[25] the plaintiff, aged seven and a half, received nothing for the lost years (because, by reason of his condition, he would not have any dependants, etc.). Nevertheless, it is possible for a young child to claim damages for the loss of earnings during the lost years if he can prove he has already been earning, for example, if he is a child prodigy and already employed as a film/television star. In *Connolly v Camden Area Health Authority,*[26] however, that loss was not proved and, therefore, no award was made for the lost years.

---

22. *Per* Lord Wilberforce in *Pickett v British Rail* [1980] A.C. 136, at p. 146. According to s.1(1), Administration of Justice Act 1982, there can be no separate claim for loss of expectation of life.
23. [1962] 2 Q.B. 210.
24. [1980] A.C. 136. See also *Harris v Empress Motors* [1983] 3 All E.R. 561.
25. [1981] 3 All E.R. 852.
26. [1981] 3 All E.R. 250.

*Future prospects*

These are also considered in increasing or reducing (as the circumstances might indicate) the damages to be awarded. Relevant factors here include whether the plaintiff is studying for further qualifications or engaged in further training that might enhance his future prospects or earning capacity and the difficulty of his finding another job if he loses his present one as a result of his injuries.

*The case of women*

In *Harris v Harris,*[27] according to Lord Denning:

(a) an unmarried woman's damages for loss of future earnings must be reduced since she may get married and give up work to have children, but

(b) young women should also be compensated for loss of amenity as regards loss of marriage prospects and consequent enjoyment of a husband's economic support.

That case was applied by O'Connor J. in *Moriarty v MacCarthy.*[28] There a young woman, aged 24, was so seriously injured in a road accident that she became paraplegic and would have to be in a wheelchair for the rest of her life. Her multiplier was reduced from 15 to 11 but she received increased general damages to compensate her for being deprived, through her loss of the opportunity of marriage, of a husband's support during the period of time she would have brought up her children. On the other hand, a different approach was adopted in *Hughes v McKeown.*[29] In that case, owing to the defendant's negligence, the plaintiff was knocked down (when she was four and a half years old) on a pedestrian crossing and suffered head injuries leading to serious brain damage. As a result of that she was not likely to live a fully independent life again; also, her prospects of working and of marriage were severely reduced. There was no such reduction of her multiplier

---

27. [1973] 1 Lloyd's Rep. 445.
28. [1978] 1 W.L.R. 155.
29. [1985] 1 W.L.R. 963.

because, even if her career was interrupted for the purpose of raising a family, the presumption was that she would be supported by her husband during that period of time. Although the husband would not be paying her in money, he would be paying her in kind (providing accommodation, food and clothing, etc.). Thus, she could be said to be earning during that period. Although the view has been expressed that the approach in *Hughes v McKeown* is "more consonant with modern notions of equality between the sexes",[30] it has been suggested that a more satisfactory one would be for courts to openly admit the unacceptability of varying the multiplier on the ground of sex and also to admit policy as the reason for not considering that factor.[31]

### (d) Miscellaneous

Where loss of earnings is incurred by a parent who gives up her job to provide care for her child disabled by the defendant's negligence, the plaintiff should be awarded a sum which will appropriately recompense, not overcompensate, that parent or carer (*Donnelly v Joyce*).

Also, damages relating to childbirth are claimable. In *Fish v Wilcox*[32] a plaintiff gave birth to a daughter suffering from spina bifida as a result of the defendant's negligence. She claimed for her loss and damage as a result of the birth and of having to look after a seriously handicapped child. The trial judge awarded her £234,387 as damages and interest thereon. The nursing care she provided to the date of judgement was assessed at £34,167. Nothing by way of loss of earnings was awarded in addition to that figure. She appealed arguing that £20,000 for such loss should have been added to the £34,387. Her appeal failed because she could not do two jobs at once and was not entitled to payment for that (otherwise she would recover twice); and moreover, the judge, by awarding the £34,387, had properly added an additional amount for the extra burden of looking after her daughter.

In the very interesting case of *Meah v McCreamer (No. 2)*[33] public policy operated to deny the plaintiff recovery of the damages sought for "pecuniary loss". There Meah was a passenger in a car driven by

---

30. Howarth, *op. cit.*, pp. 611-2.
31. See K.M. Stanton, *The Modern Law of Tort* (Sweet and Maxwell, 1994), pp. 257-8.
32. [1994] 5 Med. L.R. 230.
33. [1986] 1 All E.R. 943,

McCreamer. McCreamer's drunken driving caused Meah to suffer serious injuries, including brain damage leading to personality change. Following that, he violently and sexually attacked a number of women. He was given a life sentence for those attacks. He sued McCreamer for negligence in respect of the road accident and recovered £45,000. He was later sued for trespass to the person by two of the victims of his crimes. He admitted liability and damages of £17,560 were awarded against him. He then sued McCreamer seeking to recover a contribution from him to meet the damages to be paid to his victims. It was held that the injuries to his victims were not the direct consequence of McCreadie's drunken driving. Also, to allow Meah to recover from the defendant for the consequences of his own crimes would be "distasteful" and contrary to public policy.

In *Emeh v Kensington and Chelsea and Westminster Area Health Authority*[34] public policy did not operate to deny the plaintiff her claim.[35] The plaintiff already had three normal children. She had an abortion to terminate her fourth pregnancy and also underwent a sterilisation operation to prevent future pregnancies. That sterilisation operation was negligently carried out; thus, she later became pregnant. She refused to have an abortion because she did not want to be operated on again. She, therefore, chose to have the baby. Unfortunately, the baby she gave birth to had a congenital abnormality. She sued for damages for her loss of future earnings, maintenance of the child, pain and suffering and the extra care that would be required by the child. However, the trial judge held that her refusal to have an abortion was, by reason of being unreasonable, a failure to mitigate her loss or a factor that broke the chain of causation (a *"novus actus interveniens"*). He, therefore, awarded her only damages for pain and suffering up to the time she found she was pregnant and pain and inconvenience as a result of having a second sterilisation operation. But, the Court of Appeal allowed her appeal and awarded her all the damages she asked for originally. The reasoning of the Court was as follows:

(a) the plaintiff did not want further pregnancy and birth, and so she had the sterilisation operation; the loss she suffered as a result of the

---

34. [1985] Q.B. 1012; [1984] 3 All E.R. 1044.

35. See *Thake v Maurice* [1986] Q.B. 644; [1986] 1 All E.R. 497, and *Gold v Haringey Health Authority* [1988] Q.B. 481. See also *Walkin v South Manchester Health Authority* [1995] 1 W.L.R. 543, where the Court of Appeal held that the plaintiff's action was statute-barred.

defendant's negligent sterilisation operation, therefore, included any reasonably foreseeable financial loss flowing directly from the unexpected pregnancy;

(b) her refusal to have an abortion was neither a *novus actus interveniens* nor a failure to mitigate because the defendants, by their own negligence, had put her in the dilemma of choosing between having the child and having an abortion; and

(c) no requirement of public policy prevented her full recovery of the financial loss she suffered as the result of the defendants' negligent performance of the sterilisation operation.

*Non-pecuniary loss*

Under this head the plaintiff can claim damages for loss of amenity, pain and suffering and the injury itself. Although it may be unsatisfactory to do so, the courts assess damages for non-pecuniary loss by reference to awards made previously in comparable cases (published in, for example, Kemp and Kemp, *The Quantum of Damages*, *The Personal Injuries and Quantum Reports* and *Current Law*). Alternatively, in the absence of comparable cases, they also make references to the general level of awards. On January 4, 1996 the Law Commission issued a Consultation Paper on alternative ways of fixing general levels of damages, *Damages for personal injury: non-pecuniary loss: compensating pain and suffering*, which suggested a statutory tariff or a Compensation Advisory Board to help judges on the general levels of damages.

**(a) Loss of amenity**

This is the deprivation of the ability to enjoy life or loss of faculty, i.e., the capacity for such natural action as touching, seeing, speaking, etc. - loss of bodily function (the loss of some form of enjoyment, e.g., playing football, playing the piano, fishing,[36] etc.). This claim can be made even if the

36. *Moeliker v Reyrolle and Co. Ltd.* [1977] 1 All E.R. 9. See also *H. v Ministry of Defence* [1991] 2 W.L.R. 1192.

plaintiff is unconscious and can feel nothing because it is the fact of deprivation which is being claimed for: *Lim Poh Choo v Camden Health Authority*.[37] Loss of amenity is, therefore, objective.

### (b) Pain and suffering

Pain and suffering includes the mental distress the plaintiff will suffer as a result of knowing that his life expectancy has been reduced. Damages under this head are not awarded where the plaintiff is unconscious because he does not experience or suffer any pain.[38] Thus, in *H. West and Son v Shephard* [1964] A.C. 326, a plaintiff, who was bed-ridden but not unconscious because she could, *inter alia,* show by facial expression what she liked or did not like and she could respond to commands by movement of her right hand, was awarded damages for pain and suffering.

In *Lim Poh Choo v Camden Health Authority*, owing to medical negligence, the plaintiff, a thirty-six-year-old psychiatrist, suffered serious and irreversible brain damage and became "only intermittently, and then barely, sentient"; she also became totally dependent on others. She sued the Area Health Authority concerned. Liability was admitted, and so the only issue at trial was that of damages. The trial judge awarded her £243,000 damages, made up of £20,000 for non-pecuniary loss (pain, suffering and loss of amenities), £84,000 for loss of future earnings, £105,500 for the cost of future care and £8,000 for loss of pension. This award was ratified by the Court of Appeal.[39] In the Court of Appeal and the House of Lords fresh

---

37. See also *H. West and Son v Shephard* [1964] A.C. 326.
38. *Wise v Kaye* [1962] 1 Q.B. 638, affirmed by the House of Lords in *Lim Poh Choo v Camden Health Authority*. Pain and suffering is, therefore, subjective.
39. There Lord Denning gave a dissenting judgement. In his view (see [1970] Q.B. 196, 218-219),"... when a plaintiff is rendered unconscious or insensible, fair compensation should not include an item for loss of earnings as such ... provided also that full compensation is also given for every expense that may be incurred on his behalf and every service that may be rendered to him by relatives and friends. The cost of keeping the plaintiff for the rest of his days will exceed by far the salary or wages that he would have earned if he never had been injured. It is not fair to the defendants to make them pay both." However, with respect, it must be pointed out that His Lordship seemed not to have considered that the plaintiff, unlike the child in *Croke v Wiseman*, was already earning as a professional person, a psychiatrist, when she was injured, and that her multiplier was not the 29 years of working life she had lost.

evidence was admitted regarding the cost of future care of the plaintiff. The defendants appealed against the ruling of the Court of Appeal. The House of Lords held, *inter alia,* that:

(1) the award of £20,000 for pain, suffering and loss of amenities was not excessive because the plaintiff had suffered total loss of the amenities of her good and useful life, even though she was unaware of such loss; that sum was also not inadequate as it was substantial in the light of money values at that time;

(2) the plaintiff in such a "catastrophic" case was entitled to damages for loss of earnings because there must be compensation for a genuine deprivation; however, in order to avoid overcompensation, sums for expenses which the plaintiff would have incurred in earning a living and also her living expenses must be deducted as the "domestic element" in assessing the multiplicand; and

(3) after considering the fresh evidence relating to the cost of the plaintiff's future care, the appropriate multiplicand was £6,400 p.a., with a multiplier of 12 years' purchase from the date of the judgement of the House; the total award for the plaintiff was, therefore, reduced to £229,298.64, with interest as appropriate.

Today any child born disabled because of injuries suffered in the mother's womb can sue, among other things, for pain and suffering, according to s.1 of the Congenital Disabilities (Civil Liability) Act 1976 (which applies only to children born after 22-7-76). However, if the child is born disabled because of the failure, through negligence, to abort the foetus before death, he cannot sue for pain and suffering[40] because the claim would be against public policy in that it would constitute support for the violation of the sanctity of human life.

As already mentioned under pecuniary loss, where a sterilisation operation on a woman is negligently performed and that woman became pregnant thereafter, she can recover damages for the pain and suffering she had to face in carrying, and giving birth to, the child.[41]

---

40. *McKay v Essex Area Health Authority* [1982] Q.B. 1166.

41. *Emeh v Kensington and Chelsea and Westminster Area Health Authority*.

Lastly, it should be noted that s.1(1)(a), Administration of Justice Act 1982 abolished damages for loss of expectation of life. Instead, s.1(1)(b) of that Act requires the courts to consider, in their assessment of damages for pain and suffering, the "suffering caused to him or likely to be caused to him by awareness that his expectation of life has been reduced".

### (c) The injury itself

Damages for the injury itself may also be claimed together with the other non-pecuniary losses.[42]

*Award of interest on damages*

The present practice is mainly based on the House of Lords' decisions in Cookson v Knowles,[43] *Pickett v British Rail*,[44] and *Wright v British Rail*.[45] It is as follows: (a) pre-trial pecuniary loss carries interest at half the short-term interest rates current during that period; (b) no interest is awardable for future pecuniary loss (post-trial pecuniary loss) simply because that loss has not yet been suffered, and (c) interest is awarded on non-pecuniary loss[46] but only at 2%.

The award of interest on damages is governed today by the Supreme Court Act 1981 and the County Courts Act 1984. Section 35A(1), Supreme Court Act 1981 gives the High Court discretion to award interest on damages (and debts). S.69, County Courts Act 1984 gives the County Courts a similar discretion. However, according to s.35A(2), Supreme Court Act 1981, the High Court must include interest on damages for personal injuries or death unless it "is satisfied there are special reasons" not to do so.

---

42. It should be noted, however, that injuries without pain and suffering are not common.
43. [1979] A.C. 556.
44. [1980] A.C. 136.
45. [1983] 2 A.C. 773. Although the first guidelines were given in *Jefford v Gee* [1970] 2 Q.B. 130.
46. *Pickett v British Rail.*

*Deductions*

As regards deductions the general rule was stated in *Hodgson v Trapp*[47] in the following way: if, as the result of his injuries the plaintiff receives money which he would not have been entitled to otherwise, those sums of money, subject to exceptions, must be deducted from the total of his losses and expenses in the assessment of his damages.

### (a) Social Security payments[48]

The present position is governed by the Social Security Administration Act 1992. According to that Act, relevant benefits (nearly all benefits payable because a person is disabled or unable to work[49]) for the first 5 years (i.e., 5 years from the date the injury or illness occurred) will be deducted from the plaintiff's compensatory damages. The tortfeasor will then pay that deducted amount to the State (the Secretary of State for Social Security): s.82(1), Social Security Administration Act 1992.[50] Thus, overcompensation

---

47. [1989] AC 807, at p. 819E.
48. The pre-1992 position was governed by the Social Security Act 1989, s.22 and schedule 4.
49. See para. 2, Social Security (Recoupment) Regulations 1990. Those relevant benefits include income support, attendance allowance, invalidity pensions and allowances, unemployment benefit, sickness benefit, statutory sick pay, etc., but not housing benefit and child benefit (which are not benefits payable as a result of disability or inability to work).
50. The actual words of s.82(1) are:
"(1) A person ("the compensator") making a compensation payment, whether on behalf of himself or another, in consequence of an accident, injury or disease suffered by any other person ("the victim") shall not do so until the Secretary of State has furnished him with a certificate of total benefit and shall then: (a) deduct from the payment an amount, determined in accordance with the certificate of total benefit, equal to the gross amount of any relevant benefits paid or likely to be paid to or for the victim during the relevant period in respect of that accident, injury or disease; (b) pay to the Secretary of State an amount equal to that which is required to be so deducted; and (c) furnish the person to whom the compensation payment is or, apart from this section, would have been made ("the intended recipient") with a certificate of deduction.
(2) Any right of the intended recipient to receive the compensation payment in question shall be regarded as satisfied to the extent of the amount certified in the certificate of deduction."

or payment twice to the plaintiff is avoided.[51] One sad consequence of this statutory provision, however, is that retired plaintiffs or plaintiffs not working can be disadvantaged, as is well illustrated by *Hassall and Pether v Secretary of State for Social Security*.[52] In that case the two appellants, unemployed, were receiving social security benefits for themselves and their families. They had been involved in two separate road accidents and thereafter continued receiving social security benefits of the same amount. However, to be entitled to the benefits, they had to produce medical certificates every week in relation to their injuries caused by their accidents; that exempted them from being required to be available for work. When they sued the tortfeasors, they claimed damages for only non-pecuniary loss but not for loss of earnings because they would not have been able to find work even if they had been fit. The tortfeasors settled the action by paying compensation to the appellants. But unfortunately, the social security benefits paid to the appellants after their accident were deducted from the said compensation and recouped by the Secretary of State under s.82(1), Social Security Administration Act 1992. When the appellants appealed to the social security appeal tribunal, one of them had the deduction from his compensation payment reduced but the other's was upheld. They then appealed to the Court of Appeal arguing two things: first, that they were paid those benefits after the accident because they were still unemployed and had no income (but not as a result of the accidents) and, secondly, that the deduction made, if any, should have been of part of the benefit, i.e., that part relating to them (but not also the part of it intended for their dependants' support). However, the Court held that:

(i) The post-accident benefits which the Secretary of State recouped had been paid as a direct consequence of the accidents in that those accidents resulted in the appellants' being entitled to social security benefits on a new basis; under that new basis the payments were made after production of medical certificates which exempted them from being required to be available for work.

(ii) In addition, so far as the purposes of s.82(1), Social Security Administration Act 1992 were concerned, benefits paid "to or for the

---

51. However, after 5 years the plaintiff "may enjoy a degree of double recovery". See Brazier (ed.), *Street on Torts* (1993), p. 53.

52. [1995] 1 W.L.R. 812; [1995] 3 All E.R. 909.

victim" included those parts calculated to cater for the support of his wife and children; they were not limited to the part meant for the claimant's support because there was no such limitation in the actual words of the subsection. Besides, if only the claimant's portion was recouped (in the ordinary case of a claim for loss of earnings), there would be overcompensation in relation to the dependants' share.

The decision seems unfair to the appellants. But, Henry L.J. thought differently. He said (at page 915):

> "In my judgement the unfairness identified stems not from either the construction or the operation of Pt IV of the 1992 Act, but from the failure to claim in the original actions special damages in respect of what these men under the new statutory regime lost financially as a result of the accident. On the factual assumption that they would have been unemployed over their whole recuperation period (i.e., the period during which they were in receipt of recoupable benefits), what they lost was their entitlement to non-recoupable benefits over that period: i.e., benefits payable otherwise than in consequence of the accident."

Nevertheless, it may be asked whether the decision is not "daylight meanness" by the State. The receiving-benefits-on-a-different-basis explanation, which operated against the plaintiffs, is highly unsatisfactory and unjust because it is the innocent, non-negligent plaintiffs, who are being penalised. It is, therefore, suggested that this unsatisfactory feature of the present law be removed (and speedily, too) in the case of plaintiffs like Hassall and Pether. Until its removal lawyers must henceforth advise such plaintiffs to plead (a) loss of non-recoupable social security benefits which ceased to be paid (because of the accident and their unavailability for work) and were replaced by recoupable benefits paid as a result of the accident, and/or (b) loss of earnings which the defendant's negligence deprived them of by making them incapable of working.

It should be noted that the 1992 Act only applies to damages of £2,500 or more. Where the award is less than £2,500, s.2(1), Law Reform (Personal Injuries) Act 1948 applies to the effect that half of the sum paid in the specified benefit/s will be deducted for the first five years.[53]

---

53. See schedule 2 to the Social Security Administration Act (1992).

### (b) Statutory sick pay

Statutory sick pay is deductible.[54] This is still the position even if the employers of the plaintiff have taken out an insurance policy to reimburse them for paying the plaintiff the (statutory) sick pay.[55] The reason for this is that sick pay is a substitute (even though an incomplete one) for earnings.

### (c) Redundancy payments

A redundancy payment will be deducted if the plaintiff was made redundant because of the injury he received as a result of the defendant's negligence.[56] But, if the redundancy was not caused by the plaintiff's injury (i.e., if he would have been made redundant, irrespective of his injury), that redundancy payment will be ignored in the assessment of damages.

### (d) Other collateral benefit

*Parry v Cleaver*[57] may be said to be the leading authority on "private" collateral benefits. There the plaintiff was a 35-year-old police constable. He had been in the police force for 12 years. He was injured seriously by a vehicle driven negligently by the defendant. Out of his pay he was making compulsory contributions to a police pension fund. Those contributions entitled him to a police pension whenever he got discharged from the force. About 18 months after the accident, he was discharged from the force on the ground of disablement. He received a pension of £204 a year. If he had remained in the force until he was 48 years old, he would have received a pension of £515 a year. After leaving the police force, he started working as a clerk earning £13 16s. a week and was contributing 14s. 8d. a week to a pension fund, which would entitle him to a pension of £5 13s. 6d. a week when he reached 65 years old. The question was whether the police disablement pension should be ignored or deducted from the damages awarded. At first instance, the judge ruled that the police disablement pension

---

54. *Palfrey v G.L.C.* [1985] I.C.R. 437.
55. *Hussain v New Taplow Paper Mills* [1988] A.C. 514.
56. *Wilson v National Coal Board* (1981) S.L.T. 67, a House of Lords' decision.
57. [1970] A.C. 1.

was a collateral benefit and, therefore, non-deductible. He awarded general damages of £15,500. The Court of Appeal disagreed and cut down the damages to £7,937 4s. and 6d. But, the House of Lords rejected that ruling and held that the pension should not be taken into consideration and awarded general damages of £9,500.

That case, therefore, is authority for the proposition that private collateral benefits are not deductible.[58]

### (i) Pensions

*Contributory pensions*

Also, according to *Parry v Cleaver*, contributory pensions are non-deductible, irrespective of whether it is the employer or employee who directly pays the contributions to the pension. The reason for this is that the contributory pension is a kind of insurance whereby the employee gets back his benefits, not all at once, but slowly in the form of a pension.[59] Thus, even if the defendant is the employer or the one who is providing the pension, there will be no deduction of it because the principle that the plaintiff has purchased his pension[60] is not affected.[61]

*State retirement pensions*

In *Hewson v Downs*[62] the reasoning in *Parry v Cleaver* was applied to the effect that state retirement pensions are not deductible.

---

58. It is interesting to note that Lord Reid referred (at pp. 19-20) to s.2(1), Fatal Accidents Act 1959 (the Act then applicable) which stated that in an action thereunder insurance monies, benefits, pensions or gratuities payable as a result of the death in question are to be disregarded in the assessment of damages. He went on to say in effect that, if in an action under that statute pensions are disregarded, they should not be taken into account in a common law action.
59. *Ibid.*, p. 16.
60. That is the "fruit, through insurance, of all the money which was set aside in the past work". According to Lord Templeman in *Smoker v L.F.C.D.A.* [1991] 2 All E.R. 449 (at p. 457), the tortfeasor should not be allowed to appropriate that fruit.
61. *Smoker v London Fire and Civil Defence Authority* [1991] 2 All E.R. 449; *Wood v British Coal Corp.* [1991] 2 W.L.R. 1052 (where *Parry v Cleaver* was applied).
62. [1970] 1 Q.B. 73.

*Ex gratia pensions*

According to *Cunningham v Harrison*,[63] an *"ex gratia"* pension, which the employer of the injured plaintiff has paid, is not considered.

### (ii) Insurance monies

Payments under private insurance taken by the plaintiff or his family are not deductible (*Parry v Cleaver*) because deducting them would be unjust and unreasonable since the tortfeasor would benefit from the plaintiff's prudence in taking out a policy and premiums thereon; therefore, the plaintiff should not be left worse off than if he had never insured.

### (iii) Charitable payments, e.g., a disaster fund raised by workmates

Such payments to the plaintiff are not deductible because generosity must be encouraged (*Redpath v Belfast and County Down Railway*[64]), otherwise the "springs of private charity" will largely or entirely dry up.[65] In *Parry v Cleaver* Lord Reid pointed out that deduction of charitable payments from a plaintiff's damages to the benefit of the tortfeasor would outrage the sense of justice of the ordinary person, and so be against public policy.[66]

Also, where proceeds of an accident insurance policy (taken out by the employer who is the defendant) are used to make a benevolent payment, such payment will not be deducted.[67]

## A note - international transport by air, road and sea

The Carriage by Air Act 1961, Carriage of Passengers by Road Act 1974 and Merchant Shipping Act 1979 have imposed a limit on the damages awarded for personal injury or death relating to such modes of international transport.

---

63. [1973] Q.B. 942.
64. [1947] N.I. 167.
65. *Ibid.*, at p. 170.
66. [1970] A.C. 1, at p. 14.
67. *McCamley v Cammell Laird Ltd.* [1990] 1 All E.R. 854.

## 2. The award of damages for death

In respect of death two statutes are concerned: the Law Reform (Miscellaneous Provisions) Act 1934 and the Fatal Accidents Act 1976. Where a person is suing or is being sued, e.g., for negligence, and he dies, according to s.1(1), Law Reform (Miscellaneous Provisions) Act 1934, the cause of action will survive for the benefit of, or against, his estate. Also, where the dead person was the cause of another person's death or died as a result of someone else's negligence, action can be taken against, or by, his estate. Additionally, where a person dies as a result of, for example, negligent driving by another person, the dependants of the dead person can sue the negligent party under the Fatal Accidents Act 1976.

*Action by the deceased's estate*

At common law the position used to be that if a person was involved in an action (in tort), whether as a plaintiff or as a defendant, and he died, the action died with him.[68]

But that rule was removed by the Law Reform (Miscellaneous Provisions) Act 1934, s.1 of which provides that "all causes of action subsisting against, or, vested in [the deceased] shall survive against, or, as the case may be, for the benefit of, his estate".

### What can be claimed

The deceased's estate can claim the following:

(i) damages for non-pecuniary losses like pain and suffering and loss of amenity before the deceased died;

(ii) pecuniary losses, e.g., loss of earnings[69] and medical expenses;[70] and

(iii) funeral expenses.

---

68. In accordance with the maxim, *"Actio personalis moritur cum persona"*.
69. *Murray v Shuter* [1976] Q.B. 972; [1975] 3 All E.R. 375.
70. *Rose v Ford* [1937] A.C. 826; [1937] 3 All E.R. 359.

**What cannot be claimed**

However, the right of the dead person's estate to claim damages is limited in the following ways:

(i) No claim can be made for loss of income during the period after the death.[71] But, it must be noted that if the deceased's estate and dependants are the same persons, they can recover, under the Fatal Accidents Act 1976, damages for loss of earnings after the death. Double compensation is thereby avoided.[72]

(ii) No damages can be claimed for loss of amenity after the death; pain and suffering during the last brief moments before the death are also not claimable because they are deemed as forming part of the death.[73]

(iii) Exemplary damages cannot be claimed.[74]

(iv) The right of the deceased person to claim damages for bereavement before he died does not pass on to his estate.[75]

(v) An action for defamation dies with the deceased defamed person.

One unsatisfactory feature of the present position regarding claims by the deceased's estate[76] is that, although the estate's claim for loss of expectation of life was replaced by an award for bereavement under the Fatal Accidents Act 1976 (as amended by the Administration of Justice Act 1982), only spouses and parents of children unmarried and under the age of majority

---

71. S.1(2)(a)(ii), Law Reform (Miscellaneous Provisions) Act 1934; see also s.4(2), Administration of Justice Act 1982). Furthermore, if the victim dies instantaneously, his estate can recover, under the 1934 Act, only funeral expenses (s.1(2)(c)).
72. *Gammel v Wilson* [1982] A.C. 27.
73. *Hicks v Chief Constable of S. Yorkshire* [1992] 2 All E.R. 65. See also, A.Unger, "Pain and Anger", *New Law Journal*, March 20, 1992, 394.
74. S.4(2), Administration of Justice Act 1982.
75. S.4(1), Administration of Justice Act 1982. Damages for bereavement and exemplary damages are not claimable by a deceased's estate because those two claims are personal to the deceased person.
76. Unger, *op. cit.*

can claim for such bereavement.[77] Parents of deceased "children" who are unmarried but not minors have little to claim: if they cannot establish loss of dependency under the Fatal Accidents Act 1976, they can claim only funeral expenses.[78] Moreover, the damages for bereavement, currently £7,500, may be said to be insufficient in the case of parents who cannot establish loss of dependency resulting from their child's death because human life should be considered by the law as of more value and not otherwise. Unger,[79] after referring to the position in Scotland where "loss of society" can be claimed by children and parents (and the claim by parents is not limited by the age of the child in question), recommends the creation of: (a) an award recognising relatives' injured feelings (i.e., compensating for grief) "available to all those who have suffered grief and not just to those who fall within a very narrow concept of the nuclear family"; and/or (b) an award recognising that life has a value. Unger's first suggestion, however, is unlikely to be favoured because it would make too broad the class of claimants, especially where a deceased person has numerous relatives, all of whom suffer grief (which relatives usually suffer if another relative dies). What amount of grief, therefore, must a relative suffer before he can claim?

It is interesting to note that, in the calculation of the damages which the deceased's estate will recover, any *loss* (e.g., the termination of an annuity payment on the death of the victim) or gain (e.g., from a life insurance policy) to the estate as a result of the death are not considered.[80]

*Action by the dependants*

The Fatal Accidents Act 1976, which consolidated previous legislation, gives a new right of action to the dependants of the deceased. The action is for the loss of their dependency (loss of their breadwinner).

---

77. In the case of illegitimate children only the mother can claim therefor: s.1A, Fatal Accidents Act 1976.
78. See *Hicks v Wright*.
79. *Op. cit.*
80. S.1(2)(c), Law Reform (Miscellaneous Provisions) Act 1934.

**Requirements**

(i) According to s.1(1), Fatal Accidents Act 1976, the death should have been "caused by such wrongful act, neglect or default which is such as would (if death had not ensued) have entitled the person injured to maintain an action and recover damages in respect thereof". In other words, if the dead person would not have had any action, his dependants cannot have one. Thus, any defence pleadable against him can be pleaded against his dependants, as occurred in, for example, *Cork v Kirby Maclean*,[81] a case on contributory negligence. Where one of the deceased's dependants was partly responsible for the death (i.e., was contributorily negligent), his own share of the damages for loss of dependency will be reduced accordingly;[82] that of the other dependants will not be affected.[83]

(ii) Persons who can bring an action are listed in s.1(3). They are:

- spouses and former spouses (s.1(3)(a)),
- common-law spouses for two years (i.e., persons cohabiting as husband and wife for two years immediately before the death (s.1(3)(b)),
- a parent or other ascendant of the deceased or person treated as a parent by the deceased (s.1(3)(c) and (d)),
- any child (adopted, illegitimate, etc.) or other descendant of the deceased or any person not the deceased's child but treated by him, in respect of his marriage, as a child of the family (s.1(3)(e) and (f)), and
- any brother, sister, aunt or uncle of the deceased and his or her issue

81. [1952] 2 All E.R 402.
82. S.5, Fatal Accidents Act 1976.
83. *Dodds v Dodds* [1978] 2 All E.R. 539; [1978] Q.B. 543. He may also have to pay a contribution if the other tortfeasor applies to the Court under the Civil Liability (Contribution) Act 1978.

(s.1(3)(g)).[84]

Section 1(3) is still not wide enough because s.1(3)(f), as it stands, means that, if single persons or childless cohabitees, who are financially supporting a non-relative (not treated by them as a "child of the family"), die untimely, that dependant cannot claim for loss of dependency under the Act. It is no answer that such a dependant can, under the Inheritance (Provision for Family and Dependants) Act 1975, apply to the Court for reasonable provision to be made for him out of the estate of the deceased person since dependant relatives can also apply under that 1975 statute.[85]

---

84. This section has widened the range of claimants and follows recommendations of the Law Commission (see *Law Commission's Report on Personal Injury Litigation - Assessment of Damages* (Law Commission No. 56, 1973), paras. 257, 259 and 262(c)) and of the Pearson Commission (see *Report of the Royal Commission on Civil Liability and Compensation for Personal Injury* (Cmnd. 7054-I), 1978, para. 404). Previously only a person married to the deceased at the time of his death, parents and grandparents of the deceased, and children and grandchildren of the deceased could claim. On the inclusion of divorced persons, the Law Commission stated (*Law Commission No. 56 (1973)*, para. 259): "A divorced wife who has been awarded maintenance, particularly one who has been divorced against her will after five years' separation, may well suffer serious hardship if her former husband is killed and she is not recognised as a dependant for the purposes of a claim under the Fatal Accidents Acts. We, therefore, feel there are real grounds which justify our recommending that a divorced wife be accorded the status of a dependant. Because a divorced husband may have been receiving maintenance from his former wife we think that the class of dependants should be extended to a divorced husband as well."

85. Section 1(1) of that Act provides:
"(1) Where after the commencement of this Act a person dies domiciled in England and Wales and is survived by any of the following persons: -
(a) the wife or husband of the deceased;
(b) a former wife or husband of the deceased who has not remarried;
(c) a child of the deceased;
(d) any person (not being a child of the deceased) who, in the case of any marriage to which the deceased was at any time a party, was treated by the deceased as a child of the family in relation to that marriage;
(e) any person (not being a person included in the foregoing paragraphs of this subsection) who immediately before the death of the deceased was being maintained, either wholly or partly, by the deceased;
that person may apply to the court for an order under section 2 of this Act on the ground that the disposition of the deceased's estate effected by his will or the law relating to intestacy, or the combination of his will and that law, is not such as to make reasonable financial provision for the applicant."

It should be noted that homosexual partners are also not included. Is the law not discriminatory or guilty of double-standards here? Why should it favour cohabitees but not homosexual partners? It is admitted that this is not the place for a law-morality debate; but, it would be desirable for the law to be consistent: it must either allow or disallow both types of partners to claim under the Act.

A case that illustrates the position of the ex-wife claimant is *Shepherd v Post Office*.[86] In that case Shepherd ("S") was a dependant of the deceased who died in a fatal accident. She had been married to him but they divorced. She then remarried. After the failure of that second marriage, she went back to live with her first husband, the deceased. The Court of Appeal dismissed the argument of the defendant that S could not claim under the Fatal Accidents Act 1976 because she had remarried and was, therefore, not a former wife (within s.1(3)(a)) and also because her period of cohabitation with the deceased after her second marriage had collapsed was under two years before he died. It was held that, as the Act did not specify whether the claimant must be involved in only one marriage, S was clearly an ex-wife. Therefore, where an ex-wife cohabits with her former husband before he dies, the period of cohabitation is irrelevant because that is not a requirement in the case of former spouses who are claiming under the Act.

The suit is brought by the deceased's personal representatives (s.1(1)), or, if six months have passed after the appointment of those personal representatives, by any dependant of the deceased on his own behalf or that of others (s.2(2)).[87]

(iii) The claimant must also show actual financial dependence on the deceased. What is claimable is non-business financial loss. Business financial loss or lost business opportunities are not loss of financial dependency (loss of support) and, so, are not claimable. *Burgess v Florence Nightingale Hospital for Gentlewomen*[88] illustrates this. There the plaintiff's wife was his professional dancing partner; she died as a result of the defendant's negligence. The plaintiff's claim for financial loss resulting from the death of his wife was successful because he was able to show such loss: he lived together with the deceased as husband and wife with their joint income coming from demonstration fees and competition prizes, and they shared their

86. *The Times*, June 15, 1995.
87. See Appendix 3, *post*.
88. [1955] 1 Q.B. 349.

expenses. Through that sharing they conferred a benefit on each other, a benefit arising from their being married, and which was claimable under the Fatal Accidents Act 1846. He (the plaintiff), however, could not recover damages for the loss of earnings due to his professional relationship with his wife being interrupted. That loss was not loss of financial dependency. Another illustration is *Malyon v Plummer*.[89] There the widow of the deceased had been receiving £600 *per annum* for the services she gave to her husband's firm. Those services were assessed by the court as worth £200 *per annum*. Her actual loss of dependency (her non-business financial loss) was, therefore, £400 (not £600) *per annum*.

**What the dependants can claim**

(a) A dependant can claim for loss of actual dependency and also for loss of a potential future dependency. In *Taff Vale Railway v Jenkins*,[90] where the House of Lords emphasised that the expectation of pecuniary benefits must be reasonable, a parent successfully recovered when his daughter, aged 16, who had almost finished her dressmaking apprenticeship, died.[91]

(b) A spouse can claim damages for *bereavement* (currently £7,500)[92] if the dead person is his/her spouse; the parents of a child (but only the mother of an illegitimate child) who is a minor and unmarried can claim such damages for bereavement if that child dies (s.1A).

(c) *Funeral expenses* can also be claimed if they are actually incurred: s.3(5).

---

89. [1964] 1 Q.B. 330.
90. [1913] A.C. 1.
91. In the case of a minor who, before his death, is unmarried and supporting his parents, his parents' damages for loss of dependency may be reduced because of the uncertainty of the financial support continuing if he does not die - he might get married and from then on either stop or reduce that financial support.
92. The amount may be changed by the Lord Chancellor by statutory instrument: s.1A(5), Fatal Accidents Act 1976.

## The amount of damages for loss of dependency

It has already been noted that, if after the accident the deceased person lived for a while, his estate can recover pecuniary losses suffered during that period under the Law Reform (Miscellaneous Provisions) Act 1934.

What is recoverable in a fatal accident claim is the pecuniary loss suffered as from the date of death. In *Mallet v McMonagle*[93] Lord Diplock stated the aim of an award of damages under the Fatal Accidents Act 1976: it is to compensate the dependants for their loss of dependency over the estimated period of that dependency.

Again, just as in the case of a personal injuries action, the multiplier method is used in the assessment of damages. But, here the multiplier is assessed (not as at the date of trial but) as at the date of death because, as Lord Fraser said in *Cookson v Knowles*,[94] "everything that might have happened to the deceased after that date remains uncertain."

(a) The starting figure is the deceased's net earnings (i.e., earnings after deduction of tax and national insurance) are calculated. Promotion prospects may be taken into account.

(b) Then from this sum is deducted the amount he would have spent on his personal living expenses (but, his share of the joint expenses, e.g., payments of rent or mortgage, car-running expenses and other general household expenses, are not deducted).

(c) The appropriate multiplier is then applied. In the case of a claimant/dependant who is earning the amount of dependency will be the amount of money, if any, used by the deceased to support her or as expenditure on her.[95] Thus, it is irrelevant whether the claimant has her own income.

Where an infant dependant has lost its mother's services, the multiplicand is usually calculated by taking the notional nanny's net-in-hand wages: *Corbett v Barking, Havering and Brentwood Health Authority*.[96] According to that case (the claimant being a child) the multiplier should be

93. [1970] A.C. 166.
94. [1978] 2 All E.R. 604, at 614-5.
95. *Shiels v Cruikshank* [1953] 1 All E.R. 874.
96. [1991] 1 All E.R. 498.

assessed, not at the date of the trial but rather, at the date the mother died. In so doing, certain essential factors must be considered such as the probability of the infant not staying alive to benefit from the support of his mother and also his continuing to require that care. This was why the multiplier used by the trial judge was raised by the Court of Appeal to 15 as 12 was considered too low in respect of the pre-trial damages. As regards the post-trial damages, a multiplier of 3.5 was applied. In increasing the multiplier to 15 in respect of the pre-trial damages, the Court of Appeal took account of the chance that the dependant would go on to tertiary education when he attained the age of 18.

It is, therefore, to be noted that the likelihood of a child claimant to go on to tertiary education or to leave school on attaining 16 is also considered.

(d) After the assessment of the multiplier, the amount which is awarded is divided into *special damages* (awarded for loss/es before trial) and *general damages* (for the post-trial loss/es). Whereas special damages attract interest, general damages do not.

### Re-marriage of a widow

No account is taken by the court of a widow's remarriage or prospects of remarriage when assessing her claim in respect of the death of her husband (s.3(3), Fatal Accidents Act 1976, as amended by the Administration of Justice Act 1982). This is objectionable because (a) it can result in over-compensation in some cases, and (b) it is unsatisfactory in that it omitted widowers, whose prospects of re-marriage also ought to be disregarded in assessing damages under the Fatal Accidents Act 1976.

Also, s.3(4) of the Act provides that in assessing the damages of a cohabitee-dependant, account must be taken of the fact that a cohabitee has no enforceable right, as a result of their cohabitation, to be financially supported by the deceased. The implication of s.3(3) and (4) is, therefore, that a cohabitee's prospects of marriage are to be taken into consideration, as happened in *Greenhalgh v Smith and Shaw Transport*.[97] In that case a 24-year-old cohabitee-dependant had her prospects of marriage taken into account with the effect that her damages were reduced. It is submitted the law

---

97. (1994) C.L.Y. 380.

is here discriminating against cohabitees. Is the reason the primacy of marriage? If so, then should cohabitees be allowed to claim at all?

Although the Act does not say that a widower's prospects of remarriage will be ignored, it is submitted that the widower (unlike a cohabitee) will not be disadvantaged for two reasons: first, a husband, depending on the circumstances, has an enforceable right to financial support from his spouse and, secondly, any benefits which a widower's new wife will bring to the family can be disregarded under s.4, Fatal Accidents Act 1976.[98] Actually in one case, *Tapp v County Bus (South West) Ltd.*,[99] the reasoning in *Stanley v Saddique* (a case looked at in the section on deductions below) was applied to the effect that a widower's prospects of remarriage were not considered in the assessment of his damages.

**Apportionment of damages between dependants (s.3(1) and (2))**

According to s.3(1), "such damages may be awarded as are proportioned to the injury resulting from the death to the dependants respectively ...". Thus, where a dependant has suffered no loss under s.3, there can be no loss to be assessed. The question arose in *Auty and Others v National Coal Board*,[100] where, among other things, the fourth plaintiff's husband was killed when he was 55 years old. She would have received, under the Mineworkers' Pension Scheme, a widow's pension ("pension A") if her husband had died in service or before he reached 65. She would also have been entitled to receive a widow's pension ("pension B") if he had died after his retirement. Because he died at 55, i.e., in service and before he was 65, she received pension A but not pension B. Her argument was that she was entitled to claim (by way of loss of dependency) an amount which represented her losing the chance to claim a post-retirement widow's pension. If that was a loss and she could claim it, then by virtue of s.4, that benefit would have to be ignored in the assessment of damages.[101] However, the Court of Appeal disagreed with her because she was already receiving a widow's pension under the pensions

98. *Stanley v Saddique* [1992] 1 Q.B. 330; [1991] 2 W.L.R. 459; [1991] 1 All E.R 529.
99. November 5, 1991, unreported.
100. [1985] 1 W.L.R. 784.
101. The actual words of s.4, Fatal Accidents Act 1976, as amended, are: "In assessing damages in respect of a person's death in an action under this Act, benefits which have accrued or will or may accrue to any person from his estate or otherwise as a result of his death shall be disregarded."

scheme in question, and so she had suffered no loss under s.3(1) and was not entitled to any benefit which could be disregarded under s.4 in assessing damages. Waller L.J. explained the court's decision thus (at p. 799):

> "On the death of her husband, it is clear that Mrs. Popow qualified for, and received, a widow's pension. Furthermore her dependency was assessed by ignoring the amount of that pension. No part of her dependency either then or thereafter could arise from lack of a widow's pension because she continued to be in receipt of one. Put another way, she cannot claim for loss of an opportunity to obtain a widow's pension at a later date when she is already in receipt of a widow's pension."

## Deductions

### Section 4

According to s.4, Fatal Accidents Act 1976, the benefits which have accrued or will, or may, accrue to any person from the estate of the deceased or otherwise as a result of the death are to be disregarded when damages are being assessed.[102]

In *Pidduck v Eastern Scottish Omnibuses Ltd.*[103] the defendants' coach was involved in a road accident. The plaintiff, a retired bank employee, was a passenger in that coach. He was killed in the accident. After retirement he was receiving an occupational pension. Following his death, his widow received a widow's allowance payable under the same occupational pension scheme. It was held that the widow's allowance was a benefit that accrued to her as a result of her husband's death and, so, was to be disregarded under section 4, Fatal Accidents Act 1976 in the assessment of damages for her loss

---

102. Before the Fatal Accidents Act 1976, benefits not resulting from the death were to be disregarded in the assessment of damages. In *Hay v Hughes* [1975] 1 All E.R. 257 two boys, aged four and a half and two and a half, respectively, whose parents were killed in an accident, brought an action for loss of dependency on their father and the loss of their mother's services. Their grandmother's provision of care for them (a gratuitous, benevolent act) in replacement of that of their mother was compensable: it was not taken into account in assessing damages because it was a service not resulting from the mother's death.

103. [1990] 1 W.L.R. 993.

of dependency. Purchas L.J. said, at page 997:

> "The benefit which the widow received before the death was the financial support she received from her husband. It was incidental that her husband's financial source was another provision under the scheme. The benefits which she received after the death were benefits which were payable directly to her by the Trustees of the scheme, a right which accrued to her as a direct result of the death."

His Lordship then, at page 998, distinguished *Auty and Others v National Coal Board* from this case by saying that in *Auty* "the application of section 4 of the Act to exclude the first widow's pension received by Mrs. Popow from the calculation of damages under the Act was never in question".

In *Stanley v Saddique* the plaintiff was born a year after his mother had left her husband to cohabit with the plaintiff's father. After his mother was killed in a motor accident, his father, who had assumed responsibility for him fully, married another woman. The plaintiff was absorbed into the family: he was provided with a stable home. His step-mother's motherly services for him were of a much higher quality than the plaintiff's own mother could have provided if she had not died. When he sued (through his father and next friend) for loss of dependency on his mother, the Court of Appeal held that the benefits that had accrued to the plaintiff as a result of his being absorbed into a family unit (which consisted of his father, step-mother and step-brother and step-sisters) were benefits to be completely disregarded in assessing the damages for loss of dependency. This was because those benefits accrued as a result of the death of the plaintiff's own mother and were covered by s.4, which was not limited to direct pecuniary benefits. But, since the plaintiff's own mother's services to him in her lifetime were unreliable and it was not certain that they would have continued if she had lived, the award of damages was reduced by the Court from a total of £32,536 to £15,000.

In *Mehmet v Perry*[104] a family lost the services of the deceased lady as a wife and mother. The damages for loss of dependency were calculated according to the wages that the husband lost in giving up his job in order to look after the children at home.

*Hayden v Hayden*,[105] however, seems a difficult case. There the plaintiff was four years old. Her father negligently drove a car in which her

---

104. [1977] 2 All E.R. 529.
105. [1992] 4 All E.R. 681.

mother was a passenger; her mother was killed as a result. After the death, the plaintiff's father gave up his work to look after her. An action was brought by the plaintiff against her father for, among other things, damages under the Fatal Accidents Act 1976 for loss of her mother's services. There was evidence by the plaintiff of how much it would cost to hire a full-time nanny to care for her until she was 11 years old and after that the costs of a part-time nanny. But, the trial judge, in assessing damages under s.3(1), did take into account the father's provision of replacement care for the plaintiff between the date of her mother's death and the date of trial. Nevertheless, he still awarded the plaintiff damages of £20,000 under s.3(1) because her claim was not entirely defeated by the defendant's services. The defendant appealed on the ground that the damages were too much. The plaintiff also cross-appealed arguing that (a) the damages were too low, and (b) her father's replacement services for her after her mother's death were benefits that accrued to her as a result of the death and should, according to s.4, have been disregarded in the assessment of damages.

The Court of Appeal held first that, though the trial judge was entitled to take into account the father's replacement services so as to reduce the father's liability, the £20,000 damages were reasonable as the judge was right to award the plaintiff damages for loss of such of her mother's services as her father's services had not replaced. Secondly, as regards s.4, the father's replacement services were not benefits accruing as a result of the death of the plaintiff's mother because it was his parental duty to provide those services, some of which he had been providing before the mother's death.

*Comment*

1. In relation to s.4 this decision seems logical. But, it is unsatisfactory because it favours the defendant tortfeasor unfairly to the detriment of the plaintiff. There is nothing compelling the defendant to quit his job in order to care for the plaintiff. He chose to do so. If he had chosen instead to stay in his job but employ a nanny or persuade a relative to provide the caring, the cost of providing that care would have been recoverable (it would not have been taken into account in assessing the damages). Authority for that is *Regan v Williamson*,[106] where, following the death of the mother of the

---

106. [1976] 1 W.L.R. 305.

children in question, the care of those children by an aunt during the day and their care during the night were all compensable. Therefore, the care which a tortfeasor-parent chooses to provide and that which another relative chooses to provide are both resultant upon the death of the person who was at first providing that care, within s.4, Fatal Accidents Act 1976.

2. (This part of the comment also relates to *Hunt v Severs*, already looked at above.) The ramifications of the decision for insurers can be serious: in future an insured defendant who is also a spouse or parent of the plaintiff is likely to advise the plaintiff to hire professional care, the cost of which is claimable. The courts will be unlikely to say that hiring such professional help instead of the tortfeasor-defendant giving up his job to look after the plaintiff is failure by the plaintiff to mitigate his loss through unreasonable action. It would be subtle but unjustifiable interference by the courts on a plaintiff's freedom of choice (which is exercised reasonably) if they hold that there has been a failure to mitigate loss in such circumstances.

3. According to Rogers,[107] referring to *Hunt v Severs*:

> "... by way of analogy with the law on personal injury, it now seems that there is a simpler answer to the conundrum presented by *Hayden*. Since damages for substitute care would be held on trust for the carer, that necessarily precludes any claim where the carer is the tortfeasor".

This, it is submitted, is still unsatisfactory because of the preclusion of the claim where the tortfeasor himself is the carer in that, if no award is made (in view of the preclusion), it does not provide an answer to the question of how the plaintiff would manage if the tortfeasor-carer stops providing that care because, for example, he dies. An award, therefore, ought to be made even where the tortfeasor himself is the carer. That money can then be ordered to be held on trust so that, if the carer-husband (the tortfeasor), for example, leaves the plaintiff, there will be some money available to be used to care for the plaintiff, the victim of the tort. But, if the victim dies before any such event happens, that money will revert to the carer or his insurers.

---

107. See *Winfield and Jolowicz on Tort*, 1994, p. 696.

*Stanley v Saddique distinguished from Hayden v Hayden*

1. In *Stanley v Saddique* the death resulted in a marriage of the father to another woman. But in *Hayden v Hayden* the father was already married to the deceased mother of the child and the father was simply carrying on (although to a greater extent) his duties as a parent father.[108]

2. Whereas in *Stanley v Saddique* the child's parents were not married at the time of the death of the mother but the father soon married another woman, in *Hayden v Hayden* the parents were married at the time of the mother's death.[109]

3. Unlike *Stanley v Saddique*, in *Hayden v Hayden* the father of the child (the provider of the care) was the tortfeasor himself.

**A problem situation**

One further issue needs to be considered. If a deceased person, in his lifetime, was supporting a dependant from a capital sum and, upon his death, that dependant inherits the capital sum, can he claim for loss of dependency? It is submitted that, on grounds of public policy, he should not be allowed to recover because he has suffered no loss and there is a danger here of overcompensation. *Wood v Bentall Simplex*[110] suggests no loss has been suffered by such a dependant. In that case the plaintiff was the widow of one of the two people who died as a result of the negligence of the defendant. Liability was admitted by the defendants. Before he died, the husband of the plaintiff and his brother had both worked hard to build up the farming business of their family. According to the terms of their partnership, each of them could take out a salary of £20,319 a year. However, they did not do so for three years (1980-1982). Instead, the plaintiff's husband drew an average salary of £3,000 a year. In addition, the deceased and his family lived in a house, the improvement, maintenance and running costs of which were met by the partnership. A substantial part of the partnership's profits was used to pay off debts and in improving the farm and the buildings. That resulted in

108. According to Sir David Croom-Johnson in *Hayden v Hayden*.
109. See Brazier (ed.), *Street on Tort*, 1993, p. 542.
110. [1992] 1 P.I.Q.R. 332; The Times, March 3, 1993.

substantial improvement of the capital value of the business' assets. Thus, at the date of the death of the deceased the value of the fixed and current assets of the business was £597,503, of which £214,096 was apportioned to the share of the deceased. Because the plaintiff and her children, the dependants of the deceased, could not receive the full interest of the deceased in the farm unless the whole farm was sold, the plaintiff accepted from the administrators of the deceased's estate the house in which she lived with her children (the house having been valued at £50,000). That was in part satisfaction of her interest. 64 acres of grassland were transferred to trustees for the benefit of the deceased's children, the remainder of the deceased's share of the assets were left in the business and the respondent (the plaintiff) received in return a 12.5% share of the profits. Later she received as her share (which became 20% afterwards) approximately £5,000 a year.

Although the defendants admitted liability for the deceased's death, they argued (a) that the deceased was contributorily negligent and (b) that the loss to the deceased's dependants ought to be reduced by taking into account the income from the assets that they inherited (in other words, the income should be taken into account in assessing the size of the loss under s.3(1) of the Fatal Accidents Act 1976, which would have the effect of reducing the dependants' damages). On the facts the judge rejected both arguments and awarded the plaintiff a total of £224,593. When the defendants appealed, the Court of Appeal dismissed their appeal. The Court held that, in assessing the loss under s.3(1) of the Act, the provisions of s.4(1) were relevant. Also, where dependants claimed for loss of the expectation of a pecuniary benefit which was the very thing they had been enjoying by reason of the death, there was no loss; however, where there was clearly established a loss from one source, the fact that loss might be made good from another source by using a benefit received from the deceased's estate was to be disregarded in assessing the loss (in accordance with s.4).

## Limitation of actions

(i) Actions under the Fatal Accidents Act 1976 must be commenced within three years starting from the date of death or date of knowledge of the dependant in question (s.12(2), Limitation Act 1980).

(ii) In the case of two or more claimants, time runs against each of them separately (i.e., severally rather than jointly): s.13(1), Limitation Act 1980.

(iii) Finally, it must be noted that, according to section 33, Limitation Act 1980, the court has discretion to extend the period of limitation if it has expired, having regard to all the circumstances.

**Exercises**

1. S was knocked unconscious by a van negligently driven by D. S suffered serious injuries and would remain in bed for the rest of her life. She was aged 29 at the time of the accident. Her annual salary was £20,000 but she had very high hopes of promotion and a much bigger salary within eight years. She would not have had to go into retirement until she was 60 years old. As a result of the accident she was expected not to live beyond 61. She was bedridden for two years before the trial and was receiving 24-hour nursing care costing £12,000 a year. She would need such care until she dies. A week before trial D, one of the three nurses looking after S, married her and decided to give up his job in order to look after her at home full-time.

   Advise S and D.

2. Last year David died as a result of injuries sustained in a road accident caused by the negligent driving of Mrs. Carelessa. He was in hospital in a coma for three months before he died. David had been a struggling actor earning £12,000 a year. However, he had high hopes of being signed up for twenty episodes of a soap opera which could net him at least £250,000 over three years. After that, assuming things went well, he expected to retire from acting and open a betting shop. When he died, he was 40 years old. He had a five year old son called Winston who had relied wholly on David for material support. Prior to his death David had cohabited with Winnie for twenty-three months. Winnie was not Winston's mother. Winnie had also been dependant on David until his untimely death. Winston and Winnie have commenced legal proceedings against Mrs. Carelessa who has admitted liability.

   Advise Mrs. Carelessa on her liability in damages.

# 7 Other aspects of compensatory damages

## Introduction

Compensatory damages for breach of contract and also for tort have a much wider scope than those already discussed. Such damages are also awarded for mental distress and physical inconvenience (in both contract and tort) and loss of reputation and other losses in tort. These other compensatory damages will now be considered.

## Mental distress

Mental distress is not classified as physical injury because it is different from physical illness or mental illness like mental shock. It refers to other states like anxiety, worry, disappointment, fear, grief, upset, annoyance, etc. The courts have traditionally been unwilling to award damages for mental distress, especially, for breach of contract. For reasons like policy and the problem of accurate assessment they are still reluctant to award such damages in certain cases today for both torts and breach of contract.

### A. Contract

The award of damages for expectation loss places the injured party to a broken contract in the position, so far as money can, that he would have enjoyed if the contract had been performed. It follows, therefore, that one might expect the injured party to be provided with compensation for any distress, injured feelings, etc., caused to him by the breach. However, damages are generally not available for such non-pecuniary loss, according to *Addis v Gramophone Co. Ltd.*[1] The case concerned the wrongful

---

1. [1909] A.C. 488.

dismissal of the defendant company's manager. The latter claimed compensation for loss of commission and a sum for the wrongful dismissal which had been carried out in a harsh and humiliating manner. The House of Lords awarded compensation for the first head but not the second, Lord Loreburn stating that, where there was a dismissal without notice, the employer ought to pay an indemnity but that indemnity could not include compensation for the injured feelings of the servant dismissed.

Confirmation of the general rule, and the explanation for it, was given by the Court of Appeal in *Watts v Morrow*.[2] Bingham L.J. said (at page 959):

> "A contract-breaker is not in general liable for any distress, frustration, anxiety, displeasure, vexation, tension or aggravation which his breach of contract may cause to the innocent party. This rule is not, I think, founded on the assumption that such reactions are not foreseeable, which they surely are or may be, but on considerations of policy."

Such reactions almost inevitably accompany expectations based on promises so that a contracting party must be deemed to take the risk of experiencing them for otherwise damages for mental distress would nearly always be awarded in claims for breach of contract.

In addition to *Watts v Morrow*, other recent decisions confirm this general rule[3] which is justified by the problems associated with quantifying such damage and the possibility of false claims. However, although it is clear that such damages are not available where the object of the contract was simply carrying on a commercial activity with a view to profit,[4] the rule is not absolute and exceptions to it have evolved in two restricted areas.

## 1. Contracts to provide entertainment or enjoyment or freedom from distress

The first concerns contracts which contain an implied term to the effect that

---

2. [1991] 4 All E.R. 937.
3. *Hayes v James & Charles Dodd* [1990] 2 All E.R. 815, (breach of contract leading to failure of a business), *McConville v Barclays Bank*, *The Times*, October 13, 1993, (bank wrongly debiting customer's account), *R v Investors Compensation Scheme, ex. p. Bowden* [1994] 1 All E.R. 525, (breach of contract by broker causing financial loss to client).
4. Staughton L.J., in *Hayes v James & Charles Dodd* [1990] 2 All E.R. 815.

the promisor undertakes to give the promisee an enjoyable time by the provision of services or to relieve the promisee from distress. Here a claim for compensation for breach of such a term will succeed. A number of illustrations will now be given of this first category.

*Contracts to provide entertainment or enjoyment*

*Jarvis v Swan Tours Ltd.*[5] concerned a claim by the plaintiff for a breach of contract by the defendant holiday tour company which had failed to provide the facilities and entertainment described in the brochure as part of a skiing holiday. Lord Denning M.R. considered that, despite the problems associated with quantifying the loss, the general rule preventing the award of damages for distress was out-of-date and that, "in a proper case", damages for mental distress should be recoverable in contract. One such case would be a contract for a holiday or any other contract to provide entertainment and enjoyment. The plaintiff was entitled to damages not merely to cover the cost of the holiday but also for the lack of facilities and consequent loss of enjoyment.[6]

In the recent case of *Watts v Morrow*[7] Bingham L.J. also recognised the exception laid down by Lord Denning :

> "Where the very object of a contract is to provide pleasure, relaxation, peace of mind or freedom from molestation, damages will be awarded if the fruit of the contract is not provided or if the contrary result is procured instead. If the law did not cater for this exceptional category of case it would be defective."

In the case the plaintiffs bought a house having relied on the defendant's defective survey. The house was in need of major repairs but the Court of Appeal was unwilling to take a broad view of the exceptional category.

---

5. [1973] 1 All E.R. 71.
6. See also *Jackson v Horizon Holidays* [1975] 1 W.L.R. 1468 (sub-standard holiday), *Cook v Spanish Holiday Tours Ltd., The Times*, Feb 6, 1960 (breach of contract by travel agent to provide honeymoon accommodation), *Chandle v East African Airways Corp.* [1964] E.A. 78 (failure to transport guests to wedding), *Diesen v Samson* [1971] S.L.T. 49 (breach of contract to take wedding photographs), *Bernstein v Pamson Motors Ltd.* [1987] 2 All E.R. 220 (broken down new car which caused the buyer to suffer "a totally spoilt day comprising nothing but vexation)".
7. [1991] 4 All E.R. 937, 960.

Such a contract was not one to provide pleasure, peace of mind or freedom from molestation. Note, however, that a sum was awarded for the distress arising out of the inconvenience caused by the breach, a topic to be looked at below.

*Loss of amenity*

Compensation for loss of amenity was awarded to the plaintiff for a swimming pool, built contrary to specifications, in *Ruxley Electronics v Forsyth.*[8] Lord Lloyd was in agreement with Judge Diamond, who heard the case at first instance and took the view that the contract was one "for the provision of a pleasurable amenity" and, thus, within the exception as laid down in *Jarvis*. Lord Lloyd did not consider such an award to represent a further inroad on the general rule in *Addis v Gramophone Co. Ltd.*, instead preferring to regard it "as a logical application or adaptation of the existing exception to a new situation". In the same case Lord Mustill argued that in order to reflect the true loss suffered by the injured party, "the law must cater for those occasions where the value of the promise to the promisee exceeds the financial enhancement of his position which full performance will secure". Such "excess"[9] is not usually susceptible to precise valuation in monetary terms because it represents a personal, subjective and non-monetary gain. Even so the law should recognise it when it exists and provide compensation to the promisee when misperformance amounting to breach causes such a loss. In so doing the court is protecting the consumer's expectation interest. He saw no reason why the fact that quantification of such an intangible loss should act as a barrier to recovery.

*Freedom from distress*

An illustration of a contract to provide freedom from distress or molestation

---

8. [1995] 3 W.L.R. 118.
9. Often referred to as the "consumer surplus". See Harris, Ogus and Phillips, Contract Remedies and Consumer Surplus" (1979) 95 *L.Q.R.* 581: "Consumer surplus may arise from services as well as from possession of land or goods. Thus, a holiday is generally worth more to the tourist than the price he has to pay for it, and the value to the family of wedding photographs exceeds the price."

is provided by *Heywood v Wellers*.[10] There the defendant solicitors, Wellers, were engaged to obtain an injunction to prevent the plaintiff's former boyfriend continuing to molest her. The defendants' breach of contractual duty of care resulted in a delay in seeking the order, during which time the plaintiff was again molested. Damages for mental distress were awarded by the Court of Appeal on the basis that the very purpose of the contract was to provide relief from such a foreseeable consequence for Wellers were employed to protect the plaintiff from molestation causing mental distress and should be responsible for their failure in this regard.

## 2. Distress caused by physical inconvenience

The second exception to the general rule regarding the non-availability of damages for mental distress is where the distress arises as a direct consequence of the physical inconvenience caused by the defendant's breach of contract. In *Perry v Sidney Phillips & Son*[11] the plaintiff, having relied on a negligent survey, purchased and moved into a house subsequently finding the house to have a number of faults including a leaking roof, and a septic tank in need of repair and emitting an offensive odour. The Court of Appeal awarded damages for the mental distress sustained as a consequence of the foreseeable discomfort and inconvenience endured by the plaintiff who had to live in the poor conditions which the surveyor, in breach, had failed to identify.

As noted above, damages were awarded on the same basis in *Watts v Morrow*,[12] where the facts also concerned a defective survey of a house. The Court of Appeal rejected the trial judge's contention that such a contract was one which gave an express or implied promise to provide peace of mind and freedom from distress. Nevertheless, damages were recoverable for the distress caused by the physical inconvenience and discomfort caused by the

---

10. [1976] 1 All E.R. 300. See also *Reed v Madon* [1989] Ch. 408 (action against cemetery for breach of contract to grant exclusive burial rights) and *Mcleish v Amoo-Gottfried & C.C.*, *The Times*, October 13, 1993 (claim against solicitors for breach of contract in their alleged negligent conduct of his defence and consequent distress). The very essence of the contract to act for the plaintiff in preparation for and at his trial had been to ensure peace of mind by taking all appropriate steps to make the best possible case for him - *per* Scott Baker J.
11. [1982] 3 All E.R. 75.
12. [1991] 4 All E.R. 937.

breach and mental suffering directly related to that inconvenience and discomfort.

In cases where the contract is designed to fulfill only a commercial purpose the loss consequent on a breach will very often consist only of the monetary detriment brought about by the breach. The inappropriateness of awarding damages for mental distress arising out of a breach of a purely commercial contract was addressed by the Court of Appeal in *Hayes v James and Charles Dodd.*[13] A negligent solicitor wrongly advised a client about the existence of a right of way over premises which he then purchased for use as a car repair business. Such access which, it transpired, was not available, was vital for the well being of the enterprise. As a consequence, one year after purchase the business was closed down and the plaintiff sought damages, *inter alia*, for the anguish and vexation caused to them by the breach. At first instance £1,500 was awarded under this head.

The Court of Appeal overturned the award, Staughton L.J. making it clear that simply carrying on a commercial activity with a view to profit could not come within the exceptional categories which allowed for the provision of damages for mental distress. It is interesting to note that Staughton L.J. and Purchass L.J. both agreed with Kerr L.J. who, in *Perry v Sidney Phillips & Son.*,[14] stated that damages for vexation and inconvenience are not awardable for the tension or frustration of a person caused not by the breach itself but by the litigation process, something experienced by almost all litigants.

Short of the two exceptional categories outlined above, the general rule in *Addis v Gramophone Co. Ltd.* still prevails. That case concerned wrongful dismissal. An attempt to move the law forward in this sphere was made in *Cox v Phillips Industries Ltd.*,[15] where the defendant employers promoted an employee and then, in breach, demoted him though still paying his salary. The plaintiff claimed for the mental distress resulting from the breach and Lawson J. took the view that "damages for distress, vexation and frustration, including consequent ill-health, could be recovered for breach of contract of employment" as long as such loss was in the reasonable contemplation of the parties to the contract. In a later case, *Bliss v South Thames Regional Health Authority*,[16] a surgeon was wrongfully suspended

---

13. [1990] 2 All E.R. 815.
14. [1982] 3 All E.R. 705.
15. [1976] 1 W.L.R. 638.
16. [1987] I.C.R. 700.

from work by his employers and at first instance, the court placing reliance on *Cox v Phillips Industries,* awarded a sum of £2,000 for mental distress. The Court of Appeal reversed the award and overruled *Cox* as being contrary to the decision in *Addis v Gramophone Co. Ltd.*

The present state of the law in this matter is unsatisfactory. It may make some sense that a restrictive policy is required both to prevent the floodgates from opening and to prevent fraudulent claims succeeding. However, this protection of perceived needs is at the expense and to the detriment of innocent parties. Indeed, the argument that litigation in this area would dramatically increase is not strong for, in a commercial context, an inanimate corporation could make no such claim. Additionally, damages for mental distress do no more than compensate expectation loss and the fear of fraudulent claims should not prevent genuine claimants from receiving a justified award.

## B. Tort

Although damages are awarded for mental distress in tort, there must also be some other wrong done (e.g., physical injury, property damage, etc.). Damages for mental distress are, thus, often called "parasitic damages" - they are only awarded where they are attached to some wrong.[17] No wonder Lord Ackner said in *Alcock v Chief Constable of South Yorkshire*,[18] that "mere mental suffering ..., if unaccompanied by physical injury, is not a basis for a claim for damages".

However, the courts have traditionally been more willing to award damages for mental distress for tort than for breach of contract. This is unfortunate considering that breach of contract, like tort, is a breach of a civil obligation.

Some examples of the torts for which such damages (sometimes under the head of "aggravated damages") have been awarded for mental distress are as follows:

(a) *False imprisonment and assault*, as in *White v Metropolitan Police Commissioner*[19]

---

17. H. McGregor, Damages, 15th ed., 1988, para. 213.
18. [1992] 1 A.C. 310, at 401.
19. (1982) *The Times*, April 24, 1982. See also *Hurst v Picture Theatres Ltd.* [1915] 1 K.B. 1.

(b) *Defamation*: In *McCarey v Associated Newspapers Ltd.*[20] a patient died after being accidentally injected with surgical spirit instead of saline. The defendants (four newspapers) published reports that the plaintiff, a medical doctor (in fact a radiologist), had tried to put the blame on someone else. The court found, *inter alia*, that he had been defamed and awarded him damages of £9,000. This sum was reduced by the Court of Appeal because, although the plaintiff had suffered mental distress at the publication and injury to his reputation, on the facts exemplary damages could not be awarded.

(c) *Negligence*: The illustrations given here all concern professionals. A surveyor was involved in *Perry v Sidney Phillips and Sons*, a case already mentioned. To reiterate there the plaintiff, before buying a house, asked the defendant to conduct a survey of the house. In 1976 the plaintiff bought the house for £27,000. The surveyor's report failed to disclose serious defects including a leaking roof and a foul-smelling septic tank. The plaintiff used his own money to do minor repairs because he could not afford to do more than that. The plaintiff had to cope with inconvenience for at least 4 years. Eventually he sold the house for £43,000. Because of the defendant's negligence which misled the plaintiff to pay more for the house than its actual price and which caused the plaintiff to suffer physical inconvenience and mental distress, the plaintiff was awarded not only (i) compensatory damages reflecting the difference between the price the plaintiff paid for the house and its actual market price with the serious defects known by everyone, but also (ii) damages for the vexation and inconvenience suffered.

Also, in *Bagley v North Hertfordshire Health Authority*[21] there was medical negligence: a maternity hospital failed (i) to do a blood analysis on the plaintiff during her pregnancy at a time the hospital knew her to be suffering from blood incompatibility, and (ii) to use Caesarian section (operation) to deliver the baby early. As a result of the negligence the plaintiff gave birth to a still-born baby. She was duly awarded general damages of £18,000: (a) for being confined in hospital and for her loss of the satisfaction of bringing her pregnancy and labour to a successful end, and (b) for the

---

20. [1965] 2 Q.B. 86.
21. (1986) 136 *N.L.J.*, 1014.

loss of the child and for the physical illness and suffering she endured as a result of losing the baby.

Similarly, in *Dickinson v Jones Alexander and Co.*[22] a firm of solicitors gave negligent advice to the plaintiff in divorce proceedings. The plaintiff, who suffered mental distress, anxiety and vexation which were directly and foreseeably caused by the negligent advice, was awarded damages of £5,000.

(d) *Landlord's trespass to land or nuisance in unlawfully evicting tenant.* In *Drane v Evangelou,*[23] a case already mentioned in the chapter on exemplary damages, the defendant's behaviour was reprehensible: he showed contempt for the law and duly paid for it. The plaintiff, to whom he had rented a flat for £25 a week, applied to a Rent Officer for the rent to be fixed. The defendant then gave him notice to quit. Six days after the rent had been fixed at £16 a week, the defendant took the law into his own hands: he and his colleagues entered the flat in the plaintiff's absence, put the plainiff's belongings out in the back yard and prevented his return to the flat. The plaintiff had to stay with friends and store his belongings in a garage. Because the defendant moved his parents-in-law into the flat, the defendant was held liable for trespass. Exemplary damages were awarded against him for acting cynically in disregard of the plaintiff's rights in order to secure the property.[24]

There are, however, some instances where damages for mental distress for tort cannot be recovered:

(i) Where a person experiences only grief, anguish, upset, worry, etc., (but not nervous shock) at the sight, or on knowledge, of personal injuries inflicted *via* a tortious act like negligence on his/her spouse or child, i.e., where the plaintiff is the secondary victim rather than the primary victim.[25] *Kralj v McGrath* is a good illustration. There the plaintiff and her husband planned to have a family of three children. They already had one child.

---

22. [1993] 2 F.L.R. 521.
23. [1978] 2 All E.R 437.
24. See also *McMillan v Singh* (1984) 134 N.L.J. 1087.
25. See *McLoughlin v O'Brian* [1982] 2 All E.R. 298, at p. 301. See also *Kralj v McGrath* [1986] 1 All E.R. 54, at pp. 62-3.

Owing to the defendant's negligence, one of two twins died after birth. The plaintiff, mother of the dead child, sued the defendant in negligence, claiming, *inter alia,* damages for grief, and for the financial and other consequences of having another child to replace the deceased child. She was awarded damages including damages for nervous shock because that was the result of learning the fate of the child and seeing it. But, no damages were awarded for grief *per se*, i.e., mere grief not amounting to nervous shock.

(ii) With the exception of the tort of assault, a person cannot recover for the mental distress of being terrified for his own safety.[26]

(iii) It is not clear (though it is presumed) that, if negligent performance of services which causes pure economic loss (recoverable in *Junior Books v Veitchi Ltd.*[27]) also causes mental distress, damages for that mental distress are recoverable. However, where there is a contract to provide a service which has as its main aim the provision of mental satisfaction, damages for mental distress may be awarded; damages may also be awarded if the mental distress was caused by physical inconvenience.

## Physical inconvenience

### A. Contract

It has been established above that damages may be awarded to the injured party to a breach of contract for mental distress directly resulting from the consequent physical inconvenience. Damages are also available for the physical inconvenience itself. However, in the latter instance, the non-pecuniary harm does not necessarily come within the bounds of the plaintiff's contractual expectation losses.

A number of cases may be cited by way of illustration. In *Hobbs v London & South Western Railway*[28] the plaintiff recovered for the inconvenience of having to walk home several miles late at night and in

---

26. *Behrens v Bertram Mills Circus Ltd.* [1957] 2 Q.B. 1. See also *Reilly v Merseyside R.H.A.* [1995] Med. L.R. 246, where the Court of Appeal held, *inter alia*, that fear, apprehension and shortness of breath as a result of a couple's being trapped in a hospital lift for 80 minutes was not compensatable.
27. [1982] 3 All E.R. 201.
28. (1875) L.R. 10 Q.B. 111.

the rain with his family when taken to the wrong railway station by the defendant company. Again, in *Bailey v Bullock*,[29] a solicitor was liable under this head when, in breach of contractual duty, he failed to take proceedings for the recovering of the plaintiff's house with the result that the plaintiff suffered the inconvenience of living with his in-laws for two years. In *Perera v Vandiyar*[30] the defendant landlord, in order to persuade the plaintiff tenant to leave the property, cut off the gas and electricity. As a consequence, the plaintiff and his family had to live elsewhere for one week until the services were reinstated. The plaintiff was awarded damages for the inconvenience of having to leave the property as a result of the defendant's breach of implied covenant of quiet enjoyment.

*Watts v Morrow*[31] concerned an action by the purchaser of a house against a surveyor who had negligently failed to disclose defects. In addition to claiming for the cost of repairs to the defects, the plaintiff sought and was awarded a sum as compensation for the inconvenience suffered over a period of eight months whilst the repairs were undertaken. Referring to *Perry v Sidney Philips & Son Ltd.*,[32] a case founded on similar facts, Ralph Gibson L.J. followed Oliver L.J.'s view that, in the circumstances, an award of damages is for "vexation, that is the discomfort and so on suffered by the plaintiff as a result of having to live for a lengthy period in a defective house". Ralph Gibson L.J. stated that, for a breach of contract of this nature, the plaintiffs are entitled only to damages in respect of physical discomfort or inconvenience resulting from the breach. Such damages are recoverable where, as contemplated by the defendant, the plaintiff moves into the property and lives there in physical discomfort because of the existence of unreported defects and because of the repairs necessitated by the defects. But, in the case, there was no discomfort caused by the unreported defective roof for it did not leak or collapse and was repaired before either eventuality. Therefore, it was not appropriate to compensate for the inconvenience suffered during the course of its repair.[33]

---

29. [1950] 2 All E.R. 1167.
30. [1953] 1 W.L.R. 672.
31. [1991] 1 W.L.R. 1420.
32. [1982] 1 W.L.R. 1297.
33. Other examples of successful contractual claims for physical inconvenience include: *Hill v Debenhams Tewson & Chinnock* (1958) 171 Estates Gazette 835, *Cross v David Martin & Mortimer* [1989] 1 E.G.L.R. 154, *Calabar Properties v Stitcher* [1983] 3 All E.R. 759, *Lubren v London Borough of Lambeth* (1988) 20 H.L.R. 165 and *Roberts v Hampson* [1990] 1 W.L.R. 94.

## B. Tort

It is well established that damages for physical inconvenience are also compensable in tort. An illustration of this is *Mafo v Adams*,[34] where damages for physical inconvenience were awarded to a tenant in an action for deceit against his landlord, who had induced him to leave protected premises. The facts were as follows. The defendant gave the plaintiff (his tenant) notice to quit. The plaintiff, however, remained in occupation because he had protection under the Rent Acts. The defendant and his wife, therefore, tricked the plaintiff out of the accommodation by falsely telling him that other suitable accommodation had become vacant nearby. When the plaintiff went to inspect that new accommodation, he was met there by the defendant's wife, whom he did not know and who pretended to be the landlady of the premises. The plaintiff gave her two weeks' rent in advance. When he finally quit his accommodation, having packed all his things, in order to move into the new premises, he could not get inside that property. He realised the trickery and went to the police. He also suffered the inconvenience and distress of having to stay with a friend for a while. His wife was eight months pregnant at the time. He sued the defendant for trespass and wrongful eviction, and for breach of the covenant of quiet enjoyment. The Court of Appeal upheld the trial judge's award of £100 damages for inconvenience suffered by the plaintiff and loss of his tenancy, but refused the award of exemplary damages (£100) because the plaintiff had not shown that the defendant's motives justified their award.

In *Millington v Duffy*[35] damages for inconvenience and distress were also awarded. There the plaintiff was a tenant of the defendant for 15 years. The communal toilet at his accommodation was soiled and left uncleaned by someone in the building. The defendant thought that was done by the plaintiff and, therefore, ejected the plaintiff from the accommodation, despite the plaintiff's strong denial. The plaintiff slept rough for a while until his local authority rehoused him. He sued the defendant for, *inter alia,* exemplary damages and damages for distress and inconvenience. He was awarded compensatory damages of £500 for the latter two only.[36]

---

34. [1970] 1 Q.B. 548.
35. (1985) 135 *N.L.J.* 708.
36. He received no exemplary damages because, before the hearing, he withdrew his claim for those damages. See also *Saunders v Edwards* [1987] 2 All E.R. 651, and *Ward v Cannock Chase District Council* [1985] 3 All E.R. 537.

## Loss of reputation

### A. Contract

In *Addis v Gramophone Co. Ltd.*,[37] as already discussed, the plaintiff, the manager of the defendant's business, was wrongfully dismissed in a particularly abrupt way. He claimed for the wrongful dismissal and the loss of commission which was a consequence of his inability to work out his period of notice. The House of Lords upheld the latter claim but rejected the former, allowing the plaintiff to recover only his salary payable as part of his contractual period of notice.

Thus, at common law, damages for loss of earnings on wrongful dismissal are limited to the loss of salary and other benefits during the period until the contract could have been lawfully determined by the employer.[38] That is, only the direct pecuniary loss is compensatable whilst any detrimental effect on his reputation is not.

Additionally, in *Addis* Lord Loreburn said (at page 491):

> "If there be a dismissal without notice the employer must pay an indemnity; but that indemnity cannot include compensation ... for the loss he may sustain from the fact that his having been dismissed of itself makes it more difficult for him to obtain fresh employment."

It follows that an employee, dismissed or made redundant in breach of contract and in circumstances which leave a "black mark" against his reputation both with employment agencies and potential employers, cannot claim for loss of employment prospects.

In summary, non-pecuniary damage to the reputation itself and the pecuniary loss resulting from it will not give effect to the award of damages. The plaintiff's assertion of damage rests on the commercial consequences to him which result from injury to his reputation and for policy reasons it is considered such damage should not fall to be recovered in contract but ought properly to be claimed in an action for defamation.[39]

---

37. [1909] A.C. 488.
38. Chitty on Contracts, 27th ed. (1994), vol. 2, pp. 807-9, paras. 37-141, 142.
39. See Lord Atkinson, *Addis*, at p. 496. Although note Burrows' view that the principles of defamation law would be inapplicable to an action for breach of contract where the concern is one of damages rather than liability. See Burrows, *Remedies for Torts and Breach of Contract,* 2nd ed. (Butterworths, 1994), p. 225.

This restriction to compensation for direct pecuniary loss only has been confirmed in two recent cases.[40] In *O'Laoire v Jackel International Ltd. (No. 2)*[41] the plaintiff had been engaged as director of the defendant company with the intention to eventually appoint him managing director. This did not transpire and instead the plaintiff was wrongfully dismissed. He claimed that as a result his chances of obtaining alternative employment had been adversely affected and that, since *Addis*, the circumstances of employment and attitudes had changed. Browne-Wilkinson V.-C., in the Court of Appeal, felt considerable sympathy for the plaintiff in this regard but considered the court bound by *Addis* unless and until the House of Lords reconsidered that decision.

In *Malik v Bank of Credit and Commerce International S.A.*,[42] the plaintiffs were employed by the respondent bank, B.C.C.I., which had been involved in fraudulent activities and then went into liquidation. The employees, who were innocent of any wrongdoing, were made redundant by the liquidators and claimed damages for the stigma suffered in the search for future employment as former employees of B.C.C.I. In similar vein to Browne-Wilkinson V.-C., Morrit L.J. quoted Evans Lombe J., to whom the appellants had originally appealed with leave:

> "... the decision of the Court of Appeal in *O'Laire* and of the House of Lords in *Addis* are strictly along the same lines. It follows that, in my judgement, it is not open to me, however sympathetic I may be to the appellant's claim, to conclude ...that a case is made out for the admission of a proof of debt for what has been called stigma damages."[43]

Therefore, the inability to claim for the loss of reputation consequent on a breach of contract appears confirmed. But, a number of decisions allowing an award for pecuniary loss flowing from the loss of reputation have emerged over the years since *Addis*. Indeed, one of the bases of such partial avoidance of the principle in Addis was articulated by Ralph Gibson L.J. in *Cambridge Nutrition Ltd. v British Broadcasting Corporation*.[44] He thought

---

40. Additionally, Scott Baker J. in *Mcleish v Amoo-Gottfried & Co.*, *The Times*, October 13, 1993 could not find anything in the "later cases" making way for the retreat from the refusal of contract damages for mental distress to suggest a similar trend regarding damaged reputations.
41. [1991] I.C.R. 718.
42. [1995] 3 All E.R. 545.
43. [1984] T.L.R. 100. See, however, critique of *Addis* in chapter 3.
44. [1990] 3 All E.R. 523.

that the decision in *Addis* was not a bar to the recovery of damages for injury to reputation in an action for breach of contract, where the contractual provision proved to have been broken had as its purpose, or one of its purposes, the protection of the claimant against the sort of damage suffered.

Thus, with regard to an agreement by an artiste who engages to perform at a theatre or music-hall, the proprietor of the music-hall or theatre promises both to pay the artiste for his services and to provide him with the opportunity to play in public some part which will attract public attention. In *Withers v General Theatre Corpn. Ltd.*[45] a variety artiste had been engaged to appear at the London Palladium but the defendants, in breach, refused to allow this opportunity. It was held that damage to an already existing reputation was not a matter which could be taken into consideration when assessing damages whereas the artiste was entitled to compensation for the loss of opportunity of impressing the public with his artistic value and so enhancing his reputation.[46]

The same principle applies to an apprentice, wrongfully dismissed before the end of his agreed training period who can recover damages for the reduction in future prospects since "the very object of an apprenticeship agreement is to enable the apprentice to fit himself to get better employment".[47] The nature of such a contract is to provide for a status.

Three other cases may be identified in which the claimant relies on a different rule to that which *Addis* appears to establish, although all relate to the loss of business goodwill as a result of a breach. First, in *Aerial Advertising Co. v Batchelors Peas Ltd. (Manchester)*[48] the defendant had contracted to fly over Manchester and Salford to advertise the plaintiff's products by way of a banner. The defendants flew over Salford during the period of two minutes' silence on Armistice Day. As a consequence the plaintiff's reputation suffered and a drop in the sales of its products followed. Atkinson J. made it clear that damages were to be awarded not for the loss of reputation itself but for the damage to the business constituted

---

45. [1933] 2 K.B. 536. See also *Marbe v George Edwardes (Daley's Theatre) Ltd.* [1928] 1 K.B. 269 and *Herbert Clayton v Oliver* [1930] A.C. 209.
46. See also *Tolnay v Criterion Film Productions Ltd.* [1936] 2 All E.R. 1625, *Joseph v National Magazine Co.* [1959] Ch. 14, *Malcolm v Chancellor, Masters and Scholars of the University of Oxford*, *The Times*, December 19, 1990, all cases involving loss of publicity and authors.
47. *Dunk v George Waller & Sons Ltd.* [1970] 2 Q.B. 163.
48. [1938] 2 All E.R. 788.

by the reduction in sales: "In considering damage on this part of the case, one has to be very careful that one is not giving damages for injury to reputation and that type of thing."[49]

Next, in *Foaminol Laboratories Ltd v British Artid Plastics Ltd.*[50] the defendants failed to supply as agreed a consignment of cosmetics to the plaintiffs who, in reliance, had secured the co-operation of the the editors of a number of women's magazines who were to write favourable comments about the products in question. The breach caused, amongst other things, the loss of the promotional services of the editors, a loss which Hallett J. was, in theory, willing to compensate. He stated (at page 400):

> "I think that, if pecuniary loss can be established, the mere fact that the pecuniary loss is brought about by the loss of reputation caused by a breach of contract is not sufficient to preclude the plaintiffs from recovering in respect of that pecuniary loss."

Lastly, in *Anglo-Continental Holidays Ltd. v Typaldos Lines (London) Ltd.*[51] the plaintiff travel agents arranged cruise bookings for clients which were wrongly cancelled at the last minute. Lord Denning M.R. recognised that it is most unusual in a case of breach of contract for damages to be awarded for pecuniary loss flowing from damage to reputation but, where such loss was reasonably foreseeable as a consequence of the breach, they should be given. Damages were thus awarded for the travel agent's loss of goodwill and standing.

These cases and others were considered by Prichard J. in the New Zealand case of *Vivian v Coca-Cola Export Corp.*[52] This was a case of wrongful dismissal in which the plaintiff claimed damages for his consequent inability to obtain another suitable position. Reaching a view similar to that of Ralph Gibson L.J. in the later case of *Cambridge Nutrition*,[53] he said:

> "In such cases damages are awarded for failure to perform a specific contractual undertaking to protect or enhance the plaintiff's reputation or provide him with some amenity or source of enjoyment. They are on a different footing from cases such as the present, where the only specific undertakings broken are promises as to pay a salary for services to be rendered and not to terminate the employment without proper notice."

---

49. See also *Marcus v Myers and Davis* (1895) 11 T.L.R. 327.
50. [1941] 2 All E.R. 393.
51. [1967] 2 Lloyd's Rep. 61.
52. [1984] 2 N.Z.L.R. 289, at p. 293.
53. [1990] 3 All E.R. 523.

As with mental distress, the present position regarding damages for loss of reputation itself is questionable. Clearly there are problems associated with both proof and assessment of such loss but such difficulties do not justify the imposition of an arbitrary restriction on the ability of the plaintiff to claim a full recovery for the foreseeable harm consequent upon a breach. The cases referred to above show that the judiciary have expressed sympathy for a relaxation of the rule and it is, therefore, an issue which is ripe for review by the House of Lords.

## B. Tort

Damages for loss of reputation in tort, e.g., for defamation, are awardable, as cases like *Rantzen v M.G.M. Ltd.*,[54] *Sutcliffe v Pressdam Ltd.*[55] and *McCarey v Associated Newspapers Ltd.*,[56] etc., show.

Although defamation may be said to be the tort popularly associated with loss of reputation,[57] it must be noted that damages for loss of reputation are awarded for other torts like malicious prosecution.[58] In addition, since compensatory damages for tort are aimed at putting the plaintiff in the same position he would have been if there had been no tort, the plaintiff can also claim for all pecuniary losses resulting from the tort (i.e., consequential pecuniary losses), subject to the usual limiting factors like the duty to mitigate, etc.[59] The topic, damages for loss of reputation, is already well dealt with by the standard textbooks on tort. Readers are, therefore, referred to those texts.

---

54. [1993] 4 All E.R. 975.
55. [1991] 1 Q.B. 153.
56. [1965] 2 Q.B. 86.
57. In fact, in the early 1940's, in *Foaminol Laboratories Ltd. v British Artid Plastics Ltd.* [1941] 2 All E.R. 393 (at p. 399) Hallett J. had this to say: "... a claim for mere loss of reputation is the proper subject of an action for defamation."
58. And false imprisonment: *White v Metropolitan Police Commissioner*, *The Times*, April 24, 1982.
59. According to *Lonrho plc v Fayed (No. 5)* [1994] 1 All E.R. 188, consequential financial loss may be recovered for lawful means conspiracy but not for loss of reputation only.

## Awards for other losses in tort

As already stated, the aim of damages in tort is generally to put the plaintiff in the same position he would have been in if there had been no tort. There are other losses recoverable in tort, in addition to personal injury, death and those already dealt with. The losses to be looked at in this section include damage to land, damage to goods, wrongful interference with goods not amounting to property damage, wrongful interference with land not amounting to property damage and economic loss caused by misrepresentation, infringement of intellectual property rights, wrongful interference with contract or business and negligence.

## 1. Damage to land

Where there is damage to land, there are two approaches to the issue of damages: (i) assessment of the diminution in the value of the property, which is done by taking the difference between the market price of the damaged property and its value without the damage, and (ii) the cost of cure, i.e., the cost of repair or restoration. This position was explained by Lord Donaldson in *Dodd Properties (Kent) v Canterbury City Council*,[60] a case already looked at in connection with impecuniosity as a factor limiting an award of damages. He said that the proper approach depended on such factors as the intention of the plaintiff to cure or restore the property, how reasonable that intention was, etc.[61] Thus, in *Harbutt's Plasticine Ltd. v Wayne Tank and Pump Co. Ltd.*,[62] where the defendant's breach of contract resulted in the plaintiffs' factory burning down, the plaintiffs were awarded cost of cure, i.e., the cost of rebuilding and re-equipping the factory (£146,581) but not the difference in value. They had the intention to rebuild the factory: in fact they had already rebuilt it.[63]

---

60. [1980] 1 All E.R. 928, 938.
61. The House of Lords was of the same opinion in *Ruxley Electronics v Forsyth* [1995], a case on breach of contract.
62. [1970] 1 Q.B. 447.
63. On the other hand, in *C.R. Taylor (Wholesale) Ltd. v Hepworths Ltd.* [1977] 1 W.L.R. 659 only the diminution in value was awarded the plaintiffs, whose billiard hall had been gutted by fire caused by the negligence of the defendant company, because (a) they had no intention to cure and (b) they were holding the hall as an investment with the intention of selling it later to property developers.

## 2. Damage to goods

Also awarded here is either the diminution in value of the chattel[64] or the cost of cure, i.e., the cost of replacing or repairing it.[65]

### (i) Goods destroyed

According to Lord Wright in *The Liesbosch Dredger*, where a chattel is destroyed and the basis of the damages is the market price available when it was destroyed, no other damages for loss of use ought to be awarded. Nevertheless, in some cases there have been awards of such extra damages.[66] But, where the cost of replacement is the basis of the damages award, loss of use until the plaintiff starts using the replacement is compensatable, too.[67]

### (ii) Goods only damaged

Where the chattel is owned for the purpose of sale instead of use and it is damaged, and the cost of repair or replacement is higher than the diminution in the selling price, the latter is most likely to be awarded. On the other hand, where the chattel is owned only for use and it is damaged, the most likely award is the cost of repair or replacement.

But, the plaintiff's action in repairing his chattel or in hiring another chattel must be reasonable. If he acts unreasonably, he will only receive the market cost of repair or replacement if that is the lower sum. Examples of this are *Darbishire v Warren*[68] and *Molyneux v Gartside*.[69] In *Molyneux v Gartside* the plaintiff, after an accident involving his car, failed to mitigate his loss by hiring a different car on credit for £266 a week when he could have hired a comparable car in the same area for a cheaper sum (£146 a

---

64. As in *The Clyde* (1856) Sw. 23.
65. This is the case, especially where the chattel, e.g., a ship, is owned for use instead of for sale. See *The Liesbosch Dredger*, where the plaintiffs were awarded the market replacement cost for their dredger which sank, i.e., was destroyed.
66. For example, in *The Llanover* (1947) P. 80 an additional award was made for loss of profit on the particular voyage in which the ship was engaged.
67. See *The Liesbosch Dredger*.
68. [1963] 1 W.L.R. 1067.
69. (1995) *Current Law*, December Digest, p. 47.

week). His damages were, therefore, based on the lower hire costs.

It is, however, possible for a plaintiff, who chooses to repair his car instead of writing it off and replacing it, because it is of special value to him, to be awarded the cost of repair even if that is higher than the cost of replacement. This happened in *O'Grady v Westminster Scaffolding Ltd.*[70] although, because of the plaintiff's late commencement of repairs, a deduction was made from other damages awarded to him in that case. Nevertheless, the duty to mitigate one's loss is so strong a principle that any repair costs must, to be compensated, not be unreasonably high.

All pecuniary losses flowing from the damage to the property are also compensatable although the award may be affected by the factors limiting an award of damages, e.g., remoteness, the duty to mitigate, etc.[71]

## 3. Wrongful interference with goods (not amounting to criminal damage)

In the absence of property damage wrongful interference with goods covers loss or appropriation of goods, which may be by way of conversion, trespass or even negligence.

A plaintiff, whose chattel is wrongfully interfered with, e.g., is lost through conversion, has a duty to mitigate his loss by acquiring a replacement. Normally, the value of the chattel will be the market price of buying a replacement. But, if there is no available market and the plaintiff had the chattel for the purpose of sale only, the value of the chattel, depending on the particular facts, will be based on the market selling price[72] or the actual resale price.[73] On the other hand, if the plaintiff only had the chattel for use (not resale) and there is no available market for buying any replacement, the award likely to be made is the cost of producing a replacement and of adapting it.

Again, also claimable are all other pecuniary losses flowing from that interference. An example of other pecuniary losses is the reasonable cost of hiring a temporary chattel. Moreover, even where the chattel is

70. [1962] 2 Lloyd's Rep. 238.
71. *Ibid.* The plaintiff recovered hire costs while his car was being repaired.
72. *The Arpad* (1934) P. 189.
73. The price at which the misappropriator or converter sold it, as in *France v Gaudet* (1871) L.R. 6 Q.B. 199.

returned to the plaintiff, damages may be awarded for his being temporarily deprived of it.[74]

## 4. Wrongful interference with land (not amounting to criminal damage)

Usually through trespass or nuisance a person's land may be wrongfully interfered with by another person. This interference may temporarily prevent him from using his land or enjoying it. If he loses profit or custom as a result, he can recover compensatory damages for that. Thus, in *Hall and Co. Ltd.* v *Pearlberg*[75] damages awarded for the defendant's trespass to land represented the rent of one year which the plaintiffs would have received if they had leased the farm concerned for that period. Damages for loss of custom as a result of the defendant's nuisance which prevented free access to the plaintiff's shop were awarded in *Fritz v Hobson*.[76] Cases like *Penarth Dock Engineering Co. Ltd.* v *Pounds*[77] and *Swordheath Properties Ltd.* v *Tabet*[78] show that, where there is trespass to land, damages may be measured by the rental value of the land without the need to adduce evidence that the property will or can be let to another person but for the defendant's trespass.

Where a plaintiff is prevented from using his land as he wishes and the deprivation is a continuing one, damages in lieu of an injunction are usually based on the diminution in the selling price of the land. This was done in *Griffiths v Clay and Sons*.[79] However, there have been cases where the courts have based their assessment of damages on what the plaintiff would have accepted as a fair sum for granting the defendant the right to use his land (e.g., a right of way). *Bracewell v Appleby*,[80] *Carr-Saunders v Dick McNeil Associates Ltd.*[81] and *Jaggard v Sawyer and Another*[82] are examples of this judicial approach. In *Jaggard v Sawyer and Another* the defendants'

---

74. *Hillesden Securities Ltd.* v *Ryjak Ltd.* [1983] 2 All E.R. 184 (damages awarded, under s.3, Torts (Interference with Goods) Act 1977, for loss of use of a car).
75. [1956] 1 All E.R. 297n; [1956] 1 W.L.R. 244, 100.
76. [1880] 14 Ch.D. 542.
77. [1963] 1 Lloyd's Rep. 359.
78. [1979] 1 W.L.R. 285.
79. [1912] 2 Ch. 291.
80. [1975] Ch. 408.
81. [1986] 2 All E.R. 888.
82. [1995] 1 W.L.R. 269.

act constituted a continuing trespass and breach of covenant. The plaintiffs were awarded compensatory damages assessed, not at a ransom price but, at the price which the plaintiff might reasonably demand for the right of way and relaxation of the covenant. According to the Court of Appeal, the trial judge was right in ruling that, since (a) the injury to the plaintiff was small, (b) the value of that injury could be assessed in money and adequately compensated and, among other things, (c) the plaintiff had failed to seek an interlocutory injunction earlier on, the grant of an injunction would be oppressive to the defendant; therefore, the appropriate remedy was damages in lieu.

## 5. Pure economic loss

Because this topic has been thoroughly treated by the standard tort textbooks,[83] to which readers are referred, its coverage here will be very brief. Pure economic loss here means economic loss not flowing from physical damage (such as property damage and personal injury) or from other damage, e.g., damage to reputation, etc. The general rule in tort is that, in the absence of fraud or a fiduciary duty, pure economic loss caused by negligence is not recoverable. An exception to this is where there is a special relationship (proximity) between the parties, as shown by *Hedley Byrne v Heller and Partners*[84] and other cases.[85]

Economic loss caused by infringement of intellectual property rights like copyright, trade mark, etc., and by wrongful interference with business or contract is also recoverable. The rest of this section will deal with misrepresentation, infringement of intellectual property rights, wrongful interference with business or contract and, lastly, negligence.

### (i) Misrepresentation

Although misrepresentation is popularly associated with contract, it is actionable in tort if it is made fraudulently or negligently. In addition, under

---

83. For example, Howarth, *A Textbook on Tort* (Butterworths, 1995).
84. [1964] A.C. 465.
85. For example, *Caparo Industries v Dickman* [1990] 2 A.C. 605, where there was insufficient proximity between the plaintiffs and the defendants; see also *Henderson v Merrett Syndicates Ltd.* [1994] 3 All E.R. 506.

s.2(1), Misrepresentation Act 1967, negligent misrepresentation which induces another person to enter into a contract is a statutory tort.[86]

*Fraudulent misrepresentation*

The aim of damages for fraudulent misrepresentation or deceit, according to the leading case, *Doyle v Olby (Ironmongers) Ltd.*,[87] is to put the plaintiff in the position he would have been in if the deceit or fraudulent misrepresentation had not been made. This measure was applied in *Smith Kline & French Laboratories Ltd. v Long*.[88] In that case the defendant, the managing director of Swift Exports Ltd., by deception induced the plaintiffs to sell to Swift Exports Ltd. 16,800 packs of 500 tablets at their "ex-factory" price of £56.66 per pack. The defendant fraudulently represented that Swift Exports Ltd. would sell the drugs in Central Africa. But, contrary to that, the drugs were actually resold in Holland. Swift Exports Ltd. failed to pay £157,028 remaining of the total contract. The plaintiffs claimed that, if they had known the drugs were going to be resold in Holland, they would not have sold to Swift Exports Ltd. at any price. Swift Exports Ltd. became insolvent. The plaintiffs sued the defendant for damages for deceit. They proceeded on the basis that it had cost them nothing to produce the drugs sold to Swift Exports Ltd. and that they could have produced sufficient quantities of the drugs to meet all demand. Therefore, the trial judge held that, although the defendant had been deceitful, the plaintiffs had suffered no loss and dismissed the action. But, the Court of Appeal allowed the plaintiffs' appeal to it. The Court held, applying *Doyle v Olby*, that:

(a) in the tort of deceit the correct measure of damages was a sum to put the plaintiff in the same position which he would have been in had the deceitful representation not been made to him;

(b) where the plaintiff had been deprived of goods as a result of the defendant's deceit, the court, in assessing the damages, would ordinarily refer to only the market value of the goods (not their cost of production;

---

86. Under s.2(2), Misrepresentation Act 1967, if a misrepresentation is not negligent, then it is innocent.

87. [1969] 2 Q.B. 158. See also *East v Maurer* [1991] 1 W.L.R. 461.

88. [1989] 1 W.L.R. 1.

(c) the evidence showed that the plaintiffs had been deprived of their "ex-factory" price, which was the market value which could be properly attributed to the drugs and, therefore,

(d) the sum of £157,028, the difference between the market value of the drugs and the amount the plaintiff had actually received from Swift Exports Ltd., was the measure of the plaintiffs' loss.

The case has been criticised[89] for reaching the wrong result though it correctly applied *Doyle v Olby*. On the contrary, the decision is meritorious because of its correct application of *Doyle v Olby* and because it is logical. It is also morally appealing. Surely, fraudulent parties must bear the financial consequences of their aberrant behaviour and not be allowed to unjustly enrich themselves or third parties thereby. Accordingly, it is thought, with respect, that the criticism that the decision of the Court of Appeal was wrong is unjustified.

*Negligent misrepresentation*

Negligent misrepresentation as a tort was established by the landmark case, *Hedley Byrne v Heller and Partners* and applied in later cases like *Esso v Mardon*,[90] etc.. It was defined in *Esso v Mardon* as follows:

> "If a man who has or professes to have special knowledge or skill ... by virtue thereof ... negligently gives unsound advice or misleading information or expresses an erroneous opinion, and thereby induces the other side into a contract with him, he is liable in damages."[91]

According to *Hedley Byrne*, a duty of care will arise where there is a special relationship, that is, where a person is so placed that others could reasonably rely upon his judgement, skill or ability to make careful inquiry, and that person passes on information or advice to, or allows his information or advice to be passed on to, another person who, as he knows or should know, will place reliance upon it.[92]

---

89. Burrows, *Remedies for Tort and Breach of Contract*, 2nd ed., 1994, pp. 173-4.
90. [1976] 2 All E.R. 5.
91. *Ibid.*, *per* Lord Denning M.R., at pp. 14-16.
92. *Per* Lord Morris (at [1964] A.C. 465, at p. 503.) See also *Henderson v Merrett Syndicates Ltd.*

The aim of damages here is to put the plaintiff in the position he would have been in if no misstatement had been made.

*The statutory tort under s.2(1), Misrepresentation Act 1967*

Section 2(1) of the Misrepresentation Act 1967 provides that where a person has entered into a contract after another party to the contract has made a misrepresentation to him and the misrepresentee has suffered loss as a result of that, then, if the misrepresentor would be liable to damages had the misrepresentation been made fraudulently, that person shall be so liable even if the misrepresentation was not made fraudulently, unless he proves that, up to the time the contract was made, he believed or had reasonable grounds to believe the truth of the facts represented. The subsection is an extension of the tort of deceit and in effect creates a statutory tort. Hereunder, there is no need to prove fraud or the existence of a duty of care (as under the common law) and the burden of proof is borne by the defendant.

As in fraudulent misrepresentation, the aim of damages here is to put the defendant in the same position he would have been in had the misrepresentation not been made to him. In *Cemp Properties (U.K.) Ltd. v Dentsply Research and Development Corp.*,[93] a case concerning a contract for the sale of land, Sir Browne-Wilkinson V.-C. said (at page 200) that it was "the difference between what the plaintiff paid for the property and the true market value of what he acquired". If that is not enough to compensate the plaintiff fully, he can claim additionally for consequential loss flowing from the misrepresentation and his entering into the contract. Thus, he can claim for any expenses incurred[94] and any profits he had forgone, as in *East v Maurer*.

It should be noted that damages under the Misrepresentation Act 1967 are measured under tortious (not contractual) principles. Since the measure is that for the tort of deceit but not negligence, it includes losses that are unforeseeable.[95]

---

93. [1991] 2 E.G.L.R. 197.
94. See, e.g., *Archer v Brown* [1984] 2 All E.R. 267.
95. *Royscot Trust Ltd. v Rogerson* [1991] 3 All E.R. 294.

### (ii) Wrongful infringement of rights of intellectual property

The intellectual rights that can be wrongfully infringed are patent, trade mark, copyright and design. Those infringements are all torts. Passing off someone's product as one's own is also actionable as an economic tort.[96] Again the plaintiff here must be put in the same position he would have been in had there been no wrongful infringement. Therefore, where he has incurred expenses or lost profits as a result of the infringement, he can claim for those losses.[97] Thus, in *Cala Homes (South) Ltd. and others v Alfred McAlpine Homes East Ltd. (No. 2)*[98] it was held that the plaintiffs were entitled to an account of the profits flowing from the defendants' infringements.

### (iii) Wrongful interference with business or contract

The torts within this category include inducing breach of contract, intimidation, interference by unlawful means, conspiracy and injurious falsehood. The same measure of damages applies here because the plaintiff must be put in the position he would have been in if there had been no wrongful interference. Any expenses incurred by him or gains he has forgone as a result of the interference are generally recoverable. Thus, in *Goldsoll v Goldman*,[99] a case concerning inducement of breach of a contract, damages were awarded for the plaintiff's general loss of business.

### (iv) Negligent acts or omissions

The general rule is that economic loss, i.e., financial loss which does not flow from personal injury or damage to property, etc., caused by negligent acts or omissions, is not recoverable. Cases in point are *Spartan Steel and*

---

96. See *Hodgkinson & Corby Ltd. and Another v Wards Mobility Services Ltd.* [1994] 1 W.L.R. 1564.
97. *Catnic Components Ltd. v Hill & Smith* [1983] F.S.R. 512.
98. [1996] F.S.R. 36.
99. [1914] 2 Ch. 603.

*Alloys Ltd.* v *Martin Ltd.*,[100] *Muirhead* v *International Tank Specialities*,[101] etc.

But, there are exceptions to this general rule, as in *Junior Books Ltd.* v *Veitchi Ltd.*, a case on negligent floor-laying and a decision best restricted to the facts of that case, and *White* v *Jones*,[102] a case concerning negligent omission by a solicitor.

---

100. [1973] Q.B. 27.
101. [1986] Q.B. 507.
102. *The Times*, February 15, 1995.

**Exercises**

1. For her daughter's wedding reception, Mrs. Windsor booked Groover's club premises. She paid Groover £840, which amount included £200 for the hire of the room and a disco, and food for 80 guests at £8 per person. Excluded were alcoholic drinks which the guests could buy from the bar at the club. At the reception the food provided was sufficient for only 30 persons so that many of the guests had no food at all. Mrs. Windsor and her daughter and son in law therefore walked to the nearest fish and chip shop and purchased enough food to serve those guests who would, otherwise, have remained hungry. In addition, the toilets at the club were found to be messy with wet floors, about which some of the guests complained to Mrs. Windsor. Mrs. Windsor was unwell for one week after the reception because of these events.

   Advise Mrs. Windsor of any damages she may claim from Groover.

2. "Traditionally the courts have frowned upon recovery of damages for mental distress. Today, however, such damages are available but only 'in a proper case'."

   Discuss this statement in relation to the law of contract. Is the present situation satisfactory?

3. Critically analyse the availability of damages for loss of reputation in tort and for breach of contract.

4. Nora Bachelor, a fashion model, goes to Vivaldi's hair treatment clinic for chemical treatment to straighten her hair. As a result of the treatment, she suffers damage in the form of breakage of her hair down to scalp level. The loss of hair is in patches so that a rival of her agent describes her as looking like a "mangy dog". Nora is unable to work for three months whilst her hair grows back to its former state. Concerned at the effect of time off work on her career, she suffers considerable stress and a destruction of her self-confidence.

   Advise Nora of any damages she may claim from Vivaldi.

# PART IV
# EQUITABLE REMEDIES

# 8 Specific performance

## Introduction

At common law, the plaintiff who has proved his case is entitled as of right to an award of damages. Equity provides a range of remedies at the dispensation of the court when common law remedies prove inadequate or when, as in enforcement of an equitable right, they are not available.

Two important features of equitable remedies are that they are awarded at the discretion of the court and they act *in personam* which means that the defendant, who is within the jurisdiction of the court, is compelled personally to carry out the order of the court. The two most important equitable remedies are an order of specific performance and an injunction. Specific performance will be considered in this chapter. That will be followed in the subsequent chapters by a look at injunctions, equitable damages, rescission and rectification of contracts.[1]

## Specific performance

Specific performance is an order of the court directing a party to perform his positive contractual obligations according to the terms agreed. Given that protecting the plaintiff's expectation interest requires that he should be placed in the position he would have enjoyed if the contract had been completed, it should follow that specific performance would be the normal remedy in cases of breach of contract. However, the usual remedy in such a situation is an action for damages, except where the plaintiff seeks payment of a liquidated debt. As noted above, specific performance is a discretionary remedy, albeit according to settled principles and may, therefore, be refused by the court. The discretionary nature of the remedy is illustrated by considering the principles which bar its award and these are

---

1. Other remedies not discussed here include delivery up and cancellation of documents, account, and receivers. See e.g., Snell's *Principles of Equity* (Sweet and Maxwell) and Hanbury and Martin, *Modern Equity* (Sweet and Maxwell).

dealt with below. The reader should note how, in recent years, a number of these traditional bars have been relaxed so that the courts are more ready to award the remedy than in the past.

## 1. Where damages adequately compensate the plaintiff

Specific performance will not be ordered where the plaintiff would be adequately compensated by the award of damages under the common law.[2] In this respect the occasions where damages would prove adequate considerably outnumber those where this would not be the case but it is important to note that instances of the latter have increased in recent years so providing the first example of how the remedy is apparently becoming more readily available.[3] As Treitel observes, the recent tendency has been to ask not whether damages represent an adequate remedy but instead whether specific performance is the more appropriate response to the situation.[4]

It is not clear whether the fact that the defendant cannot pay the compensation in question causes the award of damages to be "inadequate" in the circumstances. The insolvency of the defendant has been regarded as sufficiently special circumstances for the plaintiff to obtain an order of specific performance.[5] However, the opposite view has been taken on the basis that, to hold otherwise would subject commercial life to "new and unjust hazards".[6] Burrows[7] considers that this would be so where to order specific performance would reduce the defendant's assets and, so, prejudice other creditors although, where this is not the case, for example, where the

---

2. "The Court gives specific performance of a contract only when it can by that means do more perfect and complete justice" (*Wilson v Northampton and Banbury Junction Railway Co.* (1874) 9 Ch. App. 279, *per* Lord Selbourne).
3. See Windeyer J. in *Coulls v Bagot's Executor and Trustee Co.* (1967) 119 C.L.R. 460, where he recommended a more flexible approach to the award of the remedy.
4. *An Outline of the Law of Contract*, 5th ed. (Butterworths, 1995), p. 391.
5. *Eximenco Handels A.G. v Partrederiet Oro Chief and Levantes Maritime Corporation (The "Oro Chief")* [1983] 2 Lloyd's Rep. 509; *Societe Des Industries Metallurgiques S.A. v The Bronx Engineering Co. Ltd.* [1975] 1 Lloyd's Rep. 465.
6. *Per* Goulding J., in *Anders Utikilens Rederi A/S v O/Y Lovisa Stevendoring A/B and another, The Gulfstream* [1985] 2 All E.R. at 674. See also *Re Wait* [1927] 1 Ch.D. 606.
7. Burrows, *Remedies for Torts and Breach of Contract*, 2nd ed. (1994), p. 345.

plaintiff is the defendant's sole creditor, there is justification for the order being granted.

*Contracts for the purchase or sale (or other disposition) of land*

It follows that, if the plaintiff is able to buy a substitute for the promised but unforthcoming perfomance by the party in breach of contract, then the award of damages would be perfectly adequate as a remedy. However, on the basis that each piece of land is unique, and thus an award of damages would not be adequate compensation for its purchaser, an order of specific performance is readily granted, more so than in any other contract. For instance, where the purchaser intends to reside on the land in question, damages would not accurately reflect the loss sustained if the seller breaches the contract. Also, the inconvenience of finding an alternative plot of land, negotiating for it and completing the purchase and the delay therein, are in themselves good reason for awarding specific performance instead of providing damages to buy similar property.[8]

However, in addition, specific performance will be treated as if it were the primary remedy even when the purchaser's reason for wishing to acquire the land in question is so that he may re-sell the land immediately or at some time in the future.[9] In the latter case this approach is understandable because of the problems of accurately assessing any loss incurred by the purchaser, but such an explanation does not justify the readiness to award the equitable remedy where there is an intention to sell quickly, especially if the purchaser already has a subsequent purchaser contractually committed to buy.

The apparent primacy of specific performance in this sphere[10] is illustrated by the fact that, presumably for reasons of mutuality and subject to other bars, the court will also readily grant the order against a defaulting purchaser even though a monetary award would ordinarily act as appropriate compensation for the disappointed seller. However, specific performance

---

8. Heydon, Gunmow and Austin, *Cases and Materials on Equity and Trusts*, 3rd ed., p. 1026.

9. For an Australian authority see *Pianta v National Finance & Trustees Ltd.* (1964) 38 *A.L.J.R.*, 232.

10. Note that under the Housing Act 1985, s.18 (3), a council tenant exercising his statutory right to buy can insist on specific performance if the statutory requirements have been satisfied: *Taylor v Newham L.B.C.* [1993] 1 W.L.R. 444.

is a *discretionary* remedy and, where it would be inappropriate to order performance of a contract for the disposition of land because, for example, that would be unreasonable,[11] then it will be refused. Two further and related applications of the remedy deserve mention. Firstly, in an agreement to lease land damages do not constitute an adequate remedy although the award of specific performance may be barred on the grounds of futitilty, for instance, in the case of a short-term lease and where the lease has already expired.[12] Secondly, specific performance has been granted of a contractual licence to occupy land where the licencee was unable to find any other suitable premises.[13]

*Contracts for the sale of goods*

Generally the plaintiff in a contract for the sale of goods will be able to buy substitute items in the market and so compensatory damages will provide him with an adequate remedy. Thus, even though s.52 of the Sale of Goods Act 1979 provides for the order of specific performance where the goods are specific or ascertained, damages remain the primary remedy in such contracts unless the goods in question are unique[14] or have a particular non-monetary value to the buyer. Specific performance was ordered in *Falcke v Gray*,[15] where the contractual subject matter, two china jars, was described as "articles of unusual beauty, rarity and distinction" and also in *Behnke v Bede Shipping Co.*,[16] a contract for the sale of a ship which was of "peculiar and practically unique value to the plaintiff".[17]

Section 52 of the Sale of Goods Act 1979 refers to goods which

---

11. *Wroth v Tyler* [1974] Ch. 30.
12. *Mundy v Joliffe* (1839) 9 L.J. Ch. 95.
13. *Verrall v Great Yarmouth Borough Council* [1981] Q.B. 202.
14. Perhaps it is their very uniqueness which prevents a clear market price being established.
15. (1859) 4 Drew 651; 62 E.R. 250. Yet a set of Hepplewhite chairs was not considered to be sufficiently rare or unique - *Cohen v Riche* [1927] 1 K.B. 169.
16. [1927] 1 K.B. 649. Approved in *Astro Exito Navegacion S.A. v Southland Enterprise Co. Ltd. (No. 2)* 3 All E.R. 335, c.f. *C.N. Marine Inc. v Stena A./B. and Regie Voor Maritiem Transport, The Stena Nautica (No. 2)* [1982] 2 Lloyds Rep. 336, another case concerning the sale of a ship but in which the order was not granted.
17. See also *Thorn v Public Works Commission* (1863) 32 Beav. 490 (specific performance of contract to sell stones from the old Westminster Bridge).

are "specific or ascertained" but it does not expressly restrict itself to such property. Case law shows that the order can be made available to enforce contracts for unascertained goods where to do so would be to carry out the accepted principle of granting specific performance where damages would be inadequate. Thus, it may be appropriate to order the seller of goods to deliver up to the buyer where the goods, though not unique, are urgently needed by the buyer and, because of abnormal conditions in the market, are not readily available elsewhere. The commercial buyer's difficulty in finding such alternative "unique" goods may well have serious consequences for him with regard to contractual commitments to his own customers. Thus the award of damages may not be sufficient compensation where the result of the failure to deliver has been serious disruption to the plaintiff's business such as the loss of customers and the attendant goodwill, or the laying off of staff and even possibly insolvency.

In *Sky Petroleum Ltd v V.I.P. Petroleum Ltd.*[18] the plaintiff company, who were petrol retailers, agreed to purchase all of its petrol requirements from the defendant company. The defendants, in breach, terminated the contract at a time when there was a severe world shortage of oil so making the chances of arranging alternative supplies very limited. The plaintiffs sought an interlocutory injunction to stop the defendants withholding supplies. Even though awarding such an injunction was tantamount to specifically enforcing a contract for goods which were not in themselves unique, Goulding J. granted the order. This was because of the inadequacy of awarding damages in circumstances where the plaintiff might well have been forced out of business if the defendants, who for all practical purposes were the sole means of keeping the plaintiff's business going, had not been compelled to honour their contractual obligations.

More recently, in *Howard E. Perry & Co. v British Railways Board*,[19] an order of specific performance was made against British Railways who, in breach, were refusing to deliver a quantity of steel which was in transit to the plaintiff manufacturer. The steel industry was affected by a strike and the defendants were concerned that they, in turn would suffer industrial action by their employees if they performed the contract. The court granted the order because of the serious difficulty which the plaintiffs faced in finding alternative supplies when the availability of steel was

18. [1974] 1 All E.R. 954.
19. [1980] 1 W.L.R. 1375.

very restricted.[20]

It appears then that, in regard to the sale or dealing with goods, the uniqueness or rarity of such goods may be considered as just one aspect of the general question of the inadequacy of damages. That is, there would seem to be no principle which prohibits the granting of specific performance where damages would be inadequate whether or not the goods are specific.[21]

*Contracts for the sale of stocks and shares*

As with contracts for the sale of most types of goods, contracts for the sale of stocks, shares and other securities, which are readily available in the market, do not warrant the granting of specific performance. It follows that anyone can go and buy them and, as such, damages would provide adequate compensation in the event of the buyer having to pay more than the contract price.[22]

However, specific performance will be ordered when the shares which form the subject matter of the contract in question are not available for purchase.[23] A New Zealand case echoes the point made above regarding land, that the buyer's intention behind the purchase is not of any relevance. In *A.N.Z. Executors and Trustees Ltd. v Humes Ltd.*[24] specific performance was ordered against the defendant company in a contract to allot shares, which were not readily available in the market, even though the plaintiff did not intend to keep the shares but sell them at a profit. Additionally, if the shares that were in question would give the buyer a controlling interest in

---

20. See also *Dougan v Ley* (1946) 71 C.L.R. 142, an Australian case, in which specific performance was ordered in a contract for the sale of a taxi cab together with the necessary registration and licence, the latter being very difficult to obtain at the time.
21. Note, *Societe des Industries Metallurgiques S.A. v Bronx Engineering Co. Ltd.* [1975] 1 Lloyd's Rep. 465, in which the Court of Appeal, without reference to *Sky Petroleum,* seemed to reject the principle of commercial uniqueness in the context of specific performance. However, the decision can be explained on the basis that substitute goods, though not readily available from another source (9-12 months), were more accessible than in *Sky Petroleum*, and the consequent disruption to the plaintiff's business was less severe.
22. *Re Schwabacher* (1907) 98 L.T. 127 where shares rose in value after the breach.
23. *Duncuft v Albrecht* (1841) 12 Sim.189; 59 E.R. 1104; *Langen & Wind Ltd. v Bell* [1972] Ch. 685; see also *Jobson v Johnson* [1989] 1 W.L.R. 1026.
24. [1990] V.R. 615.

the company,[25] then damages would not be an appropriate remedy and specific performance would be ordered. Note also that as with land, and for reasons of mutuality, a contract to *purchase* shares may be specifically enforceable.[26]

## 2. Contracts which require personal service

It is a clearly established principle that equity will not specifically enforce a contract that requires the performance of personal service against the will of one of the parties to it.[27] Of particular importance in this area are contracts of employment. Section 236 of the Trade Union and Labour Relations (Consolidation) Act 1992 prohibits such an order being made against an employee: "no court shall ... by way of an order for specific performance ... compel an employee to do any work or attend at any place for the doing of any work." This provision recognises that to allow an employer to force his employee to carry out the contract of employment would be an oppressive and unwarranted interference with personal liberty, being akin to slavery.[28] Also, such contracts would require constant supervision, which in itself can constitute a bar to specific performance. Note that a contract *for* service which involves an independent contractor, as opposed to a contract *of* service, is not a contract of employment and thus is not covered by the Act.

Sections 69-71 of the Employment Protection (Consolidation) Act 1978[29] recognise that it would also be inappropriate to force an employer to continue with the employment relationship when one or both parties are unwilling, for unless it is voluntary, it is likely to prove very unsatisfactory. In cases of unfair dismissal, re-instatement or re-engagement of the employee may be ordered but, if the employer wishes, he does not have to comply. In such a situation the remedy of the employee will be enhanced

---

25. *Harvela Investments Ltd. v Royal Trust Co. of Canada (C.I.) Ltd.* [1986] A.C. 207.
26. *Odessa Tramways Co. v Mendel* (1878) 8 Ch. D. 235.
27. For recent illustrations see *Thomas Marshall (Exports) Ltd. v Guinle* [1979] Ch. 227; *Provident Financial Group plc v Hayward* [1989] 3 All E.R. 298; *Wishart v National Association of Citizens Bureaux* [1990] 1.C.R. 794.
28. *De Francesco v Barnum* (1890) 45 Ch. D. 430, *per* Fry L.J..
29. As amended by Employment Act (1980), Sched. 1, Employment Act 1982, s.5 and Trade Union Reform and Employment Rights Act 1993, s.28 and Sched. 5.

damages.

Where the Acts do not apply the bar still has force. However, in *C.H. Giles & Co. v Morris*[30] Megarry J. considered that the operation of the principle was not based on any irreversible rule but was a matter of discretion which should be influenced by a strong reluctance to make the order in such circumstances. Indeed, in *C.H. Giles & Co. v Morris*, Megarry J. drew a distinction between an order to perform a contract of service and an order to procure the execution of a contract. Here the contract provided for the reorganisation of a company and included a clause which required the vendors of the company to procure the appointment of a particular person as Managing Director of the company. All that the decree of specific performance required was the procuring of a single act, namely, the execution of the service agreement. The same approach was adopted by Mervyn Davies J. in *Posner v Scott-Lewis*.[31] Additionally, specific performance may be available where the personal service in question forms but a small part of the contract under review.[32]

The courts will not permit the use of an injunction to restrain a breach and, in so doing, avoid the equitable principle that specific performance is not available as a remedy in contracts for personal sevice. In *Page One Records Ltd. v Britton*[33] the plaintiffs were managers of a pop group, The Troggs, who agreed that they would "not engage any other person, firm or corporation to act as their managers or agents or act themselves in such capacity". The group wished to appoint alternative management and the plaintiffs sought an interlocutory injunction to restrain them from doing so. It was held that allowing an injunction would have the same effect as ordering specific performance because the group were considered to be simple persons, of no business experience, and could not have survived without the services of a manager. Thus, the granting of an injunction would have compelled the group to continue to employ the plaintiff. Compulsion is a question to be decided on the facts of each case and the longer the term for which an injunction is sought, the more readily will compulsion be inferred. An injunction is less likely to be granted where there are obligations of mutual trust and confidence and the employee's

---

30. [1972] 1 All E.R. 960.
31. [1986] 3 All E.R. 413.
32. Lord Upjohn, in *Beswick v Beswick* [1972] 1 W.L.R. 307. See also *Baker v Gough* [1963] N.S.W.R. 1345 (Aus.) and *Howes v Gosford Shire Council* [1962] De G.M. & G. 604; 42 E.R. 687.
33. [1968] 1 W.L.R. 157.

trust in the employer has been betrayed or his confidence in him has genuinely gone.[34]

However, a contract of employment may contain a negative stipulation which can be enforced by a prohibitory injunction without indirectly forcing either employer or employee to continue with their personal relationship. That is, the injunction may act as an inducement to comply with the contractual obligations rather than as a means of compulsion. In *Warner Bros. v Nelson*[35] the actress, Bette Davis, agreed that for fifty two weeks she would provide her services as an actress exclusively to the plaintiffs (who had an option to renew). In breach the defendant entered into a contract with another film company in England. The plaintiffs sought an injunction which was granted on the basis that, as a person of intelligence, capacity and means, she could be employed in other, admittedly less remunerative, fields of activity and, therefore, she would not be driven to perform the contract in question. The fact that she may have been tempted to do so was no objection to the award of an injunction.[36]

Recent cases indicate that the courts are more ready to award an injunction in circumstances that would be equivalent to ordering specific performance of a contract. This may be explained by a recognition of the often impersonal relationship between the modern-day employer and employee. In *Hill v C.A. Parsons*[37] an interlocutory injunction was issued by the Court of Appeal restraining the termination of an employee's employment by the employer in line with a closed shop arrangement introduced by the trade union. The circumstances were such that the effect of the injunction was that the employee would remain in employment until protection would be given to him under the Industrial Relations Act 1971 which was about to come into effect. Also both employer and employee still enjoyed confidence in each other. However, note that the order did not allow the employee to attend work and, therefore, it did not compel the employer to provide work (only wages were to be provided).

Also, in *Powell v Brent London Borough Council*[38] the defendant employers were instructed to allow the plaintiff to continue in a promoted position, the appointment to which apparently had been in contravention of the employer's equal opportunity code of practice. Ralph Gibson L.J.,

---

34. *Warren v Mendy* [1989] 3 All E.R. 103.
35. [1937] 1 K.B. 209.
36. See also *Lumley v Wagner* (1852) 1 D.M. & G. 604.
37. [1972] Ch. 305.
38. [1987] I.R.L.R. 466.

whilst recognising that part of the basis of the general rule against specific performance of contracts of service is that mutual confidence is normally a necessary condition for the satisfactory working of such a contract, considered that such confidence is to be assessed by reference to, for example:

> "the nature of the work, the people with whom the work must be done and the likely effect upon the employer and the employer's operations if the employer is required by injunction to suffer the plaintiff to continue in the work".[39]

On the facts, it was clear that the employers had absolute confidence in the employee (even though they opposed her continuing in the post) and the relationship with her colleagues was harmonious.[40]

There are other illustrations of a willingness to enforce contracts of personal service or those based on a personal relationship.[41] An injunction was granted to restrain an employer from dismissing an employee before disciplinary proceedings had been completed. Here the employee had been suspended on full pay and, therefore, although the employer had lost all confidence in him, the order was, in the circumstances, workable.[42] However, the decision should be treated with some caution for the granting of an injunction amounted only to the equivalent of temporary specific performance in that it was restricted to ensuring only that the proper dismissal procedure was complied with and the employee was not to attend work during that period unless asked to do so by the employer.[43]

---

39. *Ibid.*, at 473.
40. Decision followed in *Hughes v London Borough of Southwark* [1988] I.R.L.R. 55 and *Wadcock v London Borough of Brent* [1990] I.R.L.R. 223.
41. See, for example, *Young v Ladies Imperial Club Ltd.* [1920] 2 K.B. 522 (expulsion from social club), *Nagle v Feilden* [1966] 2 Q.B. 633 (refusal to admit person to professional association), *Thomas v University of Bradford* [1987] A.C. 795, and *Pearce* v *University of Aston in Birmingham (No. 2)* [1991] 2 All E.R. 469 (reinstatement of university lecturers dismissed in contravention of the universities' statutes).
42. *Robb v London Borough of Hammersmith and Fulham* [1991] I.R.L.R. 72. See also *Irani v Southampton and South West Hampshire Health Authority* [1985] I.C.R. 590.
43. Distinguished in *Alexander v Standard Telephone and Cables plc* [1990] I.C.R. 291 in which a dismissed (redundant) employee would have been unable to obtain an injunction in the event of proving breach on the grounds that the employer had lost confidence in those employees who had been dismissed.

## 3. Contracts which require the continual supervision of the court

Equity does nothing in vain and it follows, therefore, that, where a contract entails continuous contractual duties which would require constant supervision by the court, an order of specific performance should not be granted for to do so would be impracticable. Thus, in *Ryan v Mutual Tontine Westminster Chambers Association*,[44] the Court of Appeal refused to order specific performance of a term of a lease of a block of flats which required the landlords to provide the services of a porter who would be "constantly in attendance". The porter, who had a number of specified duties, had been absenting himself each day to work in a club nearby. To order specific performance would have been impractical because the contract was of a continuing nature and involved the performance of a series of acts on a daily basis. Lord Esher M.R. said:

> "The contract is that those services shall be performed during the whole term of the tenancy: it is therefore a long continuing contract, to be performed from day to day, and under which the circumstances of non-performance might vary from day to day. I apprehend that the execution of it would require that constant superintendence by the Court which the Court in such cases has always declined to give."[45]

Mervyn Davies J., in *Posner v Scott Lewis*,[46] a case in which the facts were very similar to *Ryan*, considered that whether specific performance should be ordered depended on the following considerations: (a) whether what has to be done under the contract is sufficiently clear in order to comply with the order of the court, (b) whether enforcing the order will require an unacceptable level of supervision by the court and (c) the respective hardships suffered by the parties if the order is or is not made. In the circumstances the porter's duties were sufficiently defined, no protracted supervision by the court was envisaged, for if compliance was not forthcoming, then the plaintiffs could take the appropriate enforcement measures and, finally, the defendants would only be doing what they had promised to do in the first place and, so, would not be incurring any

---

44. [1893] 1 Ch. 116.
45. *Ibid.*, at 123.
46. [1986] 3 All E.R. 413. The contract simply required the landlords to appoint a porter by a specified date.

hardship.[47]

It appears that the central question is whether what has to be done under the contract is sufficiently well defined so as to make the granting of an order of specific performance a practicable matter and, with this in mind, it may be argued that, in the past, the difficulties of supervision have been exaggerated by the courts. Usually the making of a court order should in itself be enough to ensure compliance by the defendant and, if this is in doubt, it would not be difficult for the court to appoint agents to act on its behalf and ensure that the order is enforced.

A long standing exception to the constant supervision rule is illustrated by *Wolverhampton Corpn. v Emmons*,[48] in which the plaintiff corporation agreed a demolition and construction contract with the defendants. The demolition was completed and the plaintiffs sought specific performance of the covenant to build. The general rule is that a contract to build is not specifically enforceable for, ordinarily, an alternative builder can be appointed and damages would be an adequate remedy. Also, the building specifications may well lack the clarity necessary for the granting of an order whilst the degree of supervision required to enforce such a contract may be beyond that which the court is able and willing to provide.[49]

However, Romer J. in ordering specific performance, stated that, where the exact nature of the building work is defined and damages would not be sufficient because the plaintiff has a substantial interest in having the contract performed, then specific performance can be ordered as long as the defendant has by the contract obtained possession of the land on which the work is contracted to be done. The facts were that the contract plans clearly specified the defendants' obligations and, because the builders had possession of the site, which had been sold to them by the plaintiffs in pursuance of the contract, the corporation was unable to employ a replacement to complete the redevelopment of a town centre location which would have to be left vacant, unless a trespass was to be committed.

---

47. The approach in *Posner* indicates a relaxation of the requirement that, where only partial performance of the defendant's obligations is possible, then specific performance is not available. In *Ryan*, it was this that prevented the claim for merely appointing a porter. The approach in *Posner* is more pragmatic and reasonable for, where only partial performance is possible, specific performance may be ordered and damages awarded to compensate for those obligations which remain unperformed.

48. [1901] 1 K.B. 515.

49. *Carpenters Estates Ltd. v Davies* [1940] Ch. 160.

Note that in *Carpenters Estates v Davies*[50] Farwell J. modified Romer J.'s formula by holding that possession of the land by the defendant is, in itself, enough and the fact that this was not obtained by virtue of the contract was of no consequence for the fact of possession was what prevented the plaintiff entering the land and performing the building works by alternative means.

Further erosion of the bar is evidenced in Megarry J.'s judgement in *C.H. Giles Co. v Morris,*[51] where he stated that the so-called rule that contracts involving the continuous performance of services will not be specifically enforced is not absolute and without exception and not based on a narrow consideration of the difficulties of constant superintendence by the court. In addition, he recognised that breach of an order may result in repeated applications to the court for its enforcement but considered that this should not be allowed to "negative a right". Whilst accepting that, in general, the problems associated with constant supervision will outweigh the advantages of making an order of specific performance, he did not consider that the need for constant supervision in itself should result in refusal of the order. He said:

> "As is so often the case in equity the matter is one of the balance of advantage and disadvantage in relation to the particular obligations in question: and the fact that the balance will usually lie on one side does not turn this probability into a rule."[52]

In *Tito v Waddell (No. 2)*[53] Megarry J. went further in rejecting any rigid adherence to the bar in stating that the real question is whether there is sufficient definition of what has to be done in order to comply with the order of the court, an approach echoed in *Posner* by Mervyn Davies J. In *Tito v Waddell* the court actually declined an order of specific performance and it has been argued that the approach of the court in this instance is indicative of the true rationale behind the decision whether or not the order should be made.[54] That is, the order may be refused where the costs of supervision and performance are greater than any worthwhile benefit which might result from the complete performance of the defendant's obligations.

---

50. *Ibid.*
51. [1972] 1 W.L.R. 307.
52. *Ibid.*, at pp. 318-19.
53. [1977] Ch. 106.
54. Hugh Collins, *The Law of Contract*, 2nd ed. (Butterworths 1993), p.392.

In the case the defendant mining company's obligation to replant land that had been mined, and so restore it to its original state, was not ordered to be specifically performed partly because the court considered it unlikely that the scheme would be successful and also because the benefits of the replanting were not certain.

In the same way, a concern not to order specific performance of a wasteful endeavour was evident in *Wrotham Park Estate Co. v Parkside Homes Ltd.*,[55] where such an order would have resulted in fourteen homes being knocked down.

The Court of Appeal recently considered the issue in *Co-operative Insurance Society Ltd. v Argyll Stores*[56] and took a very flexible view with regard to the operation of the bar. There the plaintiff landlords of a shopping centre sought to enforce a "keep open" covenant against the defendant supermarket chain which, 19 years in advance of the termination of their lease, had decided to move out of the centre and in so doing create the risk that this would have a detrimental effect on the whole centre leading to fewer customers and consequential lower rents.

Leggat L.J. referred to Megarry J.'s observations in *Giles v Morris* that the so-called rule that contracts which involved the continuous performance of services would not be specifically enforced was not an absolute rule to be applied without exception and added that the first instance judge's decision not to order specific performance was conditioned by his belief in settled practice:

> " ... because the judge showed an unwarrantable reluctance to order specific performance the court should intervene and exercise the discretion afresh unfettered by shibboleths which would otherwise continue to be unthinkingly applied."[57]

Thus, given that the plaintiffs would have had great difficulty proving their loss, that an award of damages would be unlikely to compensate them fully, that the losses of the other tenants of the centre would be irrecoverable and that the defendants had acted with "unmitigated commercial cynicism", there was no reason why the court's willingness to grant specific performance should not be affected by a sense of fair dealing.

---

55. [1974] 1 W.L.R. 798.
56. [1996] 3 All ER 934
57. *Ibid.*, at 939

## 4. A lack of mutuality

The party in breach should not be compelled to carry out his obligations if his only remedy in the event of breach by the other party would be damages. Fry[58] states the rule as follows:

> "A contract to be specifically enforced by the Court must, as a general rule be mutual that is to say, such that it might, at the time it was entered into, have been enforced by either of the parties against the other of them."

As noted above, a contract which requires the performance of a personal service or continuous contractual duties necessitating constant supervision by the court may not lead to the granting of an order of specific performance.[59] The party seeking the remedy will be refused it on the grounds that the remedy is not available against him. For the same reason, since specific performance is not available against a minor, the minor in turn will have an application for the order against him refused.[60]

According to Fry,[61] the requirement for mutuality has to be met at the time of making the contract. However, Ames asserts:

> "Equity will not compel specific performance by a defendant if, after performance, the common law remedy of damages will be his sole security for the performance of the plaintiff's side of the contract."[62]

This means that, unless the defendant is sure that the plaintiff will himself perform his contractual obligations, then the order will not be granted against him. In other words, the defence of lack of mutuality requires the defendant to show that, if he were ordered to specifically perform his obligations, he would not be sufficiently assured that he would not suffer an injustice with regard to any unperformed obligations of the plaintiff which themselves might not be susceptible to subsequent specific performance. That is, it might be unfair to order the defendant to complete his obligations and incur the associated expense of such performance when, subsequently, he finds that the plaintiff will not perform his reciprocal duties under the

---

58. Fry, *Specific Performance* (6th ed.), pp. 219 and 386.
59. See also *Ogden v Fossick* (1862) D.F. & J. 426.
60. *Flight v Bolland* (1828) 4 Russ. 298.
61. *Specific Performance,* p. 219.
62. Ames, *Lectures in History,* p. 370.

contract and, additionally, is unable to pay damages.

Thus, it follows that the time at which the remedy should be mutual is at the trial rather than at the time of contracting. Buckley L.J., in *Price v Strange*,[63] deemed the authorities to be against Fry's proposition and supported Ames' view that the time at which mutual availability of the remedy should exist should be the time of judgement. In that case an underlease was granted by the defendant to the plaintiff, the latter agreeing to carry out certain repairs to the property in question. Some of this work was completed by the plaintiff who was quite willing to execute the remaining repairs when the defendant repudiated the contract. The defendant completed the repairs at her own expense. The plaintiff sued for specific performance, and was met with the defence that, since the obligations to repair were not specifically enforceable at the time of making the contract, the order should not be granted on grounds of mutuality. However, the Court of Appeal held that the time for considering mutuality was at the hearing and if, by that time, the defendant's obligations had been performed then specific performance should be made available to the plaintiff. Thus, as at the time of the trial, the plaintiff had carried out some of the repairs and had been prevented from completing the rest, specific performance could be granted. Since all the plaintiff's obligations had been completed, (albeit not by him alone), there was no risk of the remedy of damages being her sole security for the performance of the plaintiff's side of the contract. Buckley L.J. said (at pages 367-68):

> "... the principle to be applied can I think be stated simply as follows: the court will not compel a defendant to perform his obligations specifically if it cannot at the same time ensure that any unperformed obligations of the plaintiff will be specifically performed, unless, perhaps, damages would be an adequate remedy to the defendant for any default on the plaintiff's part."

Specific performance was, thus, ordered but on terms that would not cause unfairness to the defendant. These were that the plaintiff should pay a sum to the defendant to reflect the cost of those repairs undertaken by her.

A similar approach is evidenced in *Wilkinson v Clements*,[64] where the obligation of the plaintiff was the provision of services yet specific performance was granted to him because he had already performed the services according to the contract.

---

63. [1978] Ch. 337.
64. (1872) L.R. 8 Ch. App. 96.

Note that, this modification apart, there are certain exceptions to the bar of mutuality operating against the plaintiff who seeks specific performance. According to *Clayton v Ashdown*,[65] although specific performance is not available to a minor on grounds of mutuality, it can be granted to an adult in regard to a voidable contract made by him whilst he was a minor.[66] Also, a party who has made a contract as a result of the defendant's misrepresentation can seek specific performance against him even though, should he have wished, he could have chosen to avoid the contract and resist any reciprocal claim for specific performance from the misrepresentor.[67] According to *Horrocks v Rigby*,[68] a vendor of land who has agreed to sell a larger interest than he actually owns may be compelled to transfer that interest which he does have (at a reduced price) even though he may not enforce the contract himself. *Hoggart v Scott*[69] shows that a vendor of land may obtain specific performance if, at the time of the hearing, he has good title to the land even though at the time of the contract he had no such title. This is because the defendant could have declined the contract as soon as he had discovered that the plaintiffs had no title. The defendant was not bound to wait until they had acquired such title. In such circumstances it was enough that, at the hearing, a good title could be made.

## 5. Severe hardship

The essence of the court's equitable jurisdiction to grant specific performance is founded in the court's discretion to make the order rather than any right vested in the party seeking the remedy. In turn, such discretion has at its foundation the principle that equity will only grant specific performance if, all things being considered, it is just and equitable to do so. Specific performance is not meant to serve as a punishment and so, if the order would cause severe hardship to the defendant, the plaintiff may only be able to claim damages. This would appear to be so even where the hardship to the defendant was in no way the responsibility of the

---

65. (1714) 9 Vin. Abr. 393 (G4) 1.
66. Note, of course, that such contracts are valid and binding upon a minor unless he repudiates them during infancy or within a reasonable time after attaining majority.
67. *Winch v Winchester* (1812) 1 Ves. & B. 375.
68. (1878) 9 Ch. D. 180.
69. (1830) 1 Russ. & M. 293.

plaintiff.[70]

In *Denne v Light*[71] specific performance was refused against the purchaser of a farm which was landlocked, in that it was surrounded by land owned by others, and which was not accessible by any right of way. Again, the order may not be granted where to do so would cause the defendant to incur a forfeiture.[72] Also, specific performance was withheld where a purchaser, much against his wishes, would otherwise have become the owner of a brothel.[73]

It should be noted that an inadequate price for the subject-matter of the contract which, in itself, causes hardship to the defendant is not sufficient reason for the court to refuse specific performance. Indeed, financial difficulties in general will not act as a bar to the remedy.[74] Thus, in a rising market, the vendor of a house may have difficulty seeking an alternative property with the proceeds of the sale. However, in such circumstances specific performance will not be withheld.[75]

In the cases cited above, the circumstances which gave rise to the hardship in question prevailed before or at the time of making the contract. However, in *Patel v Ali*[76] the court decided to withhold the order because of what arose after the contract was agreed. The vendor and her husband agreed to sell their house. A four year delay, owing to the husband's bankruptcy and imprisonment, preceded completion and an action for specific performance by the purchaser. During that period, the vendor became very ill with cancer, had a leg amputated as a consequence and gave birth to two more children. Unable to speak much English and reliant on friends in the neighbourhood, having to move as a result of the order being granted would have caused her extreme hardship. Such difficulties, which arose after the contract, were not the fault of the plaintiff and did not relate to the subject-matter; yet, the court recognised that granting the remedy would lead to injustice and considered that, in the circumstances, damages were an adequate remedy.

It is also possible for the hardship suffered by a third party to act as a bar to the granting of specific performance. Indeed, in *Patel* the interests

---

70. *R.D. McKinnon Holdings Pty. Ltd. v Hind* [1984] 2 N.S.W.L.R. 121.
71. (1857) 8 D.M. & G. 774.
72. *Peacock v Penson* (1848) 11 Beav. 355.
73. *Hope v Walters* [1900] 1 Ch. 257.
74. *Francis v Cowliffe* (1976) 33 P. & R. 368.
75. *Mountford v Scott* [1975] Ch. 258.
76. [1984] Ch. 283.

of the vendor's children were considered a relevant factor in the decision not to grant the order. In *Thomas v Dering*[77] the court refused to order the defendant vendor of an estate to convey the land to the purchaser partly because to do so would have been prejudicial to others who, though they were not parties to the contract, nevertheless had an interest in the property.[78]

In *Watts v Spence*[79] the defendant wished to sell the matrimonial home to the plaintiff without the knowledge of his wife who was joint owner. The defendant, having misrepresented to the plaintiff that he was the sole owner, persuaded the plaintiff to contract to buy the property. The wife on learning of this arrangement, refused to agree to the sale. The court refused a decree of specific performance since the wife, a third party with an interest in the property, would suffer serious hardship if she were to lose her house.

## 6. Procedural irregularities

Misrepresentation, mistake or undue pressure may well act to vitiate the contract and so entitle a party to an action to rescind or rectify the contract. It follows that, in this event, any claim for specific performance made by the other party would be rejected. In *Webster v Cecil*[80] the parties negotiated for the sale of Cecil's land. Cecil, having already refused an offer of £2,000, made Webster a written offer to sell at £1,250. Webster accepted the offer aware that Cecil had almost certainly made an error and in fact had intended to offer the land for £2,250. The mistake was operative at common law. Webster sued for specific performance and the court refused to grant the decree.

However, there are circumstances where the contract has been obtained by such unfair means but not sufficient to invalidate the contract at law, and yet the court may refuse the order. In *Walters v Morgan*[81] the defendant granted the plaintiff a lease to a mine which the defendant had recently purchased. Specific performance was not granted to the plaintiff on

---

77. (1837) 1 Keen 729; 48 E.R. 488.
78. See also *Cedar Holdings Ltd. v Green* [1981] Ch. 129; *Thames Guaranty Ltd. v Campbell* [1985] Q.B. 210.
79. [1976] Ch. 165.
80. (1861) 30 Beav. 62.
81. (1861) 3 D.F. & J. 718.

the grounds that the defendant had been pressured into an early agreement to lease the mine and at the time of the contract was not aware of its true value.

The order may be withheld even where the plaintiff is in no way responsible for the procedural irregularity. The courts are more reluctant to do so and here the fundamental consideration is, as with the previous category, the hardship which would be endured by the defendant if specific performance were ordered against him. In *Malins Freeman*[82] the defendant, arriving late at an auction, purchased land in the mistaken belief that he was buying another lot. Lord Langdale M.R. regarded the defendant's actions as hurried and unconsidered and decided that it would be inequitable to compel him to perform his obligations. Thus, although he was liable at law in that the mistake was not operative, specific performance was not ordered.

The decision is, perhaps, surprising and the Court of Appeal in *Tamplin v James*[83] made clear that where a mistake has been made, the defendant cannot be allowed to evade the performance of his obligations where the contract is valid at law, unless a hardship amounting to injustice would be inflicted upon him by holding him to the bargain. In the case the fact that the defendant had no reasonable excuse for making the mistake in question, coupled with the hardship which would have been inflicted on the other party if the order was not granted, caused the court to grant the remedy.

## 7. Where specific performance is referrable to only a part of the contract

In *Ryan v Mutual Tontine Westminster Chambers Assn.*[84] Lord Esher M.R. stated the rule:

> "when the Court cannot compel specific performance of the contract as a whole, it will not interfere to compel specific performance of part of a contract. That clearly appears to be a rule of Chancery practice on the subject."[85]

82. (1837) 2 Keen 25.
83. (1880) 15 Ch.D. 215.
84. [1893] 1 Ch. 116.
85. *Ibid.*, at p. 123.

Thus, in the earlier case of *Ogden v Fossick*,[86] a contract concerned with the lease of a coal wharf contained a provision that the defendant lessor would be employed as manager of the wharf. In an action for breach the plaintiff sought specific performance, which was refused. Although an agreement for a lease is specifically enforceable, a contract of employment is not. Thus, specific performance of the whole contract not being possible, the order was withheld.

However, where the contract lends itself to severance into distinct parts independent of each other, it may be possible to enforce one part whilst not granting the order in respect of the other(s). This could occur where, in a contract for the sale of land, several lots comprise the agreement.[87] Note that the position was different in *Ryan v Mutual Tontine*. There the defendant had agreed to appoint a porter who would perform certain duties. The plaintiff not only sought specific performance in regard to such an obligation but also requested that, in the event of the order not being forthcoming in regard to the entirety of the contract, the order should at least be granted to enforce the appointment of a porter. The Court of Appeal refused to recognise that the contract consisted of two severable provisions. To enforce just part of the contract would have resulted in something quite different from that envisaged under the original agreement. Contrast this decision with that in *Posner v Scott-Lewis*,[88] referred to above.

## 8. Promises lacking consideration

At law the inadequacy of consideration is of no relevance to the validity of the contract. Equity recognises this general rule but, nevertheless, will not assist a "volunteer". This is a party who has provided no substantial consideration but who may seek to enforce a promise at law because it was supported by nominal consideration or was made in the form of a deed.[89] Thus, damages will be available to such a party but not specific performance.

An apparent exception to the rule is illustrated by the case of *Mountford v Scott*.[90] An option, exercisable within six months, to purchase

86. (1862) 4 De. G.F. & J. 426.
87. *Lewin v Guest* (1826) 1 Russ. 325.
88. [1986] 3 All E.R. 413.
89. *Jefferys v Jefferys* (1841) Cr. & Ph. 138; *Cannon v Hartley* [1949] Ch. 213.
90. [1975] 2 W.L.R. 114.

a house for £10,000 was granted in consideration for a nominal payment of £1. The defendant then purported to withdraw the option within the allotted period and the plaintiff sought specific performance of the sale of the house. The trial judge held that an order in relation to the option contract should be granted, regardless of the fact that, in this respect, the purchaser was a "volunteer". The Court of Appeal upheld the decision. However, the trial judge was criticised for placing too much emphasis on whether the option agreement was specifically enforceable. An option may be described as an offer which contains a legally binding promise not to revoke. Thus, such an irrevocable offer allows the grantee to exercise the option and purchase the land in question, regardless of the value of the consideration promised in return, and as long as, of course, the purchase price for the land is more than nominal.

## 9. Performance of the contract is impossible or futile

Where it is not possible for the defendant to perform his contractual obligations, not surprisingly the court will not order specific enforcement of what cannot be physically or legally done. Equity does not act in vain and this will be the case even where the impossibility is the fault of the defendant. In *Castle v Wilkinson*[91] specific performance was withheld against a seller of land which did not belong to the seller.[92] In the more recent case of *Warmington v Miller*[93] the Court of Appeal withheld specific performance on the grounds that it was legally impossible for the defendant lessee to comply. Contrary to his tenancy agreement, the defendant had contracted to sub-let the lease to the plaintiff. To have ordered specific performance in that case would have required the defendant to break the covenant in the head-lease. Note also that the order will not be granted to enforce a lease which has already expired by the date of the hearing.[94]

There is authority to the effect that a tenancy of short duration provides a transient interest not amenable to the granting of specific performance. *Lavery v Pursell*[95] concerned a lease for one year. Specific

---

91. (1870) L.R. 5 Ch. App. 534.
92. See also *Ferguson v Wilson* (1866) 2 Ch. App. 77.
93. [1973] Q.B. 877.
94. *Turner v Clowes* (1869) 20 L.T. 214.
95. (1888) 39 Ch. D. 508.

performance was refused because, ordinarily, it would not be possible for such an action to be heard and the award made within a year. However, this is a strange and doubtful proposition, and the Court of Appeal in *Verrall v Great Yarmouth Borough Council*[96] saw no reason why a contractual licence of short duration should not be specifically enforced. In that case an order of specific performance of a two-day contractual licence to occupy premises on a date subsequent to the hearing was affirmed by the court.

It may well be possible for the defendant to carry out his obligations at the order of the court but, if such performance would prove futile, the remedy may not be available. Thus, ordering the execution of a deed of partnership which is terminable at will might prove to be of no effect, because the defendant could subsequently dissolve the partnership. For this reason the order was refused in *Hercy v Birch*.[97]

## 10. Uncertain contracts

Of course, an agreement may not be valid on the basis that its terms are too vague.[98] Yet, though a contract may be definite enough in its terms to allow the plaintiff to sue for damages at law, specific performance may still be withheld on the grounds that the agreement is too imprecise to allow for an order which is precise enough to be enforced.

Thus, in *Tito v Waddell (No. 2)*[99] Megarry V.-C. considered that the material question to be addressed is whether or not what is required to be done by the defendant is sufficiently defined so that he can clearly comply with the order of the court. Such definition can be provided either by the terms of the contract or the terms of the court order. In the case of the latter the court must consider further if the terms of the contract sufficiently justify, by implication or otherwise, the terms proposed in the order.

This bar is linked to the unwillingness or inability of the court to supervise a contract for, obviously, the more uncertain the agreement in question, the more likely it is that the parties would be unclear as to their rights and obligations. The probability of such matters being disputed would

---

96. [1981] Q.B. 202.
97. (1804) 9 Ves. 357; 32 E.R. 817. See also *Sheffield Gas Consumers Co. v Harnson* (1853) 17 Beav. 294.
98. E.g., *British Steel Corporation v Cleveland Bridge and Engineering Co. Ltd.* [1984] All E.R. 504.
99. [1977] 3 All E.R. at 129.

be high as would the consequent need for further judicial intervention. Also, it should be noted that the courts are mindful of the fact that disobeying an order is contempt of court and may lead to imprisonment. Thus, where there is lack of clarity, it would be most inappropriate to order performance.

In *Joseph v National Magazine Co. Ltd.*[100] the defendant agreed to publish an article written by the plaintiff. The parties could not agree to the precise wording and, therefore, in an action against the publisher for breach, specific performance was denied.

## 11. Conduct of the plaintiff

We have already considered the plaintiff's conduct in relation to procedural irregularites. It remains to be considered how, in other ways, the behaviour of the party seeking equitable intervention may prevent the order of specific performance being granted.

### (a) Laches or delay

Section 5 of the Limitation Act 1980 requires an action on a simple contract to be commenced within six years of the date on which the cause of action accrued and s.8(1) decrees a period of twelve years in relation to specialty contracts. These limitation periods do not apply to an action for specific performance[101] but a party seeking an equitable remedy is expected to display a degree of promptness in so doing. According to Lord Blackburn in *Erlanger v New Sombrero Phosphate Co.*:[102]

> "... a court of equity requires that those who come to it to ask its active interposition to give them relief should use due diligence, after there has been such notice or knowledge as to make it inequitable to lie by."[103]

Thus, under the equitable doctrine of laches, "delay defeats equity" and the defendant may employ this maxim as a defence to a claim for specific performance where the plaintiff's behaviour may be regarded as

100. [1959] Ch. 14.
101. S.36(1) Limitation Act 1980.
102. (1878) 3 A.C. 1218.
103. *Ibid.*, at p. 1279.

acquiescence giving rise to affirmation of the defendant's conduct,[104] where the plaintiff's delay has caused the defendant to alter his position in reliance,[105] or where the subject matter of the contract has a value prone to fluctuation.[106]

The delay must be unreasonable but there is no definite time limit set and the approach will differ in this respect from contract to contract. Delays of a few months have been sufficient to act as a bar, as in *Pollard v Clayton*,[107] where the plaintiffs waited eleven months, after objecting to the defendant's breach, before taking action. Also, in *Huxham v Llewellyn*[108] a five month delay in respect of the sale of commercial premises was sufficient to prevent the granting of the order.

These and other cases[109] seem to indicate that action should be taken within one year but the case of *Lazard Bros. & Co. Ltd. v Fairfield Properties Co. (Mayfair) Ltd.*[110] is evidence of a more relaxed application of the doctrine. In this case the plaintiff waited over two years from the time of the breach before issuing a writ for specific performance but Megarry V.-C. said that the remedy should not be denied merely because the plaintiff has been guilty of delay. It was not a prize to be awarded to the "zealous" but denied to the "indolent". The appropriate test was to consider whether it was just between the plaintiff and the defendant that the former should be awarded the remedy. In the circumstances both parties had regarded the contract as a leisurely transaction and, therefore, it was equitable to issue the order.

If a party takes possession of land under the contract, then, by using his equitable title and regardless of any delay, he may obtain a decree of specific performance. All that he is seeking by way of the remedy is to ensure that the legal estate becomes vested in him and this will be provided by the court as long as the interest created by the contract in question is not in doubt. Specific performance was granted in these circumstances in *Williams v Greatrex*[111] despite a delay of ten years.

---

104. That is, acquiescence in the knowledge that the defendant has breached the contract.
105. For example, incurring expense on the reasonable assumption that the plaintiff has forgone his claim.
106. *Mills v Haywood* (1877) 6 Ch. D. 196.
107. (1855) 1 K.& J. 462.
108. (1873) 28 L.T. 577; 21 W.R. 570.
109. E.g., *Glasbrook v Richardson* (1874) 23 W.R. 51 (three and a half months).
110. (1977) 121 *Sol. Jo.*, 793.
111. [1957] 1 W.L.R. 31.

### (b) Acquiescence

Acquiescence refers to the plaintiff, who with full knowledge of his rights, refrains from exercising such rights against the defendant over an unreasonable period of time. The inference may be that such inaction amounts to the plaintiff waiving his rights and affirming the situation as it exists. It is in this sense that acquiescence can comprise an element in laches as described above. Acquiescence would ordinarily be synonymous with delay but in principle there seems to be no reason why the former should not constitute a bar in its own right where the plaintiff's inaction has led the defendant to alter his position on the faith of it.[112]

### (c) He who comes to equity must come with clean hands

The plaintiff will not be granted specific performance if the court disapproves of his conduct in the sense that it is considered to have been improper. It is in a general sense, rather than with reference to any procedural irregularity, that the court considers the plaintiff's behaviour in the exercise of its discretion. Thus, in *Lamare v Dixon*[113] the plaintiff landowner was refused specific performance of a lease because he had made an untrue statement of intention which amounted either to a breach or a misrepresentation.

Note that the unfair conduct does not have to amount to a breach of promise. For example, taking advantage of a superior bargaining position or of superior knowledge can persuade the court to deny the remedy.[114] Additionally, in *Shell U.K. Ltd. v Lostock*[115] the plaintiff oil company, Shell, failed to obtain an order of specific performance against the defendant garage who were parties with them to a solus agreement. This was because Shell was supplying oil to the defendant's competitors at a discount, thus making it impossible for the defendant to continue with the solus agreement without trading at a loss.

Equitable remedies, including specific performance, are, of course,

---

112. See the Privy Council case of *Nwakkobi v Nzekwu* [1964] 1 W.L.R. 1019, in which Viscount Radcliffe considered that inaction of a predecessor in title may provide some support to the defendant's equity.
113. (1873) L.R. 6 H L. 414.
114. *Falcke v Gray* (1859) 4 Drew 651.
115. [1976] 1 W.L.R. 1187.

discretionary and not available as of right. Even so, it is not possible to agree between the parties to a contract that such remedies are to be excluded in the event of breach. In *Quadrant Visual Communications Ltd. v Hutchinson Telephone (U.K.) Ltd.*[116] the Court of Appeal, in considering a clause which purported to exclude equitable remedies, decided that, once there was a request for an equitable remedy, the court's discretion could not be inhibited. The decision to grant or not to grant, in this case, specific performance was for the court alone. In the case the plaintiff company's request for specific performance, though not hampered by the restrictive clause, was nevertheless rejected. This was because of the company's unfair conduct in the form of non disclosure of material information amounting to trickery which led up to the contract being agreed.

### (d) Plaintiff substantially in breach of contract

In *Australian Hardwoods Pty. Ltd. v Commr. for Railways*,[117] a Privy Council case, Lord Radcliffe said:

> "A plaintiff who asks the court to enforce by mandatory order in his favour some stipulation of an agreement which itself consists of independent undertakings between the plaintiff and the defendant cannot succeed in obtaining such relief if he is at the same time in breach of his own obligations."[118]

Note that it is not every breach that will give rise to the operation of the bar so that trivial transgressions may be ignored.[119] Indeed the breach must be substantial and it is probable that, because of this, the plaintiff's conduct would in fact allow the defendant to discharge himself from the contract rather than have to complete performance.

### (e) He who seeks equity must do equity

The above bar to specific performance requires the plaintiff to show that he

---

116. [1993] B.C.L.C. 442.
117. [1961] 1 All E.R. 737.
118. *Ibid.*, at p. 742.
119. See *Cross v Cross* (1982) 12 Fam. Law 182; *National & Provincial Building Society v British Waterways Board* [1992] E.G.C.S. 149.

has adhered to contractual duties which arose prior to the request for equitable relief. The maxim, "he who seeks equity must do equity", focuses the court's attention on the plaintiff's future obligations. Only if the plaintiff is able to show that he is willing to perform his own contractual obligations may he seek specific performance of the other party's reciprocal duties. Thus, in *Australian Hardwoods,* Lord Radcliffe continued:

> "...where the agreement is one which involves continuing or future acts to be performed by the plaintiff, he must fail unless he can show that he is ready and willing on his part to carry out those obligations, which are, in fact, part of the consideration for the undertakings of the defendant that the plaintiff seeks to enforce."[120]

Thus, in *Martin v Pycroft,*[121] refusing to perform an agreed, but unenforceable, contractual obligation, where the term in question was not evidenced in writing, was reason for withholding the order.[122]

### Where assessment of damages is difficult

It has already been noted that the fact that measurement of damages may prove very difficult is not in itself a bar to their recovery. It follows, therefore, that, when considering the granting of an order of specific performance, such difficulties in assessment should not be a relevant factor. There are authorities to support this proposition.[123]

However, where the quantification of damages is problematic, there is an inevitable risk that losses will not be properly compensated and in such situations the granting of specific performance, by definition, is the most effective way of placing the plaintiff in the position he expected to enjoy on completion of the contract. With this in mind, it is hardly surprising that, in a number of cases, difficulties of assessment have had a bearing on whether or not the award of damages constitutes an inadequate remedy.

---

120. [1961] 1 All E.R. 737 at 742.
121. (1852) 2 De G. M. & G. 914.
122. See also *Chappell v Times Newspapers Ltd.* [1975] 1 W.L.R. 482 - refusal of trades union to promise no disruption of employment contract for which injunction amounting to specific performance was sought.
123. E.g., *Fothergill v Rowland* (1873) L.R. 17 Eq. 132; *Societe des Industries Metallurgiques S.A. v Bronx Engineering Co. Ltd.* [1975] 1 Lloyd's Rep. 465, C.A.

Thus, in *Adderley v Dixon*[124] specific performance was granted in a contract for the sale of debts proved in bankruptcy. In the same case Leach M.R. said that a contract to pay an annuity is specifically enforceable as the amount payable would be conjectural. Also, a contract to pay a debt out of specific property has been held to be specifically enforceable because of the difficulties of assessing precisely the value of obtaining security for debt.[125]

## The case of *Beswick v Beswick*

In *Beswick v Beswick*[126] a coal merchant contracted to sell his coal merchant's business to his nephew in return for a pension which was to be payable, at a slightly reduced rate, to his widow on his death. Payments ceased on the death of the uncle and the widow sued both in her own right and as the administratrix of her husband's estate.

The House of Lords held that the rule of privity prevented the widow suing in her own name. The problem facing the court was that it was the widow, rather than the estate which she represented, which had sustained the loss as a result of the breach. At first sight, all that could be awarded to the estate in the circumstances were nominal damages for to have awarded specific performance would have been to ignore the fundamental principle that such an equitable remedy should be granted when damages are inadequate to compensate the loss to the promisee and, on the facts, the estate had lost nothing by the breach.

However, the House of Lords rejected the view that the estate be barred from exercising its full contractual rights merely because in doing so it secured justice for the widow who, by a "mechanical defect of the law",[127] was unable to assert her own rights. The court, therefore, granted specific performance on the following grounds: first, the very fact that only nominal damages were available meant that the defendant would be unjustly enriched, whilst the widow had no other effective remedy, unless the nephew was ordered to pay the price for the benefit he had received; secondly, the contract was for an annuity and, as such, was one for which

---

124. (1824) 1 C. & S. 607.

125. *Swiss Bank Corporation v Lloyd's Bank Ltd.* [1979] Ch. 548; *Napier and Ettrick (Lord) v Hunter* [1993] 2 W.L.R. 42.

126. [1968] A.C. 58.

127. *Ibid.*, *per* Lord Pearce, at p. 89.

specific performance would have been granted to the uncle if it had been repudiated during his lifetime.

Thus, the remedy of specific performance was granted on the basis that to do otherwise would have been repugnant to justice.[128] The decision indicates a more flexible approach to the availability of the remedy.[129] Indeed, both Lord Pearce and Lord Upjohn subscribed to the view that the granting of specific performance should be limited by the application of a general principle rather than by pre-determined categories.[130] The principle would seem to be based on an appreciation of the impact of an award of damages on both plaintiff and defendant. According to Treitel,[131] an order of specific performance should be granted to the plaintiff when it is the most appropriate remedy for the enforcement of the contract. It would not be so appropriate where the defendant can argue that the outcome of such an order would be a situation which one of the recognised bars has been established to prevent. Whether this general principle will gain further recognition and, in the process, enable the courts more readily to grant the remedy of specific performance remains to be seen. At present, although, as noted, there has been a weakening of a number of the bars, there is no evidence of the judiciary employing the general principle laid down in *Beswick*.

## Damages instead of, or in addition to, specific performance

Under s.50 of the Supreme Court Act 1981 (the successor to the Chancery Amendment Act 1858, Lord Cairns Act), equitable damages may be awarded in addition to, or in substitution for, specific performance. Additionally, s.49 of the Supreme Court Act 1981 provides that a claim may be made for common law damages in conjunction with, or instead of, specific performance.

Prior to *Johnson v Agnew*,[132] the two categories of damages were assessed on a different basis, common law damages being quantified at the

128. Although Lord Pearce considered that instead, substantial rather than nominal damages should have been awarded.
129. The decision was applied in *Gurtner v Circuit* [1968] 1 All E.R. 328, in which the court ordered payment of single lump sum to a third party.
130. In so doing, they approved the *dictum* of Windeyer J. in *Coulls v Bagot's Executor and Trustee Co. Ltd.* (1967) 40 A.L.J.R..
131. Treitel, *The Law of Contract*, 9th ed. (Sweet and Maxwell, 1995), at p. 936.
132. [1980] A.C. 367.

time of the breach and equitable damages at the time of the judgement. The latter provided the plaintiffs with a remedy that placed them in a position as good as if the contract had been performed.[133] In *Johnson v Agnew* the principles of assessment were assimilated. Lord Wilberforce considered there that the common law method of measurement was also applicable to equitable damages. The principle that there should be no distinction between the two is founded on the assumption that both types of damages are claimed in respect of the same breach. As a result, a claim for equitable damages would only be advantageous in circumstances where they are available and common law damages are not.[134]

Note that damages in lieu will not be awarded where there has been no attempt to seek specific performance or where that remedy is not available. In *Horsler v Zorro*[135] the plaintiff withdrew his claim to specific performance and unsuccessfully sought damages. In *Surrey C.C. v Bredero Homes Ltd.*[136] specific performance was not available because the land in question had been sold on to a third party. Additionally, if the plaintiff has lost the right to specific performance, for example, because of acquiescence, delay or other conduct inhibiting its availability, the right to damages instead will also be lost.

*Specific performance - subsequent impossibility of enforcement and its effect upon the availability of damages*

If the plaintiff accepts the defendant's repudiation of the contract, he cannot subsequently seek specific performance since such acceptance releases the defendant from further performance. However, if the plaintiff obtains an order of specific performance and circumstances cause its enforcement to become impossible, the plaintiff is entitled to seek a remedy at common law since the contract remains in force after the order has been granted and the defendant commits a breach of it if he refuses to complete.

In *Johnson v Agnew*[137] the plaintiff vendors of land intended

---

133. *Wroth v Tyler* [1974] Ch. 30.
134. *Oakacre Ltd. v Claire Cleaners (Holdings) Ltd.* [1982] Ch. 197. See also the chapter on other equitable remedies.
135. [1975] Ch. 302. Also see *Wroth v Tyler* [1980] A.C. 367.
136. [1993] 1 W.L.R. 1361.
137. [1980] A.C. 367, disapproving *Capital & Suburban Properties Ltd. v Swycher* [1976] Ch. 319.

with the knowledge of the defendant purchasers, to use the purchase monies to pay off the mortgage on the land. The House of Lords ordered specific performance against the defendant but, even so, the purchase was not completed and, as a result, the vendor was forced to sell elsewhere so as to raise the proceeds to pay off the mortgage as originally intended. Unable to convey the land to the defendant, the plaintiffs were awarded damages, both equitable in lieu of specific performance and at common law.

This decision rejects the view that to to elect to pursue specific performance is an irrevocable action preventing the plaintiff from rescinding and claiming damages. Wilberforce L.J. stated:

> "A vendor who seeks (and gets) specific performance is merely electing for a course which may not lead to implementation of the contract; what he elects for is not eternal and unconditional affirmation, but a continuance of the contract under the control of the court, which control involves the power, in certain events to terminate it. If he makes no election at all, he does so when he decides not to proceed under the order of specific performance, but to ask the court to terminate the contract."[138]

Note that, in such circumstances, the plaintiff has no right to terminate the contract and claim damages. Compensation will be refused where it would be unjust to the other party to grant them, for example, where the behaviour of the *plaintiff* has been responsible for the order of specific performance not being complied with by the defendant.

Note also that, after specific performance is granted, the contract is still in existence but the performance of the contract is regulated by the order rather than by the contract.[139]

## Conclusion

It can, therefore, be seen that specific performance is available at the discretion of the court, where damages will be inadequate *and* when there is a contract for the sale of land, a contract for unique goods, a contract for the sale of stocks and shares and an agreement, the non-enforcement of which would be repugnant to justice, as in *Beswick v Beswick.* However, there are several bars or defences to it which include the requirement

138. [1980] A.C. 367, 398.
139. *Singh v Nazeer* [1979] Ch. 474.

of personal service, the need for the continual supervision of the court, a lack of mutuality, severe hardship to the defendant, procedural irregularities on the part of the plaintiff, where specific performance is referable to only a part of the contract, promises lacking consideration, where performance of the contract would be impossible or futile, uncertain contracts and the conduct of the plaintiff himself.

**Exercises**

1. When is a plaintiff unlikely to be granted the equitable remedy of specific performance on account of his own misconduct? Illustrate your answer with decided cases.

2. A number of bars to the award of specific performance have recently been weakened so that the remedy may be more freely available now than it was in the past.

   Explain.

# 9 Injunctions

## Introduction

An injunction is an order by the court to a person to the effect that he must do a particular act or refrain from doing so. At first only the Chancery Court (the Court of Equity) had jurisdiction to grant an injunction. But the Common Law Procedure Act 1854 enabled the common law courts also to grant injunctions. The position today is governed by the Supreme Court Act 1981, the statute that replaced the Judicature Acts 1873-75 which had vested the jurisdiction of the Court of Chancery and of the common law courts in the High Court.

### *The High Court*

The High Court's power to grant an injunction is presently contained in s.37, Supreme Court Act 1981, subsection (1) of which provides: "The High Court may by order (whether interlocutory or final) grant an injunction ... in all cases in which it appears to the court to be just and convenient to do so."

### *County Court*

(a) The general rule is that the county courts have jurisdiction to grant an injunction only where it is ancillary (supplementary) to a claim for a specific relief like damages (s.38, County Courts Act 1984).

(b) County courts, too, can grant an injunction if authorised by certain statutory provisions where no other relief is claimed (e.g., s.1(1), Domestic Violence and Matrimonial Proceedings Act 1976).

(c) Also, they can grant an injunction relating to land (s.22, County Courts Act 1984) if the land's value is within the county court limits.

This chapter will focus on the following topics regarding injunctions: the general principles, the classification of injunctions, interlocutory injunctions in general, Mareva injunctions, Anton Piller orders, *quia timet* injunctions and the defences (bars) to an injunction.

**General principles**

(a) An injunction is an equitable remedy, and so it is discretionary and not available as a matter of course.

(b) It will not be granted if damages will be an adequate remedy.[1]

(c) It is a remedy *in personam*.[2]

(d) Non-compliance with an injunction is contempt of court.[3]

(e) It is not available against the Crown.[4]

(f) The plaintiff must have *locus standi*, i.e., a private interest or right to protect.[5]

(g) An injunction may not be granted if it will not be in the public interest. Thus, in *Miller v Jackson*[6] the Court of Appeal refused to grant an injunction against the defendants, a cricket club, because the public interest (in enabling people to enjoy outdoor recreation like cricket) was stronger than the plaintiff's private right to quiet enjoyment of his land.[7]

---

1. Damages may be inadequate because they cannot be quantified, they will not properly compensate the plaintiff, the defendant just cannot afford to pay them, etc.
2. See, e.g., *Mareva Compania Naviera S.A. v International Bulkcarriers S.A.* [1975] 2 Lloyd's Rep. 509.
3. See Contempt of Court Act 1981. It is punishable by imprisonment, etc.
4. S.21, Crown Proceedings Act 1947. But, a declaration is so available.
5. The Attorney-General acts on behalf of the public.
6. [1977] Q.B. 966.
7. In *Kennaway v Thompson* [1981] Q.B. 88, however, where a power boat club was committing nuisance by way of excessive noise, the Court issued an injunction against the club as its interests or those of the public should not override the rights of the plaintiff. See also *Halsey v Esso Ltd.* [1961] 2 All E.R. 145.

(h) Again, like specific performance, an injunction is not likely to be granted if the case involves continuous performance of a positive obligation so that its grant would require constant supervision by the court: *Dowty Bolton Paul Ltd. v Wolverhampton Corp.*[8]

(i) An injunction may be suspended after it has been granted, depending on the circumstances (as it is a discretionary remedy).

**Classification of injunctions**

(a) *Where a wrong has been done.* Here a *final* injunction or an interlocutory or interim injunction (explained below) is granted.

A final injunction may be *prohibitory* (restraining the defendant from doing something), or *mandatory* (compelling the defendant to do something). In *Shepherd Homes Ltd. v Sandham*[9] Megarry V.-C., noted the following important differences between prohibitory injunctions and mandatory injunctions:

- first, whereas a prohibitory injunction only prevents the future continuance or repetition of what is complained of by the plaintiff, a mandatory injunction tends to look, at least partially, to the past: it frequently undoes what has already been done; and

- secondly, whereas a prohibitory injunction only requires a defendant not to act, a mandatory injunction requires him to take positive steps (which may involve the pulling down of something already constructed).

It must be pointed out here that mandatory injunctions are less readily granted by the courts because, as already stated, (a) a prohibitory injunction prevents future action or repetition of it, unlike a mandatory injunction which compels a party often to undo something already done, and (b) a prohibitory injunction, therefore, may not be as burdensome to a defendant as a mandatory injunction usually is.

---

8. [1971] 1 W.L.R. 204 (where an injunction to enforce a covenant to maintain some land as an airfield was not granted).
9. [1971] 1 Ch. 340, at p. 348.

An interlocutory or interim injunction may also be prohibitory (e.g., a Mareva injunction) or mandatory (e.g., an Anton Piller order).

(b) *Where no wrong has been done yet but one is feared or threatened.* Here a *quia timet* injunction is the type of injunction granted.

**Final prohibitory injunctions - tort**

A final prohibitory injunction is discretionary. It may be granted if it will be unfair to leave the plaintiff to his remedy in damages.[10] It is usually a primary remedy in nuisance and trespass, as shown by *Shelfer v City of London Electric Lighting Company*. In that case the defendants were an electric lighting company. They erected powerful engines, etc., on land close to the plaintiffs' premises. Structural damage was done to the plaintiffs' house as a result of the digging of foundations for the defendants' engines and of noise and vibration from the working of those engines. That also caused annoyance and discomfort to the lessee of the premises, Shelfer. Therefore, Shelfer and the lessors of the building, Meux's Brewery Company, commenced separate proceedings against the defendants. They sought an injunction and damages for the nuisance and injury they had been caused. The trial judge found both nuisance to the lessee and structural damage to the house. However, under the circumstances, he granted Shelfer and the Brewery Company only relief by way of damages. The Court of Appeal allowed the plaintiffs' appeal to it and granted them the injunction sought because there was no justification for the court's refusal of an injunction to aid the established legal rights of the plaintiffs.

But, a final prohibitory injunction may not be granted:

(i) if damages are an adequate remedy;

---

10. *Express Newspapers Ltd. v Keys* [1980] I.R.L.R. 247 (where interlocutory injunctions were granted). Also, in *Shelfer v City of London Electric Lighting Co.* [1894] 1 Ch. 287 Lindley L.J. said:

> "...Neither has the circumstance that the wrongdoer is in some sense a public benefactor (e.g., a gas or water company or a sewer authority) ever been considered a sufficient reason for refusing to protect by injunction an individual whose rights are persistently infringed."

(ii) where the defendant gives the court an undertaking not to do the act the plaintiff complains of[11] and

(iii) where the court considers that no injustice has been suffered by the plaintiff, even if there is no other suitable remedy.[12]

The court, at its discretion, may suspend or restrict the operation of the injunction, as in, for example, *Halsey v Esso* and *Kennaway v Thompson.*

**Final prohibitory injunctions - contract**

This has already been considered in the chapter on specific performance.

**Final mandatory injunctions**

A final mandatory injunction is also discretionary. Therefore, hardship to the defendant could be an important factor to be taken into account.

It may be *restorative* - to compel a party to undo a wrongful act in circumstances where a prohibitory injunction might have been granted to prevent that act initially. But, it may also be *mandatory* - to compel the performance of some positive obligation. A few examples will now be given.

**Tort**

In *Kelsen v Imperial Tobacco*[13] the defendants' advertising sign which projected into the plaintiff's airspace was not only a nuisance but also a trespass, which warranted the grant of a mandatory injunction.

Also in *Allen v Greenwood*[14] an injunction was issued against the defendants, who had caused diminution of access of light to the plaintiff's greenhouse by keeping a caravan and a fence along the boundary of their property. The injunction (a restorative one) restrained them from causing a

---

11. *A-G v Times Newspapers*, *The Times*, June 27, 1975.
12. *Glynn v Keele University* [1971] 1 W.L.R. 487.
13. [1957] 2 Q.B. 334.
14. [1980] Ch. 119.

nuisance by their said conduct.[15]

## Contract

*Charrington v Simons & Co.*[16] concerned a breach of a covenant. Although the defendant company was in breach, it had not tried to take undue advantage and had not behaved dishonourably but rather stood to suffer inconvenience which was grave and probably far in excess of the cost of taking remedial action. Therefore, only one of the two injunctions sought by the plaintiff was granted; the other was suspended for three years in order to enable the defendant to carry out the necessary remedial works.

However, in *Woolworth plc v Charlwood Alliance Properties Ltd.*,[17] because of the problem of supervision, an injunction to enforce a covenant in a lease to keep a retail shop open in trading hours was not issued. It has also been held, in *Harold Stephen & Co. v Post Office*,[18] that the court should not intervene in industrial disputes by granting a mandatory injunction. Thus, no injunction was issued in that case. However, in very exceptional circumstances, e.g., where there is risk to life and health, a mandatory injunction may be granted.[19]

## Interlocutory injunctions

### (a) General points

Interlocutory injunctions are granted before trial; they are temporary injunctions in that they last until the actual trial of a case.

Their object is, according to Lord Wilberforce in *Hoffman La Roche (F.) & Co. A.G. v Secretary of State for Trade and Industry*[20]: "to prevent a litigant, who must necessarily suffer the law's delay, from losing by that delay the fruit of his litigation."

---

15. Such a restorative injunction (a mandatory injunction to compel a party to undo a wrongful act) may be said to concern usually acts and tangibles.
16. [1970] 1 W.L.R. 725.
17. [1987] 1 E.G.L.R. 53.
18. [1977] 1 W.L.R. 1172.
19. *Parker v Camden London Borough Council* [1986] Ch. 162.
20. [1975] A.C. 295, at 355.

They are advantageous in that they are quick to obtain. For example, if a certain act has been threatened and a plaintiff wants to prevent it, he can do so *via* an interlocutory injunction rather than wait until trial.

They may be mandatory, prohibitory[21] or *quia timet*. But it must be noted that a prohibitory interlocutory injunction will be more readily granted than a mandatory interlocutory injunction because the "balance of convenience" (explained below) is more likely to favour the issuing of an interlocutory injunction of the prohibitory type than of the mandatory type.[22]

An interlocutory injunction usually lasts until trial, but an interim injunction may also be granted. The interim injunction is a more limited, modified form of injunction and it lasts for a shorter, specified period of time. For example, in *Eringford Properties Ltd. v Cheshire County Council*,[23] although an interlocutory injunction was refused by the court, it subsequently granted an interim injunction to restrain the defendant for a shorter period of time.

If a plaintiff fails to apply for an interlocutory injunction to stop a wrongful act by the defendant, he can still get a final injunction to compel the defendant to undo that wrongful act.[24] In such circumstances, however, the defendant may want to plead acquiescence by the plaintiff.[25]

### (b) Procedure

Ordinarily, the plaintiff should give the defendant at least two hours' notice in order to afford him the opportunity of opposing the motion when it is heard. In exceptional circumstances, however, the injunction may be granted *ex parte* (i.e., without notice being given to the defendant) where the matter is urgent and the normal procedure would result in damage that cannot be remedied.[26]

---

21. For a recent illustration see *Themehelp Ltd. v West* [1995] 4 All E.R. 215.
22. *Shotton v Hammond* (1976) 120 S.J. 780; *R v Kensington and Chelsea Royal London Borough Council, ex. parte Hammell* [1989] Q.B. 518.
23. [1974] Ch. 261.
24. See *Wrotham Park Estates v Parkside* [1974] 1 W.L.R. 798, where damages in lieu of a mandatory injunction were awarded against the defendants.
25. *Shaw v Applegate* [1977] 1 W.L.R. 970.
26. See the *ex parte* procedure in Mareva injunction applications.

### (c) Principles governing interlocutory injunctions

These may be found in *American Cyanamid Co. v Ethicon*,[27] a case on prohibitory interlocutory injunctions. There the plaintiffs had a patent which covered certain sterile surgical sutures that were absorbed by the body. When the defendants (American manufacturers like the plaintiffs) were about to market in Britain surgical sutures, the plaintiffs alleged that the defendants had infringed their patent. They, therefore, sued the defendants and asked for an interlocutory injunction to restrain them from marketing their sutures in Britain. The injunction was granted at first instance (by the trial judge) but it was discharged by the Court of Appeal. The plaintiff's subsequent appeal was allowed by the House of Lords which held that in every case the court must decide the issue in accordance with the balance of convenience (the inconvenience to the plaintiff if the injunction is refused and that of the defendant if the injunction is granted); there was no rule saying it must first be satisfied that the plaintiff, with only the evidence then available, would get a final injunction if the case did go to trial. The House saw no reason to disagree with the way the judge at first instance assessed the balance of convenience. Since, therefore, the balance of convenience favoured the granting of the injunction, it was duly granted.[28] According to the House of Lords, the principles or guidelines governing interlocutory injunctions, were as follows:

(i) The court must be satisfied that there is a serious question to be tried: i.e., the plaintiff must show that his cause of action is real and has substance,[29] and, therefore, it is not frivolous or vexatious.

(ii) The court must consider whether damages to the plaintiff will not be adequate compensation.

---

27. [1975] A.C. 396.

28. If the injunction was issued, there would be no closure of any factory or factories. But, its refusal would result in the plaintiffs failing to increase their market and losing in effect the benefit of their patent; in addition, if it was refused but the plaintiffs succeeded in their claim when the case was tried, it might not have been commercially possible for them to seek withdrawal from the market of the defendants' sutures.

29. See *Porter v National Union of Journalists* [1980] I.R.L.R. 404, where there was a serious issue to be tried.

(iii) Also to be considered by the Court is the question whether the plaintiff's undertaking in damages will adequately protect the defendant. The purpose of the undertaking in damages is to safeguard the defendant in case the plaintiff's action fails or the injunction is later found to have been wrongly issued.[30]

(iv) Also, all the circumstances must be looked at, including difficulties of compliance with the injunction and other matters, e.g., the deprivation of employment,[31] preservation of confidential information,[32] damage to business,[33] etc. No exhaustive list, however, can be drawn. Indeed, as Lord Diplock said in *American Cyanamid*, it would not be wise to list all the different matters which may have to be considered, varying, as they do, from one case to another.[34]

(v) The balance of convenience, too, must be considered.[35] Then, if that balance of convenience favours the issue of the injunction, it will be granted. In *American Cyanamid*, as noted above, the balance of convenience favoured the granting of the injunction.

---

30. It must be noted, however, that no undertakings are required when an interlocutory injunction is sought: (a) by the Crown or a local authority in order to enforce the law (*Kirklees M.C.B. v Wickes Building Supplies Ltd.* [1993] A.C. 227), or (b) by the Securities and Investments Board in order to enforce any provision/s of the Financial Services Act 1986 (unless there is a strong prima facie case that the defendant acted lawfully: *F. Hoffman-La Roche and Co. A.-G. v Secretary of State for Trade and Industry* [1975] A.C. 295).
31. *Fellowes and Son v Fisher* [1976] Q.B. 122.
32. *X.A.G. v A Bank* [1983] 2 All E.R. 464.
33. *Hubbard v Pitt* [1976] Q.B. 142.
34. [1975] A.C. 396, at 408.
35. But, the court can, in exceptional circumstances, refuse an injunction without considering the balance of convenience: *Morning Star Co-operative Society Ltd. v Express Newspapers Ltd.* (1979) F.S.R. 113 (where the plaintiff's cause of action was weak and that plaintiff was so much in debt that it was unlikely it could honour its undertaking in damages).

### (d) Situations where *American Cyanamid* does not apply

The *American Cyanamid* guidelines do not apply in the following situations:

(i) *Defamation actions*: In defamation cases they do not apply where the defendant intends to plead the defence of justification,[36] fair comment[37] or privilege (unless, as regards qualified privilege, he is malicious).

(ii) *Copyright proceedings*: The defendant in copyright proceedings, who has a defence of fair dealing, according to Lord Denning in *Hubbard v Vosper*,[38] should not have an injunction issued against him. His Lordship said (at pages 96-97):

> "We never restrain a defendant in a libel action who says he is going to justify. So in a copyright action, we ought not to restrain a defendant who has a reasonable defence of fair dealing. Nor in an action for breach of confidence, if the defendant has a reasonable defence of public interest. The reason is because the defendant, if he is right, is entitled to publish it: and the law will not intervene to suppress freedom of speech except where it is abused."

Today the reasonable defences of fair trading are contained in s.30, Copyright, Designs and Patents Act 1988.

(iii) *Proceedings against public authorities:* Where a plaintiff's case against a public authority is not an extremely strong *prima facie* case, that public authority should not be restrained by an injunction from carrying out its statutory duties or exercising its statutory powers: *Smith v Inner London Education Authority*.[39]

---

36. *Bestobell Paints Ltd. v Bigg* (1975) F.S.R. 421. The reason for this is the supreme public interest in the preservation of freedom of speech. In a similar way a defendant in proceedings for breach of confidence, who has a reasonable defence of public interest, should not be restrained by an injunction.
37. *Fraser v Evans* [1969] 1 Q.B. 349.
38. [1972] 2 Q.B. 84.
39. [1978] 1 All E.R. 411. There, at page 418, Lord Denning actually said that "a local authority should not be restrained, even by an interlocutory injunction, from exercising its statutory powers or doing its duty towards the public at large, unless the plaintiff shows that he has 'a real prospect of succeeding in his claim for a permanent injunction at the trial'".

(iv) *Compelling medical treatment*: It has been held by the Court of Appeal in *Re J. (A Minor) (Child in Care: Medical Treatment)*,[40] a case concerning the treatment of a sixteen-year-old girl suffering from anorexia nervosa, that an interlocutory injunction should not be granted to compel medical doctors to give a special type of treatment to a child in an intensive care unit.

(v) *Anton Piller Orders and Mareva Injunctions*: Both of these are forms of interlocutory injunctions and will be looked at in detail below. In the case of an Anton Piller order (an interlocutory *mandatory* injunction) there must be an extremely strong *prima facie* case (not just a serious issue to be tried): because (i) applications for such injunctions are made *ex parte* and (ii) the Anton Piller order is "Draconian" in nature. It may, therefore, be said that *American Cyanamid* does not apply to Anton Piller orders. Arguably, *American Cyanamid* does not also apply to Mareva injunctions to the extent that Mareva injunctions require much more safeguards for the defendant than is the position under *American Cyanamid*. Indeed, Lord Donaldson, M.R. said in *Polly Peck International plc v Nadir (No. 2)*[41] that "the approach called for by the decision in *American Cyanamid Co. v Ethicon* ... has ... no application to the grant or refusal of Mareva injunctions which proceed on principles which are quite different".

Lastly, it must be noted that in trade union (i.e., labour) disputes, the rule in the *American Cyanamid case* has been modified by section 221(2), Trade Union and Labour Relations (Consolidation) Act 1992. Previously, the unmodified application of the rule in *American Cyanamid* in labour disputes tilted the balance of convenience constantly in favour of the employer and so denied the unions their power to put pressure on employers. What the 1992 legislation does is simply ensure consideration of the merits of the statutory defences[42] before an injunction is issued against a trade union.

---

40. (1993) Fam. 15.
41. [1992] 4 All E.R. 769, at p. 786.
42. Which include protection from certain tortious liabilities and peaceful picketing.

## The Mareva injunction

### *Introduction*

Before 1975 the Mareva injunction was simply unknown. According to the law then, as represented by *Lister v Stubbs*,[43] a plaintiff could not get an injunction restraining the defendant from dealing with his (the defendant's own) property if a court judgement had not yet been given against that defendant. Moreover, the defendant's intention during that period was immaterial. In *Lister v Stubbs* Lord Cotton said:

> "I know of no case where, because it was highly probable that if the action were brought to a hearing the plaintiff could establish that the debt was due from the defendant, the defendant has been ordered to give security until that [debt] has been established by the judgement or decree."[44]

According to him,[45] such an order "would be introducing an entirely new and wrong principle, even though we might think that, having regard to the circumstances of the case, it would be highly just to make the order".

Also, in *Jagger v Jagger*[46] Lord Scrutton said he was "not aware of any statutory or other power in the court to restrain a person from dealing with his property at a time when no order against him has been made".

Then forty-nine years later (in 1975) the position changed - the Mareva injunction was born (although it was to be in 1981 that it was given a statutory basis).[47]

### *Definition*

The Mareva injunction is an interlocutory injunction which temporarily freezes the assets of a defendant (or a potential defendant) so that he cannot frustrate any likely judgement by removing his assets from the jurisdiction or by disposing of them.

---

43. [1890] 45 Ch. D. 1.
44. *Ibid.*, at p.13.
45. *Ibid.*, at p.14.
46. (1926) P. 93, 102.
47. By s.37, Supreme Court Act 1981.

*Types of the order*

Three types of the order may be made: the first is *a general Mareva order or injunction* covering all the assets of the defendant; secondly, *a maximum sum order* may be made (this is the order that is usually granted and it covers the defendant's assets only up to the maximum sum of the plaintiff's claim plus interest and costs); and thirdly, there is the type of order which covers only *specific assets*, e.g., a ship, aeroplane, etc.

***The Mareva case***

The name of the injunction comes from the case, *Mareva Compania Naviera S.A. v International Bulkcarriers S.A.*[48] There the plaintiffs, ship-owners, hired a vessel to the defendants. The vessel was delivered on 12-5-75. The defendants sub-chartered the vessel to another party. Under the (first) hire agreement the defendants were to pay the hire charges half-monthly in advance at the rate of 3850 dollars a day from 12-5-75. However, only the first two instalments were paid. The plaintiff, therefore, sued the defendants for the unpaid hire and damages for repudiation of the contract, and also sought, *ex parte,* an injunction to restrain the defendants from disposing or removing out of the jurisdiction any money they had been paid under the sub-charter. Donaldson J., granted the injunction only until 5.00 p.m. on 23-6-75. When the plaintiffs appealed to the Court of Appeal for the period of the injunction to be extended, the Court distinguished *Lister v Stubbs* and held that, where a person owed a debt which was due and he was likely to dispose of his assets so as to frustrate it before judgement was issued, the court could, in a proper case like the present,[49] grant an interlocutory injunction to help avoid injustice to the plaintiff. The period of the injunction was, accordingly, extended.

Here are a few judicial statements referring to this type of injunction:

In *Bank Mellat v Nikpour*[50] Sir John Donaldson M.R., stated that "the Mareva injunction is in effect, together with the Anton Piller order, one of the law's 'nuclear' weapons".

---

48. [1975) 2 Lloyd's Rep. 509.
49. Because the defendants had money in a London bank.
50. [1985] F.S.R. 87, at 92.

Also, in *Siporex Trade S.A. v Comdel Commodities Ltd.*[51] Bingham J. (as he then was) stated:

> "The advent of the Mareva injunction has, as is notorious, led to *ex parte* applications for injunctive relief becoming common-place, hundreds being made each year and relatively few refused."

In *The Siskina*[52] Lord Diplock said:

> "A *Mareva* injunction is interlocutory, not final; it is ancillary to a substantive pecuniary claim for debt or damages; it is designed to prevent the judgement ... for a sum of money being a '*brutum fulmen*'."[53]

## Main points

(a) The usual purpose of the Mareva injunction is to stop the defendant from dissipating, removing or hiding his assets before trial.[54]

(b) It is an interlocutory injunction and application for it is usually made *ex parte*, i.e., without the defendant being present. The application is made in the High Court. (County Courts have no power to make that type of order: County Courts Remedies Regulations 1991.)

(c) It is often sought together with an Anton Piller order.

(d) The present basis of the court's jurisdiction to grant the injunction is s.37, Supreme Court Act 1981.

(e) The plaintiff, as is the position regarding interlocutory injunctions generally, must first satisfy the requirements laid down in *American Cyanamid* by the House of Lords, i.e., (i) he must have a good

---

51. [1986] 2 Lloyd's Rep. 428.
52. [1979] A.C. 210 at 253.
53. A *brutum fulmen* is a threat to which no effect can be given.
54. However, a Mareva injunction can also be granted to aid execution of a judgement (*Orwell Steel (Erection and Fabrication) Ltd. v Asphalt and Tarmac (U.K.) Ltd.* [1984] 1 W.L.R. 1097) or to aid the enforcement of an order for taxed costs (*Faith v Panton Property Plan Ltd. v Hodgetts* [1981] 1 W.L.R. 927).

arguable case, and (ii) the balance of convenience must be in favour of the grant of the injunction. However, because of the draconian nature of the Mareva injunction, the plaintiff must do much more in that certain safeguards must be provided for the defendant (as contained in the guidelines in The *Rasu Maritima*, the "*Babanaft* proviso" and the Practice Direction 1994, all to be looked at below).

(f) As a safeguard to the defendant, the plaintiff must make an undertaking in damages and, in appropriate cases, must support this by paying money into court in case the order is refused.[55] He must also undertake: (a) to let the defendant know, by fax or telex, etc., the terms of the injunction and, in *ex parte* applications, to serve him with the affidavit and exhibits supporting it (because the defendant was not present in court to see them), (b) to pay the expenses any bank or innocent third party incurs as a result of complying with the injunction, and (c) to indemnify that bank or innocent third party as regards any liability it is exposed to in complying with the injunction. In addition, he must notify the defendant/s and third parties that they have the right to apply to the court to set the order aside.

**The guidelines**

In *Rasu Maritima S.A. v Perusahaan etc.*[56] the plaintiffs sued the defendants for breach of contract (repudiation of a charterparty) for the hiring of an oil tanker. The plaintiffs also obtained an injunction to restrain the defendants, who were abroad, from disposing of assets in England. Those assets were part of a fertiliser factory which was going to be built in Indonesia. As such part, they were valued at $12m. However, their scrap value was only $350,000. The plaintiffs' application for a continuation of the injunction failed because, considering the character and circumstances of the assets (their nominal scrap value, uncertain ownership, etc.), it would not be just and convenient to order so.

Lord Denning suggested the following guidelines to be followed by the court:

---

55. See Practice Direction 1994.
56. [1978] Q.B. 644.

(a) the plaintiff must have a good arguable case;[57]

(b) the injunction may cover both money and chattels (goods); and caution must be taken so as not to bring the defendant's business to a halt;

(c) if the grant would be likely to force the defendant to provide security, the court should favour it;

(d) the plaintiff should make full and frank disclosure of all material matters in his knowledge;

(e) the plaintiff should give full particulars of his claim and the amount thereof, and (where his application is made *ex parte*) he must fairly state any points the defendant has made against it;

(f) the plaintiff should give grounds for believing that the defendant has assets within the jurisdiction;

(g) he should give some grounds for believing that there is a risk that the assets will be removed before the claim is satisfied; it is not enough to state that the defendant is abroad (outside the jurisdiction);[58]

(h) the plaintiff must give an undertaking in damages in case his claim fails.[59]

---

57. "A good arguable case", according to *Ninemia Maritime Corp. v Trave Schiffahrtsgesellschaft mbH and Co. KG.* [1983] 1 W.L.R. 1412 (affirmed [1983] 2 Lloyd's Rep. 600), is "a case which is more than barely capable of serious argument, and yet not necessarily one which the judge believes to have a better than 50 per cent chance of success". Thus, mere anticipation of the defendant breaching his contract in the future is not enough to constitute a "good arguable case": *The Veracruz* [1992] 1 Lloyd's Rep. 353.

58. An indication of the risk of dissipation of assets by the defendant is evidence that he had already taken steps for the transfer or dissipation of those assets (*Aiglon Ltd. v Gau Shan Co. Ltd.* [1993] 1 Lloyd's Rep. 164.

59. These guidelines were restated again by Lord Denning in *Third Chandris Shipping Corporation v Unimarine S.A.* [1979] 2 All E.R. 972; [1979] Q.B. 645.

Now, according to the Practice Direction 1994,[60] in appropriate cases, he must, *inter alia*, support his undertaking by paying money into court and must deposit the papers to the judge at least 24 hours before the hearing.

Further, as part of the safeguards to protect the defendant, there is a proviso in the order that the assets will be frozen up to only the amount the plaintiff is reasonably likely to recover.[61]

**Procedure**

1. The application is made usually *ex parte* (i.e., without informing the defendant). This is because, if he is alerted, he may dispose of his assets or dissipate them.

2. The plaintiff makes the application to a judge in chambers. This is done usually before a writ is served on the defendant (in order not to tip him off). The application must contain:

(a) a draft statement of claim,

(b) a draft order, and

(c) an affidavit.

3. The affidavit attached to the application must show:

(a) a good arguable case for the plaintiff (a serious question to be tried);

(b) any evidence or arguments which the defendant may present;

(c) that the plaintiff's claim is justiciable or triable in this jurisdiction (England and Wales) either because the defendant

---

60. [1994] 4 All E.R. 52.

61. *Per* Lord Denning in *Z. v A.Z. and A.A.-L.L.* [1982] 2 W.L.R. 288, at p. 298. This is very likely only where the defendant has assets far exceeding the amount claimed by the plaintiff. It will be unjust to freeze all the assets of such a defendant.

is resident in England and Wales or the cause of action arose in England and Wales, etc.[62]

(d) that the defendant has assets within the jurisdiction; and

(e) evidence that the defendant is likely to dispose of, or dissipate, the assets unless restrained.[63]

*Additional points*

The following additional points, too, should be noted:

(i) The court has jurisdiction to grant a Mareva injunction only to aid or support a cause of action which is already existing at the time the injunction is sought. In other words, the Mareva injunction is ancillary to a substantive claim (for damages or for a debt). Where, therefore, there was no existing cause of action in aid of which it could be granted, the Mareva injunction was not granted in *The Siskina*.[64]

(ii) Under s.37(3), Supreme Court Act 1981 the injunction can be granted even if the defendant is not based in this jurisdiction, i.e., England and Wales. Section 37(3) provides that the power of the courts to grant an interlocutory injunction to restrain a party to any proceedings from removing from the jurisdiction, or otherwise dealing with, assets located within the jurisdiction, can be exercised whether or not that party is domiciled, resident or present in England and Wales.[65] In *Mercedes-Benz A.G. v Leiduck*[66] the Privy Council held that Order 11, r.1, of the Rules of the Supreme Court (which allows service of a writ out of the jurisdiction) did not give the court

---

62. Rules of the Supreme Court, Order 11, r.1 enables service of a writ outside the jurisdiction where the defendant is abroad.

63. See Appendix 5 (d) and (e), *post*, showing a draft Mareva injunction and an affidavit supporting the application for it.

64. [1979] A.C. 210. See also *Veracruz Transportation Inc. v V.C. Shipping Co.* ("*The Veracruz*") [1992] 1 Lloyd's Rep. 353; *Zucker v Tyndall Holdings* [1992] 1 W.L.R. 1127; and *The P* [1992] 1 Lloyd's Rep. 470.

65. "Domicile" means physical presence in the jurisdiction with the intention of remaining (i.e, of not going back, "*animus non revertendi*").

66. [1995] 3 All E.R. 929.

extra-territorial jurisdiction to allow service of a writ on a foreigner out of the jurisdiction if the only relief the plaintiff was seeking was a Mareva injunction to freeze the defendant's assets in the jurisdiction while waiting for proceedings brought against him in a foreign court to be concluded. This was because, *inter alia*, a claim for a Mareva injunction was only to prepare the ground for enforcement of a judgement: it was not a means of enforcing a judgement.

**Where the defendant is abroad**

In such a situation the plaintiff can sue the defendant in England and Wales in one of three ways:

(a) first, by getting leave to issue and serve the writ or other proceedings out of the jurisdiction under Rules of the Supreme Court, order 11, r.1(1),

(b) secondly, if the defendant himself yields or assents to the jurisdiction; and

(c) thirdly, he can serve the writ in another contracting state to the Brussels and Lugano Conventions without leave under the Civil Jurisdiction and Judgement Acts of 1982 and 1991.

However, where proceedings are pending (i.e., have already been, or will be, started) in another contracting state (and, therefore, another substantive action cannot be started in England and Wales), the English court has power under s.25(1), Civil Jurisdiction and Judgement Act 1982 to grant an interim relief, which may include a Mareva injunction. Thus, if the facts of *The Siskina* (where a Mareva injunction was not granted because there was no substantive claim which the plaintiff could bring in England and Wales and, *inter alia,* exclusive jurisdiction had been conferred on the Italian courts) were to recur today, the High Court in England would have jurisdiction to grant an interim relief in the form of a Mareva injunction (as Italy is a contracting state to the Brussels Convention and the Lugano Convention, both of which relate to jurisdiction and enforcement of judgements in civil and commercial matters).[67]

**What happens if the assets in question are abroad?[68]**

The Mareva injunction may still be granted even where the assets in question are abroad providing third-party rights will be protected: *Babanaft International Co. v Bassatne*[69] (where there was a post-judgement Mareva injunction which bound the defendant alone and s.37(3), Supreme Court Act 1981 was held not to restrict the geographical scope, etc., of s.37(1)). Without protection of third-party rights such an injunction would be a serious extension of extra-territorial jurisdiction over third parties. In fact Nicholls L.J. said in *Babanaft International Co. v Bassatne*:[70]

> "It would be wrong for an English court, by making an order in respect of overseas assets against a defendant amenable to its jurisdiction, to impose or attempt to impose obligations on persons not before the court in respect of acts to be done by them abroad regarding property outside the jurisdiction. That, self-evidently, would be for the English court to claim an altogether exorbitant, extra-territorial jurisdiction."

Also, in *Derby & Co. Ltd. v Weldon*[71] a world-wide Mareva injunction was granted. In such a case, i.e., where a world-wide Mareva injunction is sought:

(a) the plaintiff must show that any assets within the jurisdiction are insufficient and that the defendant has assets abroad, and

---

67. The member states of the European Community are the contracting states of the Brussels Convention (i.e., The Brussels Convention on Jurisdiction and the Enforcement of Judgements in Civil and Commercial Matters). That Convention was given effect to by s.2 of the Civil Jurisdiction and Judgements Act 1982. The Lugano Convention was entered into by the European Community states and members of the European Free Trade Association (Austria, Finland, Iceland, Norway, Sweden, and Switzerland). Effect to it was given by the Civil Jurisdiction and Judgements Act 1991, to which it appears as schedule 1. The date it came into force in the United Kingdom was 1st May 1992 (see S.I. 1992/745).
68. See Appendix 5 (d) and (e), *post*.
69. [1990] Ch. 13.
70. [1990] Ch. 13, at p. 44.
71. [1990] Ch. 48.

(b) the plaintiff must satisfy the court *via* an undertaking or proviso that:

(i) the injunction will not be oppressive to the defendant (in that it will not expose him to multiple proceedings abroad); one form of oppression is oppressive enforcement by a multiplicity of applications in different countries worldwide;[72] the other form (as illustrated by *Morris and ors. v Mahfouz and ors.*)[73] is the issuing of fresh proceedings in a foreign court arising out of the same subject-matter.[74]

(ii) third-party rights are protected (i.e., unspecified individuals or companies and persons not resident in the jurisdiction, even if they have notice of the injunction, should not be liable for a breach of it by acts done abroad unless the injunction has been declared enforceable by a court outside the jurisdiction - this is known as the "*Babanaft proviso*"); and

(iii) any information obtained from the order for disclosure of assets by the defendant will not be misused against the defendant.

In *Derby v Weldon*[75] the amount of money involved was a huge one (£25m.), the defendant's assets within the jurisdiction were inadequate, and the plaintiff was able to show the defendant was very likely to dissipate the foreign assets through various companies abroad. That was why the Mareva injunction applied for was granted by the Court of Appeal.

The court can also exceptionally order the defendant to transfer his assets from one jurisdiction to another in order to stop them from being disposed of or dissipated before trial (*Derby v Weldon (No. 6)*[76]).

---

72. *Ashtiani v Kashi* [1986] 2 All E.R. 970; *Babanaft v Bassatne* [1989] 1 All E.R. 433; *Republic of Haiti v Duvalier* [1989] 1 All E.R. 456; *Derby v Weldon (No. 1)* [1989] 1 All E.R. 469.
73. (1993) *N.L.J.*, December 10, 1993, p. 1748.
74. That is why an undertaking is required that no such application will be made to, or fresh proceedings be commenced in, a foreign court without first obtaining leave of the English court.
75. [1990] Ch. 48.
76. [1990] 1 W.L.R. 1139.

Once the injunction has been granted, the defendant has the right to apply to the court to vary it or to set it aside. An example of where, on the application by the defendant, a Mareva injunction was discharged is *Cheltenham and Gloucester Building Society (formerly Portsmouth Building Society) v Ricketts and others.*[77] What happened in that case was that the plaintiff, the building society, made an *ex parte* application for interlocutory injunctions against the defendants because, they alleged, the defendants were involved in serious mortgage fraud. The judge who heard the application granted a Mareva injunction against three of the defendants (and an injunction against all four defendants) whereby the defendants were restrained from dealing with or alienating the properties concerned. However, the plaintiff had to give an undertaking in damages. The first and fourth defendants then applied for the injunctions to be discharged. Although both injunctions were discharged, the judge went on to order an inquiry into the plaintiff's liability in damages to those two (the first and fourth) defendants. When the plaintiff appealed against the judge's decision, the Court of Appeal held, *inter alia,* that the judge was wrong in ordering an inquiry into the plaintiff's liability in damages before deciding whether the undertaking in damages ought to be enforced. The application was, therefore, adjourned to be dealt with at the trial.

**The privilege against self-incrimination**

A defendant faced with a Mareva injunction may be able to invoke the privilege against self-incrimination in order to avoid complying with it (or with an order for discovery). Such non-compliance will not be contumacious or stubborn defiance because it has a legitimate basis. But, he cannot rely on the privilege if a term in the order adequately protects him by preventing the disclosures from being used in a prosecution.

**The Practice Direction [1994] 4 All E.R. 52**

The effect of the Practice Direction 1994 on Mareva injunctions (apart from the draft order) is as follows:

---

77. [1993] 1 W.L.R. 1545.

1. If practicable, the applicant should lodge the relevant papers with a judge at least two hours before the application is heard.

2. Where appropriate, the applicant's undertaking in damages should be supported by actual payment of money or a bond being provided by an insurance company to the court or to the plaintiff's solicitor, as an officer of the court, to hold pending a further order by the court.

3. If there is an application for the order to be varied/discharged, such application should, if practicable, be dealt with on the return date.

4. If the injunction is discharged on that return date, the judge must always consider the appropriateness of immediately assessing damages and directing payment thereof by the applicant.

**Implications of the Mareva injunction**

It must also be noted that the Mareva injunction operates only *in personam*. It prohibits the defendant personally from transferring, removing or otherwise dealing with his property/assets. Failure to comply with it generally constitutes contempt of court. It does not give the plaintiff any proprietary right in the asset/s. It also does not give any priority over other creditors. Therefore, the rights of a third-party with an interest in the assets will not be affected, as can be seen below on the limits of the injunction.

**Limits of the Mareva injunction**

The Mareva injunction, despite being a "nuclear weapon" of the law, has some limitations. They include the following:

1. The Mareva injunction does not create any priority. It simply prevents a defendant from removing his assets from the jurisdiction so as to make them unavailable to satisfy any judgement against him. According to Goff J. (as he then was) in *Iraqi Ministry of Defence v Arcepey*,[78] "the purpose of the Mareva jurisdiction is not to improve

---

78. [1980] 2 W.L.R. 488, at 494.

the position of claimants in an insolvency" and it is "not a form of pre-trial attachment, but a relief *in personam* which prohibits certain acts in relation to the assets in question".[79]

2(a). It does not hinder or block a judgement creditor: therefore, against any frozen assets a judgement creditor can enforce his judgement.

(b). It also does not block a pre-existing creditor: *Iraqi Ministry of Defence v Arcepey*. In that case the plaintiffs owned cargo on a ship, the Angel Bell. The ship was owned by the defendants. The ship sank and the plaintiffs lost their cargo. They sued the defendants for £3m. for that loss. Then three and half months later they obtained a Mareva injunction against the defendants. Creditors of the defendants had (two years before then) loaned the defendants £270,000 to buy ships including the Angel Bell. The Angel Bell and other ships were mortgaged to the creditors and an insurance policy on the Angel Bell was assigned to the creditors. The creditors obtained leave to intervene in the action. The defendants' only assets were the proceeds of insurance policies in respect of the ship which the brokers were holding. On the issue between the plaintiffs and the interveners (the defendants' creditors) it was held, before the plaintiffs obtained the Mareva injunction, that the interveners were equitable mortgagees of the Angel Bell and assignees of the insurance policies who could sue on them. The interveners then applied for the Mareva injunction to be varied to allow the brokers to pay back the loan from the insurance moneys they were holding. It was held that the injunction would be varied because its purpose was not to improve a claimant's position to an insolvent debtor's property; rather, it was to prevent the defendant from removing his assets from the jurisdiction in order to defeat any judgement against him. According to Goff J., a plaintiff who had not yet proceeded to judgement but is merely claiming an unliquidated sum from a defendant, should not be allowed to stop that defendant from using his assets to pay his debts. Therefore, to allow the Mareva injunction to be used to prevent such payment of a defendant's debts *bona fide* "would be to stretch it beyond its original purpose so that instead of preventing abuse it would rather prevent businessmen conducting their businesses as they are entitled

---

79. See also *Cretanor Maritime Co. v Irish Marine Management* [1978] 1 W.L.R. 966.

to do".[80]

3. On the position of banks, according to Lord Denning M.R., in *Z. Ltd. v A.-Z. and A.A.-L.L.*,[81] the juristic principle is that, as soon as notice is given to a bank of a Mareva injunction, the bank must freeze the bank account of the defendant and not allow any sum to be drawn on it by way of a cheque, etc. However, this does not apply to payment under a letter of credit or a bank guarantee, although "it may apply to the proceeds as and when received by or for the defendant". It also does not apply to a credit card issued to, and used by, the defendant. In the same case (at page 583) Lord Eveleigh stated:

> "The fact that the bank is under an obligation to others to make a payment should be strong evidence that the bank was not contumacious where that obligation emanates from a relationship between the bank and such other people as was established before the making of the order. Thus, to honour a cheque drawn with the support of a banker's card should not be treated as contempt ... ."

Also, according to *Polly Peck v Nadir (No. 2)*,[82] the court will not grant a Mareva injunction against a bank before any liability had been imposed if the effect of the injunction will be to interfere with its normal course of business as a bank. In the words of Lord Scott:[83] "a Mareva injunction ought never to prevent a defendant from paying his creditors their due debts. A bank must repay its depositors in accordance with the terms on which the deposits are held." Lord Donaldson M.R., too, had this to say:

> "... no defendant, whether a natural or a juridical person, can be enjoined in terms which will prevent him from carrying on his business in the ordinary way or from meeting his debts or other obligations as they come due prior to judgement being given in the action."[84]

---

80. *Per* Goff, J. (as he then was) in *Iraqi M.O.D.*, at p. 495.
81. [1982] 1 Q.B. 558, at p. 574.
82. [1992] 4 All E.R. 769.
83. *Ibid.*, p. 782.
84. *Ibid.*, p. 785.

4. The property of a defendant's spouse does not also get frozen if there is no evidence that the defendant in fact owns those assets: *Allied Arab Bank Ltd. v Hajjar.*[85] A joint bank account will only be affected if the order is so worded as to cover it specifically. For example, in *S.C.F. Finance Co. Ltd. v Masri*[86] the order in question referred specifically to all accounts "held by or on behalf the defendant or by or on behalf of the defendant jointly with any other persons or by nominees or otherwise howsoever" at three named banks in London.

5. Good title to assets frozen by a Mareva injunction can be obtained by a *bona fide* purchaser for value without notice of the injunction.[87]

**The Anton Piller order**

This order, which took its name from the case, *Anton-Piller KG v Manufacturing Processes Ltd.*,[88] permits the plaintiff's solicitors to search the defendant's premises and seize items and documents found there which could constitute evidence in the action of the plaintiff against that defendant. Its purpose is, therefore, simply to prevent the defendant from frustrating a fair trial by destroying documents and other items of evidence before the case is tried, and by not giving proper discovery.[89]

The Anton Piller order is a very useful device for victims of breaches of confidence and of copyright as well as victims of passing off. However,

---

85. (1989) 19 Fam. Law 68. There the plaintiff, a bank, could not show that the assets in question were in truth assets of the husband and not the wife.
86. [1985] 1 W.L.R. 876.
87. This is because equity always does what is conscionable and "equity will not assist a volunteer".
88. [1976] 1 Ch. 55.
89. "Discovery" is the process by which parties to an action are obliged to exchange documents which they possess or are in their custody or control. In an action begun by writ a list of documents must be served by each party after the close of pleadings. Also, each party who is entitled to have discovery can serve a notice requiring an affidavit which verifies the list of documents. The court, too, may, in any action, make an order requiring any party to make and serve a list of documents, and to make a verifying affidavit. See Rules of the Supreme Court, Ord. 24 and County Court Rules, Ord. 14.

it has also been made in respect of accounts and a diary,[90] documents relating to a husband's earnings and capital,[91] etc.

The application for the order is usually made *ex parte*. This is because, if the defendant is forewarned, he would destroy or remove the evidence before trial.

The order has been variously described:

- as "an illustration of the adaptability of equitable remedies to new situations" (by Lord Wilberforce in *Rank Film Distributors Ltd. v Video Information Centre*;[92]

- as "a draconian power which should be used only in exceptional cases" (by Lord Donaldson in his dissenting judgement in *Yousif v Salama*;[93] and

- as "an innovation which has proved its worth time and time again" (by Lord Denning in *Rank Film Distributors Ltd. v Video Information Centre*).[94]

*E.M.I. Ltd. v Pandit*[95] is the first reported modern case in point. There, in an action for breach of copyright, the plaintiff applied *ex parte* for an injunction to enable him to enter the defendant's premises for the purpose of inspecting and removing items showing infringement by the defendant. The order (under order 29, Rules of the Supreme Court) was duly granted because the court thought that would ensure the defendant could not frustrate a fair trial by destroying or removing damaging evidence. That case was approved in *Anton Piller KG v Manufacturing Processes Ltd*. In that case the plaintiffs were German manufacturers of frequency converters for computers and the defendants were the plaintiffs' agents in the United Kingdom. The plaintiffs claimed the defendants were infringing their copyright. Therefore, to prevent the defendants from disposing, before trial, of documents they had which related to the plaintiffs' designs, etc., the plaintiffs made an *ex parte*

---

90. *Yousif v Salama* [1980] 1 W.L.R. 1540.
91. *Emmanuel v Emmanuel* [1982] 1 W.L.R. 669.
92. [1982] A.C. 380, at 439.
93. [1980] 1 W.L.R. 1540, at 1544.
94. [1982] A.C. 380, at 406.
95. [1975] 1 W.L.R. 302.

application for an interim injunction to stop the defendants from breaching their copyright and disclosing confidential information. They also applied for an order to permit them to enter the defendants' premises to inspect documents and remove them into the custody of their (the plaintiffs') solicitors. The order for inspection and removal of documents was refused and the plaintiffs appealed *(ex parte)*. The Court of Appeal referred to *E.M.I. v Pandit* and held that, where, in most exceptional circumstances:

(a) the plaintiffs' case was, *prima facie,* very strong,

(b) there was very serious actual or potential damage to the plaintiffs, and

(c) there was clear evidence of the defendants' possessing vital material which they might destroy or dispose of (before an *inter partes* application was made), and so defeat the ends of justice, the court had inherent jurisdiction to order the defendants to allow the plaintiffs' solicitors to enter their premises and inspect and remove such evidence/items.

In contrast with a search warrant, the Anton-Piller order does not authorise the plaintiff to enter the premises against the defendant's will. It only orders the defendant to permit the plaintiff to enter, and non-compliance with it constitutes contempt of court.[96]

**Requirements**

In the *Anton Piller case*, Lord Ormrod laid down three requirements for the making of the order:

(a) the plaintiff must have an extremely strong *prima facie* case;

(b) he has to show real or potential damage which is very serious;

---

96. In *Bhimji v Chatwani* [1991] 1 W.L.R. 989, however, where the defendant failed to comply with the injunction in question, that failure was, on the facts, not contumacious. It, therefore, did not justify the infliction of any penalty.

(c) there must be clear evidence of the defendant's having incriminating documents or other property and also a real possibility of their destruction before any *inter partes* application can be made;

Lord Denning added another:

(d) it must be shown that the inspection will do no real harm to the defendant.

The order must, thus, not be sought as a "fishing expedition".

**Safeguards for the defendant**

In *Universal Thermosensors v Hibben*[97] the plaintiff, which had commenced proceedings against the defendants for damages for loss of profits caused by misuse of confidential information by the defendants, obtained an Anton Piller order and an interlocutory injunction against the defendants. The Anton Piller order was, however, executed by the plaintiff in a very questionable manner: (a) it was executed very early (at 7:15 a.m.) in the homes of the first three defendants, (b) one home, where the order was executed by a lone male, a stranger, was occupied by an unaccompanied woman (her children were in bed at the time), (c) there was no responsible officer or employee of the fourth defendant present at its premises when they were searched and (d) the search, a thorough one, was carried out there by a person with considerable interest in the plaintiff firm (in other words, by a competitor of the defendants, a person who was not independent), a situation described by the court (at p. 276) as "most unsatisfactory". The defendants were duly awarded damages of £20,000 against the plaintiff in accordance with the plaintiff's undertaking in damages made to the court. According to the court (*per* Sir Nicholls V.-C.) , the grant of an Anton Piller order must be subject to the following safeguards:

1. the order should be executed only on working days in office hours when a solicitor will be available for the defendant to seek legal advice;

---

97. [1992] 3 All E.R. 257.

2. if the order is to be executed at a private house and a woman may be alone there, the solicitor serving the order must be a woman or must be accompanied by a woman;

3. the order should provide expressly that, unless it is not practicable, a list of all documents and items removed should be made at the premises and checked by the defendant;

4. an injunction prohibiting those on whom the order is served from telling others about the order should be for a limited time and not as long as a week;

5. the order should provide that it should be served at only business premises in the presence of a representative of the company, unless there is good reason for not doing so;

6. consideration should be given to some means of preventing the plaintiff from conducting a thorough search of a competitor's documents when executing the order.

   Also, judges should consider the desirability of ordering that the service and execution of the order be supervised by a solicitor who is experienced in the practice of such orders.

These guidelines have, however, been modified slightly by the Practice Direction 1994.

**The effect of the Practice Direction on Anton Piller order (apart from the draft order)**

1. If practicable, the applicant should lodge the relevant papers with a judge at least two hours before the application is heard.

2. Where appropriate, the applicant's undertaking in damages should be supported by actual payment of money or a bond being provided by an insurance company to the court or to the plaintiff's solicitor, as an officer of the court, to hold pending a further order by the court.

3. If there is an application for the order to be varied/discharged, such application should, if practicable, be dealt with on the return date.

4. If the injunction is discharged on that return date, the judge must always consider the appropriateness of assessing damages and directing payment thereof by the applicant immediately.

5. The specimen order is to be served by a supervising solicitor. It must also be carried out before him and supervised by him. He should be:
   (a) an experienced solicitor familiar with Anton Piller orders, and
   (b) not a member/employee of the firm representing the plaintiff.

   But, if the court does not want the order to be served by a supervising solicitor, it should state its reason/s in the order.

6. Where the place of service of the order is occupied by an "unaccompanied woman", and the supervising solicitor is a man, the persons accompanying him should include a woman.

7. The applicant should be required to insure the items if, because of their nature, that is appropriate.

8. The applicant should promise to inform no third party of the proceedings until the return date has passed.

9. In the Queen's Bench Division, applications are no longer to be heard by the judge in chambers. Moreover, so far as practicable, applications to the Chancery and Queen's Bench Divisions will be so listed before a judge as to afford him enough time to read and consider in advance the papers.

10. On the circuit, the application can be heard by either:

    (a) a High Court judge, or

    (b) a Circuit Judge, sitting as a High Court judge and who the Presiding Judge has duly designated to hear such applications.

As can be seen, the main differences between the Practice Direction 1994 and the principles stated in *Universal Thermosensors v Hibben* are contained in paragraphs 7-9 above (regarding insurance, undertaking not to inform any third party until after the return date, and future applications to the Queen's Bench Division not being heard by a judge in chambers, etc.).

**The procedure followed**

1. The application will be made *ex parte* (and to a judge in chambers, if made to the Chancery Division).

2. The solicitor of the plaintiff prepares the following:

   (a) a *writ* indorsed (if time so allows) with a statement of claim. If it is not possible to issue the writ, an undertaking is given to the court that it will be issued as soon as the court office is open;

   (b) an *affidavit*:

      - showing that there is clear evidence to justify the substantive claim of the plaintiff (the plaintiff's extremely strong *prima facie* case, full and frank disclosure of all material facts, etc.);

      - showing that the plaintiff will suffer very serious actual or potential damage if an order is not made; and

      - justifying the claim that the defendant is likely to destroy or dispose of the property in question if the order is not made;[98]

   (c) a *draft order* to be made by the court.[99]

---

98. See Appendix 5(b), *post*.
99. See Appendix 5(c), *post*.

In very urgent cases the plaintiff's counsel may attend before a judge and state orally what his evidence is.

**Other points to be noted:**

1. Because of the draconian nature of the order, the plaintiff must make full and frank disclosure of all relevant matters to the court.

2. The plaintiff's solicitor also must make undertakings relating to the return of material seized, etc.

3. When executing the order, the plaintiff must act with caution, as shown by *Columbia Picture Industries Inc. v Robinson,*[100] a case concerning breach of copyright. There the defendant was making pirate copies of films on video cassettes. The plaintiffs had originally made the films. The defendant had earlier allowed some videotapes of his to be taken away and checked by the chief investigation officer of the plaintiffs' trade organisation. The plaintiffs applied for and obtained an Anton Piller order against the defendant. However, they (the plaintiffs) did three things wrong:

    (a) their solicitors (in their affidavit supporting their application) did not make full and frank disclosure of all relevant matters; for example, they did not disclose that not all the tapes, which the defendant had permitted the chief investigation officer of the plaintiffs' trade organisation to take and check for breach of copyright, actually breached the plaintiffs' copyright;

    (b) some documents and video cassettes taken and retained were not listed in the order; and

    (c) some of the items that were seized were lost while in the custody of the plaintiffs' solicitors.

    The defendant was put out of business as a result of the order.

---

100. [1987] Ch. 38.

The court held, *inter alia,* that, although the plaintiffs' breach of duty to make full and frank disclosure of all relevant matters was enough reason to discharge the order, doing so would serve no purpose. Therefore, because the plaintiffs had caused the shutting down of the defendant's legitimate business (in addition to the illegal one), compensatory and aggravated damages of £10,000 should be paid to him by the plaintiffs.

4. The plaintiff must be able to specify or particularly identify the trade secrets or other confidential information which the defendant should be prevented from using. If the plaintiff cannot do so, the injunction may not be granted: *Lock International v Beswick.*[101]

5. The order may relate to premises situated abroad, e.g., a flat in Paris, as in *Cook Industries Inc. v Galliher.*[102]

6. The plaintiff, after execution of the order, is subject to an implied undertaking not to use the documents or other items for any collateral purpose without the consent of the defendant.

**The privilege against self-incrimination**

The order may be set aside if the defendant invokes the privilege against self-incrimination: *Tate Access Floors Inc. v Boswell.*[103]

However, the privilege has been affected by the Supreme Court Act 1981, s.72(3), as regards disclosure of information relating to an intellectual property right (breach of copyright, passing off, etc.) to the effect that matters which are disclosed as a result of an Anton-Piller order are

---

101. [1989] 3 All E.R. 373, where the plaintiff failed to disclose relevant information when the order was applied for and the evidence did not justify the making of the order.
102. [1979] Ch. 439.
103. [1990] 3 All E.R. 303.

inadmissible as evidence against the defendant if he is prosecuted.[104] It can, thus, be said that the privilege against self-incrimination is now not claimable in cases involving intellectual property rights. But, it may be claimed in other cases, e.g., revenue offences or where the plaintiff's case suggests there is conspiracy to defraud (as in *Tate Access Floors v Boswell*), etc. It is not surprising, therefore, that the privilege could not be invoked successfully in *Coca-Cola v Gilbey*.[105] There the plaintiff, in an action for breach of trademark, passing off, etc., obtained an Anton-Piller order against the defendant. Under the order the defendant was to allow searching of his premises by the plaintiff, to deliver up specific documents and other items and to give information about the whereabouts of certain other items and the addresses the breaching organisation used and the names of the individuals who were involved therein. The defendant failed to give information about the whereabouts of items and addresses used by the organisation because, he argued, that would incriminate him in criminal proceedings and those persons involved were likely to be violent towards his family if he gave that information. His argument was, however, held to be inferior to the plaintiff's interests and that of the public and, so, did not prevail.

### Variation or discharge of the order

The following are some common grounds on which an Anton Piller order may be varied or discharged:

- failure by the plaintiff to make full and frank disclosure of any argument or point the defendant might make if he were present;

- plaintiff's failure to show:

---

104. It is interesting to note that in *Istel Ltd. v Tully* [1993] A.C. 45, a case where the claim in question did not relate to rights pertaining to commercial information within the meaning of section 72, Supreme Court Act 1981, the House of Lords held, *inter alia,* that a defendant in a civil action should not be allowed to rely on the privilege against self-incrimination where compliance with an order for disclosure would not cause any real danger of prejudice for that defendant in criminal proceedings or where his own protection was adequately made safe by other means.
105. *The Independent*, October 10, 1995.

(a) an extremely strong *prima facie* case,

(b) that he will suffer very serious actual or potential damage unless the order is made; or

(c) that the defendant has vital, incriminating evidence and is likely to destroy or dispose of it/them unless the order is made;

- when the privilege against self-incrimination is invoked.

## *Quia timet* injunction[106]

Where the infringement of the plaintiff's right has not yet occurred but is threatened or feared, a *quia timet* injunction may be granted. It may be (a) perpetual or interlocutory, or (b) prohibitory or mandatory.

The plaintiff must show a strong case of probability of imminent danger and there must be proof that the damage feared will (if it comes) be very substantial.[107] In *Litchfield-Speer v Queen Anne's Gare Syndicate (No. 2) Ltd.*,[108] a case on nuisance which necessitated a judicial visit to the premises concerned, Lawrence J. said:

> "In all cases of apprehended nuisance the authorities show that if the plaintiff proves that he will certainly sustain substantial damage by what the defendant is about to do the Court will restrain the defendant from doing the act and will not wait until the plaintiff has sustained the damage."

### *Principles*

In *Redland Bricks v Morris*[109] the respondent's eight acres of land was next

---

106. *Quia timet* means "because he fears".
107. *A.-G. v Nottingham Corp.* [1904] 1 Ch. 673.
108. [1919] 1 Ch. 407, 412.
109. [1970] A.C. 652.

to, and sloped down, the land of the appellants (a brick company). The appellants carried out excavations on their land some 60 feet away from the respondent's boundary. A big hole was left in the land of the appellant brick company. That hole became filled with water up to about nine feet high. Later the respondent's land started slipping on to the land of the appellants. Further slips occurred, despite remedial work done by the appellant brick company. The respondent was awarded, *inter alia,* (a) a prohibitory injunction against the appellants' further excavations which would interfere with the support of the respondent's land, and (b) a mandatory injunction to compel the appellants to do all that was necessary to restore support to the respondent's land in six months' time. The brick company appealed to the House of Lords against the mandatory injunction. That appeal succeeded because the mandatory injunction imposed a totally unconditional duty to restore the support required but did not specify the work that had to be done.

The principles to be applied to the granting of a mandatory *quia timet* injunction were stated by the House as follows (even though the injunctions awarded earlier were not themselves *quia timet*):

1. the plaintiff must show a very strong probability that grave damage will come to him in the future;

2. if the damage does happen, damages will not be an adequate remedy;

3. the cost to the defendant to do works to prevent or to reduce the likelihood of a feared future wrong must be taken into consideration; and

4. the court must make sure that the defendant knows exactly what he has to do if a mandatory injunction is granted.

### *Discretionary remedy*

The *quia timet* injunction is, like all injunctions, a discretionary remedy, as shown by *Torquay Hotel Co. Ltd. v Cousins*.[110] In that case the Court of Appeal refused to grant an injunction against a union because of s.4(1), Trade Disputes Act 1906 which, at that time, prohibited an action for an injunction against such unions. But, it dismissed the appeal of certain union officials

110. [1969] 2 Ch. 106; [1969] 1 All E.R. 522.

against the grant of an interlocutory injunction restraining them from interfering with the supply or delivery of fuel oil to the plaintiff hotel because those officials had no immunity from liability.

Another illustrative case is *Redland Bricks v Morris*, already referred to for above.

Finally, a *quia timet* injunction will not be granted if there is only a mere possibility of future injury, or mere speculation of possible injury or damage which may never occur at all. Thus, in both *A.-G. v Manchester Corporation*[111] and *A.-G. v Nottingham Corporation*[112] the plaintiff failed to obtain an injunction restraining the defendants, local authorities, from establishing smallpox hospitals.

**Bars/defences to an injunction**

This section focuses on the bars or defences to an injunction. They are:

**1. Delay (*laches*)**

According to section 36(1), Limitation Act 1980, the limitation period for torts does not apply to an action for an injunction.

However, an injunction is (just like specific performance) an equitable remedy. Therefore, in accordance with the maxim, "delay defeats equities", where a plaintiff has delayed unreasonably before bringing his action (for an injunction), that delay may defeat his claim. For example, as regards interlocutory injunctions, in *Shepherd Homes Ltd. v Sandham*[113] it was held, *inter alia,* that, because of the plaintiff's delay in bringing the motion in question, it would be wrong to grant the injunction sought.

Concerning perpetual injunctions, there seem to be conflicting authorities. Thus, in *Brooks v Mucleston*[114] the plaintiff's own delay defeated his claim. On the other hand, in *Kelsen v Imperial Tobacco* the plaintiff's case was not defeated by delay because, as McNair J. said in that case (at p. 342), the defendant did not get the plaintiff's permission before encroaching

---

111. [1893] 2 Ch. 87.
112. [1904] 1 Ch. 673.
113. [1971] Ch. 340.
114. [1909] 2 Ch. 519.

on the plaintiff's airspace and any such permission was generally revocable:

> "... if the Imperial Tobacco Co. had come direct to the plaintiff as the owner of the airspace above his shop and asked him expressly for his permission and he had granted his permission expressly, ... such an express liberty given by the plaintiff would be revocable at least on reasonable notice unless by the express terms of the agreement or licence the plaintiff had debarred himself from terminating on reasonable notice. If that is the position with regard to express notice it is very difficult to see, however the case was put, that the position of the plaintiff can be worse if the permission relied upon is merely an implied permission, as indeed it must be, because there is no evidence or suggestion that he ever expressly granted permission."

Perhaps the common factor that can reconcile the conflicting decisions is the fact that, although the court considers all the circumstances of each case in making its decision, an equitable remedy is discretionary.

## 2. Acquiescence

Acquiescence (as can be seen above in the section on specific performance), is assenting to rights being infringed. Such assent may be express, implied or by conduct. Thus, in *Sayers v Collyer*,[115] where the plaintiff had known for three years that, in breach of covenant, the defendant was using his premises to sell beer and the plaintiff himself had bought beer from there, the plaintiff's action was, accordingly, barred by acquiescence on his part.

For acquiescence to be a defence to an injunction the circumstances must be such that it would be dishonest or unconscionable for the plaintiff to seek enforcement of his legal right. In *Shaw v Applegate,*[116] where the defendant breached a covenant not to use his property as an amusement arcade, there was no such dishonesty or unconscionability on the part of the plaintiff. However, as he had failed to ask for an interlocutory injunction and the defendant had incurred expenditure, etc., over a period of time, it was held that damages in lieu of an injunction should be the proper remedy.

---

115. [1885] 28 Ch.D. 103.
116. [1977] 1 W.L.R. 970.

### 3. Hardship to the defendant

This may be illustrated, as regards interlocutory injunctions, by the *American Cyanamid case* and, as regards *quia timet* injunctions, by *Redland Bricks v Morris*, where Lord Upjohn stated, *inter alia*:

> "Unlike the case where a negative injunction is granted to prevent the continuance or recurrence of a wrongful act the question of the cost to the defendant to do works to prevent or lessen the likelihood of a future apprehended wrong must be an element to be taken into account ... ."[117]

### 4. Conduct of the plaintiff ("clean hands")

An example of this is *Shell U.K v Lostock Garages*,[118] where the injunction sought was not granted because the "solus agreement" in question, though a reasonable restraint of trade at the start, became unreasonable and, therefore, could not be enforced while the unreasonable element (i.e., a support scheme which was prejudicial to the defendants) remained. The decision is well in accordance with the maxim, "He who comes to equity must come with clean hands," which is similar to another maxim dealt with in the previous chapter, "He who comes to equity must do equity".[119]

### 5. Contract of employment

As already noted, specific performance will not be granted where there is a contract of employment. An injunction will, therefore, not be granted to an employer to restrain a defendant from breaching a covenant in a contract of employment if the effect of the injunction will be indirect specific performance. Thus, *Ehrman v Bartholomew*[120] an injunction was not granted to stop an employee from breaching his promise "not to engage in any other

---

117. [1970] A.C. 652, 666.
118. [1976] 1 W.L.R. 1187.
119. See *Measures Bros. Ltd v Measures* [1910] 2 Ch. 248; and *Agricultural Supplies Ltd. v Rushmere* (1967) 111 *Sol. Jo.*, 683.
120. [1898] 1 Ch. 671.

business for ten years".[121]

Today section 236 of the Trade Union and Labour Relations (Consolidation) Act 1992 restates the rule against indirect specific performance in cases where the plaintiff is suing his employee.

Also, if an injunction granted against a third party would have the effect of indirect specific performance of a contract of employment, as in *Warren v Mendy*,[122] it would not be granted.

**Exercises**

1. Is it true that no account is taken by the court of the defendant's hardship or the public interest when granting a prohibitory injunction?

2. L, A, P and D left the employment of X. On leaving, they took with them certain confidential documents including information about customers of X. L, A, P and D started their own business which competed with X's. Within 6 months they achieved sales of over £2 million. When X suspected that his ex-employees were making extensive use of his client list he decided to commence legal proceedings to sue L, A, P and D for breach of confidence and breach of contract.

   On Friday at 4.59 p.m., L, A, P and D, fearing that X was about to take action against them, instructed their solicitors to start transferring the bulk of their assets to MIL Ltd., a company owned by L's mother-in-law, from the following Wednesday. Unknown to L, A, P and D, their solicitors' secretary, Cassandra, was engaged to X's son. She knew of L, A, P and D's instructions to her law firm and so promptly telephoned X and told him about the situation.

   Advise X.

3. What is a Mareva injunction? Describe the procedure and safeguards attached to the granting of such an order.

---

121. But, see *Lumley v Gye* (1852) 1 De. G.M. and G. 604, where the court granted an injunction.
122. [1989] 3 All E.R. 103.

# 10 Other equitable remedies

## 1. Equitable damages

Prior to the passing of the Chancery Amendment Act 1858,[1] where the Court of Chancery refused specific performance or an injunction, it had no power to award damages and a separate action in a common law court was necessary for damages to be recovered. However, s.2 of the Chancery Amendment Act ("Lord Cairn's Act") altered the position and gave discretion to the Chancery Court to award damages. It stated :

> "In all cases in which the Court of Chancery has jurisdiction to entertain an application for an injunction against a breach of any covenant, contract or agreement, or against the commission or continuance of any wrongful act, or for the specific performance of any covenant, contract or agreement, it shall be lawful for the same court, if it shall think fit, to award damages to the party injured either in addition to or in substitution for such injunction or specific performance, and such damages may be assessed in such manner as the court shall direct."

The power to award "equitable damages" is now contained in s.50 of the Supreme Court Act 1981. It is not an unlimited power and such damages are not available in lieu at equity when the action in question is pursued only at common law.[2] Additionally, the court may not award equitable damages where, at the time the action is brought, it does not have the jurisdiction to issue an injunction or order specific performance.[3] However, the court will have the necessary power where an injunction or specific performance is barred for some discretionary reason. The distinction between jurisdiction and discretion can lack clarity but the trend towards recognising jurisdictional defences as discretionary should extend the power of the

---

1. Repealed by Statute Law Revision Act 1883. But, this did not affect the jurisdiction of the court. See *Leeds Industrial Co-operative Society Ltd. v Slack* [1924] A.C. 851.
2. *Horsler v Zorro* [1975] Ch. 302.
3. *Ferguson v Wilson* (1866) L.R. 2 Ch. App. 77; *Sayers v Collyer* (1884) 28 Ch. D. 103.

courts to award equitable damages.[4] Note that, where the court has the jurisdiction to award an injunction or specific performance at the time the action commences, it may award equitable damages, regardless of the fact that the equitable remedy is no longer available at the time of judgement.[5]

*Availability of equitable damages*

Given the above restricted power, when will the courts award equitable damages in lieu of providing specific relief? In *Shelfer v City of London Electric Lighting Co.*[6] A.L. Smith L.J. stated that, as a working rule, damages should be awarded in lieu of an injunction if:

(i) the injury to the plaintiff's rights is small,

(ii) the injury is capable of being estimated in money,

(iii) the injury is one which is capable of being adequately compensated by a small money payment, and

(iv) the granting of an injunction would be oppressive to the defendant.

The bias is, therefore, towards the granting of specific relief and against the defendant being able to purchase the plaintiff's rights where they are of some consequence. A greater willingness to award damages would favour the defendant in possession of large resources, in particular, the wealthy corporation, which would be able to disregard the interests of the plaintiff safe in the knowledge that all the court will demand of it is a cheque, the amount for which may well already have been built into its costing calculations.[7]

Note that damages will be awarded as an *addition* to specific

---

4. See *Price v Strange* [1978] Ch. 337, where want of mutuality was regarded as a discretionary bar to specific performance.
5. *Cory v Thames Iron Works & Shipbuilding Co. Ltd.* (1863) 8 L.T. 237.
6. [1895] 1 Ch. 287.
7. However, see *Miller v Jackson* [1977] Q.B. 966, where the Court of Appeal disregarded this rationale and compare with *Kennaway v Thompson* [1981] Q.B. 88, where the same court, in turn, disregarded *Miller*.

performance only in circumstances where there has been some special damage, as in *Jacques v Millar*,[8] where the plaintiff received compensation for loss of business profits.

The Judicature Act 1873 made available common law damages in the Chancery Division. Given that the method of quantifying each category of damages is the same, the only reason for seeking equitable damages is when no damages are available at common law. This will occur, of course, when no action at common law may be pursued because the infringement in question is concerned with a purely equitable right. It is useful to refer to a number of examples.

### (a) Breach of confidence

It is a broad principle of equity that someone who has received information in confidence shall not take unfair advantage of it to the prejudice of the person who gave it without obtaining that person's consent. In *Seager v Copydex (No. 1)*[9] the defendant company employed in their own product an idea devised by the plaintiffs and discussed with them in confidence. The usual remedies for breach of such a duty are an injunction and an account of profits but the Court of Appeal considered that, in the circumstances, damages in lieu of an injunction were the fairest remedy.

In *Peter Pan Manufacturing v Corsets Silhouette*[10] an account of profits was granted (in addition to an injunction), but the plaintiff was given the option of damages. The jurisdiction under which such damages were made available in the two cases above was not made clear. However, in *Att.-Gen. v Observer Ltd.*[11] Lord Goff considered that a benign interpretation of the Chancery Amendment Act 1858 allowed for damages to be made available in cases of breach of confidence notwithstanding the fact that the duty in question was equitable.

### (b) Restrictive covenants

The rule of privity of contract is subject to a modification entirely founded

---

8. (1877) 6 Ch.D. 153.
9. [1967] 2 All E.R. 415. Also *Saltman Ltd. v Campbell Ltd.* [1948] 65 R.P.C. 2033.
10. [1963] R.P.C. 45.
11. [1990] 1 A.C. 109.

in equity. This is the doctrine that a restrictive covenant, which binds a purchaser of land not to perform certain acts of ownership thereon, may be enforced not only against him as the contracting party but also against subsequent purchasers of the land.[12]

Restrictive covenants consist of a negative contractual undertaking and it follows that in such cases an injunction is the appropriate equitable remedy available almost as a matter of course.[13] However, in *Eastwood v Lever*[14] the power of the court to award damages, as an addition to or in substitute for an injunction, was recognised. The availability of a monetary award is determined by the surrounding circumstances in each case[15] so that, for example, in *Baxter v Four Oak Properties Ltd.*[16] the effect of awarding an injunction against the defendants, who were innocently in breach of a covenant, would have been to make them particularly vulnerable to a claim from the plaintiff for a money payment to release the defendants from the restrictions imposed by an injunction. In effect the plaintiffs would receive "damages" and the sum in question would probably be greater than if no injunction were granted.

Again, in *Wrotham Park Estate Co. v Parkside Homes Ltd.*[17] a subsequent purchaser of land proceeded to build 14 houses in breach of a covenant. Brightman J. held that he could not shut his eyes to the fact that the houses existed and that to direct that they be pulled down would be an unjustifiable waste of much needed accommodation. Thus, damages were awarded in substitution for a mandatory injunction. It would have been wrong to allow the defendants to retain the fruits of their wrongdoing and, so, the measurement of such damages was based on the sum which the plaintiffs might hypothetically have been willing to receive to relax the covenant.

### (c) *Quia timet* injunctions

It will be necessary to rely on Lord Cairn's Act where no damages would

---

12. *Tulk v Moxhay* (1848) 2 Ph. 774.
13. *Doherty v Allman and Dowden* (1878) 3 App. Cas. 709.
14. (1863) 4 De G.J. & Sm. 114. See also *Crabb v Arun District Council (No. 2)* [1977] 121 S.J. 86.
15. *Shaw v Applegate* [1977] 1 W.L.R. 970.
16. [1965] Ch. 816.
17. [1974] 2 All E.R. 321.

be available at law. However, is this possible where a *quia timet* injunction is sought? In such cases the legal wrong in question is merely apprehended and no legal injury has yet occurred whilst the Act refers to damages only being awarded "to the party injured". It was decided by the House of Lords in *Leeds Industrial Society Co-operative Society Ltd. v Slack*[18] that equitable damages are available in addition to or instead of an injunction under Lord Cairn's Act in such circumstances. The case concerned an action to prevent the construction of a building which, on completion, would obstruct the plaintiff's right to light. Damages were awarded in lieu of a *quia timet* injunction, Viscount Finlay stating:

> "The words 'to the party injured' seem to me quite apt, according to the ordinary use of language, to denote parties injured or to be injured, including those who will be injured by buildings against which the court refuses an injunction ... If an injunction is granted the obstruction will never take place. If damages are given instead of an injunction, they must be in respect of an injury which is still in the future."[19]

### (d) Anticipatory breach

In *Hasham v Zenab*[20] specific performance of a contract for the sale of land was granted even before the contractual completion date where the defendant had been guilty of anticipatory breach of contract. The breach had not been accepted by the plaintiff, and so no action and no damages were available at common law.

This inability to pursue an action at law allows for the application of Lord Cairn's Act and, indeed, in *Oakacre Ltd. v Claire Cleaners (Holdings) Ltd.*,[21] following a *dictum* in *Phelps v Prothero*,[22] equitable damages were awarded in addition to specific performance even though there was (when the proceedings were commenced) no right to damages at common law since the writ for damages in addition to specific performance was issued before the breach.

Therefore, equitable damages have an advantage over common law damages simply because they may be available where common law damages

---

18. [1924] A.C. 851.
19. *Ibid.*, at 859.
20. [1960] A.C. 316, (Privy Council).
21. [1982] A.C. 851.
22. (1855) 7 De G.M. & G. 722.

are not for reasons such as an action not lying at common law, as shown above.

## 2. Rescission

The equitable remedy of rescission entitles a party to a contract to have the transaction set aside and be restored to the position he would have been in had the contract not been entered into. It is used where a contract has been affected by a flaw in its formation. Thus, its availability in relation to mistake, misrepresentation, contracts *uberrimae fidei*, undue influence and failure to perform will be considered in outline below. Strictly speaking, rescission is not a judicial remedy but the act of the party entitled to rescind and, therefore, a party can rescind a contract without taking legal proceedings at all. However, the party seeking rescission may well need to enlist the aid of the court to confirm that he is actually entitled to rescind and/or to ensure that property which has changed hands is returned.

### (a) Mistake

The common law rules regarding mistake lack clarity and this, in turn, makes the analysis of equity's role imprecise and confusing. Nevertheless, it can be stated that, as a general rule, the mistake of the plaintiff is, in itself, not a ground for recission. Instead entitlement to the remedy must be based on the reason for the mistake that has been made, for example, the misrepresentation of the other party. In considering the role of rescission, albeit briefly, reference will be made to the threefold classification of mistake at common law adopted by Cheshire, Fifoot and Furmston.[23]

*Mutual mistake*

Here, the parties are at cross-purposes but neither realises it.[24] Unless the mistake of one party has been induced by some fraud or misrepresentation on the part of the other equity will deny rescission.[25] This reflects the

---

23. *Law of Contract*, 12th ed. (Butterworths, 1991), pp. 228-61.
24. *Raffles v Wichelhaus* (1864) 2 H. & C. 906.
25. *Riverlate Properties Ltd. v Paul* [1975] Ch. 133.

general maxim, *caveat emptor*, underpinning the law of mistake. Therefore, as equity operates on conscience and conscience is clear at the time of the transaction, why should equity disrupt the transaction?

### *Unilateral mistake*

Here, the mistake of one party as to a fundamental term of the contract is known to the other party. Such a mistake causes the contract to be void at common law and equity follows the law in this respect. However, where the contract is valid at law equity may intervene and set it aside. In the Australian case of *Taylor v Johnson*,[26] where there was a contract for the option to buy a piece of land, the purchaser was mistaken as to the value of the land in question. Even so the contract was held to be valid at common law. However, it was decided that where a party has entered into a written contract under a serious mistake concerning a fundamental term and the mistake was both known to and deliberately obscured by the other party, then the mistaken party will be entitled to an order of rescission.

### *Common mistake*

Common mistake is pleaded where the parties are actually in agreement but, owing to some common error as to a serious matter, the agreement is fundamentally undermined. The common law regarding common mistake is uncertain and is not an appropriate subject for discussion in this text. Of more concern is the role of equity and in this regard, the court will if it thinks fit, set aside a contract on terms that are fair and just, regardless of whether it is void at law or not.

In *Cooper v Phibbs*[27] Cooper agreed to take a lease of a fishery from Phibbs which, it transpired, and because of an innocent mistake made by both parties, already belonged to Cooper. The House of Lords set aside the agreement on the grounds of common mistake but on terms that Phibbs should have a lien on the fishery for the amount she had spent on making improvements during the time which she believed it to be hers.

Lord Westbury stated (at page 170):

---

26. (1983) 151 C.L.R. 422.
27. (1867) L.R. 2 H.L. 149.

> "If parties contract under a mutual[28] mistake and misapprehension as to their relative and respective rights, the result is that the agreement is liable to be set aside as having proceeded upon a common mistake."

Such a wide principle allows equity to respond to cases of mistake which are beyond the domain of the common law. However, any attempt to define more precisely the impact of equity on common mistake proves problematic. Indeed, Treitel observes: "In the present confused state of the authorities one can only conclude that the courts recognise the existence of the equitable jurisdiction; but no clear answer can be given to the question just when a contract valid at common law will be rescinded in equity."[29]

Case law will illustrate, but not conclusively, the scope of the equitable jurisdiction. In *Solle v Butcher*[30] both parties to a lease of a flat mistakenly assumed that the property was not subject to rent control under the Rent Restriction legislation. Although the lease was valid at common law, the Court of Appeal held that the lease could be rescinded on the following terms: the lessee could surrender the lease entirely or he could remain in possession but pay the higher rent which, with appropriate statutory notice, the landlord would have charged had he been aware the contract was subject to rent control. In language similar to that of Lord Westbury in *Cooper* Denning L.J. said (at page 693):

> "A contract is also liable in equity to be set aside if the parties were under a common misapprehension either as to facts or to their relative and respective rights, provided that the misapprehension was fundamental and that the party seeking to set it aside was not himself at fault."

This principle laid down by Denning L.J. refers to the requirement that the party seeking rescission should not be at fault. This may serve to define more clearly the scope of the equitable jurisdiction although, as Treitel observes,[31] the meaning of "fault" in this regard is itself unclear. In *Leaf v International Galleries*,[32] *Rose v Pym*,[33] *Oscar Chess Ltd. v Williams*[34] and *Magee v Pennine Insurance Co. Ltd.*,[35] Lord Denning reiterated his view as

---

28. I.e., "common".
29. Treitel, *The Law of Contract*, 9th ed., (Sweet and Maxwell 1995) p. 284.
30. [1950] 1 K.B. 671.
31. Treitel, *The Law of Contract*, 9th ed.(Sweet and Maxwell, 1995), p. 296.
32. [1953] 1 Q.B. 646.
33. [1953] 2 Q.B. 450.
34. [1957] 1 W.L.R. 370.
35. [1969] 2 Q.B. 507.

stated in *Solle v Butcher*. Additionally, in *Grist v Bailey*[36] a house was sold at a low price because both parties mistakenly thought that a tenant could not be removed and vacant possession was not available. The contract was set aside but on terms that the plaintiff purchaser should have the chance to buy the property "at a proper price for vacant possession".

It should be emphasised that rescission will not be granted as of right but only if it is reasonable to do so and reference to the facts of the cases above seems to indicate that the requirement of reasonableness is very much concerned with the hardship which a mistaken party would incur if the contract in question were to be enforced on its original terms.

### (b) Misrepresentation

Misrepresentation renders a contract voidable at the option of the representee. This allows him to either affirm or rescind the contract.

*Fraudulent misrepresentation*

Where a misrepresentation has been made knowingly or recklessly, the representee may sue for damages in the tort of deceit or fraud and, in addition, the contract can be set aside both at common law and in equity.

*Non fraudulent misrepresentation*

Until the Misrepresentation Act 1967 rescission was the general remedy for misrepresentation though, as stated above, damages were available for fraudulent misrepresentation. Section 2(1) of the Misrepresentation Act 1967 provides a statutory right to damages for "negligent misrepresentation" in addition to rescission.[37] This will be the case where the misrepresentor had an honest but unreasonable belief in the truth of his statement. Additionally, s.2(2) provides the court with a discretion to declare the contract as still

36. [1967] Ch. 532.

37. An action for negligent misstatement is also available at common law. See *Hedley Byrne & Co. Ltd. v Heller & Partners Ltd.* [1964] A.C. 465 and *Caparo Industries plc v Dickman* [1990] 1 All E.R. 568.

subsisting and award damages for wholly innocent (i.e., "non-negligent") misrepresentation in lieu of rescission where it is equitable, to do so. In this respect, the court should pay regard to the nature of the misrepresentation, the loss which would be caused by it if the contract were to be upheld and the loss that rescission would cause to the other party. It seems that the object of providing the court with such discretion is to encourage the award of damages where such would provide an adequate remedy so avoiding what may be the serious effects of rescission.[38] However, the discretion to award damages in lieu under s.2(2) is removed if the availability of rescission is barred.

Note that rescission is effected either when the representee commences legal proceedings or when he gives notice to the other party. It may be difficult to give such notice where, for example, the representor is a criminal and cannot be traced. In such a case notice given to the police or some other body should suffice. An illustration is *Car and Universal Finance Co. Ltd. v Caldwell*,[39] where the owner of a car sold it to a rogue who paid for it with a dishonoured cheque. On discovering this and the fact that the rogue had disappeared, the vendor notified the police and the Automobile Association in order that they could help trace the car. Such notification, which took place before the car was sold to a third party, was found to be sufficient to constitute rescission.

*Indemnity*

An equitable remedy available in addition to that of rescission is an indemnity. This is the award of a sum of money which will compensate the plaintiff for expenses necessarily incurred as a result of obligations created by the contract in question and which will help to restore the plaintiff more fully to his pre-contractual position.

In *Whittington v Seale-Hayne*[40] the plaintiffs leased the defendant's premises in order to breed poultry. They relied on the defendant's innocent misrepresentation that the premises were in a sanitary condition. The lease imposed certain obligations upon the plaintiff including any repairs which

---

38. See *William Sindall plc v Cambridgeshire C.C.* [1994] 3 All E.R. 932. Note also that, where a misrepresentation has become incorporated as a term of the contract, the right to rescind remains available.
39. [1965] 1 Q.B. 525.
40. (1900) 82 L.T. 49.

might be ordered by the local authority. The water supply was contaminated, the plaintiff's manager became ill, most of the poultry died and those that survived were of no use for breeding purposes. Additionally, the local authority ordered that the drains be put in good order. The plaintiffs were awarded rescission but, additionally, claimed an indemnity against the following: value of poultry lost, loss of profit on sales of poultry, loss of a breeding season, removal expenses and medical expenses for the manager. All these claims were rejected on the basis that none was a loss arising out of an obligation *created* by the lease, for the plaintiff was not obliged to use the farm in the way that he had done and to employ a manager to run it. However, the plaintiff was indemnified against expenditure on rent, rates and repairs, all of which were required by the agreement.

Note that, with the greater availability of damages for non-fraudulent misrepresentation under the Misrepresentation Act 1967, the need to claim an indemnity has been reduced.

### (c) Contracts of the utmost good faith

Generally silence does not constitute misrepresentation. However, a duty to disclose all material facts exists in the case of contracts *uberrimae fidei* (contracts of the utmost good faith)[41] which include contracts of insurance[42] and family settlements. The remedy for a breach of the duty of disclosure is rescission and not damages.[43] In *Gordon v Gordon*[44] a family settlement based upon the assumed illegitimacy of the elder son was set aside upon the discovery that the younger son had concealed the fact that his parents had secretly married.[45]

---

41. Also where the contracting parties have a fiduciary or other special relationship: *van Gestel v Cann*, *The Times*, August 7, 1987; *Guiness plc v Saunders* [1990] 2 A.C. 663.
42. *Lindenau v Desborough* (1828) 8 B. & C. 586.
43. *Banque Financiere de la Cite S.A. v Westgate Insurance Co. Ltd.* [1989] 2 All E.R. 252; *Banque Keyser Ullman S.A. v Skandia (U.K.) Insurance Co. Ltd.* [1991] 2 A.C. 249; *Bank of Novia Scotia v Hellenic Mutual War Risks Ass. (Bermuda) Ltd.* [1990] 1 Q.B. 818.
44. (1821) 3 Swan 400.
45. See also *Harvey v Cooke* (1827) 4 Russ. 34; *Roberts v Roberts* [1905] 1 Ch. 704.

## (d) Undue influence and unconscionable bargains

Equity provides relief where an agreement has been obtained as a result of improper pressure not amounting to duress. This may occur between the original parties or in certain cases where one party has notice of a third party's undue influence.[46] Contracts affected by undue influence are voidable and therefore a party who is successful in seeking relief will be awarded rescission.

Additionally, imprudent transactions made, without independent advice, by poor and ignorant persons may be set aside in the absence of proof by the other party that the contract is fair and reasonable.[47]

## (e) Rescission for failure to perform

A contract may be broken by a failure of one party to perform his contractual obligations and in such circumstances the injured party may, instead of seeking to be placed in the position he would have enjoyed if the contract had been performed, request to be put in the position in which he would have been if the contract had not been performed. Indeed, even where there is no breach, for example in the event of the contract being frustrated, the latter remedy may be available.

Treatment of this aspect of rescission is outside the scope of this text and readers are recommended to refer to, e.g., Treitel's detailed consideration of the matter.[48]

## (f) Substantial misdescription of land

If, in a contract for the sale of land, the vendor substantially misdescribes the property, the purchaser may rescind the contract. In *Walker v Boyle*[49] the vendor stated that the land in question was not subject to any boundary

---

46. *Barclays Bank plc v O'Brian* [1993] 4 All E.R. 433, where a wife had an equity against her husband to set aside a transaction induced by his undue influence (and indeed misrepresentation) and such right was enforceable against a third party bank with notice.
47. *Fry v Lane* (1888) 40 Ch. D. 312.
48. Treitel, *The Law of Contract*, 9th ed. (Sweet and Maxwell 1995), p. 674.
49. [1982] 1 All E.R. 634. See also *Re Brine and Davies's Contract* [1935] Ch. 388.

disputes. The purchaser was able to have the contract set aside.

*Bars to rescission*

The right to rescission may be lost in a number of ways:

**(a) By acquiescence**

This arises where the party seeking rescission has, with full knowledge of the facts which give him the right to the remedy, nevertheless, chosen to waive such right and affirm the contract.[50] For example, delay defeats equity and so a lapse of time may indicate waiver[51] although in the case of fraud mere lapse of time is, in itself, not a bar for time does not run until discovery of the truth. Therefore, at most it might provide some evidence of affirmation.

**(b) *Restitutio in integrum* not possible**

The object of rescission is to return the parties to their pre-contractual positions (*restitutio in integrum*) and it follows that the right to rescission will be lost if this is no longer possible.[52] However, precise restoration to the original position is not necessary for the availability of the remedy as long as substantial restitution is possible.[53] The court seeks a just solution and this may be achieved by imposing terms such as ordering an account of profits or making an allowance to reflect any deterioration of the subject matter.[54]

---

50. *Payman v Lanjani* [1985] Ch. 457.
51. *Leaf v International Galleries* [1950] 2 K.B. 86.
52. *Clarke v Dickson* (1858) E.B. & E. 145.
53. *Cheese v Thomas* [1994] 1 All E.R. 35.
54. *Erlanger v New Sombrero Phosphate Co.* (1878) 3 App. Cas. 1218; *O'Sullivan v Management and Music Ltd.* [1985] 3 All E.R. 351.

### (c) Intervention of third party rights

Where an innocent third party acquires an interest for value under the contract before the innocent party seeks to set the contract aside, the right to rescission is lost. If the third party is a volunteer in that he did not provide value for the property in question, then no bar operates. Thus, in *Re Eastgate*[55] the third party was the defendant's trustee in bankruptcy who enjoyed no better position than the defendant in respect of the plaintiff's ability to rescind.

## 3. Rectification of documents

Because of a mistake in its execution, a contractual document may fail to express the true intentions of the parties as previously agreed. In these circumstances the court may rectify the document so that it may accurately record the earlier agreement. Note that the court does not have the jurisdiction to rectify the contract; it may only reform the instrument which mistakenly expresses the parties' agreement.[56]

*Common mistake*

Generally the document must fail to express the intentions of both parties. It matters not that no enforceable contract had been agreed previously as long as the parties were in agreement right up until the time that the provision was later recorded erroneously in writing.[57]

The courts are loth to interfere with the construction of a contract. Therefore, if rectification is to be granted, two requirements must be satisfied: first, the document must not accurately express the true agreement of the parties which remained unchanged until the document was drawn up and secondly, the rectification requested, if implemented, must represent the agreement.

---

55. [1905] 1 K.B. 465. Also *Lewis v Averay* [1972] 1 Q.B. 198 and *Phillips v Brooks Ltd.* [1919] 2 K.B. 243.
56. *McKenzie v Coulson* [1869] L.R. 8 Eq, 368.
57. *Joscelyn v Nissen* [1970] 2 Q.B. 86.

In *Frederick E. Rose (London) Ltd. v William H. Pym Jnr. & Co. Ltd.*[58] the parties orally agreed to buy and sell horsebeans but both mistakenly believed horsebeans to be the same as feveroles. The written document which was subsequently drawn up again referred to "horsebeans". In fact horsebeans were not feveroles and the plaintiff purchasers sought to rectify the written contract so that it included the word feveroles and they could then sue for breach. The Court of Appeal held that there was no cause for this since the document accurately recorded the previous oral agreement.

By contrast, in *Craddock Brothers Ltd. v Hunt*[59] the parties orally agreed to the sale of a house exclusive of an adjacent yard. A mistake in the execution of the written documents which were subsequently drawn up caused the yard to be included as part of the land to be sold. It was held that the plaintiff was entitled to rectification of the documents. In *Craddock Brothers* there was a disparity between the words used in the oral agreement and those in the written documents, whereas in *Rose* there was merely a misunderstanding of the meaning of the language used.[60]

The burden of proof is on the party who seeks rectification. He must bring to the court strong and convincing evidence that the document fails to record accurately the original intention of the parties though the standard of proof required is not that of a criminal trial (i.e., beyond reasonable doubt).[61] It follows that, if the dealings between the parties were uncertain, rectification is unlikely for then the disputed document actually represents the strongest evidence of their intentions. Oral evidence on the part of the plaintiff alone makes it difficult, though not impossible, to obtain rectification.[62]

A lack of evidence of common intention was found in *Whiteside v Whiteside*,[63] where a covenant between husband and wife was enforced without rectification. However, an additional reason for withholding the remedy was that the parties had already addressed and corrected the error by executing a supplementary deed expressing their true intention.

---

58. [1953] 2 Q.B. 450.
59. [1923] 2 Ch. 136.
60. See also *Re Slocock's Will Trusts* [1979] 1 All E.R. 358.
61. *Joscelyn v Nissen* [1970] 2 Q.B. 86.
62. A limited exception, therefore, to the parol evidence rule. *Mortimer v Shortall* (1842) 2 Dr. & War. 363; *Cook v Fearn* (1878) 48 L.J. Ch. 63.
63. [1950] Ch. 65.

*Unilateral mistake*

Generally, rectification is available only where the mistake results in the contractual document failing to express the intention of *both* parties. In *Riverlate Properties Ltd. v Paul*,[64] the plaintiff landlords intended to make the defendant tenants liable for one half of the cost of expenditure on certain repairs to the property. This intention was unknown to the defendant and the document containing the lease failed to include such a provision. It was held that the landlord was unable to have the contract rectified.[65]

Rectification will be available in cases of unilateral mistake where the mistake in question is attributable to the fraud of the other party[66] or where the other party knew of the mistake and did not bring it to the attention of the plaintiff.[67] The Court of Appeal has considered this matter in a number of recent cases. In *Thomas Bates & Son Ltd. v Wyndham's (Lingerie) Ltd.*[68] it upheld the plaintiff's claim for rectification in a case of unilateral mistake known to the other party but not pointed out to the plaintiff. Reference was also made to the need to establish that the other party had obtained some unfair benefit as a result of the mistake.

Buckley L.J. referred to the principle stated in *Snell's Principles of Equity* as follows:

> "By what appears to be a species of equitable estoppel, if one party to a transaction knows that the instrument contains a mistake in his favour but does nothing to correct it, he (and those claiming under him) will be precluded from resisting rectification on the ground that the mistake is unilateral and not common."[69]

In *The Nai Genova*[70] Slade L.J. declared that, in the absence of estoppel, fraud, undue influence or a fiduciary relationship between the parties, actual

---

64. [1975] Ch. 133.
65. Thus, effectively overruling the decision in *A. Roberts and Co. Ltd. v Leicestershire County Council* [1961] Ch. 551 and also the suggestions in *Harris v Pepperell* (1867) L.R. 5 Eq. 1 and *Paget v Marshall* (1882) 28 Ch.D. 255 that in cases of unilateral mistake the defendant could be made to choose between rectification and rescission.
66. *Blay v Pollard & Morris* [1930] 1 K.B. 628.
67. *A. Roberts and Co. Ltd. v Leicestershire County Council* [1961] Ch. 555.
68. [1981] 1 All E.R. 1077.
69. 25th ed. (1960), p. 569; 29th ed. (1990), p. 630.
70. [1984] 1 Lloyd's Rep. 353.

knowledge of the plaintiff's mistake at the time when the contract was signed was required if rectification was to be granted in cases of unilateral mistake. He justified this requirement as follows: "In view of the drastic nature of such an order, so far as the non-mistaken defendant is concerned, the consequences of any such conclusion may not appear unduly harsh."More recently, the Court of Appeal has given further consideration to this matter in *Commission for New Towns v Cooper*.[71] Stuart-Smith L.J. referred to the relevance of "unconscionable conduct" on the part of the party attempting to enforce the written contract. This could be evidenced by the fact that he had diverted the other party from discovering the mistake although in the process he was merely suspicious rather than aware that the other party had no knowledge of the mistake.

*Defences to rectification*

As with other equitable remedies rectification is granted at the discretion of the court. However, note that, since the purpose of rectification is to give effect to the agreement of the parties rather than to return them to their pre-contractual positions, impossibility of *restitutio in integrum* is not normally a bar to rectification.[72] The following may bar the claim:

1. Lapse of time or acquiescence.[73]

2. Where a *bona fide* purchaser without notice and for value has acquired an interest under the instrument.[74]

3. If the contract is no longer capable of performance or it has already been performed under the judgement of the court.[75]

4. Where the rights under a contract have been assigned, it is

---

71. [1995] 2 All E.R. 929.
72. *Cook v Fearn* (1878) 48 L.J. Ch. 63 - rectification of marriage settlement *after* marriage had taken place.
73. *Beale v Kyte* [1907] 1 Ch. 564.
74. *Lyme Valley Squash Club Ltd. v Newcastle-Under-Lyme Borough Council* [1985] 2 All E.R. 405.
75. *Borrowman v Rossell* (1864) 16 C.B. (N.S.) 58; *Caird v Moss* (1886) 33 Ch. D. 22.

suggested that the assignee cannot seek rectification for otherwise he could receive an unjustified benefit.[76]

**Exercises**

1. When are equitable damages available either instead of or in addition to an injunction or specific performance?

2. Gullible purchased a picture for £50,000 from Melchester Gallery described by the gallery's representative as "by Confield", a well known 19th century artist. In fact, the picture was worth only £20 because it was painted by Shane, a law student who painted for fun in his spare time.

   Advise Gullible whether rescission would be available to him in the following circumstances:

   (a) He discovered the misrepresentation five years after the purchase.

   (b) He discovered the misrepresentation five years after the purchase and is confident that he could prove that the representative knew who had actually painted the picture.

   (c) The painting has been badly damaged in a fire at Gullible's house.

   (d) He employed someone to restore the painting.

---

76. *Napier v Williams* [1911] 1 Ch. 361, although note the Law of Property Act 1925, s. 63(1), allows for rectification where the assignment forms part of a conveyance.

# PART V
# OTHER REMEDIES

# 11 Other Remedies

## 1. Restitutionary remedies

As already stated in the Preface, this chapter will deal with the restitutionary and other remedies in outline only. Restitutionary remedies are basically remedies which reverse unjust enrichment by a party.

### *Restitutionary remedies for tort*

Such remedies are to reverse the enrichment the defendant has gained by his tort rather than to compensate the plaintiff for his loss. So, where the defendant has gained more from the tort than the loss suffered by the plaintiff, a restitutionary remedy is advantageous to the plaintiff.

A restriction on when restitutionary remedies may be awarded for a tort was imposed in *Phillips v Homfray*.[1] There the Court of Appeal held that a remedy reversing a gain made by a defendant could only be awarded where the defendant's gain is property the plaintiff had or proceeds of that property.

However, restitutionary remedies/damages or account for profit have been awarded in some cases where the defendant's gain did not consist of property of the plaintiff or proceeds thereof. Examples of those are the following cases illustrating restitutionary damages: *Strand Electric Engineering Co. v Brisford Entertainments Ltd.*,[2] *Penarth Dock Engineering Co. Ltd. v Pounds*[3] and *Swordheath Properties Ltd. v Tabet*.[4]

There is also the equitable remedy of account of profits. This is the remedy whereby the defendant has to render an account of the profits he has gained by his wrong-doing and to pay the same. The remedy is available for violations of intellectual property rights, e.g., patent (s.61(1)(d) of the

1. [1883] 24 Ch. D. 439.
2. [1952] 2 Q.B. 246 (a case on wrongful interference with goods).
3. [1963] 1 Lloyd's Rep. 359.
4. [1979] 1 W.L.R. 285 (trespass to land).

Patents Act 1977) or breach of confidence.[5]

*Restitutionary remedies for breach of contract*

The general position is that the law does not award restitutionary remedies to reverse the gain a defendant has made from his breach of contract.[6] There is, however, academic opinion that would welcome such remedies.[7]

The point has been made, for example, by Birks,[8] that remedies like the recovery of money had and received (where there is total failure of consideration) and *quantum meruit* claimable by a non-breaching party to a contract after he has terminated the contract for breach of it, are not remedies for breach of contract; and that they are rather to be seen as belonging to the province of "autonomous unjust enrichment by subtraction". That is a topic comprehensively treated by the standard texts on the law of restitution, to which readers are referred. Those texts have similarly covered the restitutionary remedies for equitable wrongs.

## 2. Tracing

The tracing of property (i.e., following or identifying property) is, strictly speaking, not a remedy but a method by which a plaintiff establishes his claim to the actual remedy of having his property or the value of it restored to him. For example, if A's money is stolen by B and the money finds its way into C's hands, C will be liable to A if A can trace that money into C's hands.

Tracing is available at common law as well as in equity.

*Tracing at common law*

Tracing at common law depends on the receipt by the defendant of the

---

5. *Peter Pan Manufacturing Corpn. v Corsets Silhouette Ltd.* [1963] R.P.C. 45; *Ansell Rubber Co. Pty. Ltd. v Allied Rubber Industries Pty. Ltd.* (1972) R.P.C. 811.
6. *Tito v Waddell (No. 2)* [1977] Ch. 106.
7. See, e.g., Jones, "The Recovery of Benefits Gained from a Breach of Contract", *Law Quarterly Review*, vol. 99 (1983), 443, at p. 459.
8. *Introduction to the Law of Restitution*, at p. 334.

plaintiff's property.[9]

It is a personal claim (not a proprietary one like tracing in equity). It is, therefore, not relevant where the defendant has subsequently disposed of the property of the plaintiff.

Under s.3, Torts (Interference with Goods) Act 1977, the court has discretionary power to order specific delivery of a plaintiff's chattel or goods to him by the defendant if the plaintiff applies to it.

The plaintiff's right subsists even if his property is changed for some other property or is sold by the defendant and the proceeds thereof used to buy another property. Provided the plaintiff can show that what the defendant has is a product of, or substitute for, his property, he can claim. Thus, in *Taylor v Plumer*[10] the plaintiff (P) handed money over to a stockbroker (S) and instructed S to buy him Exchequer bonds with it. S rather bought U.S. investments and bullion with the money and tried to go abroad with them. After S had been caught, P seized the U.S. investments and bullion. The assignees of S sought to recover the property from P. They failed because P's money had been traced into the investments and bullion.

*Taylor v Plumer*, therefore, illustrates the position where there is a straightforward exchange of property.

Where the property or its proceeds have been placed in a bank account, the plaintiff can trace the money if it is in a substantially unmixed account and is, therefore, deemed by the court as identifiable, as happened in *Banque Belge Pour L'Etranger v Hambrouck.*[11] In that case Hambrouck, while a clerk in the employment of M. Pelabon, had forged cheques in favour of himself although the cheques were supposed to have been drawn by his employer. Hambrouck paid the cheques into his own bank account. His bank, Farrow's Bank, collected the money from Banque Belge, M. Pelabon's bankers, Hambrouck drew certain cheques on his bank account with Farrow's cheque. Those cheques were in favour of his mistress, Miss Spanoghe. She paid the cheques into her deposit account at the London Joint City and Midland bank. When Hambrouck's fraudulent activities were discovered, only £315 was left in his mistress' account. Banque Belge sought a declaration that the £315 was their property, and an order for it to be paid to them. The Court of Appeal affirmed the judgement of Salter J. that the

---

9. See *Lipkin Gorman v Karpnale* [1991] A.C. 548.
10. (1815) 3 M. & S. 562 .
11. [1921] 1 K.B. 321.

bank was entitled to both the declaration and the order sought because the money paid into the mistress' account could be identified as "the product of the original money".[12]

However, tracing at common law is not possible if the property cannot be followed at every stage from its original form to the current one (i.e., if the chain is broken at any stage): *Agip (Africa) Ltd. v Jackson.*[13]

The limits of tracing at common law can, therefore, be seen:

(i) where the plaintiff's property is mixed with the defendant's in a bank account, and so is not identifiable, and

(ii) where there is a break in the chain so that the property cannot be followed at every stage.

*Tracing in equity*

In equity, property mixed with the defendant's in a bank account, etc., can be traced even if the mixed fund has itself been converted into other property. Therefore, the methods of tracing in equity are more flexible and sophisticated than common-law tracing so far as dealing with mixed funds is concerned.

Tracing in equity usually applies where property is in the hands of trustees/fiduciaries (and often when they go bankrupt). According to *Re Diplock's Estate*,[14] the general principle regarding equitable tracing is that whenever a fiduciary relationship exists, the beneficial owner of an equitable interest in property can trace that property into the hands of any person holding it, unless that person is a *bona fide* purchaser for value without notice.[15] In *Re Diplock* the executors of a will made an error of law, as a result of which the defendants, which were charities, received certain sums of money *bona fide*. The defendants mixed those sums with their own money.

---

12. *Per* Atkin L.J. at p. 335.
13. [1992] 4 All E.R. 451.
14. [1948] Ch. 465; [1948] 2 All E.R. 318.
15. See *Sinclair v Brougham* [1914] A.C. 398. The title of such a *bona fide* purchaser is not violable. See also *Chase Manhattan Bank N.A. v Israel-British Bank (London) Ltd.* [1981] Ch. 105 - where it was held that a person who pays another person money under a mistake of fact retains an equitable property/interest in it and that recipient has a fiduciary duty to respect that proprietary right.

Some of the defendants (charitable institutions) used the money given to them in error to alter or improve existing buildings on their own lands. The plaintiffs, the next-of-kin of the deceased, who should have received the money paid in error to the defendants, made a claim against the charitable institutions. It was held, *inter alia,* applying *Sinclair v Brougham*, that, where trust money had been mixed with other property (such as charity money, etc.), there was an equitable right of tracing; also, where a recipient (a defendant institution) had mixed its money with trust money it had received and used the mixed fund to buy property, e.g., land, the next-of-kin would have a right to a charge on that property; but, where the recipient charity used the mixed funds to alter or improve a building or assets it already owned, there could be no tracing of the money in a true sense and it would be inequitable to declare a charge on the property.

Note that, according to the Court of Appeal in *Bishopsgate Investment Management Ltd. v Homan*, where money is paid into an overdrawn bank account, it has disappeared and, therefore, cannot not be traced.[16]

## 3. Subrogation

Subrogation is the technique whereby one person steps into another person's shoes in order to obtain that other person's rights and remedies against a third person. The types of subrogation include the following:

(a) subrogation rights of indemnity insurers;

(b) subrogation rights of sureties (e.g., where a surety, who pays off the debt which a principal debtor owes, is subrogated to any securities the debtor has given to the creditor as security for the debt);[17]

(c) subrogation rights of business creditors dealing with trustees;

(d) subrogation rights of lenders; and

(e) subrogation rights of bankers.

---

16. [1995] 1 All E.R. 347 (*per* Dillon and Leggatt L.J.J.).

17. See, for example, *Ghana Commercial Bank v Chandiram* [1960] A.C. 74; see also *Re Byfield* [1982] 1 All E.R. 249, where subrogation was refused.

*An illustration*

**Subrogation rights of indemnity insurers**

There are two types of the indemnity insurers' right of subrogation.

(i) The first is entitlement to take over the remedies which the assured person has against another party so as to recover the sum paid to the assured person by the insurers; this avoids overcompensation of the assured person. This right is usually exercised by the insurer taking action in the assured person's name against another (a third) party). Examples of this can be found in *Morris v Ford Motor Co.*[18] and also *Esso Petroleum Ltd. v Hall, Russell & Co. Ltd.*,[19] where it was held that the plaintiff's action against the tortfeasor, because of the indemnifiers' right of subrogation, had to be brought in the assured (plaintiff)'s name by the indemnifiers (but not in the indemnifiers' own name even though they had already paid out to the plaintiff).

(ii) Secondly, there is the entitlement of the insurers to recover from the assured person, up to the amount they paid out to him, money he has received already or receives later from another party; again, this avoids overcompensation of the assured person.

## 4. Delivery up, recovery of land and appointment of a receiver

Under s.4, Torts (Interference with Goods) Act 1977 and also R.S.C., order 29, r.2A, the court can order delivery up of goods which could be or actually are the subject-matter of a subsequent action concerning tortious interference with them. There can also be, in addition, (a) delivery to a plaintiff of material which contains confidential information belonging to him, and (b) an action for the recovery of land, whereby the court can order the defendant to yield his possession of the land.[20]

---

18. [1973] Q.B. 792.
19. [1989] A.C. 643.
20. The limitation period for such an action is 12 years: s.15(1), Limitation Act 1980.

Moreover, under section 37 of the Supreme Court Act 1981, the High Court has power to appoint, in any case it deems proper to do so, a receiver, i.e., a person to receive rents and profits or real estate, to recover property and to protect property until ascertainment of the parties' rights.

# PART VI
# JUDICIAL REVIEW

# 12 Judicial review

In this chapter only a bird's eye-view will be given of the judicial remedies which are available against administrative bodies. Those remedies may be statutory or non-statutory.

The main non-statutory remedies are:

- *habeas corpus* (a prerogative writ),
- *certiorari*,
- prohibition,
- *mandamus*,
- injunction,
- damages, and
- declaration.

*Certiorari*, *prohibition* and *mandamus* are prerogative orders. Since injunctions and damages have been dealt with in the earlier chapters, this chapter will only look at the other five remedies in outline.

## *Habeas corpus*

This is a prerogative writ which is directed to a person detaining another person in custody and which commands the detainer to produce the detainee before the court. It is used to test the legality of a detention or imprisonment.

Some illustrative cases are *In re S.-C. (Mental Patient)*,[1] *R. v Home Secretary, ex parte Muboyayi*[2] and *R. v Governor of Durham Prison, ex parte Hardial Singh*.[3]

### *Certiorari*

Certiorari, a prerogative order, is used to remove civil causes or indictments from the inferior courts to the High Court to be better tried or re-tried in the case of abuse or error (*R. v Haringey Justices, ex parte Director of Public Prosecutions*).[4]

### **Prohibition**

Prohibition (now a prerogative order) is used:

- to restrain an inferior tribunal or court from acting *ultra vires* or exceeding its power/jurisdiction, or from breaching the rules of natural justice, and

- to control the exercise of judicial or quasi-judicial functions by a minister or a public authority (e.g., a local authority).[5]

It must be noted that *certiorari* is issued to quash and prohibition to prohibit or prevent a decision if there is:

(a) excess or want of jurisdiction,

(b) breach of the rules of natural justice,

(c) error of law on the face of the record, or

---

1. [1996] 2 W.L.R. 146.
2. [1992] 1 Q.B. 244.
3. [1984] 1 W.L.R. 704.
4. [1996] 2 W.L.R. 114; see also *R. v Wandsworth London Borough Council, ex parte Beckwith* [1996] 1 W.L.R. 60.
5. See, for example, *R. v Kent Police Authority, ex parte Godden* [1971] 2 Q.B. 662.

(d) fraud, duress or perjury in obtaining a decision.

### *Mandamus*

*Mandamus* is now another prerogative order. It is issued by the High Court to compel the performance of a public duty, if no other effective redress is available. Illustrations of it are *R. v Bristol Corporation, ex parte Hendry*[6] and *R. v Commissioner of Police for the Metropolis, ex parte Blackburn.*[7]

### Declaratory judgement

A declaratory judgement is a judgement declaring conclusively the pre-existing rights of the parties without appending any coercive decree or order.[8]

---

6. [1974] 1 W.L.R. 5093.
7. [1968] 2 Q.B. 118.
8. *Ridge v Baldwin* [1964] A.C. 40.

# Appendices

**Preface**

It is important to note that the precise form of pleadings is a very personal matter. There is no absolutely correct wording. But, the essential thing is: (a) to plead all the things one has to plead and (b) to assert facts not plead evidence.

**Details**

1. Breach of Contract
   - (a) Task
   - (b) Statement of Claim.

2. Personal Injuries
   - (a) Task
   - (b) Statement of Claim.

3. Fatal Accident
   - (a) Task
   - (b) Statement of Claim.

4. Exemplary damages
   - (a) Task
   - (b) Statement of Claim.

5. Mareva injunction and Anton Piller order
   - (a) Task
   - (b) Draft affidavit in support of an application for an Anton Piller order.
   - (c) A draft Anton Piller order (in accordance with Annex 1 of the Practice Direction 1994).
   - (d) A draft Mareva injunction in (accordance with Annex 2 of the Practice Direction 1994).
   - (e) Draft affidavit in support of an application for a Mareva injunction.

# Appendix 1

## Breach of contract

### (a) Task

In anticipation of her daughter's wedding, Mrs. Do, a resident of Islington, north London, who had inherited £5.5m. from her Arsenal-supporting mother, made a contract on 1-1-94 with Puttemup Co., a firm of contractors. According to the terms of the contract, in consideration of the sum of £250,000, Puttemup Co. were to build a recreation hall with proper toilet and other facilities for Mrs. Do in Highbury in the London Borough of Islington. The building was to be completed on 11-3-96. Puttemup Co. also agreed to provide a bar and a disco on the day of the wedding, 1-4-96, between 3.00 p.m. and 10.30 p.m. for the plaintiff and her invitees as well as food for 150 guests or invitees of the plaintiff at £6 per person. Excluded were alcoholic drinks which the guests could buy from the bar. It was a term of the contract that there would be reasonably sufficient food for the guests. However, Puttemup Co. failed to complete the said building by 11-3-96. Mrs. Do, therefore, had to pay another firm £150,000 to complete it. Puttemup had, however, by then installed all the toilet facilities there and assured Mrs. Do that they were proper and in good working condition. It happened at the wedding reception on 1-4-96 that the food provided by Puttemup was sufficient for only 69 guests and the toilet facilities in the building were improper because the toilets were messy with wet floors caused by seriously leaking taps and faulty flushing mechanisms. The bride and groom and Mrs. Do were very embarrassed, emergency caterers had to be engaged at the cost of £800 to provide food for the other guests and mobile toilets hired at the cost of £400. Mrs. Do's embarrassment caused her to be unwell for one week after the reception.

Advise Mrs. Do.

**(b) Statement of claim**

IN THE HIGH COURT OF JUSTICE 19... C. No. ...

QUEEN'S BENCH DIVISION

| | | |
|---|---|---|
| BETWEEN | Mrs. Do | Plaintiff |
| AND | Puttemup Co. | Defendant |

STATEMENT OF CLAIM

1. On January 1, 1994 a contract in writing was made between the Plaintiff and the Defendant.

2. By the said contract, in consideration of the sum of £250,000, the Defendant agreed:

   (a) to build a recreation hall with proper toilet and other facilities for the Plaintiff in Highbury, north London, the said building to be completed on or before 11th March 1996;

   (b) to provide a disco at the said recreation hall on 1st April 1996 between 3.00 p.m. and 10.30 p.m. for the Plaintiff and her invitees; and

   (c) to provide food for 150 invitees of the Plaintiff at £6 per person at the said disco.

3. In breach of the said contract:

   (a) the Defendants, although they had installed toilet facilities which they represented to the plaintiffs were in good working order, failed to complete the said building on or before the said 11th March 1996.

(b) the Defendants provided food for only 69 of the guests of the Plaintiff at the said disco, and

(c) the defendants failed to provide proper toilet facilities in the said recreation hall in that, in breach of their aforementioned representations, the floors in the said toilets were wet and messy as a result of leaking taps and faulty flushing mechanisms, whereby the plaintiff was obliged to hire mobile toilets for use at the said disco.

4. By reason of the matters aforesaid the Plaintiff was occasioned mental distress and humiliation and has suffered loss and damage.

**Particulars of pain and suffering**

Following the said breach of contract by the said Defendant and the events during the afternoon of that breach, the Plaintiff:

(a) felt ashamed and was mentally distressed and depressed,
(b) could not go out was generally unwell for a week, and
(c) could neither eat nor sleep well.

**Particulars of special damage**

| | | |
|---|---|---|
| 1. | Cost of employing another builder to complete the said building including the installation of proper working toilet facilities: | £ 150,000 |
| 2. | Cost of emergency catering for 81 guests: | £ 800 |
| 3. | Transport to and from shops: | £ 50 |
| 4. | Hire of emergency mobile toilets: | £ 400 |
| 5. | Cost of emergency cleaning: | £ 140 |
| 6. | Loss of net earnings for one week: | £ 900 |
| | Total: | £ 152,290 |

Further the Plaintiff claims interest pursuant to section 35A of the Supreme Court Act 1981 on the damages to which she is entitled at such rate and for such period as the Court thinks fit.

And the Plaintiff claims:

1. Damages
2. Interest as aforesaid

Signed:

Counsel for the Plaintiff

Served this ... day ... 19... .

## Appendix 2

### Personal injuries

#### (a) Task

Ponvus, a 19-year-old professional footballer earning £240,000 per annum, became a paraplegic as the result of a road accident, caused by the negligent driving of Mr. Riches. He (Ponvus) will also not be able to play football again. In addition, he was in and out of hospital for 10 months, during which time he received invalidity benefit totalling £590. He is now in a wheelchair and will remain so for the rest of his life. He will also require nursing care at night. He is still receiving some state benefits because of his disability. His workmates themselves have managed to contribute, and to raise, funds amounting to £20,000 for him. His accident insurance policy, which he had taken with A.R. Senal Insurance Co. two years ago, also nets him £75,000. Liability has been admitted by the negligent driver, Mr. Riches.

Advise Ponvus on the measure of damages he is likely to recover.

### (b) Statement of claim

IN THE HIGH COURT OF JUSTICE 19... C. No. ...

QUEEN'S BENCH DIVISION

| | | |
|---|---|---|
| BETWEEN | Mr. Peter Ponvus | Plaintiff |
| AND | Mr. Ronald Riches | Defendant |

STATEMENT OF CLAIM

1. On April 1, 1995 the Plaintiff was a passenger in a motor car, registration number VIV999, owned and being driven by the defendant along High Street, New Town, Newshire, in the direction of Old Town, when the Defendant so drove his motor car as to collide head on with a motor lorry parked on the Defendant's offside of the road.

2. The said collision was caused by the negligence of the Defendant.

**Particulars of Negligence**

The Defendant was negligent in that he:

(a) Drove too fast;
(b) Drove on the wrong side or part of the road;
(c) Failed to keep a proper outlook;
(d) Failed to have any or any sufficient regard for any traffic that might be or was on the road;
(e) Failed to stop, slow down or swerve or otherwise avoid the said collision.

3. As a result of the Defendant's aforementioned negligence the Plaintiff, who until the said collision was a professional footballer earning £240,000 a year, suffered injury, pain, loss and damage.

**Particulars of injury**

In the said collision the Plaintiff, who was then 19 years old, sustained a fracture of the spine, as a result of which he is now a paraplegic with paralysis of both legs. He is in a wheelchair and will remain so for the rest of his life. He will never again be able to work as a professional footballer.

**Particulars of special damage**

| | |
|---|---|
| Loss of earnings from April 1, 1995 to December 1, 1995 (and continuing): | £200,000 |
| Fares to and from hospital | £ 90 |
| Cost of wheelchair | £ 90 |
| Cost of nursing care from April 1, 1995 to December 1, 1995 (and continuing): | £ 20,000 |
| Total | £220,180 |

4. The Plaintiff claims interest pursuant to section 35A of the Supreme Court Act 1981 on the damages to which he is entitled at such rate and for such period as to this Honourable Court may appear just.

And the Plaintiff claims:

1. Damages
2. Interest as aforesaid

Signed:

Counsel for the Plaintiff

Served this 1st day of December 1995.

## Appendix 3

## Fatal accident

### (a) Task

Mr. Defend ("D") was negligently driving a heavy goods vehicle which struck a car in which Mr. Plainte ("P"), a self-employed plumber, was travelling.

P, who was 40 years old and earning £600 a week, died on the following day as a result of severe head injuries caused by the accident. Liability has been admitted by D. P left behind a wife and two 10-year-old twin sons called Mark and Arthur.

Advise P's widow and two sons.

## (b) Statement of claim

IN THE HIGH COURT OF JUSTICE 19... C. No. ...

QUEEN'S BENCH DIVISION

| BETWEEN | Mrs. Paula Plainte | Plaintiff |
|---|---|---|
| AND | Mr. Den Defend | Defendant |

STATEMENT OF CLAIM

1. The plaintiff is the widow and administratrix of the estate of Mr. Phillipo Plainte, deceased, and she brings this action for the benefit of the dependants of the deceased under the Fatal Accidents Act 1976 as amended, and for the benefit of the deceased's estate under the Law Reform (Miscellaneous Provisions) Act 1934. Letters of Administration were granted to the Plaintiff out of the Principal Registry of the Family Division on ... .

2. At all material times the deceased was a self-employed plumber trading from No. 10 Boning Street, ... .

3. On or about ... 19..., there was a collision in Low Street, Low Town between a heavy goods vehicle, registration no. ..., driven by the Defendant, and a motor car in which the deceased was a passenger. As a result of the said collision the deceased sustained injuries involving pain and suffering from which he died the following day.

**Particulars of injuries**

(a) Severe head injuries
(b) Fractured ribs.

4. The said collision and the said injuries, pain, suffering and death of the deceased were caused by the negligence of the Defendant.

## Particulars of negligence

The Defendant was negligent in that he:

(a) Drove too fast;

(b) Drove on the wrong side or part of the road;

(c) Failed to keep a proper outlook;

(d) Failed to see in time or at all the car in which the deceased was a passenger.

(e) Failed to stop, slow down or swerve in order to avoid colliding with the said car.

5. Particulars pursuant to the Fatal Accidents Acts 1976, as amended, are:

(a) Names of persons for whose benefit this action is brought:

The Plaintiff, Mrs. Paula Plainte, born on ... 19..., the widow of the deceased,

Mark Plainte, aged 10, born on ..., 19... , and

Arthur Plainte, aged 10, born on ..., 19... .

(b) The nature of the claim in respect of which damages are sought:

The deceased was at the time of his death a healthy and happy man aged 40, self-employed and earning an average of £600 a week. The Plaintiff received from the deceased the sum of £100 per week out of which she paid some of the household expenses. Furthermore, the deceased made the mortgage payments of £800 per month and Council Tax of £80 a month, and the cost of clothes and holidays for the family, and sundry other expenses amounted to £120 a week.

The Plaintiff and the children of the deceased were dependent on the deceased for support and by his death they have lost this means of support, and they have thereby suffered loss and damage.

6. Further the Plaintiff claims damages for bereavement.

7. Further, by reason of the matters aforesaid, the deceased's estate has suffered loss and damage.

**Particulars**

Funeral expenses £ ....

And the Plaintiff claims:

(i) under the Fatal Accidents Act 1976, as amended, damages for the dependants,

(ii) under the Law Reform (Miscellaneous Provisions) Act 1934, for the benefit of the estate of the deceased,

(iii) interest on damages pursuant to section 35A of the Supreme Court Act 1981.

Signed:

Counsel for the Plaintiff

Served this ... day ... 19 ... .

## Appendix 4

## Exemplary damages

### (a) Task

Last week on Monday at about 11 a.m. there was an armed robbery at Bill's shop in Notting Hill Gate, west London. The robbers escaped in an old Fiat car. Fifteen minutes after the robbery, Otto von Lombroso, a medical student, was stopped outside his flat in his new VW car by two police constables at Ladbroke Grove in west London. The constables asked him to get out of his car. They then asked him where he had been. He said he had just got out of bed and was going to the public library. They did not believe him but did not enquire any further. Instead, they forced his wrists behind his back, handcuffed him, told him he was under arrest and took him to the police station. He was put in a police cell. When he asked the officers who had arrested him the reason for his arrest, they punched him in the ribs and kicked him in the shin. He sustained a badly bruised shin and two broken ribs. After being kept in the police cell for six hours continuously, he was released. During that time he was given neither food nor drink and was denied access to a solicitor although he did make a request to do so.

### (b) Statement of claim

IN THE HIGH COURT OF JUSTICE 19... C. No. ...

QUEEN'S BENCH DIVISION

| BETWEEN | Otto von Lombroso | Plaintiff |
|---|---|---|
| AND | The Metropolitan Police Commissioner | Defendant |

STATEMENT OF CLAIM

1. The Plaintiff was at all material times a student.

2. The Defendant is and was at all material times the Chief Officer of the Metropolitan Police Force, London.

3. On or about ... 19... , at about ... 11.15 a.m. while the Plaintiff was sitting in his car on Oblong Road, Ladbroke Grove, west London, P.C. Nosey-Parker and P.C. Hit (hereinafter called "the police constables") wrongfully and without reasonable cause arrested the Plaintiff forcibly and took him in custody to the Notting Hill Gate Police Station. The Plaintiff was detained there for six hours continuously before he was released.

4. At the said Police Station the Plaintiff was punched in the ribs and kicked in the shin by the police constables.

5. The police constables were at all material times being directed and controlled by the Defendant in the performance or purported performance of his functions.

6. In the premises, the Plaintiff was wrongfully imprisoned and deprived of his liberty and assaulted, and the Defendant is liable to the Plaintiff in respect of the said wrongful imprisonment assault.

7. By reason of the matters aforesaid, the Plaintiff sustained injuries and has suffered loss and damage.

**Particulars of injuries**

(a) Badly bruised shin

(b) Two broken ribs

**Particulars of special damage**

Fares to and from hospital for three months: £150

8. Further, in the premises the said conduct was arbitrary, oppressive and/ or unconstitutional and the Plaintiff claims exemplary damages.

**Particulars**

(i) The Plaintiff repeats the facts and matters set out above;

(ii) The police constables failed and refused to listen to the Plaintiff but used unreasonable force on him, thereby causing his injuries aforesaid;

(iii) The police constables made false accusations against the Plaintiff to the custody officer as a result of which the Plaintiff was detained;

(iv) The Plaintiff was detained without food or drink or access to a lavatory during the said period and was not allowed to contact or communicate with a solicitor although he requested to do so.

9. Further pursuant to section 35A of the Supreme Court Act 1981 the Plaintiff is entitled to and claims interest on the amount found due to him at such rate and for such period as to this Honourable Court may

appear just.

And the Plaintiff claims:

(i) Damages including exemplary damages;

(ii) Interest pursuant to section 35A of the Supreme Court Act 1981.

Signed:

Counsel for the Plaintiff

Served this ... day ... 19 ... .

## Appendix 5

## Mareva injunction and Anton Piller order

### (a) Task

Mr. Pele Smith ("P") owns Pelefe Ltd. which produces Lefe Port. He has registered that trade mark in accordance with the Trade Marks Act 1994. He employs over 200 people. Two years ago, Dhee and Chee ("D and C"), who used to work for him as chemists, left his employment to go and start a rival business. Clause 13 of each of their contracts of employment stated:

"1. The employee covenants:

(a) that he will not engage in a trade similar to that of the employer in any part of east London before the expiration of three years beginning with the date of his resignation from the employment of P, and

(b) that, if he should go into business similar to that of the employer, he will not approach any client of the said employer before the expiration of three years beginning with the date of his leaving the said employment."

In fact, when they left, they took away with them P's list of clients (retailers). D and C kept the list of clients in a locked safe in their office in Upton Lane, London E7. They also produced port which they called Lefee Port. They approached P's clients, who had very extensive overseas connections, and, granting them generous concessions, persuaded them to choose to do 70% of their business with them (D and C) and only 30% (instead of 90%) with P. Last year D and C made £13m. profit while P's profits went down to £3m. D and C also managed to buy a hotel in London's West End and two casinos in Las Vegas, U.S.A., and Monte Carlo, respectively. P later received a letter from Mr. Betray, who was a disgruntled employee of D and C, detailing the activities of D and C against P's business interests. The letter disclosed (i) that D and C had been using P's label or label similar to P's for making port as well as P's list of clients and (ii) details of D and C's profit margin over the years and also their assets in the United Kingdom and abroad. Mr. Betray is willing to give evidence in court against D and C and has actually sworn an affidavit deposing to the facts in his letter to P. P thereupon rang his solicitor, Mr. Laws, and instructed him to start legal proceedings against D and C for violating his intellectual property rights and using his list of clients. Mr. Laws' private secretary, however, carelessly left on her desk a formal letter from P to Mr. Laws requesting the commencement of legal proceedings against D and C. Miss Reveal, an enterprising contract cleaner at the offices of Mr. Laws, saw the letter when she was cleaning Mr. Laws' offices. Because she knew D, she told him about the letter and was given a handsome reward.

D and C, realising they stood to lose a lot if they were sued by P, and wishing to teach P a lesson, instructed their solicitor, Mr. Noconscience, to sell off their hotel and casinos within two months and transfer the money to an account in a bank in Switzerland. In addition, they decided to remove and then destroy all documents that might incriminate them (P's list of clients, etc.) at the end of two months because they calculated that any action against them would not come to trial before that time, which meant they could make some real profit in the interim. The minutes of their meeting, during which all these measures were decided on, were recorded by D and C's secretary, Miss Efficient. However, soon after that meeting Miss Efficient forgot to lock away the original printed copy of the minutes (signed by both C and D). She left it on her desk when she was going home that evening. Miss Tellall, a cleaner at the offices of D and C and also of P, saw the minutes on Miss Efficient's desk and promptly photocopied it. She then sent a copy of it to P and assured P she would be prepared to give evidence in court against C and D.

Advise P.

### (b) Draft affidavit in support of an application for an Anton Piller order

| | |
|---|---|
| Filed on behalf of: | Plaintiff |
| Name of deponent: | Lorenzo Laws |
| No. of Affidavit: | 1 |
| Date sworn: | 1 April 19... |

DOC 1,2,3 and 4.

IN THE HIGH COURT OF JUSTICE
CHANCERY DIVISION
In the Matter of an Intended Action
Between

| | |
|---|---|
| PELE SMITH | Intended Plaintiff |
| and | |
| DHEE and CHEE | Intended Defendant |

AFFIDAVIT

I, Lorenzo Laws of 13 Oliver Street, London E5, make oath and say as follows:

1. I am a senior partner in the firm of Laws and Co. of 13 Oliver Street, London E5, solicitors for the Intended Plaintiff. I have the care and conduct of this matter and I am duly authorised to make this Affidavit on behalf of the Intended Plaintiff.

2. The contents of this Affidavit are obtained from documents and information supplied to me by or on behalf of my client, in particular by Mr. Betray, an employee of the Intended Defendants, and Miss Tellall, a contractor, and are true to the best of my information and belief.

**Application**

3. I make this Affidavit in support of an application by the Intended Plaintiff for:

   (1) Leave to be granted to issue a Writ of Summons for service on the Intended Defendants at their registered office at 333 Upton Lane, London E7 or elsewhere in the United Kingdom;

   (2) An Anton Piller order to be granted against the Intended Defendants in the terms of the draft order, or in such other terms as may be just and convenient.

**Facts relating to the claim**

4. The Intended Plaintiff trades at 11 Oliver Street, London E5, as a manufacturer and exporter of Lefe's Port. The Intended Plaintiff has registered under the Trade Marks Act 1994 a trade mark, namely, "Lefe Port". There is now produced and shown to me marked "DOC 1" a copy of the Intended Plaintiff's audited accounts for the past year. The Intended Plaintiff has been making profits of at least £6m. per year and has assets totalling £20m., as shown by his audited accounts of last year (page 2 of DOC 1).

5. The Intended Defendants were employed as chemists by the Intended Plaintiff between November 1, 1989 and April 1, 1994. There is now produced and shown to me marked "DOC 2" a copy of the Intended Defendants' contracts of employment. Clause 13 of each of the said contracts (at pages 3 and 7 of DOC 2) states:

   "1. The employee covenants:

      (a) that he will not engage in a trade similar to that of the employer in any part of east London before the expiration of three years beginning with the date of his resignation from the said employment, and

(b) that, if he should go into business similar to that of the employer, he will not approach any client of the employer before the expiration of three years beginning with the date of his leaving the said employment."

6. On April 1, 1994 the Intended Defendants resigned from the employment of the Intended Plaintiff.

7. On April 10, 1994 the Intended Defendants started manufacturing port in their premises, in breach of clause 13 of their contracts of employment aforementioned.

8. The Intended Plaintiff has reason to believe that his trade mark is being infringed by the Intended Defendants, contrary to s.10(2)(b) of the Trade Marks Act 1994. The said reason is that the Intended Defendants have been using the Intended Plaintiff's trade mark by calling their port "Lefee Port" without his consent. Section 10(2) of the Trade Marks Act 1994 provides:

   "A person infringes a registered trade mark if he uses in the course of trade a sign where because -

   (a) the sign is identical with the trade mark and is used in relation to goods or services similar to those for which the trade mark is registered, or

   (b) the sign is similar to the trade mark and is used in relation to goods or services identical with or similar to those for which the trade mark is registered,

   there exists a likelihood of confusion on the part of the public, which includes the likelihood of association with the trade mark."

9. The Intended Plaintiff also believes his list of clients has been used since April 10, 1994 and is still being used by the intended Defendants, contrary to clause 13(1)(b) of their contracts of employment aforementioned.

10. There is now produced and shown to me marked "DOC 3" a sworn statement of one Mr. Betray, an employee of the Intended Defendants. The said Mr. Betray, who had and still has access to the

documents of the Intended Defendants, made the said sworn statement voluntarily.

11. The Intended Plaintiff appreciates that the Intended Defendants are likely to claim that the sworn statement of Mr. Betray was in breach of trust and actuated by malice. However, the Intended Plaintiff stresses that the said sworn statement was made out of Mr. Betray's own free will and without any prior inducement whatsoever by any person or persons.

12. Therefore, I truly believe that the Intended Plaintiff has a strong *prima facie* case against the Intended Defendants in support of a claim for damages and an injunction for breach of contract and for infringement of trade mark [DETAILS OF THE ALLEGED BREACHES ...]

**Quantum of the claim of the Intended Plaintiff**

13. The Intended Plaintiff wishes to claim:
    (a) For loss of profits of £3m. per year for two years totalling £6m. [FURTHER DETAILS RELATED TO THE LOSS ...].

    (b) Interest pursuant to section 35A of the Supreme Court Act 1981, and

    (c) Costs.

**Possible defences to the claim**

14. The Intended Defendants are likely to argue that clause 13 of their contracts of employment aforesaid was void for being contrary to public policy because it interfered with their freedom of contract, or freedom to trade or otherwise to do business.

15. However, the Intended Plaintiff states that the said clause 13 was not against the public interest but was rather reasonable and aimed at protecting his trade secrets, custom and, therefore, business.

**Documents**

16. I am informed by the Intended Plaintiff that he was also informed by Mr. Betray aforementioned that the Intended Defendants had in their possession, locked in their safe, and were using (a) the Intended Plaintiff's trade mark in that they had labels bearing the name, "Lefee Port", the trade mark of the Intended Plaintiff, which they were putting on their bottles of port and (b) the Intended Plaintiff's list of clients. A sworn statement deposing to that is on page 1 of DOC 3.

**Risk of removal and/or destruction of documents**

17. The Intended Defendants, Dhee and Chee, own a firm incorporated in the United Kingdom and have their registered office at 333 Upton Lane, London E7.

18. I am informed by the Intended Plaintiff that he was informed by Miss Tellall, who is a contract cleaner at the offices of the Intended Defendants and also at the offices of the Intended Plaintiff, that:
    (a) the Intended Defendants know that the Intended Plaintiff has instructed his solicitor to commence legal proceedings against them; and

    (b) the Intended Defendants, in order to frustrate a trial, have decided to remove from their premises and destroy (i) the labels bearing the name "Lefee Port", which is the Intended Plaintiff's registered trade mark and (ii) the Intended Plaintiff's list of clients.

    A sworn statement deposing to the matters aforesaid has been produced and shown to me marked "DOC 4".

19. The Intended Defendants are likely to argue that the said sworn statement of Miss Tellall was made with malice or under duress or after inducement by the Intended Plaintiff or his agent or agents.

20. However, the Intended Plaintiff states that the said sworn statement was made by Miss Tellall out of her own free will and without

malice, duress or any inducement whatsoever.

21. In all the circumstances, I truly believe that unless an Anton Piller order is granted to search the premises of the Intended Defendants and remove therefrom (i) the Intended Defendants' labels bearing the name "Lefee Port", (ii) the Intended Plaintiff's list of clients [LIST OTHER DOCUMENTS, IF ANY], there is real risk that the Intended Defendants will destroy the documents aforementioned and thereby frustrate trial of the Intended Plaintiff's action.

Sworn, etc.

## (c) A draft Anton Piller order (in accordance with Annex 1 of the Practice Direction 1994)

(It is assumed that the premises to be searched are likely to be occupied by an unaccompanied woman and the supervising solicitor is a man. See paragraph 2(3) of Restrictions on the service and carrying out of paragraph 1 of the Order.)

[Heading]

*Order to allow entry and search of premises*

IMPORTANT:

NOTICE TO THE DEFENDANTS

(1) This Order orders you to allow the persons mentioned below to enter the premises described in the Order and to search for, examine and remove or copy the articles specified in the Order. This part of the Order is subject to restrictions. The Order also requires you to hand over any of the articles which are under your control and to provide information to the Plaintiff's solicitors, and prohibits you from doing certain acts. You should read the terms of the Order very carefully. You are advised to consult a solicitor as soon as possible.

(2) Before you the Defendants or the person appearing to be in control of the premises allow anybody onto the premises to carry out this Order you are entitled to have the solicitor who serves you with this Order explain to you what it means in every day language.

(3) You are entitled to insist that there is nobody [or nobody except Mr. ...] present who could gain commercially from anything he might read or see on your premises.

(4) You are entitled to refuse to permit entry before 9.30 a.m. or after 5.30 p.m. or at all on Saturday and Sunday.

(5) You are entitled to seek legal advice, and to ask the Court to vary or discharge this Order, provided you do so at once, and provided that meanwhile you permit the supervising solicitor (who is a solicitor acting independently of the Plaintiff) and the Plaintiff's solicitor to enter, but not start to search: see paragraph 3.

(6) If you, Dhee Dhee and Chee Chee, the Defendants disobey this Order you will be guilty of contempt of Court and may be [sent to prison or] fined or your assets seized.

THE ORDER

An application was made today [date ...] by solicitors for Pele Smith the Plaintiff to Mr. Justice [...]. Mr. Justice [...] heard the application and read the affidavits listed in Schedule 6 at the end of this Order.

As a result of the application IT IS ORDERED by Mr. Justice [...] that:

*Entry and search of premises and vehicles on the premises*

1. (1) The Defendants must allow Mr./Mrs./Miss ... ("the supervising solicitor"), together with Mr. ... a solicitor of the Supreme Court, and a partner in the firm of the Plaintiff's solicitors (Laws and Co.) and up to ... other persons being [their capacity ...] accompanying them, to enter the premises mentioned in Schedule I to this Order and any vehicles on the premises so that they can search for, inspect, photograph or photocopy, and deliver into the safekeeping of the Plaintiff's solicitors all the documents and articles which are listed in Schedule 2 to this Order ("the listed items") or which Mr. ... believes to be listed items. The Defendants must allow those persons to remain on the premises until the search is complete, and if necessary to re-enter the premises on the same or the following day in order to complete the search.

(2) This Order must be complied with either by the Defendants themselves or by a responsible employee of the Defendants or by the person appearing to be in control of the premises.

(3) This Order requires the Defendants or their employee or the person appearing to be in control of the premises to permit entry to the premises immediately the Order is served upon them, except as stated in paragraph 3 below.

*Restrictions on the service and carrying out of paragraph 1 of this Order*

2. Paragraph 1 of this Order is subject to the following restrictions.

(1) This Order may only be served between 9.30 a.m. and 5.30 p.m. on a weekday.

(2) This Order may not be carried out at the same time as any police search warrant.

(3) This Order must be served by the supervising solicitor, and paragraph I of the Order must be carried out in his presence and under his supervision. [At least one of the persons accompanying him as provided by paragraph 1 of this Order shall be a woman.][1]

(4) This Order does not require the person served with the Order to allow anyone [or anyone except Mr. ...] who could gain commercially from anything he might read or see on the premises if the person served with the Order objects.

---

1. This only applies where the premises are likely to be occupied by an unaccompanied woman and the supervising solicitor is a man.

(5) No item may be removed from the premises until a list of the items to be removed has been prepared, and a copy of the list has been supplied to the person served with the Order, and he has been given a reasonable opportunity to check the list.

(6) The premises must not be searched, and items must not be removed from them, except in the presence of the Defendant or a person appearing to be a responsible employee of the Defendant.

(7) If the supervising solicitor is satisfied that full compliance with sub-paragraph (5) or (6) above is impracticable, he may permit the search to proceed and items to be removed without compliance with the impracticable requirements.

*Obtaining legal advice and applying to the Court*

3. Before permitting entry to the premises by any person other than the Supervising Officer and the Plaintiff's solicitors, the Defendants or other person appearing to be in control of the premises may seek legal advice, and apply to the Court to vary or discharge this Order, provided they do so at once. While this is being done, they may refuse entry to the premises by any other person, and may refuse to permit the search to begin, for a short time (not to exceed two hours, unless the supervising solicitor agrees to a longer period).

*Delivery of listed items and computer print-outs*

4. (1) The Defendants must immediately hand over to the Plaintiff's solicitors any of the listed items which are in their possession or under their control.

(2) If any of the listed items exists only in computer readable form, the Defendants must immediately give the Plaintiff's

solicitors effective access to the computers, with all necessary passwords, to enable them to be searched, and cause the listed items to be printed out. A print-out of the items must be given to the Plaintiff's solicitors or displayed on the computer screen so that they can be read and copied. All reasonable steps shall be taken by the Plaintiff to ensure that no damage is done to any computer or data. The Plaintiff and his representatives may not themselves search the Defendants' computers unless they have sufficient expertise to do so without damaging the Defendants' system.

*Disclosure of information by the Defendants*

5. (1) The Defendants must immediately inform the Plaintiff's solicitors: (a) where all the listed items are; and (b) so far as they are aware: (i) the name and address of everyone who has supplied them, or offered to supply them, with listed items; (ii) the name and address of everyone to whom they have supplied, or offered to supply, listed items; and (iii) full details of the dates and quantities of every such supply and offer.

(2) Within ... days after being served with this Order the Defendants must prepare and swear an affidavit confirming the above information.

**Prohibited acts**

6. (1) Except for the purpose of obtaining legal advice, the Defendants must not directly or indirectly inform anyone of these proceedings or of the contents of this Order, or warn anyone that proceedings have been or may be brought against them by the Plaintiff until [...].[2]

---

2. The return date or, if sooner, 7 days from the date of the order, whichever is shorter.

(2) The Defendants must not remove from the premises stated in schedule 1 of this Order or destroy (i) the labels bearing the name "Lefee Port" and (ii) the list of clients belonging to the Intended Plaintiffs and called ...

(3) Until [...] or further Order the Defendants must not (i) use any "Lefee Port" label or (ii) contact any person or persons on the list of customers belonging to the Intended Plaintiffs.

EFFECT OF THIS ORDER

1) A Defendant who is an individual who is ordered not to do something must not do it himself or in any other way. He must not do it through others acting on his behalf or on his instructions or with his encouragement.

2) A Defendant which is a corporation and which is ordered not to do something must not do it itself or by its directors officers employees or agents or in any other way.

UNDERTAKINGS

The Plaintiff, the Plaintiff's solicitors and the supervising solicitor gave to the Court the undertakings contained in Schs. 3, 4 and 5 respectively to this order.

DURATION OF THIS ORDER

Paragraph 6(2) of this Order will remain in force up to and including [ : :19 ] (which is "the return date"), unless before then it is varied or discharged by a further Order of the Court. The application in which this Order is made shall come back to the Court for further hearing on the return date.

VARIATION OR DISCHARGE OF THIS ORDER

The Defendants (or anyone notified of this Order) may apply to the Court at any time to vary or discharge this Order (or so much of it as affects those persons), but anyone wishing to do so must first inform the Plaintiff's solicitors.

NAME AND ADDRESS OF PLAINTIFF'S SOLICITORS

The Plaintiff's solicitors are:

Laws and Co.,
13 Oliver Street,
London E5.
(Phone: DAY - 0171...
NIGHT - 0171...)

[INTERPRETATION OF THIS ORDER

1) In this Order "he" or "his" include "she" or "her" and "it" or "its".
2) Where there are two or more Defendants then (unless the context indicates differently) (a) references to "the Defendants" mean both or all of them; (b) an Order requiring 'the Defendants' to do or not to do anything requires each Defendant to do or not to do it; (c) a requirement relating to service of this Order, or of any legal proceedings, on "the Defendants" means on each of them; and (d) any other requirement that something shall be done to or in the presence of "the Defendants" means to or in the presence of one of them.]

SCHEDULE I
*The premises*

333 Upton Lane, London E7.

SCHEDULE 2
*The listed items*

1. Bottle labels bearing the name "Lefee Port".
2. List of Clients, called "...".

SCHEDULE 3
*Undertakings given by the plaintiff*

1) If the Court later finds that this Order or carrying it out has caused loss to the Defendants, and decides that the Defendants should be compensated for that loss, the Plaintiff will comply with any Order the Court may make.

[2) As soon as practicable to issue a Writ of Summons [in the form of the draft writ produced to the Court] [claiming appropriate relief.]]

3) To [swear and file an Affidavit] [cause an Affidavit to be sworn and filed] [substantially in the terms of the draft produced to the Court] [confirming the substance of what was said to the Court by the Plaintiff's counsel/solicitors.]

4) To serve on the Defendants at the same time as this Order is served upon him (i) the Writ (ii) a Notice of Motion/ Summons for ... 19 and (iii) copies of the Affidavits and copyable Exhibits containing the evidence relied on by the Plaintiff. [Copies of the confidential exhibits need not be served, but they must be made available for inspection by or on behalf of the Defendants in the presence of the Plaintiff's

solicitors while the order is carried out. Afterwards they must be provided to a solicitor representing the Defendants who gives a written undertaking not to permit the Defendants to see them or copies of them except in his presence and not to permit the defendants to make or take away any note or record of the Exhibits.]

5) To serve on the Defendants a copy of the supervising solicitor's report on the carrying out of this Order as soon as it is received and to produce a copy of the report to the Court.

6) Not, without the leave of the Court, to use any information or documents obtained as a result of carrying out this Order except for the purposes of these proceedings or to inform anyone else of these proceedings until after the return date.

SCHEDULE 4

*Undertakings given by the plaintiff's solicitors*

1) To answer at once to the best of their ability any question whether a particular item is a listed item.

2) To return the originals of all documents obtained as a result of this Order (except original documents which belong to the Plaintiff) as soon as possible and in any event within two working days of their removal.

3) While ownership of any item obtained as a result of this Order is in dispute, to deliver the article into the keeping of solicitors acting for the Defendants within two working days from receiving a written undertaking by them to retain the article in safe keeping and to produce it to the Court when required.

4) To retain in their own safe keeping all other items obtained as a result of this order until the Court directs otherwise.

## SCHEDULE 5

*Undertakings given by the supervising solicitor*

1) To offer to explain to the person served with the Order its meaning and effect fairly and in everyday language, and to inform him of his right to seek legal advice and apply to vary or discharge the order as mentioned in paragraph 3 of the Order.

2) To make and provide to the Plaintiff's solicitors a written report on the carrying out of the Order.

## SCHEDULE 6

*Affidavits*

The judge read the following Affidavit before making this order:

1) Affidavit of Lorenzo Laws.

All communications to the Court about this order is to be sent to Room ..., the Royal Courts of Justice, Strand, London, WC2A 2LL and should quote the case number. The office is open between ... and ... Monday to Friday. The telephone numbers are ... .

**(d) A draft Mareva injunction (in accordance with Annex 2 of the Practice Direction 1994)**

[Heading]

*Injunction prohibiting disposal of assets worldwide*

IMPORTANT

NOTICE TO THE DEFENDANT

(1) This order prohibits you from dealing with your assets up to the amount stated. The order is subject to the exceptions at the end of the order. You should read it all carefully. You are advised to consult a solicitor as soon as possible. You have a right to ask the court to vary or discharge this order.

(2) If you disobey this order you will be guilty of contempt of court and may be [sent to prison or] fined or your assets may he seized.

THE ORDER

An application was made today [date ...] by solicitors for Pele Smith, the Plaintiff, to Mr. Justice [ ... ]. Mr. Justice[ ... ] heard the application and read the affidavits listed in Schedule 2 at the end of this order.

As a result of the application IT IS ORDERED by Mr. Justice [ ...] that:

1. *Disposal of assets*

1) The Defendants must not (i) remove from England and Wales any of their assets which are in England and Wales whether in their own names or not and whether solely or jointly owned up to the value of £4m. or (ii) in any way dispose of or deal with or diminish the value of any of their assets whether they are in or outside England or Wales whether in

their own names or not and whether solely or jointly owned up to the same value. This prohibition includes the following assets in particular:

(a) the properties known as (i) The Bemis Hotel, 1313 Regent's Street, London W1, (ii) Casino Lefe, Monte Carlo and (iii) Lefe's Casino, Las Vegas, Nevada, United States of America or the net sale money after payment of any mortgages if they have been sold;

(b) the property and assets of the Defendants' business known as "Dhee and Chee Manufacturing" (or carried on at 333 Upton Lane, London E7) or the sale money if any of them have been sold; and (c) any money in the accounts numbered ... at VT Bank, Lucerne, Switzerland.

2) If the total unincumbered value of the Defendants' assets in England and Wales exceeds £6m. the Defendants may remove any of those assets from England and Wales or may dispose of or deal with them so long as the total unincumbered value of their assets still in England and Wales remains above £4m. If the total unincumbered value of the Defendants' assets in England and Wales does not exceed £4m., the Defendants must not remove any of those assets from England and Wales and must not dispose of or deal with any of them, but if they have other assets outside England and Wales the Defendants may dispose of or deal with those assets so long as the total unincumbered value of all their assets whether in or outside England and Wales remains above £6m.

2. *Disclosure of information*

1) The Defendants must inform the plaintiff in writing at once of all their assets whether in or outside England and Wales and whether in their own names or not and whether solely or jointly owned, giving the value, location and details of all such assets. In the case of any bank, building society or

similar account the Defendants must give:

(i) the name or names in which it is held;

(ii) the name of the bank, building society or other institution;

(iii) the address of the branch at which the account is held;

(iv) the number of the account;

(v) the balance in the account;

2) The information must be confirmed in an affidavit which must be served on the Plaintiff's solicitors within 7 days after this order has been served on the Defendants. The affidavit is also to contain both the information which is up to date when the affidavit is served and the information as at the time of service of the order.

EXCEPTIONS TO THIS ORDER

1) This order does not prohibit the Defendants from spending £ ... a week towards their ordinary living expenses [and £... a week towards their ordinary and proper business expenses] and also £ ... a week [*or* a reasonable sum] on legal advice and representation. But before spending any money the Defendants must tell the Plaintiff's solicitors where the money is to come from.

[2) This order does not prohibit the Defendants from dealing with or disposing of any of their assets in the ordinary and proper course of business.]

3) The Defendants may agree with the Plaintiff's solicitors that the above spending limits should be increased or that this order should be varied in any other respect but any such agreement must be in writing.

EFFECT OF THIS ORDER

1) A Defendant who is an individual who is ordered not to do something must not do it himself or in any other way. He must not do it through others acting on his behalf or on his instructions or with his encouragement.

2) A Defendant which is a corporation and which is ordered not to do something must not do it itself or by its directors officers employees or agents or in any other way.

THIRD PARTIES

1) *Effect of this order.* It is a contempt of court for any person notified of this order knowingly to assist in or permit a breach of the order. Any person doing so may be sent to prison, fined, or have his assets seized.

2) *Effect of this order outside England and Wales.* The terms of this order do not affect or concern anyone outside the jurisdiction of this court until it is declared enforceable or is enforced by a court in the relevant country and then they are to affect him only to the extent they have been declared enforceable or have been enforced UNLESS such person is:
   (a) a person to whom this order is addressed or an officer or an agent appointed by power of attorney of such a person; or
   (b) a person who is subject to the jurisdiction of this Court and (i) has been given written notice of this order at his residence or place of business within the jurisdiction of this Court and (ii) is able to prevent acts or omissions outside the jurisdiction of this Court which constitute or assist in a breach of the terms of this order.

   Nothing in this Order shall, as regards assets situated outside England and Wales (and especially including assets in Monte Carlo and Nevada, U.S.A.) prevent any bank or its subsidiaries from complying with:
   (1) what it believes reasonably to be its contractual or other obligations under the laws and obligations of

the country or state in which those assets are situated or under the proper law of the account in question;

(2) any orders made by the Courts of that country or state.

3) *Set off by banks.* This injunction does not prevent any bank from exercising any right of set off it may have in respect of any facility which it gave to the Defendants before it was notified of the Order.

4) *Withdrawals by the Defendants.* No bank need inquire as to the application or proposed application of any money withdrawn by the Defendants if the withdrawal appears to be permitted by this Order.

UNDERTAKINGS

The plaintiff gives to the Court the undertakings set out in Schedule I to this Order.

DURATION OF THIS ORDER

This Order will remain in force up to and including : :19... ("the return date"), unless before then it is varied or discharged by a further order of the court. The application in which this Order is made shall come back to the Court for further hearing on the return date.

VARIATION OR DISCHARGE OF THIS ORDER

The Defendants (or anyone notified of this Order) may apply to the Court at any time to vary or discharge this Order (or so much of it as affects that person or persons), but anyone wishing to do so must first inform the Plaintiff's solicitors.

NAME AND ADDRESS OF PLAINTIFF'S SOLICITORS

The Plaintiff's solicitors are:

Laws and Co.,
13 Oliver Street,
London E5.
(Phone: DAY - 0171...
NIGHT - 0171...).

[INTERPRETATION OF THIS ORDER

1) In this order "he", "him" or "his" include "she" or "her" and "it" or "its".

2) Where there are two or more Defendants then (unless the context indicates differently) (a) references to 'the Defendants' mean both or all of them; (b) an order requiring 'the Defendants' to do or not to do anything requires each Defendant to do or not to do it; (c) a requirement relating to the service of the order, or of any legal proceedings, on 'the Defendants' means on each of them.]

SCHEDULE I

*Undertakings given to the court by the plaintiff*

1) If the Court later finds that this Order has caused loss to the Defendants, and decides that the Defendants should be compensated for that loss, the Plaintiff will comply with any Order the Court may make.

2) As soon as practicable the Plaintiff will issue and serve on the Defendant the Writ of Summons in the form of the draft Writ produced to the Court [claiming appropriate relief] together with this Order.

3) The Plaintiff will cause an affidavit to be sworn and filed substantially in the terms of the draft affidavit of Mr. Lorenz Laws produced to the Court.

4) As soon as practicable the Plaintiff will serve on the Defendants a [notice of motion] [summons] for the return date together with a copy of the Affidavit and exhibits containing the evidence relied on by the Plaintiff.

5) Anyone notified of this Order will be given a copy of it by the Plaintiff's solicitors.

6) The Plaintiff will pay the reasonable costs of anyone other than the Defendants which have been incurred as a result of this Order including the costs of ascertaining whether that person holds any of the Defendants' assets and that if the Court later finds that this order has caused such a person loss, and decides that the person should be compensated for that loss, the Plaintiff will comply with any Order the Court may make.

7) The Plaintiff will not without the leave of the Court begin proceedings against the Defendants in any other jurisdiction or use information obtained as a result of an Order of the Court in this jurisdiction for the purpose of civil or criminal proceedings in any other jurisdiction.

8) The Plaintiff will not without the leave of the Court seek to enforce this Order in any country outside England and Wales or seek an Order of a similar nature including Orders conferring a charge or other security against the Defendants or the Defendants' assets.

SCHEDULE 2

*Affidavits*

The judge read the following affidavits before making this Order:

1) The draft Affidavit of Mr. Lorenz Laws.

Any communication about this Order is to be sent to Room ... , Royal Courts of Justice, Strand, London WC2A 2LL and should quote the case number. The office is open between ... and ... Monday to Friday. The telephone numbers are ... .

### (e) Draft affidavit in support of an application for a Mareva injunction

| | |
|---|---|
| Filed on behalf of: | Plaintiff |
| Name of deponent: | Lorenzo Laws |
| No. of Affidavit: | 1 |
| Date sworn: | 1 April 19... |

DOC 1,2,3 and 4.

IN THE HIGH COURT OF JUSTICE
CHANCERY DIVISION
In the Matter of an Intended Action
Between

| | |
|---|---|
| PELE SMITH | Intended Plaintiff |
| and | |
| DHEE and CHEE | Intended Defendant |

AFFIDAVIT

I, Lorenzo Laws of 13 Oliver Street, London E5, make oath and say as follows:

1. I am a senior partner in the firm of Laws and Co. of 13 Oliver Street, London E5, solicitors for the Intended Plaintiff. I have the care and conduct of this matter and I am duly authorised to make this Affidavit on behalf of the Intended Plaintiff.

2. The contents of this Affidavit are obtained from documents and information supplied to me by or on behalf of my client, in particular by Mr. Betray, an employee of the Intended Defendants, and Miss Tellall, a contractor, and are true to the best of my information and belief.

**Application**

3. I make this Affidavit in support of an application by the Intended Plaintiff for:

   (1) Leave to be granted to issue a Writ of Summons for service on the Intended Defendants at their registered office at 333 Upton Lane, London E7 or elsewhere in the United Kingdom;

   (2) A Mareva injunction to be granted against the Intended Defendants in the terms of the draft order, or in such other terms as may be just and convenient.

**Facts relating to the claim**

4. The Intended Plaintiff trades at 11 Oliver Street, London E5, as a manufacturer and exporter of Lefe Port. The Intended Plaintiff has registered under the Trade Marks Act 1994 a trade mark, namely, "Lefe Port". There is now produced and shown to me marked "DOC 1" a copy of the Intended Plaintiff's audited accounts for the past year. The Intended Plaintiff has been making profits of at least £6m. per year and has assets totalling £20m., as shown by his audited accounts of last year (page 2 of DOC 1).

5. The Intended Defendants were employed as chemists by the Intended Plaintiff between November 1, 1989 and April 1, 1994. There is now produced and shown to me marked "DOC 2" a copy of the Intended Defendants' contracts of employment. Clause 13 of each of the said contracts (at pages 3 and 7 of DOC 2) states:

   "1. The employee covenants:

   (a) that he will not engage in a trade similar to that of the employer in any part of east London before the expiration of three years beginning with the date of his resignation from the said employment, and

(b) that, if he should go into business similar to that of the employer, he will not approach any client of the employer before the expiration of three years beginning with the date of his leaving the said employment.

6. On April 1, 1994 the Intended Defendants resigned from the employment of the Intended Plaintiff.

7. On April 10, 1994 the Intended Defendants started manufacturing port in their premises, in breach of clause 13 of their contracts of employment aforementioned.

8. The Intended Plaintiff has reason to believe that his trade mark is being infringed by the Intended Defendants, contrary to s.10(2)(b) of the Trade Marks Act 1994. The said reason is that the Intended Defendants have been using the Intended Plaintiff's trade mark by calling their port "Lefee Port" without his consent. Section 10(2) of the Trade Marks Act 1994 provides:

"A person infringes a registered trade mark if he uses in the course of trade a sign where because -

(a) the sign is identical with the trade mark and is used in relation to goods or services similar to those for which the trade mark is registered, or

(b) the sign is similar to the trade mark and is used in relation to goods or services identical with or similar to those for which the trade mark is registered,

there exists a likelihood of confusion on the part of the public, which includes the likelihood of association with the trade mark."

9. The Intended Plaintiff also believes his list of clients has been used since April 10, 1994 and is still being used by the intended Defendants, contrary to the clause 13(1)(b) of their contracts of employment aforementioned.

10. There is now produced and shown to me marked "DOC 3" a sworn statement of one Mr. Betray, an employee of the Intended Defendants. The said Mr. Betray, who had and still has access to the

documents of the Intended Defendants, made the said sworn statement voluntarily.

11. The Intended Plaintiff appreciates that the Intended Defendants are likely to claim that the sworn statement of Mr. Betray was in breach of trust and actuated by malice. However, the Intended Plaintiff stresses that the said sworn statement was made out of Mr. Betray's own free will and without any prior inducement whatsoever by any person or persons.

12. Therefore, I truly believe that the Intended Plaintiff has a strong *prima facie* case against the Intended Defendants in support of a claim for damages and an injunction for breach of contract and for infringement of trade mark [DETAILS OF THE ALLEGED BREACHES ...]

**Quantum of the claim of the Intended Plaintiff**

13. The Intended Plaintiff wishes to claim:

    (a) For loss of profits of £3m. per year for two years totalling £6m. [FURTHER DETAILS RELATED TO THE LOSS ...].

    (b) Interest pursuant to section 35A of the Supreme Court Act 1981, and

    (c) Costs.

**Possible defences to the claim**

14. The Intended Defendants are likely to argue that clause 13 of their contracts of employment aforesaid was void for being contrary to public policy because it interfered with their freedom of contract, or freedom to trade or otherwise to do business.

15. However, the Intended Plaintiff states that the said clause 13 was not against the public interest but was rather reasonable and aimed at protecting his trade secrets, custom and, therefore, business.

**Assets**

16. I am informed by the Intended Plaintiff that he was informed by Mr. Betray aforementioned that the Intended Defendants own: (i) Bemis Hotel, 1313 Regent Street, London W1, (ii) The Casino Lefe, Monte Carlo, and (iii) Lefe's Casino, Las Vegas, Nevada, U.S.A. A sworn statement deposing to that is on page 1 of DOC 3.

**Risk of disposal of the assets**

17. The Intended Defendants, Dhee and Chee, own a firm incorporated in the United Kingdom and have their registered office at 333 Upton Lane, London E7.

18. Paragraph 16 of this Affidavit is repeated.

19. I am informed by the Intended Plaintiff that he was informed by Miss Tellall, who is a contract cleaner at the offices of the Intended Defendants and also at the offices of the Intended Plaintiff, that:
    (a) the Intended Defendants know that the Intended Plaintiff has instructed his solicitor to commence legal proceedings against them; and

    (b) the Intended Defendants, in order to make any judgement that may be obtained against them unsatisfied, have decided to sell all their assets both in the United Kingdom and abroad and to deposit the sale money in a secret bank account in Switzerland. A sworn statement deposing to the matters aforesaid has been produced and shown to me marked "DOC 4".

20. The Intended Defendants are likely to argue that the said sworn statement of Miss Tellall was made with malice or under duress or after inducement by the Intended Plaintiff or his agent or agents.

21. However, the Intended Plaintiff states that the said sworn statement was made by Miss Tellall out of her own free will and without malice, duress or any inducement whatsoever.

22. In all the circumstances, I truly believe that unless a Mareva injunction is granted in appropriate terms against the Intended Defendants there is a real risk that any judgement obtained by the Intended Plaintiff against the Intended Defendants would be unsatisfied.

Sworn, etc.

# Select Bibliography


*Actuarial Tables for Use in Personal Injury and Fatal Accidents Cases.* H.M.S.O., May 1985.

ALDRIDGE, T.
"Life is Priceless", *S.J.* 138 (1994): 1174.

ANDERSON, L.
"An exemplary case for reform". *Civil Justice Quarterly* 11 (July 1992): 233-260.

ATIYAH, P.S.
*Accidents, Compensation and the Law.* Ed. by P. Cane. 5th ed., London. Butterworths, 1993.

BEALE, H.G.
*Remedies for Breach of Contract.* Sweet and Maxwell, 1980.
"Damages for Rebuilding". *L.Q.R.* 111 (1995) 54.

BEALE, H.G., BISHOP, W.D. and FURMSTON, M.P.
*Contract: Cases and Materials*, London. Butterworths, 1995.

BEAN, D.
*Injunctions.* 6th ed., Longman, 1994.

BEATSON, J.
"Discharge for Breach: The Position of Instalments, Deposits and Other Payments Due Before Completion." *L.Q.R.* 97 (1981) 389.

BEATSON, J.
"More Proposals on Damages Law Reform from the Law Commission: Punitive and Other Non-Compensatory Damages". *Quantum*, Issue 6/93, Nov. 11, 1993, 1-2.

BEATSON, J. and MATTHEWS, M.H.
*Administrative Law: Cases and Materials.* 2nd ed., Oxford. Clarendon, 1993.

BIGGART, J.

"The Assessment of Damages in Actions against Valuers". *Int. I.L.R.* 11 (1994): 401.

BIRKS, P.

"Restitutionary Remedies for Breach of Contract". L.M.C.L.Q. (1987): 421. *An Introduction to the Law of Restitution.* Oxford. Clarendon, 1993.

BIRTLES, W.

"The Privilege against Self-incrimination". *S.J.* 138 (1994): 342.

BISHOP, H.G., BEALE, W.D. and FURMSTON, M.P.

*Contract: Cases and Materials.* 3rd ed., London. Butterworths.

BISHOP and KAY.

"Taxman and Damages: The Rule in Gourley's Case". *L.Q.R.* 105 (1987): 366. Blackstone.

*Commentaries on the Laws of England*, Book III, ch. 1.

BULLEN, E. and LEAKE, S.M.

*Precedents of Pleadings.* Ed. by Sir J.H. Jacob and I.S. Goldrein. 13th ed., London. Sweet and Maxwell, 1990.

BURROWS, A., ed.

*Essays on the Law of Restitution.*
Oxford. Clarendon Press, 1991.

*The Law of Restitution.* 2nd ed.,
London. Butterworths, 1993.

*Remedies for Torts and Breach of Contract.* 2nd ed.,
London. Butterworths, 1994.

BUSHE, K.

"A single guiding rule for damages awards in the presence of collateral benefits". *H.K.L.J.* 25(1), (1995): 51-63.

CHESHIRE and FIFOOT.

*Law of Contract.* Ed. by M.P. Furmston. 12th ed., London. Butterworths, 1991.

CHITTY, J.

*Law of Contracts.* Ed. by A.G. Guest and others. 27th ed., London. Sweet and Maxwell, 1994, Vol. 1.

CLAYTON, R., and TOMLINSON, H.

*Civil Actions Against the Police.* 2nd ed., 1992.

"Civil actions against the police: recent developments in the law". *Legal Action*, October 1993, 15-18.
CLERK AND LINDSELL.
*On Torts*. 27th ed., Ed. by M. Brazier and others. London. Sweet and Maxwell, 1995.
COLLINS, H.
*The Law of Contract*. 2nd ed., London. Butterworths, 1993.
COMMITTEE ON DEFAMATION.
*Report*. (The Faulks Committee Report). Cmnd. 5909. (1975).
COOKE, J. and OUGHTON, D.
*The Common Law of Obligations*. 2nd ed., London. Butterworths, 1993.
CRAIG, I.
"Anton-Piller Orders after Universal Thermosensors", *Solicitors' Journal*, 30th October 1992, 1078-9.
CRAIG, P.P.
*Administrative Law*. 3rd ed., London. Sweet and Maxwell, 1994.
CURRAN, P.
*Personal Injuries Pleadings*. London. Sweet and Maxwell, 1995.
DOCKRAY and LADDIE.
"Piller Problems". *L.Q.R.* 106 (1990) 601-20.
DOGGETT, R. "Hunt v Severs - A Pyrrhic Victory for Insurers?"
*Quantum*. Issue 3, May 6 (1994): 6-7.
DOWNES, T.A.
*Textbook on Contract*. 4th ed., Blackstone Press, London, 1995.
FLEMING, J.G.
*The Law of Torts*. The Law Book Company (Australia), 8th ed.
GALINSKY, R.
"Interlocutory Injunctions and Damages". *Solicitors' Journal*, 30th October 1992, 1086-7.
GEE, S.
*Mareva Injunctions and Anton Piller Relief*.
FT Law and Tax, 1995.
"Mercedes and Mareva". *Solicitors' Journal*,
27th October 1995, 1076-7.

"Diving in at the deep end". *LSG* 92(30), (1995): 23.
GHANDHI, P.R.
"Punitive damages against the police".
*Solicitors' Journal* 134(13), (30th March 1990): 357-8.
"Exemplary Damages in the English Law of Tort".
*Legal Studies* 10(2), (1990): 182 - 200.
GOFF and JONES.
*The Law of Restitution*. 4th ed., London. Sweet and Maxwell, 1993.
HANBURY and MAUDSLEY.
*Modern Equity*. Ed. by Jill Martin. 14th ed., London. Sweet and Maxwell, 1993.
HARRIS, D.
*Remedies in Contract and Tort*. London. Weidenfeld and Nicolson, 1988.
HARRIS, OGUS and PHILLIPS,
"Contract Remedies and the Consumer Surplus". *L.Q.R.* 95 (1979): 581.
HART and HONORE,
*Causation in the Law*. 2nd ed., Oxford. Clarendon.
HARVEY, B. and MARSTON, J.
*Cases & Commentary on Tort*. Pitman, 1994.
HOLDSWORTH, W.S.
*A History of English Law*. 3rd ed. (Methuen: London, 1923), vol. II.
HOWARTH, D.
*Textbook on Tort*. London. Butterworths, 1995.
INGHAM, T.
*The English Legal Process*.
5th ed., Blackstone Press.
JACOB, Sir J. and GOLDREIN, I.S.
*Pleadings: Principles and Practice*. London. Sweet and Maxwell, 1990.
JONES, G. "The recovery of Benefits gained from a Breach of Contract", *Law Quarterly Review*, 99 (1983): 443-60.

JONES, G. and GOODHART, W.
*Specific Performance*. Butterworths, 1986.
JONES, M.A.
"Calculating the Widow's Dependency". *Law Quarterly Review,* 101 (1985): 21.
"The Widow's Dependency Again". *Law Quarterly Review*, 111 (1995): 223-8.
JOWITT, W.A.
*Dictionary of English Law*. Ed. by J. Burke. 2nd. ed., Sweet and Maxwell, 1977.
KEMP and KEMP.
*The Quantum of Damages in Personal Injuries and Fatal Accident Claims*. Sweet and Maxwell, 1992.
KEMP, D.
"Voluntary Services Provided by Tortfeasor to His Victim", *The Law Quarterly Review* 110 (1995): 524-6.
KIDNER, R.
*Casebook on Torts*. 3rd. ed., Blackstone Press.
LAW COMMISSION.
*Aggravated, Exemplary and Restitutionary Damages*.
Consultation Paper No. 132. HMSO, 1993.
*Contributory Negligence as a Defence in Contract.*
Law Com. No. 219, 1993.
*Report on Personal Injury Litigation - Assessment of Damages*,
Law Com. 56, 1973.
*Report on Structured Settlements and Interim and Provisional Damages*.
Law Commission No. 224. Cm. 2646. HMSO, 1994.
*Rights of Access to Neighbouring Land.*
Law Comm. No. 151, 1985.
*Working Paper*. No. 54.
LAWSON, F.H.
*Remedies of English Law*. 2nd ed., London. Butterworths, 1980.
LEWIS, R.
"Structured Settlements in Practice".
*Civil Justice Quarterly* 10 (July 1991): 212-219.

"The Merits of a Structured Settlement: The Plaintiff's Perspective".
*Oxford Journal of Legal Studies* 13(4), (1993): 530-547.
"Structured Settlements: An Emergent Study".
*Civil Justice Quarterly* 13 (Jan. 1994): 18-28.
*Structured Settlements: The Law and Practice.*
London. Sweet and Maxwell, 1994.

LOWE, R. and WOODROFFE, G.
*Consumer Law and Practice*. 3rd ed., Sweet and Maxwell, 1991.

LUCIOLI, P.
"Avoiding the Benefits Trap". *Gazette*, Jan. 18 (1995): 18.

McLEAN, S.A.M.
*Law Reform and Medical Injury Litigation*. Aldershot. Dartmouth, 1995.

MacGREGOR, G.
"Cruise Missiles from the Courts". *Accountancy* 116(1228), (1995): 156.

MacQUEEN, H.
"Unjustified Enrichment and Breach of Contract". *J.R.* (1994): 127.

McBRIDE, N. J.
"A case for Awarding Punitive Damages in Response to Deliberate Breaches of Contract". *Anglo-American Law Review* 24(3), (1995): 369-390.

McGREGOR, H.
*McGregor on Damages*. 15th ed., Sweet and Maxwell, 1988.

MADDAUGH, P.D. and McCAMUS, J.
*The Law of Restitution*, 1990.

MARKESINIS, B.S. and DEAKIN, S.F.
*Tort Law*. Oxford. Clarendon Press, 1994.

MATTHEWS, P. and LUNNEY, M.
"A Tortfeasor's Lot is not a Happy One?". *Modern Law Review* 58(3)3, (1995): 399.

MEAGHER, R.P., GUMMOW, W.M.C. and LEHANE, J.R.F.
*Equity - Doctrines and Remedies*. 3rd ed., Sydney.

Butterworths, 1992.
MORRIS, R.
"Anton Pillers and Marevas in Hong Kong". *J.I.B.L.* 11 (1994): 480.
O'DAIR, R.O.
"Remedies for Breach of Contract: a wrong turn (Surrey County Council v Bredero Homes)". *R.L.R.* (1993): 31.
ODGERS.
*High Court Pleading and Practice*. Ed. by D.B. Casson. 23rd. ed., London. Sweet and Maxwell, 1991.
OGUS, A.
*The Law of Damages*. Butterworths, 1973.
OUGH, R.N. and FLENLEY, W.
*The Mareva Injunction and Anton Piller Order*. Butterworths, 1993.
OUGHTEN, D. and DAVIS, M.
*Sourcebook on Contract Law*. Cavendish, 1996.
OWEN, R.
"Personal Injury Astrologers". *S.J.* 139(41), (1995): 1068.
PALMER, N.E.
*Bailment*. London. Sweet and Maxwell, 1991.
PEARCE, R.A. and STEVENS, J.
*The Law of Trusts and Equitable Obligations*. Butterworths, 1995.
PIPE, G.S.
"Exemplary damages after Camelford". *The Modern Law Review* 57 (1st Jan. 1994): 91-101.
POOLE, J.
*Casebook on Contract*. 2nd ed., Blackstone Press.
PRITCHARD, J., and SOLOMON, N.
*Personal Injury Litigation*. 8th. ed. FT Law and Tax, 1995.
REED, A.
"Exemplary Damages: A Persuasive Argument for their Retention as a Mechanism for Retributive Justice". *Civil Justice Quarterly* 15, April 1996, 130-140.

ROYAL COMMISSION

*Report on Civil Liability and Compensation for Personal Injury* (The Pearson Report). Cmnd. 7054-I. London. H.M.S.O., 1978. Vol. 1.

SALMON, Sir J. and HEUSTON, R.F.V.

*Law of Torts*. Ed. by R.F.V. Heuston and R.A. Buckley. 20th ed., 1992.

SHERIDAN, L.A.

*Injunctions in General*. Chichester. Barry Rose, 1994.

*Chancery Procedure and Anton Piller Orders*. Chichester. Barry Rose, 1994.

SILVERTOWN. *The Law of Lien*. 1988.

SIME, S.

*A Practical Approach to Civil Procedure*. 2nd ed., London. Blackstone Press, 1995.

SMITH, J.C.

*Smith and Thomas, A Casebook on Contract*. 10th ed., Sweet and Maxwell.

SNELL, E.H.T.

*Principles of Equity*. Ed. by P.V. Baker and P.J. Langan. 29th ed., London. 1990.

SPRY, I.C.F.

*Equitable Remedies*. 4th ed., Sweet and Maxwell, 1990.

STANTON, K.M.

*The Modern Law of Tort*. London. Sweet and Maxwell, 1994.

STREET, H.

*Torts*. Ed. by M. Brazier. 9th ed., London. Butterworths, 1993.

TREITEL, G.H.

*Remedies for Breach of Contract*. Clarendon, 1988.

*The Law of Contract*. London. Sweet and Maxwell, 1995.

*Outline of the Law of Contract*. 1995.

WADDAMS, S.M.

*The Law of Damages*. Toronto. Canada Law Books Ltd., 1983.

WADE, H.R.W. and FORSYTH, C.F.

*Administrative Law*. 7th ed., Oxford. Clarendon, 1994.

WATSON, A.
"Reforming Anton-Piller Orders". *Litigation* 12(6), May 1993, 229-235.
WEIR, A.
*Casebook on Tort*. 7th ed., London. Sweet and Maxwell, 1992.
WHITFIELD, M.
"Cost pressures keep safety on the sidelines", *The Independent*, 9 December 1992.
WINFIELD, Sir P.H. and JOLOWICZ, J.A.
*Tort*. Ed. by W.V.H. Rogers. 14th ed., London. Sweet and Maxwell, 1994.
WORKING GROUP OF THE SUPREME COURT PROCEDURE COMMITTEE.
*Report on the Practice and Procedure in Defamation*, 1991.

# Index